THE POLK
CONSPIRACY

ALSO BY KATI MARTON

An American Woman
Wallenberg

THE POLK
CONSPIRACY

Murder and Cover-up in the
Case of CBS News
Correspondent George Polk

KATI MARTON

TIMES 𝕿 BOOKS

All rights reserved under International and Pan-American Copyright
Conventions. Published in the United States by Random House, Inc.,
New York and simultaneously in Canada by Random House of Canada
Limited, Toronto.

This work was originally published in hardcover in the United
States by Farrar, Straus & Giroux, Inc., New York, and in Canada
by HarperCollins*CanadaLtd*., Don Mills, Ontario, in 1990.

Library of Congress Cataloging-in-Publication Data

Marton, Kati.
The Polk conspiracy : murder and cover-up in the case of CBS
News correspondent George Polk / Kati Marton.
p.   cm.
Originally published: 1st ed. New York : Farrar, Straus & Giroux,
1990.
Includes index.
ISBN 0-8129-2047-3
1. Murder—Greece—Thessalonikē—Case studies.   2. Polk, George,
1913–1948.   3. Murder victims—Greece—Thessalonikē—
Case studies.   4. Journalists—Greece—Thessalonikē—Case studies.
5. Greece—Politics and government—1935–1967.   I. Title.
[HV6535.G83T46   1992]
364.1'523'094956—dc20   91-50973

Manufactured in the United States of America
9   8   7   6   5   4   3   2
First Paperback Edition

This reporter's tale, a missing chapter in the chronicle of foreign correspondents, is for my son and daughter, Christopher and Elizabeth Jennings, children and grandchildren of foreign correspondents

Preface to This Edition

I could not have predicted, when I set out some half a dozen years ago to attempt to piece together the brief life and violent death of a relatively obscure American journalist, the sort of reaction *The Polk Conspiracy* would provoke. In the year since the book's first publication, *The Polk Conspiracy* has been scrutinized and argued over, praised to the skies and severely chastised. Clearly, the book touched an unexpected nerve for many Americans. Though I was unprepared for the strong reactions I stirred up in writing this story, I believe the debate it has provoked has been a healthy one for all concerned.

But why the sound and fury expended over the forty-three-year-old murder of a reporter? In part, I think, because of what George Polk's story reveals about ourselves. This is a cautionary tale about us, our government, our media, and our icons. *The Polk Conspiracy* reminds us, and some would prefer not to be reminded, that we Americans have very little cause for either smugness or complacency regarding our own behavior during the Cold War. We are all too familiar with Stalinist terror and those nauseating parodies of justice, the notorious show trials of the thirties, forties, and fifties. But they took place east of the divide.

Polk's murder and the subsequent show trial of the man charged with the crime were stage-managed by one of our allies. In the case of the murder trial, as *The Polk Conspiracy* makes abundantly clear, Washington itself played an active part in subverting justice. It is this, and the weak-kneed—if not duplicitous—reponse that the murder of a brave and honest reporter elicited from revered members of our government and media, which has angered so many readers of *The Polk Conspiracy*.

This is a book of secrets held close to the vest for over four decades by officials in three countries: the United States, Great Britain, and Greece. Some of the people named in *The Polk Conspiracy* have cried foul at the revelations contained in this book. Some have even threatened to sue me. Though this is never a pleasant experience for a writer, I have no regrets regarding the contents of this book. I believe that secrets rarely do damage to anyone but the secret-keeper. By the time most such revelations reach the public, "the facts on the ground," as they say in the intelligence world, will have changed sufficiently so that the contents of classified material endanger only reputations, not lives. A far larger cause is served, I believe, in the telling, after so many years of disinformation and secrecy, of the full story of George Polk's brutal murder and its subsequent cover-up. I firmly believe, as did George Polk during his too brief lifetime, that if a democracy is to be more than a paper tiger, its constituency must be well informed. How, otherwise, will we be fit to weigh and judge before we make our choices? Secretive government by a few powerful men is not the point of the exercise called America.

For me, as a Hungarian-born American who experienced those chilly years of Cold War paranoia from the other side, unraveling this elusive case had a definite down side. Like most immigrants, I am a fervent American patriot. I would have liked nothing more than for my investigation of the Polk case to confirm Washington's official story: that Polk fell victim to a Communist plot, that his murder was the work of Greek guerrillas bent on overthrowing the U.S.-supported right-wing government in Athens. Polk's assassination, so ran the official version, was just another Moscow-inspired skirmish in the Cold War.

In sifting the evidence, I tried to leave my personal baggage at the door, where it belonged. I approached this case with as much detachment as I could muster. I followed the murder trail where it led, not where I would have wished it to lead. Along the way I discovered some unpleasant truths about my adopted country, the United States. I learned that the Cold War had exacted as high a cost in human and official values in Washington as it had in my native city, Budapest.

The Polk conspiracy was not the first or last attempt by our government to get away, if not with murder, then with a murky conspiracy—all in the name of some higher purpose. Richard Nixon attempted to quash the *New York Times'* publication of *The Pentagon Papers* in the name of national security. If the *Times* had not gone ahead anyway, we would not have learned what a fragile being this system is, and how nearly it was fatally subverted.

The Polk Conspiracy, the story of a restless, gifted journalist, is also a timely reminder that the role of a reporter is not to echo his own or any government's current policy. The role of the journalist is never to "get on the team," nor to advance any official's agenda. Quite the contrary: a reporter's task is to get at the truth even if in the process he reveals things neither his own government nor the public really wants to know.

George Polk was that sort of journalist. He paid with his life for the high standards he set for himself and for his profession. For forty years nobody talked much about how and why this good and brave man died. We are talking about him now. Through his story we are reliving those poisonous times of Cold War–induced terror and blindness. The most painful lesson of *The Polk Conspiracy* is that sometimes in uncertain, fearful times we cannot rely on our own government, or even on our own profession. Polk was betrayed by both. If we draw a lesson from his tragedy, we are paying George Polk the only sort of tribute he would have approved.

Dramatis Personae

FREDERICK AYER: special investigator on leave from the FBI, assigned by Secretary of State George Marshall to the Polk case.

MARY CAWADIAS BARBER: *Time* magazine Greek stringer.

WILLIAM O. BAXTER: assistant chief of the State Department's Division of Greek, Turkish, and Iranian Affairs.

HOMER BIGART: Pulitzer Prize-winning correspondent for the New York *Herald Tribune*.

WINSTON BURDETT: CBS correspondent assigned to investigate the Polk murder for CBS News. Burdett also covered the murder trial of Gregory Staktopoulos.

RANDOLL COATE: British information officer in Salonika.

MATTHEW COCCONIS: Rea Polk's father and George Polk's father-in-law.

WILLIAM E. COLBY: a former agent of the OSS, the wartime intelligence agency, Colby was assistant to General Donovan and a member of his law firm, Donovan and Leisure. Colby was director of the Central Intelligence Agency in 1973–76.

DR. CARL COMPTON: dean of Anatolia College, the secondary school attended by Gregory Staktopoulos in Salonika.

WAIDE CONDON: U.S. Information Service officer in Athens and friend of George Polk who identified Polk's body.

PANAYOTIS CONSTANTINIDES: Attorney General for the Greek Court of Appeals.

WILLIAM ("WILD BILL") DONOVAN: former head of the OSS who conceived the idea for the CIA. As a New York lawyer, he was recruited by Walter Lippmann to be counsel to the Overseas Writers Special Committee to Inquire into the Murder of George Polk.

GERALD DREW: U.S. delegate on the United Nations Special Committee on the Balkans, in session in Salonika at the time of the Polk case.

GEORGE DROSSOS: deputy Greek liaison officer to the United Nations Special Committee on the Balkans.

RALEIGH GIBSON: American Consul General in Salonika.

HENRY GRADY: American Ambassador in Greece during most of the Polk case.

COSTAS HADJIARGYRIS: Greek journalist and *Christian Science Monitor* correspondent from Athens who also worked as George Polk's stringer.

JAMES KELLIS: OSS war hero recruited by General Donovan as investigator in the Polk case on behalf of the Overseas Writers.

ALEXANDER KENDRICK: CBS correspondent who, along with Winston Burdett, covered the trial of Gregory Staktopoulos.

THEODORE LAMBRON: Greek-American medical student engaged by General Donovan as his assistant in Athens following the removal of Colonel Kellis.

ERNEST K. LINDLEY: *Newsweek* Washington bureau chief, friend of Walter Lippmann, and president of the Overseas Writers.

WALTER LIPPMANN: eminent columnist and Washington elder who chaired the Overseas Writers Special Committee to Inquire into the Murder of George Polk.

LINCOLN MACVEAGH: longtime American Ambassador in Athens (1943–48).

HELEN MAMAS: Associated Press stringer in Salonika during the Polk case.

GEORGE C. MARSHALL: Secretary of State during the Polk case.

COLONEL THOMAS MARTIN: British Police Mission officer in Salonika who supervised the Greek investigation of the Polk case.

DONALD MATCHAN: correspondent for the York, Pennsylvania, *Daily Gazette*, in Salonika during the Polk case.

ANNA MOLYVDA: sister-in-law and mistress of one of the men accused of Polk's murder, Adam Mouzenides.

NICHOLAS MOUSCOUNDIS: chief of the Salonika security police.

STYLIANOS MOUZENIDES: the dentist brother of the accused Communist, Adam Mouzenides.

EDWARD R. MURROW: the distinguished CBS commentator and friend of George Polk.

JOHN PANOPOULOS: chief of the Athens town police under the Ministry of Public Order.

STYLIANOS PAPATHEMILES: Minister for Northern Greece, who led Gregory Staktopoulos' effort to win a retrial and found crucial evidence raising serious questions regarding his first trial.

DREW PEARSON: Washington *Post* columnist and friend of George Polk.

ADELAIDE ROE POLK: mother of George Polk.

GEORGE W. POLK: CBS chief Middle East correspondent.

REA COCCONIS POLK: George Polk's widow.

WILLIAM R. POLK: George Polk's younger brother.

CONSTANTINE POULOS: foreign correspondent for the Overseas News Agency who (along with William Polk) represented the Newsmen's Commission at the Polk (Staktopoulos) murder trial and covered it for *The Nation*.

RUPERT PROHME: U.S. Information Service officer in Salonika and friend of George Polk.

Karl Rankin: chargé d'affaires and for a period (before the arrival of Ambassador Grady during the summer of 1948) the ranking American diplomat in Greece.

Constantine Rendis: Greek Minister of Public Order.

John Secondari: CBS Rome bureau staffer who assisted Winston Burdett in the Polk murder investigation.

Themistocles Sophoulis: Prime Minister of Greece during the Polk case and stepfather of Costas Hadjiargyris.

Anna Staktopoulos: Gregory Staktopoulos' mother.

Gregory Staktopoulos: Salonika reporter and Reuters stringer accused of having played a part in the murder of George Polk.

Daniel Thrapp: United Press correspondent in Salonika just prior to the Polk murder, posted to Rome during the murder investigation.

Athanasios Tsaldaris: son of Constantine Tsaldaris.

Constantine Tsaldaris: Greek Prime Minister in 1946, Foreign Minister during the Polk case.

Markos Vafiades: Communist guerrilla general.

Evangelos Vasvanas: Communist guerrilla leader accused of Polk's murder but never brought to trial.

Despina Vroutsis: George and Rea Polk's maid in Athens who provided investigators with a description of one of the key participants in the Polk murder.

Sir Charles Wickham: chief of the British Police and Prisons Mission in Greece.

Nikos Zachariades: the secretary-general of the Greek Communist Party.

THE POLK
CONSPIRACY

Introduction

At noon on a bright day in May 1948 they lowered George Polk's coffin, draped in the Stars and Stripes, into the dry Athenian ground. Polk, the chief Middle East correspondent for CBS News, had been dead for almost two weeks, but his body had surfaced in Salonika Bay just six days before. His arms and legs had been bound and the back of his skull had been blown away by a bullet fired point-blank.

The Greek Orthodox cemetery overflowed on this late-spring day with Greek cabinet ministers, much decorated officers, and the ranking members of the American Embassy. A short distance away, the tall cypresses that framed the cemetery's iron gates barely sheltered the dignitaries' bodyguards and Rolls-Royces.

An observer of this serene setting and the display of conspicuous affluence might have been surprised to learn that this was a country in the throes of civil war.

Equally startling was the fact that all these dignitaries had gathered, not for the final rites of a general or a civic eminence, but for a reporter, murdered while carrying out an assignment.

Like the country in which it occurred, George Polk's murder posed a critical problem for Washington. Greece had recently become the front line of the Cold War—the place chosen by Harry S. Truman in which to draw the line against Soviet expansion. The murder in Salonika of an American reporter known to be an irritant to Washington's new friend threatened to erupt into a diplomatic nightmare.

These final rites in the shadow of the Acropolis were meant to bury not only a man but what he had stood for. The men who planned the funeral, Greeks and Americans, very nearly achieved both those aims.

Leading the funeral procession were the Greek Minister of Justice, George Melas, and, flanking him, the Minister of Public Order, Constantine Rendis. Melas and Rendis had the responsibility of overseeing this delicate case. Six gendarmes, members of the most reactionary of the country's many security forces, bore Polk's coffin on their muscular shoulders. Karl Rankin, chargé d'affaires at the American Embassy, at the time the highest-ranking American diplomat in Greece, followed the procession. Rankin knew his future in the foreign service depended on how adroitly he advanced Washington's interests among the many elements of the volatile Greek political landscape.

Washington had thrown its full weight behind a coalition of anti-left politicians, which, although nominally headed by a Liberal, was actually dominated by the Royalists (called "Populists"). The coalition's chief virtue, in Washington's view, was its determination to crush the Communist insurgents. It was a risky business, meddling in another nation's civil war. The risk was heightened by the odious practices of the oligarchy Washington felt compelled to support. But Rankin firmly believed that American interests were best served by maintaining the Royalists in power. To guarantee that end, he supported massive infusions of American aid.

Rankin felt comfortable with his role as American proconsul in Athens. He made no secret about this, nor about his view of the man they had come to bury. Rankin felt George Polk had been uncooperative and unpatriotic. It was too bad men of his sort were placed in positions of trust by their employers. Rankin had done everything in his power to call that fact to the attention of those who counted in Washington.

The Greeks who had gathered at this funeral were, like Melas and Rendis, members of the Athenian elite, born into the great shipping and trading houses, scions of the banking, merchant, and political dynasties. They were not prepared to share their wealth and property. They particularly did not wish to cede anything to the Communist guerrillas, their countrymen, who, having fought for Greece against the Nazi occupation, now demanded some significant share of economic and political power. The origins of the Greek Civil War were vastly more complex than this, of course. But from the American government's point of view, what counted was the current Greek regime's determined resistance to any form of Communist encroachment. George Polk had questioned this oversimplification. His repeated probing and his exposures of corruption among the Greek ruling elite had become a threat to sustaining this new Greek-American alliance.

Both Washington and the current Greek regime agreed on this point. As they saw it, during those days of hardening East-West tensions, the press was meant to serve a higher cause than the mere reporting of events. The press was meant to be harnessed to foreign and domestic policy. The man they had come to bury in Athens' most important cemetery had not played by those rules.

George Polk's twenty-year-old Greek widow, her eyes fixed on the flag-draped coffin as it slowly disappeared under mounds of earth, seemed almost abstracted in her grief. She and George had been married only eight months. It was simply not possible that she should already be his widow. He was too young, only thirty-four. They had planned to begin the long journey to America, a place she had never seen, the following week. Rea Polk leaned on the arm of a young Greek woman, who squeezed her hand in support. Mary Cawadias Barber hadn't left Rea's side since the day the widow returned to Athens from Salonika with her husband's coffin. Rea did not question Mary Barber's sudden devotion. Rea Polk needed a friend. Only later, when Mary Barber, a stringer for *Time*, vanished from her life as abruptly as she had appeared, did the young widow wonder.

Now, with all these strangers hovering around George's coffin, Rea Polk was not even allowed to say a private goodbye to her husband. She knew what these men stood for and how George had felt about them, but had been too weak to stop them from making this their ceremony. They had even insisted on the gold inscription for the white marble tombstone. "George W. Polk, Lieutenant, U.S. Navy," it read. They were men impressed by George's military record, the medals and citations he had earned for his heroic performance as a World War II Navy fighter pilot at Guadalcanal, the Pacific's bloodiest battlefield. The men gathered at Polk's grave site were themselves run by military men, the country's invisible government. But that was not how Polk would have wished to be remembered. He had only enlisted out of wartime patriotism and had since been in the Naval Reserve. "George Polk, Reporter"— that would have suited him.

The final testament of a man who loved his profession, Polk's will specified that he be buried in whichever country he died. He had begun drifting from his native Fort Worth, Texas, a decade before. Though born into a proud Southern family that claimed a President, an Under Secretary of State, and a Civil War general, Polk was really a child of the Depression. Scarred by his father's ruin in the Great Crash, and by his parents' divorce, which followed, George Polk never really considered any place home.

His first and most passionate love had been reserved for his profession. It was a mutual affection. Edward R. Murrow, Polk's mentor at CBS, considered Polk the best prospect of the new crop of foreign correspondents. "His copy is clean, hard, and well documented," Murrow said of Polk's broadcasts when the State Department and the Greek Embassy in Washington began to put the heat on CBS to rein in Polk. "And his stories stand up," Murrow had stated in attempting to counter the charge that Polk's reporting was biased, "every last one of them."

George Polk had been driven by an unusual appetite for experience and knowledge, invaluable traits for a foreign correspondent. His innate rootlessness was also an asset. He was always an outsider. Polk believed you could not maintain objectivity and watchfulness if you made a comfortable place for yourself in any society. He rarely socialized with the people he wrote about. In all the places he lived and worked—Washington, New York, Cairo, Athens—he kept his distance.

In May 1948, George Polk was finally coming home. A Nieman Fellowship awaited him at Harvard. CBS wanted him for an important job in Washington.

Edward R. Murrow, Howard K. Smith, Eric Sevareid, Charles Collingwood, and William Shirer had dominated CBS's news coverage during the war years. Murrow of the golden voice and the prickly conscience had Polk in mind as one of his natural successors. The volatile postwar political climate required a cool observer, immune to the zealot's urgings, a man of proven courage like Polk.

But the times also favored a quality that Polk did not possess. With the clouds of fanatical anti-Communism gathering, Americans were expected not only to love their country but to love it blindly. George Polk believed his job was to report both sides of every story, no matter what the consequences. And so he had in Greece, transformed into the vortex of the Cold War. America had very little prior experience in Greece, had not until very recently deemed Greece to be even remotely important to her national security. But by 1948 Washington had become enmeshed in nearly every facet of Greek life.

The Truman administration became entangled in the Greek Civil War for the sake of "preserving Democracy." Greece was a strange candidate for this rescue operation in the name of democracy. It was ruled by a discredited king and a graft-ridden oligarchy. What resources had not been bled by Nazi occupation were controlled by 2 percent of its population. But Washington was determined to "save" Greece at any cost, partly because there weren't too many places left in Central Europe or the Balkans to save from Stalin's grasp. "From Stettin in the Baltic to Trieste in the Adriatic an iron curtain has descended across the continent," Churchill had warned in his historic March 1946 speech at Fulton, Missouri. "Behind that line lie all the capitals of the ancient states of Central and Eastern Europe. Warsaw, Berlin, Prague, Vienna, Budapest, Belgrade, Bucharest, and Sofia . . . Athens, Greece, alone," Churchill intoned, "with its immortal glories, is free to decide its future."

One year after Churchill sounded those alarms, Washington responded with the Truman Doctrine. "I believe," Truman told Congress on March 12, 1947, "that it must be the policy of the United States to support free peoples who are resisting attempted subjugation by armed minorities or by outside pressures." The speech signified a turning point in American foreign policy, which, since George Washington's early admonishment, had stayed clear of the entangling alliances of European politics. America now pronounced itself ready, willing, and able to rush to the aid of any "free peoples" regardless of geographic or strategic considerations. But unlike other imperial powers, its motive for this far-flung policy was not exploitation but democracy's sacred trust. Or so it was said.

Washington had few illusions about its client's commitment to the rights of "free peoples." But in 1947 the United States was ready to back almost any government willing to resist Russia's drive to expand its territorial control. Much of Greece, ideally suited for guerrilla warfare with its craggy, impenetrable mountain ranges, was, by 1947, dominated by the Communist guerrillas. Only the cities belonged to the Athens government.

It was not a time when subtle or even obvious distinctions were made between a Communist Party run from the Kremlin and one that sprang from its own national roots. The Greek left had never had more than the Kremlin's grudging approval. In 1944, Stalin had struck a good bargain with Churchill, in effect trading Greece for most of the rest of the Balkans. In this matter, Stalin meant to keep his end of the bargain.

But Washington, gripped by Cold War fever, saw the world in terms of two categories: Communist and non-Communist. If Greece fell to a Communist regime, warned Dean Acheson, one of the Truman Doctrine architects, "like apples in a barrel infected by one rotten one," Iran, Asia Minor, Egypt, Italy, and France would fall prey. Acheson's rhetoric was prophetic of Dean Rusk's domino theory of two decades later.

America's massive intervention in Greek life was its first such experiment outside the Western Hemisphere and the Philippines in saving a country from itself. It was not its proudest moment. In many ways the United States continues to pay the price today for its policies of four decades ago.

In 1990, an armed guard must still stand a twenty-four-hour vigil beside the statue of Harry S. Truman on a broad Athens boulevard. Though the inscription on its pedestal reads: "Statesman, Humanitarian, Pan-Hellene," Truman, whose doctrine was meant to make Greece safe for democracy, is, to many Greeks, a symbol of colonial manipulation. The statue is a frequent target of vandals and terrorists. The embattled monument is only an outward symbol of a far deeper rancor.

In 1947 and 1948, George Polk was one of the few to openly question the wisdom of some of our government's political decisions. He was appalled at the choice of America's new ally, and in his frequent broadcasts showed why.

Murrow claimed that George Polk knew more about Greece than any other foreign correspondent. But George Polk was not the lone critic of a regime even her supporters found sinister. The critical question is: Why was George Polk murdered? Why not any of the other tough-minded reporters covering America's growing involvement in Greek life? What did George Polk know? Who killed him? And why?

I. F. Stone said that George Polk was the first casualty of the Cold War. His brutal murder had more than Polk as its victim, however. America lost much of its innocence in that piercingly beautiful land. The crime of murder was soon to be compounded by other crimes.

Though largely played out on Greek soil, the Polk affair is the story of the age-old conflict between the press and the government. George Polk stood for the kind of open society Thomas Jefferson and Woodrow Wilson envisioned. He was ultimately defeated by forces more comfortable with secrecy, by people advocating a closed government, in which power is held by a few.

As a former foreign correspondent, the child and the wife of foreign correspondents, I found myself drawn to the unsolved murder of one of the profession's most accomplished practitioners. There was another pull as well. In a way, George Polk altered the course of my life. In 1957, my mother and father, having recently escaped with their children from post-revolt Budapest to Vienna, traveled to New York for the sole purpose of receiving the George Polk Award for their coverage of the Hungarian uprising. It was the first time the Polk Award had been presented to a married couple. It was also the first time any member of my family had set foot in the New World. On that early spring day, my family made the decision to start our lives anew here.

If I have brought a particular sensibility to this subject, it has been the result of having experienced the Cold War as a child. The murder trial that followed Polk's assassination reminded me of the more notorious show trials of my Budapest childhood. My parents, Hungarian nationals employed as correspondents by two American wire services during the 1950s, were victims of a similar court performance. They, like Gregory Staktopoulos, who was ultimately convicted of the murder of George Polk, were dispatched on the flimsiest "evidence" to serve long prison terms. In my parents' case the charge was the catchall crime of being CIA agents. Cold War paranoia had its mirror image east and west of the divide.

They gave George Polk a hero's funeral on that beautiful day in Athens. But the elaborate wreaths and the solemn-faced dignitaries were there for all the wrong reasons. While it is doubtful any of those reliable bureaucrats who followed his coffin with measured steps will be remembered, the man they buried surely will. And whatever his official epitaph, he will be remembered the way he would have wished: George Polk, Reporter.

1

―――――

"You won't be hearing from me for a couple of days, Bob," George Polk said, his voice crackling over the transatlantic line into Robert Skedgell's earphone. Skedgell, a young CBS editor, was lining up the morning news spots from around the world. It was 7:55 a.m. in New York on Thursday, May 6, 1948.

"Where are you off to now, George?"

"Up north, to have a last look around . . . see some places I've never seen . . . Kavalla . . . Konitsa . . ." Polk said, ticking off datelines the Greek Civil War had put on the CBS map. "Rea's coming with me, though her mind is already on New York," Polk added, laughing. It was an easy laugh that Skedgell would remember for years.

"I'll bring her in to meet you in a couple of weeks. She's a beauty, Bob."

"O.K., George. Stand by, please." Skedgell gave Polk the countdown cue. "Three, two, one, go . . ."

"Here in Greece," Polk began, "this capital city has a slight case of the jitters. So far today, and it's only early afternoon in Athens, forty-four alleged Communists have been executed.

"The British government has indicated an official protest, saying the shootings have come 'as a great shock for all in London.' "

Though less deliberate than Edward R. Murrow's famous staccato, Polk's pared-down delivery owed much to the man whose career he hoped to emulate. He tried not only to sound like his mentor but to be as uncompromising in his reporting.

"There has been no official reaction from American authorities,"

George read on. "Since Monday, more than two hundred persons have been put to death by Greek Army firing squads. . . ."

Skedgell did not want to interrupt the reporter's flow, but the editor was concerned about the broadcast's air quality. Polk's voice kept fading out under the transatlantic hum.

"These executions," George Polk continued, "followed the assassination last Saturday of an important Greek cabinet minister, Christos Ladas, Minister of Justice. The assassin was a twenty-two-year-old Greek. He allegedly is a member of the Communist Party and was working under the instructions of Communist guerrilla chieftain Markos . . . according to Greek police. . . . The Greek government's anti-Communist measures include martial law, curfew at night, and heavy guards at strategic places. Today, a tommy gun is a more ordinary sight in Athens streets than a cigar. . . . This is George Polk reporting from Athens, and now back to CBS in New York."

"O.K., George, we got all that." Skedgell came back on. "Fine report. Lousy broadcast quality. Can't do much about the line, I'm afraid. Unusable."

"Oh well," Polk said, disappointed, but accustomed to the erratic temperament of transatlantic telephone lines, "Tomorrow's another day, right?"

"Have a good trip, George." Skedgell switched off the Athens line.

Polk had just signed off the air for the final time. The subject of the next CBS report from Athens would be George Polk's own assassination.

Two days earlier, Polk had gone to Athens' Ministry of Information seeking permission to travel to the north of Greece. The air had the soft warmth of summer that morning. The heady perfume of hyacinths and wild lupines wafted from the flower vendors' carts. Dazzling anemones and poppies brimmed from boxes everywhere on the square the Greeks call Syntagma, the heart of Athens. Polk inhaled it all as he walked toward the Ministry of Information, his reactions sharpened by his imminent departure.

The best hotels and two of the most important government offices face this handsome square. Dominating Syntagma is the Parliament House, once a palace, still radiating an air of self-conscious grandeur. The cafés squeezed together in the center of the square were crowded that morning with women already in their summer silks, the men looking prosperous in gray suits. Some of them fingered worry beads as they engaged in Athens' favorite pastime: passionate conversation. Waiters in long white aprons snaked between the tiny marble-topped tables.

This was a society addicted to news and rumor. A dozen different newspapers were strewn on tables. Silver pots filled with coffee, which was available in thirty-three varieties of strength and sweetness, gleamed in the sun. Here and there a flash of khaki muddied the pastel tableau, the only sign that this was the capital of a country at war against itself.

Turning down a narrow cobblestoned street toward the Ministry of Information, Polk saw a line of U.S. Army trucks covered with camouflage-colored canvas. A clutch of servicemen waited for the PX to open. Since the arrival of AMAG, the American Mission for Aid to Greece, some months before, the ancient winding street had been transformed into one more U.S. Army base.

Polk approached the ministry warily. It had been quite some time since he had encountered any response but icy formality, frequently followed by rejections of his many travel requests. Under martial law, travel was restricted primarily to military personnel and those favored by the Greek government. Polk was not among them.

Polk was regarded by most officials as a troublemaker. He did not take no gracefully, a dangerous quality in a police state. He liked to tease bureaucrats who had no intention of either changing their minds or appreciating his humor.

But on this day a man named Kavanides, who handled travel permits for the press, looked up from behind his baroque mahogany desk and smiled encouragingly at the lanky, blond American. "Your travel permit has been approved. You can fly to Kavalla on Friday," he said.

"And my wife and friends?" Polk asked. For he hoped to travel with Rea as well as his Greek stringer, Costas Hadjiargyris, and his English wife, Aileen. Hadji, as Hadjiargyris was known, was Polk's closest friend in Athens. This would be their last chance to take a trip together before Polk's return to America.

They, too, could travel north, Kavanides assured Polk.

Not long before, Polk had written to Ed Murrow that things had gotten so poisonous between certain members of the press and Greek and American officials in Athens that "somebody was likely to get hurt." Just the week before, he had received several threatening phone calls. "Watch out, Polk. We know you are a Communist," the hard-edged voice threatened before hanging up. But Polk wasn't overly concerned, regarding this as just one more attempt on the part of the Royalists to intimidate him.

On May 6, two days after Polk received his travel permit, his friend Hadji informed him that he and his wife would not be able to accompany him on the trip after all. The embattled north did not hold the same allure for Hadji as it did for the American reporter, and since Aileen felt she should stay home that week to help her new maid settle in, Hadji had decided to remain in Athens as well.

Polk was disappointed, but determined to go anyway. Rea would come along. Though relations between husband and wife had been volatile for some time, Polk was not comfortable with solitude. He was often plagued by pain from the war wounds that had never healed; at those times he appreciated company.

On the eve of their scheduled departure for Kavalla, George and Rea had one of their bad times. They had gone to a party around eight o'clock. Nobody ever thought of dinner until ten in Athens. There were the usual people in attendance. A handful of reporters, British and American, and a few Greeks accustomed to mixing with foreigners. While most of Greece was suffering from malnutrition, for this privileged group food and drink were always plentiful. In the shelter of a cosmopolitan capital, they lived as if in a colonial outpost.

George Polk was one of those men whose presence in a room is immediately felt. Tall and muscular, he had an unselfconscious elegance and a somewhat tentative smile that disarmed both men and women. Moreover, Polk seemed unaware of his power over people, which only enhanced his magnetism. People liked to please him.

On this particular evening, mostly from boredom, Polk engaged a cousin of Rea's, a pretty woman he barely knew, in conversation. Rea, watching from across the room, recalled how he had captivated her with his effortless charm not so very long before. Rea wondered why things weren't working out between them. She knew so little about him, except that she loved his looks and his endless ability to surprise and beguile. And now he seemed lost to her, caught up in some other woman's story.

Later, they exchanged a few hard, careless words. Upset, she said, "Go on your trip by yourself. I am staying home." It was the only way she could think of to repay hurt with hurt. These scenes were not uncommon between them. She hoped things would be better once they reached America. He needed a rest. Greece had gotten under his skin.

Still later that night, George stopped off at his friend Hadji's house. He hated the night. He never got through one without a nightmare. It was always the same: An ambush. The awful human scent of the Japanese soldier in the foxhole. The man's hot breath on his face. Just the way it had happened in Guadalcanal. He usually woke up screaming.

Polk counted on Hadji, not only for friendship but also for his knowledge of and remarkably dispassionate judgments about the labyrinthian world of Greek politics. As the stepson of the aged but respected Liberal Prime Minister, Themistocles Sophoulis (who referred to himself as the "captive Liberal" in the Royalist-dominated coalition), Hadji also had excellent connections. In addition to stringing for Polk and CBS News, Hadji was a correspondent for the *Christian Science Monitor* and also worked as a stringer for the Pulitzer Prize–winning reporter Homer Bigart, then of the New York *Herald Tribune*. Hadji, too, had his troubles with the authorities for resisting their attempt to spoon-feed him the news. He, like Polk and Bigart, had been called on the carpet by the American chargé d'affaires, Karl Rankin, who was incensed by the reporters' criticism of the regime America had chosen to support.

The regime itself took a more devious route in expressing its displeasure. Knowing how the *Christian Science Monitor* felt about reporters who imbibed, the Royalist disinformation people put out the word that Hadji, who rarely drank liquor, was a drunk. But there wasn't much more they could do to Hadji, not while his stepfather was in office.

The two friends talked about Polk's trip. Hadji told him Kavalla was the only really lush part of Greece. Polk said he would spend a few days there before pushing on to Konitsa, near the Albanian border. He wanted to get close to the battleground. Too many reporters were covering the civil war from the bar of Athens' swank Hotel Grande Bretagne. Polk planned to do some descriptive broadcasts about Greece as soon as he was back in America, the kinds of pieces that capture the smell and sound and feel of a place. Murrow loved that kind of broadcasting. George wanted to be prepared.

Polk arose early the next morning, May 7. He had already telexed CBS London bureau chief Howard K. Smith: "I am northward because unscheduled presently, plus Athens news paucity. Expecting return Tuesday. Hadjiargyris bystanding. Regards, Polk." In those pre-technological-revolution days, foreign correspondents informed the home office what their plans were. Not the other way around.

Rea did not stir, but the man both she and her husband called Baba, her father, was already up. He made George a cup of the thick, strong Greek coffee he loved. They sat in the small kitchen and chatted quietly.

Baba, whose wife had left him the year before, knew something about loneliness. He was always ready with coffee and quiet conversation. In this gentle, wise Greek George found the father he had lost so many years ago. He could talk to Baba about anything. He could even talk about the woman to whom he had been married before he met Rea, the woman who had left him in Cairo two years earlier.

Athens still slept when Polk's taxi drove him to the airport. He breathed in that gummy scent, unique to Athens, that comes from its many evergreens and their dried needles. A faint orange light glowed on the horizon. The Acropolis Hill seemed suspended in the soft early-morning light. The marble columns shone pink and apricot, and Polk thought he had never seen anything so breathtaking.

The airfield, overgrown with tufts of grass, made no pretense about its business: military transport. British Spitfires were the dominant aircraft, a reminder that though Washington was now the chief giver of aid, London had been here first.

Polk was booked on an American military plane. These bookings were much prized, as air was the only way to reach the north, apart from a long and arduous boat trip. The guerrillas owned much of the countryside between Athens and Kavalla. After signing a waiver agreeing that in case of accident, death, or injury he wouldn't hold the United States responsible, Polk took one of a long row of bucket seats.

In less than two hours, he could see the magnificent sweep of Salonika Bay, bounded on the west by the mountains that were the dwelling place of the gods of Greek mythology, Mount Olympus. It was the bay itself, calm, deep blue, and filled with colorful little vessels known as caïques, each with a jaunty sail of a different color, that transfixed Polk.

Polk loved arrivals, felt his pulse quicken at the possibility they held out for the unexpected. Descending the steep steps that had been wheeled up to the AMAG plane, he inhaled the soft sea air of Salonika. He strolled over to the information counter inside the shabby terminal to ask the Greek Army officer how soon the flight would push on for Kavalla. The Greek answered in English. "Didn't you know? The Kavalla airport is closed. The airfield is flooded." No, Polk hadn't been told in Athens.

"What about a room in Salonika?" the officer inquired. Polk decided he might as well stay on for a few days. The obliging officer picked up the phone. Within minutes, Polk was booked in Room 25 of the Astoria Hotel. It was not one of the city's best, but it was very close to the bay. It was a hotel favored by Greek Air Force personnel, the officer informed Polk.

Carrying his bag out of the terminal, Polk recognized the erect bearing and always crisp khakis of Colonel Allen "Ace" Miller, assistant Air Force attaché at the U.S. Embassy in Athens. "Hello, Ace," Polk said, extending his hand. "Ride into town with me?"

"No, thanks, George, I'm headed back to Athens. But I'll be back Monday." Miller and Polk fixed a date for Monday. "What are you up to, George?" the colonel asked with the easy familiarity they had established since discovering they had attended the Virginia Military Institute at roughly the same time. Miller didn't pay attention to the embassy gossip about Polk bending over too far to see the dark side of things in Greece. He thought Polk was one of the best reporters he'd met in the field.

Polk told him he didn't have any real plans, that he hadn't expected to stay on in Salonika. But he'd been there before, so he'd look up some friends, talk to some sources.

"Got any contacts you could pass on, Ace?" Polk inquired, knowing the colonel had been around longer than most Americans. "Of course, I'd like to get to the other side before I go home."

Miller said yes, he'd built up some good contacts to the *andartes*, the Greek name for the guerrillas. Almost everybody else at the embassy called them bandits, the Greek right's name for them. "It's been some time since I've used those names. I'll have to look them up for you, George. But I'll bring them along on Monday."

They shook hands goodbye.

Another American officer, whom Polk knew only slightly, a Colonel Smith, was also headed toward the Astoria, and offered George a lift in his jeep.

The Astoria was located on Agias Sofias Street, a few minutes' walk from Nikis Street, the wide promenade that hugged the corniche and the harbor. The hotel was a place of no particular style or taste, neither very old nor new, just a place to stay. The Astoria's clientele was not the kind who made a fuss about decor. They were almost all Greeks, almost all connected to the military. But then most people who moved around Greece in 1948 were either fleeing an army or on military business.

The blond American who checked in at midmorning on Friday must have been a curious sight in the Astoria's faded lobby, though later no one would claim any memory of him.

Polk, a meticulous man, unpacked his small suitcase, opened his portable typewriter on the little desk the hotel provided, and hurriedly left the small room. His first stop was the U.S. Consulate, which faced the bay, a short walk from the Astoria.

On a prior trip Polk had befriended Rupert Prohme, the young U.S. Information Service man in Salonika. Prohme was in a conference when Polk stuck his head in the door. They made a date to meet later that day. Prohme, who knew Polk would be restless until he found a story to cover, suggested he stroll over to the Mediterranean Hotel, where a United Nations committee was holding hearings on the *pedomazoma*, the kidnapping of children by the Communist forces.

Polk was soon having lunch with a Dr. Ahmed, a Pakistani official of the United Nations Special Committee on the Balkans. Ahmed briefed him on the committee's findings on this latest and perhaps most grotesque in a long list of outrages foisted on the Greek population.

In March 1948, the Provisional Government of Greece, as the Communist forces chose to call themselves, had announced a new policy over its radio. All children between the ages of three and fourteen in the regions under guerrilla control would be collected and sent to "People's Democracies" behind the Iron Curtain. The *pedomazoma*, the gathering up of children, was "for their own good," the rebel radio assured the highly skeptical Greek population. The guerrillas said they wanted to safeguard the new generation of Greeks, to protect them from the ravages of hunger and the "monarcho-fascists."

The *pedomazoma* ultimately did the Communists a great deal of harm. The policy backfired. After years of war and Nazi occupation, Greeks were not about to condone similar cruelties carried out by their own countrymen. The world at large was outraged when it learned of children being forcibly torn from their parents.

As he listened to Dr. Ahmed describe scenes of villages in the Grammos Mountains resisting the guerrillas' demand that they hand over their children, Polk felt a familiar surge of excitement. It was the electric feeling brought on by the prospect of a big story. This one touched him in a personal way.

Although childless and, for a number of reasons, determined to remain so, Polk loved children. Everywhere he moved around the world, he befriended them. He was still helping a black student he knew in New York with checks and long letters full of paternal advice. There was an orphanage in Cairo which had come to depend on Polk's generosity. The *pedomazoma* was not just another news release for Polk. He would stay on in Salonika, he decided, until the UN committee released its final report.

After lunch Polk went to look in on the Associated Press stringer in Salonika, Helen Mamas. Massachusetts-born but of Greek origin, the blond reporter was very young, not much past twenty, the only woman among the foreign correspondents in Salonika, and anxious not to be bested by any of them. She caught Polk just as he was leaving her hotel, the Cosmopolit, where he had left his card for her.

"What's new?" she asked, having seen him just the week before at the USIS office in Athens. "The *pedomazoma* story is shaping up," Polk answered. "How about dinner tonight?" Helen agreed and then asked if George would mind taking a small package to America for her parents. "You are still planning on leaving for New York soon?" she asked. "Yes, absolutely." They decided to meet at the bar of the Mediterranean Hotel later and wait for the UN press release on the children before having dinner.

"Helen," Polk asked as he was leaving, "got any good contacts to the other side?" She shook her head. "I use official sources only," she answered carefully.

He had time to kill now, so George ambled along Nikis Street, where the afternoon strollers had already begun their timeless ritual. In an hour or so the boulevard would be teeming with promenaders.

The arched windows of the six- and seven-storied buildings that lined Nikis Street recalled the long Ottoman occupation of this port city. Salonika, which joined the modern Greek state eighty years after Athens, still showed much of the influence of Byzantium. Many of the street signs, however, were in German, a legacy of the port's most recent army of occupation.

By six o'clock in the evening Polk had made his plans. He sent a message to Rea, using the abbreviated language of telegramese: "Decided remain Astoria Hotel Salonika because United Nations story upshaping on child abduction. Perhaps continuing Kavalla Monday or Tuesday then returning Athens. Don't forget advise me here any word Nieman Fellowship . . . Eyell cable departure Love Baba You, George."

At 7:30, Polk and several other correspondents, including Helen Mamas, met at the bar of the Mediterranean Hotel to await the UN press release. Rupert Prohme, the USIS man, arrived, bringing with him a young American diplomat named Oliver Crosby, up from Athens for the weekend. Don Matchan, a North Dakotan who was a reporter for the York, Pennsylvania, *Daily Gazette*, on his first trip to Greece, spotted the group and pulled up a chair.

It was a high-spirited circle, drinking, laughing, and swapping war stories. Crosby and Matchan both recall George as an almost incandescent spirit that night, weaving tales of Palestine, of close calls with Arabs, Jews, and the British. The CBS man dominated the conversation without seeming to do so.

Around 9:30, Ahmed, press release in hand, joined them. "The committee agrees that the task is an urgent one . . . practical measures on the abduction of children must be taken as soon as possible." Ahmed paused to let them finish scribbling his words verbatim into their notepads. "The committee will meet tomorrow at 10 a.m.," he concluded. The language of the communiqué was as strong as anybody could dare hope for from a UN committee, but it was not strong enough to make a reporter spring to his feet and abandon a pleasant gathering.

In 1948, serving as a foreign correspondent was a far more leisurely business than it is now. Without the benefit of satellites, or video cameras that have eliminated film-processing time, or fax machines, or even reliable phone service, the correspondent could vanish for days at a time from the long reach of the home office. As George Polk and his colleagues saw it, there would be time enough to pursue the *pedomazoma* tomorrow.

Shortly before they left the bar for dinner, a Greek journalist approached the table and asked Helen Mamas, whom he knew, to introduce him to the rest.

Gregory Staktopoulos spoke perfect English, which he learned at Salonika's only English-speaking school, Anatolia College. Like so many other survivors of armies of occupation Staktopoulos had learned to accommodate himself to new regimes. He was perhaps too pliant a man. He liked to please a bit too much. His politics had wavered from left to right to center and now again to the right, that being the safest course at the moment.

Staktopoulos declined to join the group for a drink. He never touched alcohol, he explained. As the sole supporter of a widowed mother and two sisters, he was always working, always in a hurry. Smiling and bowing, Staktopoulos left them with their drinks and their gaiety and returned to the city room of *Makedonia*, the newspaper where he worked the night shift.

The alcohol-warmed group made its way from the Mediterranean down Nikis Street to the Olympus Naoussa restaurant. Large, noisy, and unpretentious, it was the kind of hangout reporters around the world inevitably find and make their own. The seafood was fresh and the wine reasonable. The group feasted on fried eels and mussels and white Macedonian Korona wine. Polk regaled them with details of his recent trip to Iraq. Raising his glass, he said this might be the last time they all gathered at this table, as he was scheduled to fly home in less than two weeks. They drank to his safe trip and his continued good fortune.

Halfway through the meal, a waiter approached and told Helen Mamas she was wanted on the telephone. She returned moments later. "It was Greg Staktopoulos," she informed the group. "He wanted to know everybody's name. He's doing a piece about newly arrived foreign correspondents in Salonika."

At 11:30, Polk, Prohme, and Crosby left the restaurant together and strolled along the bay in the direction of the American Consulate, where the two diplomats were staying. Matchan and Mamas returned to their hotel. Polk walked the short distance to the Astoria alone.

The next morning, Saturday, May 8, Polk arose at 7:00, his habit when on a story. There is strong evidence pointing to Polk's making contact between 7:00 and 9:30 a.m. with the people who, before the day's end, would lead him to his death. For by 9:30 a.m. Polk had made appointments (details of which he would not share with any of his friends or colleagues in Salonika) for both Saturday and

Sunday evenings. This much he told Rupert Prohme when he called on him at the USIS offices at 9:30 Saturday morning.

Declining invitations for Saturday and Sunday, Polk made a date with Prohme for Monday night.

The abduction of children was still very much on Polk's mind later that morning when he saw Gerald Drew, the American delegate on the UN committee. But he also asked Drew if he had good contacts to the Communists. Drew, a recent arrival in Salonika, said he did not.

Down the street from the American Consulate, also facing the bay, was the seven-story building that housed the British Consulate. Reporters arriving in Salonika made a point of stopping off there for their first briefing on the civil war. There was good reason for this. The British were much better connected and had far deeper roots in Greece than the Americans, relative newcomers on the scene. Randoll Coate, British information officer at the consulate, had a reputation as the best source on northern Greece in the country.

An Oxford University–nurtured love of the classics and the image of Lord Byron felled at Missolonghi for the cause of Greek independence had first attracted Coate to the ancient land. In this he was not unlike scores of other British agents and diplomats in Greece. During the war, Coate had been attached as an intelligence officer to the left wing of the resistance, the so-called ELAS guerrillas. ELAS, organized in 1942 to repel the Nazi occupiers, was made up primarily of anti-monarchist leftists who in a very vague way shared a vision of a new "people's Greece." The movement constituted about 90 percent of the wartime resistance. In the early days of the war, when defeating the Nazis was the Allies' overwhelming purpose, Churchill had called ELAS "those gallant guerrillas."

As the war progressed, however, so did British opposition to ELAS—based on fear of a postwar Communist power grab in Greece. The British were determined, once the Nazis had been routed, to restore the Greek monarchy, and the "gallant guerrillas" became, in Churchill's words, "miserable banditti."

Randoll Coate, a maverick diplomat, was not in step with the new order from his own capital. But then he had seldom been in step. Considered a bit eccentric, he preferred the company of visiting journalists to that of the "old duffers," as he referred to his fellow diplomats. "I never served under an ambassador whose first questions were not 'Do you play golf? Polo? Cricket?' " Coate later recalled. He played none of those games. And he loathed Britain's high-handedness in dealing with Greece, its protectorate.

To Polk, the thirty-eight-year-old Coate must have appeared to be the portrait of the English squire. Randoll Coate had the breezy manner and clipped tones of an Old Etonian who had whiled away the day at his London club.

"My colleagues in Athens urged me to come see you," the young American began. "I'd like to get to the other side." The Englishman studied him closely. "You have helped others before . . ." Polk's voice trailed off.

Coate, who had lived with the guerrillas, did not think George Polk was ready for the mountains. He looked too young and inexperienced. He seemed to be in too much of a hurry. It took weeks and even months to lay the groundwork for such a trip. The confidence of so many hard and deeply suspicious people had to be won. The police, uniformed and not, were everywhere.

"I have one name I can give you," Coate said, for he did not wish to send the young man away empty-handed. "The one you gave Barber?" Polk asked. Steve Barber, an English newspaperman, husband of Mary Barber of *Time* magazine, had told Polk about a contact of Coate's.

"He didn't pan out. I want a direct contact," Polk said, his voice edgy with impatience. Coate shook his head. "I really can't help you," he said, convinced now the man was in too much of a hurry for such a perilous mission. Coate stood up to indicate he considered the interview over.

Still concerned with the story of the abduction of children, George Polk returned twice to the Mediterranean Hotel, where the UN committee continued to meet behind closed doors. He sent his card in to Ahmed, but by the time the Pakistani official came out to look for him, Polk was gone.

Between 12:30 and 1:00 Polk was at the bar of the Mediterranean

Hotel, hoping to catch Matchan for lunch. Matchan did not return to his hotel until 7 p.m., when, too late, he found Polk's card inviting him to lunch. No one remembers seeing Polk at the lunch hour. After lunch, when the city of Salonika, faithful to Mediterranean custom, pulled in its shutters for the afternoon siesta, Polk was seen at his own hotel. A passionate letter writer, he wrote two sometime that afternoon and evening. The first was to his mother, Adelaide, who had recently returned to her home in California after spending five weeks with him. The second was to his friend and mentor, Ed Murrow.

"One of my reasons for coming north," Polk wrote his CBS colleague, "has been to get into some kind of direct, businesslike contact with the Markos government crowd. Since 1946, I've not had a contact with the Greek Communist Party that I believed was a real contact. Lots of persons have presented themselves to me claiming to speak authoritatively, but I think they were all phonies. So, with a contact through a contact, *I'd like to get in touch with persons who count*. If necessary, I'll go outside Salonika, to any other town or village 'they' may designate."

A "contact," this time a convincing one, had been in touch with Polk. But still nothing had been pinned down, no firm date set. Neither the American Consulate nor CBS News need yet be alerted that he was embarked on a high-risk expedition. The discussions were at a preliminary stage.

Around 6 p.m., Polk left the Astoria to send a cable to Rea: "Planning to go to Kavalla by air on Wednesday. Why don't you join me there for a couple of days' stay . . . Suggest you fly via Greek Airlines Wednesday or Thursday . . . Please reply Astoria Hotel Salonika Love Baba You George."

At 7 p.m., he kept a date for drinks with Gerald Drew, the American delegate on the UN committee meeting in Salonika. They met at Drew's apartment and parted about an hour later, having agreed to have lunch together the next day. Drew was the last American to see George Polk alive.

Seven days later, after Polk had been missing for one week, the Associated Press in Athens reported on its wires: "Police saying Polk making effort contact guerrillas. Press Minister confirmed this, adding not unusual for American correspondents to be out of contact for week, American Information Service officer Athens said Polk planning make direct contact with guerrilla forces. From Salonika American Consulate and Greek military security officials watching northern Greece for Polk. Security officials began investigating several days ago after Salonika police received by mail the American war correspondent's credentials."

On Sunday, May 16, at 1 p.m. Washington time, the following telegram clattered over the State Department's wire: "Please inform the Columbia Broadcasting System George Polk's body washed ashore in Salonika Bay. Foul play indicated. Further details to follow. Signed, Raleigh Gibson, Consul General."

2

More than miles separated the dusty cow town of 1930s Fort Worth, Texas, where fifty years was history, from Salonika, a teeming port with a twenty-five-hundred-year memory. The distance George Polk traveled was enormous: from the self-satisfied insularity of the plains of north-central Texas into the tangled web of several millennia of Byzantine history. In many ways George Washington Polk's journey mirrored his country's own plunge from secure isolationism into the unfamiliar entanglements of a global superpower.

But then, over the past two centuries Polks had been part of every critical development in the American odyssey. They had been public servants and military leaders for generations.

None of the members of the Polk clan or their friends who celebrated the birth of the first child of George Washington and Adelaide Polk on October 17, 1913, could predict that the newborn would find his happiness outside Fort Worth. Life, they felt sure, did not get much better than Fort Worth after World War I. Just-tapped Breckenridge oil was gushing. Cotton and cattle were still king. The town's rough-and-ready character was beginning to evolve into a more disciplined vitality that supported cultural pursuits alongside the pursuit of money. There was still nothing refined about the north side of Fort Worth, along the stockyards, where the air hung foul and heavy. But the stockyards and the oil and the cotton made the rest happen.

Great houses, many in the Tudor style, sprouted along the perimeters of the River Crest Country Club, the heart of Fort Worth society. The Polks lived in Edgehill Manor, the biggest house of them all: a twenty-room mansion with leaded-glass windows and polished parquet floors and a playroom spacious enough for the children to ride their bicycles within its boundaries.

George Polk, Jr., the child of this new prosperity, possessed a beautiful mother, a handsome and rich father, ten dogs, a pony, and two black servants, children of his grandfather's slaves, to look after him. His father, a Fort Worth lawyer, loved to take him hunting and fishing. There was neither much crime nor much traffic in Fort Worth, the kind of town where dogs slept in the street. Everyone knew everyone else, knew when their ancestors' wagon trains had pulled into town, and what they had done in the war meant to end wars.

When he was eleven, George wrote in his diary: "My father is a lawyer. His law firm is Polk and Samson. He was a captain in the World War. He is my pal. He is big and tall. . . ."

Of his mother, young George wrote in his diary: "I think I love her with all my heart and she loves me with all her heart. She has long brownish golden hair and it is so beautiful. She reads to me and plays games with me."

Three sisters, Adelaide, Milbry, and Jeanne Marie, came along in rapid succession. When George was sixteen, a brother, William Roe, was born. In those early years, when George was growing up with the sons and daughters of ranchers and oilmen, regularly winning silver cups at the country club swimming meets, the Polks' good fortune seemed as large and constant as the Texas sky.

The Carters, the Richardsons, the Van Zandts, and the Polks formed this enclave. Bloodlines were almost as important as money to these families. Far from the more European Eastern cities, they craved legitimacy and culture. The more time that elapsed since a man made his first million, the higher his family was ranked in the social pecking order.

They thought anybody who left Fort Worth for more than a few weeks, even if only to travel as far as Houston, was of dubious character. Fort Worth society prided itself on its absence of curiosity about the rest of the world. Texas was all the world they needed.

The Polk family had all the required qualifications to belong to this aristocracy. Everybody knew that President James Polk was George Polk, Sr.'s great-uncle. Lesser-known forebears included

Frank Polk, an Under Secretary of State at the time of the Versailles Treaty, and General Leonidas Polk, killed at Pine Mountain during a spectacularly bloody Civil War battle.

Young George's grandfather, James, a Civil War captain by the time he was seventeen, had made the journey west from Tennessee. George loved Papa, as he called his grandfather, who lived with the growing family in Fort Worth. Papa made the Civil War seem very real, a chapter of family history. Papa instilled in the boy, as he had in his own son, pride in the past, in the glories of the Polk forebears.

Young Polk was tremendously proud of his somewhat distant father and used to clip newspaper articles for his bulging scrapbook whenever G. W. Polk put up another office building in Fort Worth.

At Stripling High School, one of the two elite public schools in Fort Worth, George played football and romanced a lot of girls. His grades, particularly in English and the sciences, were good enough to gain him admission to the college several generations of Polk men had attended, the Virginia Military Institute in Lexington, Virginia.

Part Southern gentlemen's finishing school and part rigorous training for future officers, VMI had for generations prepared pedigreed Southerners for public service. General Stonewall Jackson was once a physics instructor at VMI. General of the Army and Secretary of State George C. Marshall graduated in the Class of 1901.

But, unlike his father and his grandfather, George would never graduate from VMI. Before the end of George's junior year, the Polk family had been swept up in a disaster as powerful as the Civil War had been for George's grandfather: the Depression.

George Polk's father, raised on the American work ethic that held if you worked diligently, you would succeed, found he had no cash, no credit, and no reputation left among his peers. Like a man caught in an earthquake, he didn't understand what he had done to bring about this calamity.

What made the elder Polk's ruin all the more personally rancorous was that it was not his own money he had invested and lost. His ambitious real estate schemes had been financed by Adelaide's inheritance. Now, when there was nothing left, he was overwhelmed by guilt and a sense of failure. He could no longer live up to his society's most fundamental expectation of a man: the ability to provide.

A man like Polk might have been able to endure lack of income for a few months or even a year or two. But after three or four years with no hope of being able to pay off his debts and no recourse except bankruptcy, he sank into a prolonged depression. His father's death-in-life fundamentally altered the father-son relationship just as George was reaching manhood.

Adelaide Polk, coddled daughter of a lumber millionaire, now tapped her own remarkable inner resources. There had been clues along the way that this woman was no mere Fort Worth country club matron. At a time when young ladies were not expected to finish high school, she had earned a liberal arts degree from the University of Chicago. It was there that Adelaide met and fell in love with the quiet, stern-faced Texan with the proud heritage.

Now, with her family bankrupt, Adelaide returned to school and earned a more practical sort of degree: in library science. She was soon making a living, a bare one at $900 a year, but enough to keep the family together.

The sight of his privileged and cherished wife taking over as head of the household, going off every morning to a school on the shabby side of town, destroyed whatever self-respect George Polk, Sr., had left.

George Polk's childhood effectively ended with the Depression and his father's ruin. He was not yet twenty. He saw his father, the man he had called "my pal," transformed from a loving but firm figure into a distraught and irritable presence in the family's midst. What made it worse was that Fort Worth had weathered the Depression relatively well and few among his set had been hit as hard as Polk.

The ranchers and the oilmen could wait out the Depression, their assets intact. All Polk had left was the big house in the best neighborhood in town. The only reason he still owned it was that there were no buyers for a house that size in the early 1930s. So they suffered the ignominy of taking in boarders. The Polks could not keep up payment of their country club dues. Soon they were no longer deemed to be among the "right" families of Fort Worth.

Nor could they afford to send their son back to VMI. Henceforth, Fort Worth assumed a different character for George. It was now a place to flee, not a place to build a life.

George spent the summer of 1933 pumping gas. That fall, he was hired by Conoco, the Continental Oil Company, to sell gas to stations in northern Texas. These were the early days of America's burgeoning car culture, and in spite of the depressed economy, gas stations were springing up like mushrooms after rain all over the West. The oil company sent him on to California, Oregon, and Washington State to keep new stations supplied.

The snappy VMI cadet's blues were replaced by oil-smeared khakis, his new uniform.

Like many people during those years of constricted dreams, Polk found some escape through listening to the radio, which was replacing the hearth as the center of the American home. More than just providing laughter and music, radio in the 1930s was a gateway to other worlds. It was in radio that Polk would ultimately find salvation.

People in those days did not just turn on their Atwater Kent wireless sets for background sound, the audible wallpaper radio would become. Radio was an event. You listened when Lowell Thomas or Elmer Davis or Jack Benny or Amos 'n' Andy came on.

Urging his used Conoco Chevrolet from one gas station to the next, indifferent to the spectacular beauty of the Northwest, a landscape unaltered by suburbs or superhighways or shopping malls, young George Polk listened to some of the century's most entrancing music. Gershwin, Berlin, Armstrong, and Copland were in his mind forever mingled with those hot, empty roads, the dust that seeped into his pores and mouth.

Polk's easy charm and good manners made the job of selling to gas station managers an unchallenging occupation. Unchallenging and deadly dull. He did not much miss the military drilling of VMI. He missed learning. He missed his books. He feared the effects of the corrosive boredom on his mind.

Once as he drove up to customs at the Canadian frontier the puzzled official asked, "What's that, sonny?"—pointing to a weighty tome that George kept within reach of the steering wheel. "A dictionary," the Conoco man replied matter-of-factly. "Study it every night," he said in his still thick Texas drawl. He'd made a pledge to himself. Each day he'd learn a new word. What's more, he'd use it.

In 1936, at the age of twenty-three, he was still without a dream to grab hold of. He was then living in Sacramento and considered a comer by Conoco. He could see no other prospect than the life of a businessman. He drew up some principles to follow. "I shall not lie," he wrote at the top of his list.

"I shall not waver from the truth for a second. . . . I shall never consider anything or be interested in anything that is doubtful or even approaching the shady side. I shall not talk . . . I resolve to pump all I can without saying anything about my thoughts or plans. Your best friend may give you away without meaning to. Talking has ruined many a big 'deal.' . . . I shall be fair. . . . I want to place myself in the other man's shoes and see his angle. I shall attempt to be a step ahead of the other fellow. Anticipate his moves and thoughts. . . . Hope for a little luck . . . and say a little prayer once in a while."

He was no longer the young innocent whose future was guaranteed by a good name and a loving family. To deaden the loneliness of the road, he had started drinking. His diary has many references to drunken bouts, followed by periods of agonizing self-doubt.

I sometimes wonder what life holds for me . . . at times it seems most baffling and terrifying. . . . I think I see my way for a time leaving Conoco . . . going to Alaska . . . a trip by slow freighter to Japan, China, and Manila . . . maybe working there. Then what?

It was the beginning of his dreams of travel, the ultimate escape. For the rest of his life the prospect of boarding a ship or plane was

Polk's means of evading himself when life—or he—hadn't measured up.

And always there was an ache for what he had left behind.

> The grand times in Texas . . . I think I might do well there
> . . . my family name . . . good luck with older men . . . to
> help . . . but I wish I knew what I could do. I do need my
> trip to give color and background to my life after it. I might
> be able to settle down to work and to seriousness . . . build
> towards something . . . I wish I knew.

His habit of writing down his every dream and every fear, documenting every move, would also become permanent, an act of self-confirmation.

He fell in and out of love with dizzying speed; love, like alcohol, provided another quick fix. On March 22, 1937, Polk wrote in his journal:

> Perfect cloudless sky. Maxine and I went to the Del Mar
> Club (Sacramento) and spent the entire day . . . There has
> been a death. My love for Maxine has died without any rhyme
> or reason . . . I don't understand. But I'm kind of glad . . .
> she still remains that wonderful, tender sweet person . . . but
> not to me. It must prove that I'm still a child. Still incapable
> of making decisions that are important. I see a beautiful woman
> . . . wonder if I'll know her . . . meet her . . . become familiar
> . . . kiss her? Maybe seduce her. And then she loses all mystery
> for me. She turns out to be like all the rest. They all go for
> the same line. And just a few days ago I stood in awe. I'm
> tired of it all . . . sick of women. I wonder if I ever will be
> satisfied with one woman always?

"I wish I had a little more money . . . or were proposed certain work . . . as a geologist . . . a mechanic . . . anything but an 'all around.' " George, acutely aware of his lack of preparedness for anything but an "all around" position, had not, however, given up on making up for the loss.

Again and again, the longing for home washed over him, at night when there was no one left to charm or seduce. "I'm sick for family and for Texas," he wrote in his journal. There was nothing of promise to go back to.

"I'm hot to go," he wrote, as if in movement there was salvation. "I'm always hot to go, just after a picture show or a book. . . . I'll get over it. But not my desire for escape from the city and the hard streets and groping tradespeople. Everybody sees me coming and wants my money because they know I won't be back. I'm a traveling salesman!" he wrote, as if it had just dawned on him that this was how he made a living.

In June 1937, the twenty-three-year-old Polk, with savings of one thousand dollars in his pocket, finally quit Conoco and took off for Alaska. For the rest of his short life, he would rarely mention his four years with Conoco. Nor did that experience find its way into any of his résumés. It was as if those four unhappy, lonely years never happened.

The beauty of Alaska and its distance from reminders of home and family satisfied Polk for a while. He grew a beard and was inevitably dubbed "Tex" by his fellow workers at the Wrangell salmon canneries. "Manhood attained" reads one caption in his photo album of the summer of 1937. George is standing in front of the Ace of Spades Mining Company in Happy Creek, Alaska. He looks happy and relaxed, as if in the outdoors, among woodsmen and fishermen, he found he could hold his own.

Still nagged by his lack of a college degree, Polk decided to stay on in Alaska, long past the term he had set for his adventure, and finish his education. He enrolled at the University of Alaska in Fairbanks. The school, a rough sort of institution of dubious academic standing, was only too pleased to have the pedigreed Texan with three years of credits from VMI. He was promised a degree in one year.

It was a sometimes tedious year in the small mining town. But it was there that Polk finally found what he loved to do and had a natural flair for: reporting.

His hometown paper, the Fort Worth *Press*, asked him to write a column on Alaska and on his own adventures as a displaced Texan in the wilds. The columns, of which only the accompanying photo of Polk decked out in black tie remains, were, according to his family, a fairly self-conscious attempt at Hemingwayesque prose. Still, he loved the writing. To be paid for doing something that gave him such pleasure was wonderful.

He was getting mail from people back home. They liked his style. They enjoyed his stories. For the first time, he felt the stirrings of promise about the future. He liked the sound of "George Polk, Reporter." There was pride in that, and the possibility of redeeming his name.

3

Nothing could have prepared George Polk for the city where his freighter, a Japanese vessel carrying mostly scrap iron and twelve uncomfortable passengers, made its final stop in the fall of 1938. Shanghai, the name resonant with the unpredictable, was enough to revive the weary traveler.

In 1938, Shanghai was not really a single city. Three million Chinese lived under joint British, American, and Japanese rule. The French, just adjacent to the others, also had a slice of this imperial pie. So the Chinese of Shanghai, China's largest city, were ruled by foreigners, under laws imposed thousands of miles away. The deafening sounds of the harbor were nothing less than stunning: the crashing of cargo being unloaded; the screech of rigging being raised and lowered on junks and clipper ships; the eerie wail of a steamer coming in. Coolies, bent and panting under the weight of foreigners in rickshaws, sped around the Bund.

The young Texan was shocked and captivated. He instantly fell in love with the wild contrasts of the place. The prostitutes strolled nonchalantly at all hours, in full view of passing missionaries and black-robed women, some still hobbled by their bound feet. The unabashed depravity of Shanghai was unlike anything he'd ever seen.

Armed now with a college degree, perhaps not from a great institution of learning but legitimate nonetheless, and with a folder of clips confirming his title of reporter, Polk set off in search of work. Shanghai, with its rich mine of stories waiting to be tapped, its unlimited local color, was a good place for an amateur to learn the ropes.

For all its intrigues and bloody colonial rivalries, China was a far less dangerous place for a cub reporter than many other parts of the world had become. Everywhere, change was assaulting the old order. Spain, where so many other foreign correspondents would find instant fame covering a civil war, held immeasurably greater risks in 1938. Europe was being transformed, as Hitler began extorting territory, from first one weak country, then another, on a continent that still preferred peace at any cost. *Time* magazine's Man of the Year, that portentous year of 1938, was Adolf Hitler.

China was pulled in many directions. The Japanese Army had invaded in 1931, seizing Manchuria first of all, but raiding and ravaging many of the coastal cities, so that by 1939 they occupied Shanghai, Canton, Tientsin, and Peking, all of northern China, and the cities of the Yangtze Valley up through Hankow. Here, too, civil war was simmering just beneath the surface; the Nationalists and Communists had struck a truce which would hold only until the loathed foreign invaders were repelled.

For Polk, however, these upheavals were distant rumblings. Shanghai held out what he had most sought: a job. The foreign press in Shanghai was not afraid of inexperienced reporters. Three English-language newspapers catered to the huge foreign community, and they were none too particular about a reporter's résumé. Eric Sevareid and Edgar Snow, Teddy White and John Hersey would all sharpen their craft here in the late 1930s. Polk was hired as a reporter for the Shanghai *Evening Post*.

His wages were well below what he had earned selling gasoline, but that wasn't the point. He was doing something he loved. He relished the craft and the kinship that came with the job and reveled in the status it conferred. He bought himself his first typewriter, a Remington portable, the talisman of his good fortune.

He was too busy now to keep up his journal, and his letters home were rare. His last communication with his father had been terse. The elder Polk had tried to dissuade him from his trip. "Your future's with Conoco, George," he told his son, urging the secure path that had eluded him. Young George had already booked passage on the freighter. Their parting had been cool.

Thoughts of his mother, divorced now from his father and making a life for herself as a public-school librarian, would occasionally intrude on his happiness, filling him with sadness and remorse. Just before he had boarded his freighter in Los Angeles, George had received a phone call from her which would haunt him throughout his journey East.

"George," she began, "I do not intend for this to change your plans."

"What is it, Mother?" he asked, suddenly worried by her tone.

"Edgehill Manor caught fire and burned to the ground last night," she said too evenly.

"My God, Mother, are you all right?"

"Yes, we're all fine. No one was at home. I don't know how it started. But there is nothing left. Nothing . . ." Her voice trailed off.

"I'm coming right home, Mother. Oh, my poor little mother . . ."

"You will do no such thing," she insisted, her voice calm and firm. "You will stick to your plans. You will get on that freighter. You would only be in the way here. Where would I put you? Your sisters are with their friends . . . Daddy is next door . . . Billy and I are at the Orrs' . . ."

"I will tear up my ticket," George said, and his mother heard the rip in her earpiece.

"You must go on, George," she said, desperate now, as if his adventure was hers also.

"All right," he sighed, "I didn't tear it up."

"I know, George. I know your flair for the dramatic. Travel safe."

He loved this about his mother. She never tried to hold him back. She wanted him to find his own happiness, however far that might take him.

Restless after six months in Shanghai, he resigned from the *Evening Post* and found passage on a small freighter headed for Manila, with stops along the way in Hong Kong and Singapore.

Everywhere he wandered, symbols of the British Empire, waning but still conspicuous, abounded—pith-helmeted Hong Kong policemen, steamers bringing the cargo of colonial trade from India and Australia, the lions and unicorns which invariably capped the proudest buildings of the port, all reminders that the sun still never set for London. Polk was struck by this world in transition, caught between the blind excesses of colonialism and, swirling beneath the surface, the temptation of independence.

In Manila, George Polk lost his heart. They met at the rambling, colonial Army-Navy Club. Twenty-three years old, Mary Catherine Phillips, daughter of a U.S. Army doctor, exuded the confidence of a woman every soldier on the base wants to romance.

Polk was nearly three years older, but his own self-confidence did not run nearly as deep as hers. Kay, as she was called by everyone but Polk, who called her Catherine, had something he had never encountered in a woman. She did not try to please or seduce. And she had an appetite for adventure that matched his. She knew about things he did not, however. With a master's degree in medieval and Renaissance art from the University of Chicago, she opened subjects like so many birthday presents for Polk, the insatiable learner.

As for Kay, she found Polk far more intellectually challenging than any of the military men who had been her beaux in Manila. He was handsome and unconventional enough to suit her. But she had plans of her own. She was determined to see the world before she returned to America to pursue a doctorate in fine arts. So they parted without making any real commitment. Each was convinced, however, that the parting would be temporary.

Deaf to her parents' loud protestations, Kay sailed from Manila in the spring of 1939, the year the world was on the brink of war. She was fulfilling her life's dream, to travel unchaperoned around the world. Her French liner made stops in Saigon, Singapore, Colombo, Djibouti, and Suez.

Polk, too, had been traveling since he left Manila, his general direction, by no coincidence, matching hers.

Reunited in Venice, Polk and Kay Phillips were in their own world. Together they moved on to Athens, where they clambered up the Acropolis to the Temple of Athena. There, on those ancient crumbling steps, George asked Kay to marry him.

"Give me some time," she said, her "no" tentative enough for him to persist. In Rome, where the young couple again came together, she promised him an answer if he turned up in Paris.

Polk arrived in Paris well ahead of Kay. He was full of purpose now, his wanderlust behind him. He needed a job. The war, which was now a matter of days away, provided the opportunity.

In August 1939, Paris was in the throes of full military fever. Every adult French male under the age of fifty had been called up. The subways were jammed with soldiers, many of them wearing uniforms of their own manufacture. Berlin and Moscow had just jointly announced their nonaggression pact. The import of that agreement, even to die-hard isolationists back home, was clear: Poland, caught in the Nazi-Soviet vise, would go next. Munich and its tarnished policy of appeasement were dead.

George Polk marched into the offices of the New York *Herald Tribune*, off the Champs-Elysées, and within minutes sold himself to the paper as a radio specialist and sometime Far Eastern foreign correspondent. His job at the *Trib* was to monitor all shortwave radio stations as well as the wires of the UP, AP, and Reuters. Not a glamorous position, but it was a start.

On his second day on the job, the lowly radioman was dispatched to cover a news conference called by the American Ambassador, William Bullitt.

"Gentlemen," the former Ambassador to Moscow intoned to the newsmen gathered in his ornate office off the Place de la Concorde, "the Department of State tells me the day has come. I am advising all Americans to leave Europe. We can no longer be responsible for them. My staff and I," he proclaimed with pride, "shall remain at our posts until we are bombed out."

Polk was more excited at sitting just a few feet from Bullitt than by the dramatic announcement. After the other reporters left, Bullitt showed Polk, John Elliott, and Walter B. Kerr of the *Trib*'s Paris bureau his cables from all over Europe. The new man on the *Trib* was ecstatic.

Polk wrote his family on August 24, 1939:

> Without wishing to appear dramatic, I think I may safely say that Paris is a bit exciting at the moment. I wish to further say I think that I am in the most exciting part of it all. . . . On my right is a ticker belonging to the United Press. Across

the room is one belonging to the Associated Press. Various other machines bring us news from AFP [Agence France-Presse] and Reuters. They are all chattering away at a furious rate, for this may be a big day for France . . . general mobilization. The subway this morning was jammed with soldiers, many of them with only half uniforms, half mufti. There were over 100 recruits aboard the train I took to Châtelet. Just at the moment I have been interrupted to handle the radio. I forgot to tell you about this new job. In fact I shall never be able to tell you all that has happened to me in the last few days.

Gas masks were already sold out in Paris. Nor were there any places left on ocean liners or planes heading home. George Polk, however, had never been so happy in his life. He wrote his mother: "I've interviewed Helen Hayes and John Roosevelt. What a wonderful job! I'm having a marvelous time. I'm calling Cornelius Vanderbilt, our news and political writer, 'Neil'!"

At 5:20 a.m. Polish time on September 1, 1939, a German warplane bombed Puck, a fishing village and air base on the northwestern coast of the Gulf of Danzig. A Wehrmacht infantry division rolled across the Polish frontier under a gentle rain that had begun falling over much of the continent but which did not obscure the lines of tanks and armored cars.

The day after, on September 2, 1939, George Washington Polk and Mary Catherine Phillips were married in the Normandy village of Etretat. George had brought a local priest to Kay's bedside in the hospital where she was convalescing from appendicitis surgery.

Telegrams to her parents in Manila and his family in Fort Worth were the first news their relatives had of the nuptials. It was wartime, however; ordinary rules of conduct were suspended.

Those months in the feverish atmosphere of Paris under full mobilization were another chance for George to prove himself. He cultivated the friendships of seasoned *Tribune* correspondents like John Elliott and Walter Kerr and worked hard to emulate their style. Eric Sevareid and David Schoenbrun, both in Paris at the time and soon to join CBS, recall the young Texan as brimming with almost unseemly enthusiasm for his new craft. "When you were with George, you had this feeling that anything was possible," recalled Schoenbrun. Polk's job, transcribing radio broadcasts, would have been deemed a lowly position under normal circumstances, but war made radio crucial.

"Polk was in love with all of it," Schoenbrun remembered, "the pounding of the news bulletins on the wires, AP, UP, Reuters, and Agence France-Presse. He romanticized the news business, as only an inexperienced newsman can."

While the rest of the world was in turmoil that terrible winter of 1940, George Polk—now twenty-six, married at last to the woman he had pursued across several continents, and employed by a legendary newspaper—was supremely happy.

By June, Denmark, Norway, and the Low Countries had crumbled before Hitler's field-gray columns. Just one step ahead of the German advance, the reluctant Polk and his new bride were evacuated by an American refugee ship.

On June 22, France capitulated and the Champs-Elysées was wrapped in the victor's red and black.

America was still only observing from the sidelines when the Polks' ship pulled into New York Harbor. But a powerful voice rumbled over the Atlantic, urging "the New World with all its power and might" to step forth "to the rescue and the liberation of the Old." Winston Churchill had replaced the timorous Neville Chamberlain as wartime Prime Minister.

It was radio that enabled Polk, like the rest of the country, to be drawn to the edge of Europe's nightmare. Now holding a desk job at the New York *Herald Tribune*, Polk followed news of the Battle of Britain on his shortwave. One voice, emphatic and richly cadenced, masterful at the use of the meaningful pause, captured the London blitz almost as vividly as Churchill.

"This . . . is London . . ." Edward R. Murrow of the Columbia Broadcasting System began his daily report. "I am standing on a rooftop looking out over London. I think probably in a minute we shall have the sound of guns in the immediate vicinity. The lights are swinging over in this general direction now. You'll hear two explosions. There they are. . . ."

Murrow became the human bridge between America and the beleaguered island. Polk was transfixed by the broadcaster's ability to make distant battle scenes seem alarmingly close.

"These things must be seen," Murrow insisted, and then painted his word pictures of night bombers and antiaircraft barrages which "seemed to splash blobs of daylight down the streets."

Polk listened to Murrow's words and, through him, discovered the power of radio not only to inform but to move. "Those black-faced men . . . with bloodshot eyes . . . fighting fires . . . the girls who cradle the steering wheel of a heavy ambulance in their arms . . . the policemen who stand guard over that unexploded bomb . . ."

In New York, the *Herald Tribune* put Polk to work as a desk assistant. It was a heady experience, working for the newspaper which from pre–Civil War days had drawn talented writers of staggering diversity to its pages. From Walter Lippmann and Walter Kerr to Homer Bigart and Marguerite Higgins, the *Trib* occupied a central place in the country's nascent days as Big Power. Under such editors as Joseph Barnes and George A. Cornish, George Polk served his apprenticeship among some of the profession's most respected figures. Cornish, a smooth, gallant Southerner like Polk himself, remarked on the young Texan's promise. But promotions at the venerable *Tribune* were as measured in their pace as in the foreign service.

Polk was willing to put in his time as he moved from desk jobs to editorial work, taking whatever shifts came his way. What he longed for was to get out in the field and do real reporting.

Propelled by his zeal for self-improvement, George enrolled in night school at New York University in the fall of 1940, while still working full-time at the *Tribune*. He signed up for writing and journalism courses, performing well enough so that by the end of the term he was offered a job teaching journalism at NYU. He grabbed the chance and discovered a genuine vocation for teaching. His students, only five years his junior, were captivated by his stories of Alaska, Shanghai, and Paris before the fall. His journalism classes were among the most popular on the campus. "My name is George Polk," he began his class, "and I am not a teacher."

Kay, who spent her days doing war-related charity work for Bundles for Britain, was discovering the underside of the charm that so beguiled his students: a bottomless insecurity. He was plagued by feelings of self-doubt and an endless need to prove himself. There was about him the uncomfortable restlessness of a new arrival, a strange cast of mind for the pedigreed son of a distinguished old line.

The restlessness prompted his request for a year's leave of absence from the *Tribune* in the summer of 1941. He planned to spend the year earning a master's degree in modern history at NYU while continuing to teach at the journalism school. In a hurry to make up for the lost years with the oil company, he hoped to return to the *Tribune* in a higher position.

4

George and Kay Polk were having lunch in Montclair, New Jersey, at the home of George's cousins Bill and George Price on December 7, 1941. It was a lively gathering, full of spirited needling, as the three male cousins reverted to adolescent habits. The competition between the two branches of the family, the Polks and the Prices, reached back many years. The Price cousins, George, an airline pilot, and Bill, a reporter on the New York *Daily News*, were down-to-earth young men of no vaulting social aspirations. They found the Polks a shade too grand.

The Polks displayed their Southern aristocratic lineage a bit too much for their East Coast cousins. The Price boys didn't have much use for those stories of President Polk's coffee urn and pocket watch, the sole remnants of the plantation which made Tara look small.

But George they saw as different. George didn't take himself or any of that family mythology too seriously. Whatever he had become had been his own doing.

At three o'clock in the afternoon, the family was just settling into easy chairs in the living room, mellow from the wine and warm family feelings. They tuned the radio to the Dodgers-Giants game on the Mutual Broadcasting System. Len Sterling, the announcer, broke into the football game, and right away they knew from his funereal voice that the news was bad:

"The White House has just announced that Japanese forces have attacked the naval base at Pearl Harbor."

A stunned silence descended on the room. Nobody was expecting a strike at Hawaii. Manila, yes, but Pearl Harbor, never. It was a brilliant move. Without knowing anything more, the cousins assumed the American fleet must have been caught by surprise.

So the debate that had for so long rent the country was over. Isolationism was no longer an option.

"That's it," George Polk, the first to speak, said. "That's war. I'm signing up."

His cousins agreed. They would all enlist. The war had been a long time coming. It was a just war, if there was such a thing. They were almost relieved now that the waiting was over.

"Goodbye, Mama, I'm Off to Yokohama," jukeboxes began bellowing that day, and "I'm Gonna Slap a Dirty Little Jap," as war fever replaced soul searching and the country geared up for the business of war.

Polk, who had acquired a pilot's license somewhere along the way, tried to enlist as a pilot in the Army but flunked the eye examination. He next went to the Navy, this time having had himself fitted out with contact lenses. He passed the eye test and would spend much of his time during the war as a fighter pilot, the only Navy man (originally charged with reconnaissance) with a Marine unit at Henderson Field, Guadalcanal.

Polk, like hundreds of thousands of other young men fired by patriotic zeal, had never heard of Iwo Jima or Wake Island or the Solomons as he marched around the dusty fields of Fort Bragg and Fort Dix, preparing for war in the Pacific. Nor were his commanding officers much better prepared. The Marine Corps had to survey those islands, the new front, as they went along. There were simply no maps in existence.

Polk, who had already crossed the Pacific and had seen many of the great cities around its rim, had no idea what kind of war he would fight. He just wanted to get there, close to the action. One month after Pearl Harbor, he received his commission: Ensign, U.S. Navy.

Consumed like the rest of the country by war fever, he nonetheless made certain the New York *Herald Tribune* would have his job as rewrite man waiting when he returned from the war. George Cornish assured him his job would be safe.

Gregory Mason, chairman of New York University's Department of Journalism, was more than a little reluctant to let the

promising new instructor leave the faculty. "It gives me great pleasure to testify that Mr. Polk has proved himself a highly capable
teacher of journalism," Mason wrote on February 7, 1942, in his
final report on George Polk, "as well as a gentleman whose character
is marked by integrity, initiative, intelligence, and cooperativeness.

"It happens that I know something, too, about Mr. Polk's work
on the Foreign News Rewrite Desk of the New York *Herald Tribune*,
and I know that he is extremely well founded in the practice of
journalism, as well as in the theory of journalism."

War, in the early stages at least, has a way of taking people out
of themselves, of reducing their own lives to manageable proportions. So, for George Polk, whose marriage had started showing
signs of strain, war was something he could believe in, excel in.

There had been unpleasant scenes with Kay. He had not stayed
faithful to her for very long. She had a way of making him feel a
little wanting, a little less educated and polished than she was. He
still seemed to need the exhilaration of conquest. Women were too
accessible, the habit of seduction too hard to break.

On his way to California, where his ship for the Far East would
take to sea, Polk stopped off in Fort Worth to spend a few days
with his mother. He and his younger brother, Bill, called on their
father, now living by himself on a ranch outside of town. His father,
whose military bearing had been replaced by an old man's slump,
faced his son with a vacant look. George had not written him in
years. Still, he was off to fight a war. They shook hands stiffly.

"He's a coward," George remarked bitterly to his brother as they
were leaving. "And I'll never see him again." He was right. Captain
Polk died that summer.

At first, Polk was exultant at being back in the Far East, the
scene of his first adventures abroad. But already he was discovering
that, more than anything else, war was "organized boredom."

"I've had to learn to stand bridge watches on the trip out. I find
myself totally unable to understand why anyone on earth would
go to sea for a living. To me it is a terrible life of waiting (fearful
and bored) for the next four-hour watch to roll around and when
the watch time does come up, a period of four hours when you

peer at the sun, raise the deuce with a bunch of farm boys (who love the sea no more than I) for not keeping a sharp lookout, finally you count the minutes until the watch is over."

By the summer of 1942, Polk's wish to see real fighting was answered. Guadalcanal, one of the Solomon Islands off the coast of New Guinea, was his final destination. It was a thickly forested volcanic island where the temperature never dropped below a hundred degrees in the summer; it stayed well above that for most of Polk's time there.

In 1942 this steamy tropical jungle was transformed into one of the Pacific's ugliest battlegrounds. This was a war without rules, and the American side was at a disadvantage in men and matériel. But Guadalcanal, like Stalingrad, would mark a turning point.

Polk would shortly learn that "the Jap," the little man in the rumpled uniform he had been seeing on newsreels, was actually a ruthless fighting machine. "The Nip," as General MacArthur called him, was an uncanny sharpshooter, carrying twice as many rounds of ammunition as a GI. The belief that dying for the Emperor was the greatest glory one could gain on earth made him a fearsome enemy.

Operating on ridiculously skimpy supplies (every modern weapon was headed for Europe), with a jerry-built corrugated-steel hut for headquarters and a temporary airstrip made of perforated steel strips, one hundred and twenty men (one hundred and nineteen of them Marines) and fifteen light planes took on the mighty "Tokyo Express."

After Emperor Hirohito announced that Guadalcanal would be a "decisive battle," the little island became a magnet for enemy forces far out of proportion to its strategic importance. For the Japanese troops, surrender was out of the question; it was deemed the ultimate act of humiliation. Guadalcanal turned into a conflict in which few prisoners on either side were taken, as the enemy thought it equally shameful for the Americans to surrender. Captured Marines were frequently beheaded; others were led on "death marches" after their surrender, with the weak and wounded literally marched to death.

Polk's unit of Marines managed to hang on to Guadalcanal, despite being stretched beyond the limits of endurance. The rule was that nobody left the island unless he was running a fever of 102 degrees. "We must hate with every fiber of our being," Lieutenant General Lesley J. McNair told his troops in the Pacific. "We must lust for battle; our object in life must be to kill."

Polk, too, had been transformed into a killing machine. He wrote his mother about the enemy: "What I took to be brute courage and endurance is blind obedience without a bit of intelligence behind it. I respect them only as savages . . . as that they are well qualified."

Polk did not write home about the incident that would haunt him for the rest of his life. Polk and his Marine unit were dug into foxholes one night, a net on four poles the men's only protection, when a musky aroma stirred him from a light sleep. A Japanese soldier, a giant curved knife in hand, fell on top of him as Polk fumbled for the .45 under his "mattress." His shots and screams woke his comrades in other foxholes, and soon the night rang out with the sound of whistling bullets. The next morning they found the Japanese soldier's bullet-sprayed body at the fringe of the camp. That night was the beginning of Polk's nightmares.

By the spring of 1943, George Polk, credited with shooting down eleven Japanese planes, wracked by combat fatigue, malaria, and improperly treated shrapnel wounds, finally qualified for leave.

While laid up in an Australian hospital, Polk discovered he had become a war hero. Surviving Guadalcanal, not winning medals, had become his primary goal while in the war. But now newspapers, including his own, the *Herald Tribune*, were running his photograph in full Navy dress with the word "hero" listed among his credits. He was awarded the Purple Heart and a presidential citation.

Much sought after by newspapers for his eyewitness accounts of the battle of Guadalcanal, he gave this one while still in the hospital:

> The "Tokyo Express" was still persistently and viciously active in attempting to shell our forces off Guadalcanal and destroy our shipping which was reinforcing and supplying those forces. The Jap ships came down the "slot" every night when the moon waned. . . . We had our 15 scout seaplanes but independently they were of little offensive use. . . . Some

of us got together with the PT boys and formed a team. We devised our own signals for teamwork, and our own system of coordinated attack, and then we went to work. Supplies, gasoline, oil, ammunition, tools, etc., were scarce. We solved that problem. Agreeing that the PT stockpile and our stockpile were sacred, we decided that every other stockpile in the area was fair game for "borrowing."

Our planes would go out and find the "Express" coming down the "slot." We immediately radioed the PTs the position of the Jap ships. We couldn't carry bombs so all we could do was skim low over their decks and strafe 'em. We had one other weapon: empty Japanese beer bottles, left behind by the enemy when we took the islands. These we tossed down on the "Express." Our object was to get the Nips to open up on us so that they would reveal themselves by their gun flashes. When they did cut loose, our PT boats, which had been lying in ambush, would let go their torpedoes. The PT boys hit several destroyers and at least one cruiser, damaging all severely and sinking some.

Back at our base we tried to get some sleep while "Washing Machine Charlie" clanked around upstairs. Charlie was also known as "Maytag Charlie," who also was known as "Louis the Louse," a Jap light bomber who cruised around overhead hour after hour with an engine that sounded like a washing machine. He carried a 500-pound bomb but was careful never to drop it until he had been overhead for four or five hours. This meant many hours of lost sleep below until the bomb was deposited safely. You will understand why "Charlie" was called many other names, none printable.

Early in 1944, Lieutenant George W. Polk was discharged from the military hospital where he had spent as much time as he had in combat. He was expected, like so many thousands of other returning GIs, to pick up the pieces of his life as if he had never left. Polk, trained for two years to be a killer, had experienced the most primitive form of combat. He was permanently scarred in body and spirit.

5

———

In the fall of 1944, Polk came to Washington, D.C., to find his wife, who had been living there with her parents, and to reclaim his job on the *Herald Tribune*. The war still raged and scores of men and women in Washington were in uniform. Polk did not like the fit of civilian clothes. Nor did he feel relief at having survived. A feeling that he had served too short a time nagged at him. He felt depressed thinking about his dead comrades. He could not forget the fellows in the wretched fox-holes of Guadalcanal while he dressed for another Washington dinner party.

Nor was there anybody to talk to about these things. He and Kay, apart for two years and separated by an unbridgeable gulf of experience, had drifted apart. Nobody made much fuss about a soldier's reentry problems. His nightmares were his private de-mons. It was regarded as somehow unmanly to admit to such things. The psychic wounds of war were simply not understood in 1944. It would take more than three decades and another jungle war to coin the term "post-traumatic stress disorder."

Good Housekeeping magazine, the bible of the American housewife, counseled patience, but only up to a point. "After two or three weeks the returning GI should be finished with the talking, with oppressive remembering. If he still goes over the same stories, reveals the same emotions, you had best consult a psychiatrist."

But psychiatry carried with it a stigma that few Americans were prepared to face in the 1940s. "Home must be the greatest reha-bilitation center of them all!" *House Beautiful* trumpeted. And yet the tabloids daily ran lurid headlines like "CRAZED VET RUNS AMOK."

The military, for its part, wished only to wash its hands of this dark residue of war. The services offered skimpy help for shell shock. A story that made the rounds concerned General George S. Patton, commander of the U.S. Seventh Army. "Old Blood and Guts," as Patton was known, was touring a military hospital in Sicily in 1943. The general asked a private what ailed him. "Nerves," the GI replied hesitantly. "You yellow bastard," the general barked, slapping the shaken man across the face with a pair of kid gloves, and kicking him in the behind for good measure. "No such thing as shell shock," Patton announced to the doctors on duty. "It's an invention of the Jews." At the time, the story provoked more laughter than revulsion.

Polk felt demeaned by receiving naval retirement pay. He paid a call on Howard University, the capital's black college, and arranged for half his monthly retirement check of $125 to go to a scholarship fund. The other half he sent to NYU for the same purpose.

The news business, too, had been shaken by the war. The Washington press corps, swollen from a prewar few hundred, was now two thousand strong. Women had joined the ranks of journalists, though they were conspicuously absent from the airwaves. NBC News confidently pronounced women "biologically incapable of total objectivity" and refused to put them on the air.

In the 1940s reporters earned about $5,000 a year and seemed always to hang out in packs, waiting for press releases. Skepticism toward government pronouncements was almost nonexistent. An atmosphere of cozy gentlemen's clubbiness pervaded the Washington press corps, which served the government perhaps better than it did its readers. "The job of briefing the press," Under Secretary of State Dean Acheson would later write, referring to a major foreign policy shift on Greece and Turkey in 1947, "I took on myself, talking on the evening of February 27 off the record, and with the greatest frankness to a group of twenty men regularly assigned to the Department."

No journalist or commentator occupied a more hallowed position in the nation's esteem than Walter Lippmann. Lippmann had risen far above the rank of a mere journalist. He was a man politicians and government officials went to for counsel. Walter Lippmann embodied the delicate position of a member of the Fourth Estate who attempted to retain his objectivity while working very much within the walls of the Washington Establishment.

Shoehorned with a dozen seasoned Washington hands into the *Tribune*'s crowded Room 1285 in the old National Press Building, George Polk was now officially a full-time reporter. His pieces, though often routine Washington stories built around government handouts and the predictable pronouncements of officials, gave him a steady flow of ego-boosting bylines.

Alongside the intoxication of doing a job he really loved there lurked anxiety over the possibility of failure. Polk was haunted by feelings of being a fraud, of putting one over on the world. He wasn't sure he had the substance to back up the winning appearance.

He had been passing himself off as a reporter for years before he actually earned the title. "I shall try to do an intelligent and American-like job of reporting honestly the news as I see it," George wrote his cousin Bill Price on March 12, 1944. "I shall try to do a better job of writing about the war than some of the copy I see every day. . . . It will be a stiff haul for me here, though," he wrote, "for I never was much of a newsman and as you (you alone, you great secret keeper) know, I've had damn little experience."

Perhaps because he had cut ties with his own father long before the latter's death, Polk was always looking for mentors. Early on in Washington, he sought out Drew Pearson and Walter Lippmann, and listened avidly to their professional advice and counsel. Being an "insider," dining with the powerful, interested him less than learning from the most eminent in his profession.

On November 11, 1944, George Polk savored victory. His story, topped by his byline, on President Roosevelt's return to Washington after his election win was carried on the *Herald Tribune*'s front page, just beneath the paper's logo.

President Roosevelt, arriving here today after his election weekend stay at his Hyde Park, NY, home, was greeted by an officially estimated crowd of 330,000 persons, who lined rain- and wind-swept streets to cheer the successful fourth-term Presidential candidate. . . . The President then turned to an accumulation of international and domestic problems pressing for his attention. Mr. Roosevelt, accompanied by Vice President Elect Harry S. Truman and Vice President Henry A. Wallace, who met him at Union Station, drove to the White House in an open touring car under dark skies that failed to damp the spirits of the Presidential party or spectators, many of whom had waited almost two hours to salute the President.

Polk impressed editors like Joe Barnes with his eagerness to be where the story was, no matter how minor, and with his unflinching determination to get at unpleasant truths. Fellow *Tribune* reporter Ruth Gruber, a friend and Washington neighbor of the Polks, recalls that George was "adversarial at news conferences. He would dive into the deep sea if the story required it. He was not the sort of reporter who liked to travel in a pack."

At the end of November 1944, Polk was back on the *Tribune*'s front page, this time with detailed evidence of what was still a murky subject for many Americans: the horrifying extent of Nazi atrocities. Auschwitz was still a functioning death camp when Polk wrote:

The War Refugee Board, in what is regarded as the most shocking document ever issued by a United States government agency, made public today an official report on German atrocities that have caused the death of "millions of innocent civilians . . . Jews and Christians alike . . . all over Europe."

The "revolting and diabolical" German atrocities were described as a "campaign of terror and brutality which is unprecedented in all history and which even now continues unabated and is part of the German plan to subjugate the free peoples of the world."

The 25,000-word indictment of Germany was assembled by the WRB as one of the agencies under the executive office of the President of the United States. . . . The report reveals that 1,765,000 Jews were gassed to death at Birkenau alone between April 1942 and April 1944, including 900,000 Poles, 100,000 Dutch, 45,000 Greeks, 150,000 French.

On December 6, 1944, in a story that subsequent events would make ironic, Polk reported:

> The U.S. will keep hands off in Italy and Greece. . . . In what was interpreted as criticism of British actions in Greece . . . dispatches from London said the State Department policy statement came as a "stunning surprise," although it had been known that there was a wide difference of opinion between Washington and London . . . Rep. John M. Coffee of Washington declared, meanwhile, that the Greek people "deserve better of us than to have to continue shedding blood for democracy because Greek police, backed by British patrols, fired on them." Mr. Coffee added: "The first guns used in the current struggle were, according to reports from two American eyewitnesses, used by Greek police against unarmed men, women, and children who were attempting to demonstrate peacefully against the Greek government's unfair edicts." Rep. Coffee asserted that "these same police were those who kept order for the Germans when Athens was occupied by Germans."

In spite of his professional success, Polk was deeply unhappy. Some of the optimism that had propelled him forward had been spent. He told Kay he did not want to have children, and she did not dissuade him from getting a vasectomy. She felt their fragile marriage would not bear up under the weight of family life. Polk was often ill-humored, seemingly unable to absorb life's normal irritations. He was only thirty-one, but he no longer had a young man's stamina and had to get to bed early to do a day's work.

It was at night that Polk and Kay had their worst moments. Once Kay awoke to find herself being dragged by her long hair along the floorboards. "George," she screamed, "wake up, George, you're hurting me."

Finally, she resorted to tying him to his bedposts at night.

Riding his bicycle under a Connecticut Avenue bridge one morning, he suddenly lost control and slumped over the handlebars. He fell unconscious in the middle of the road. His malaria, never completely cured, had flared up. A stranger dragged him to safety. He spent the rest of the day sleeping, the sweat pouring so hard from him that Kay had to throw out his soaked pillow.

In the spring of 1945, there was another death in the Polk family. Milbry, his second-youngest sister, a bright, sweet-natured redhead, died of multiple sclerosis while still in her twenties. George had flown to Fort Worth to be with her during her last days. From there, he went on to cover the birth of the United Nations in San Francisco.

Another death, this one in the American family, followed. On April 12, 1945, at 5:47 p.m., Polk was in the city room of the *Trib*'s San Francisco bureau. A small bell, signifying a wire service "flash," rang out. History's briefest news bulletin followed: "FDR Dead."

FDR had intended the San Francisco Conference to be the scene of a jubilant show of great-power unity. He fully expected the Alliance to survive the war's end. After all, hadn't Moscow, Washington, and London worked together to achieve great victories during the war's final year? At Yalta, FDR thought he had laid the groundwork for a durable peace.

America was now the unrivaled naval power in the world. Backed by its newly tapped industrial and military muscle, Washington would be the benign but undisputed mediator between the two imperialist powers: the Soviet Union and Britain. All this was to be certified in San Francisco.

Now, even while celebrating the birth of the United Nations, the big powers set about drawing the lines of a cold, hard peace. Walter Lippmann, also in San Francisco for the conference, attributed its failures to the maneuverings of the British. Lippmann saw Churchill's hand behind the State Department's hard line toward Moscow.

Lippmann called it essentially "a British-Russian" conflict. Churchill's insistence on supporting "ultraconservative" forces in Southern Europe and the Middle East would, he wrote, eventually play into the Soviets' hands. "I do not believe," Lippmann wrote, "that the pre-war Rightist elements can continue to govern Europe. I do not think it is ideology, but realism, to argue that the support of governments somewhat left of center has the greatest promise . . ."

Lippmann warned his readers that British foreign policy was essentially colonial, imperialistic, and hostile to any form of radicalism. As an example to illustrate the divergence of British and American values, he pointed to the blatant attempt on Churchill's part to force a discredited monarchy on Greece and exclude the leftist guerrilla forces that had led the anti-Nazi resistance.

Polk was uncomfortable with the geopolitical pronouncements of others. He wanted to go to places like Nuremberg and Athens and see for himself. And anyway, Washington under the new Truman administration lacked the allure of FDR's magnetic presence.

Overseas, in a shifting postwar landscape, he would make his name. Kay, working as a researcher at the Office of Indian Affairs, agreed that travel might do them good. They had been happy once before exploring strange places together. Maybe it would work again.

In May 1945, Polk resigned from the *Herald Tribune*, where his chances of landing a foreign assignment at this early stage in his career were remote. The paper was not happy to see him leave. Managing editor George A. Cornish wrote him: "It was the opinion of all the editors on our staff that you did an excellent job for us, both on our New York cable desk and in our Washington bureau. All of us regret your decision to leave . . ."

Both Polks signed on with the Los Angeles *Daily News* as foreign correspondents. Their pay was $100 a week each, plus expenses. Their ultimate destination would be a part of the world each had been exposed to and was fascinated by: China.

They also signed a contract to write pieces from wherever they traveled for United Features Syndicate. It was going to be a grand adventure.

Before sailing for Europe, George visited Harvard University. The world of Cambridge was a place he both hankered for and feared. With a letter of recommendation from Walter Lippmann in his pocket, he called on Professor Arthur Schlesinger, Sr., a member of the prestigious Nieman Foundation. Polk was drawn to the idea of applying for a Nieman Fellowship for journalists. Such a fellowship, which grants tuition to pursue studies at Harvard for a year, would fill in the void left by his spotty education. Above all, it would establish him in both his own and the world's eyes as a serious man. He longed, like so many from his part of the world, for the legitimacy which in his eyes only an Eastern institution could bestow.

Though he did not apply for a fellowship during this visit, for the rest of his life the Harvard year remained something of an *idée fixe*.

George and Kay Polk sailed for Southampton, England, on the *Queen Mary* in early October 1945.

6

London, the Polks' first stop, was a heartbreaking place that fall. One had to look hard to find any signs that this was the capital of a triumphant nation. Over 400,000 British men and women had lost their lives in the war. Britain had been fighting longer than any of the Allies and had borne the brunt of the German bombs. Its cities were scarred and reduced to rubble, and one-quarter of its national wealth was gone.

"Seldom if ever," Edward R. Murrow reported, "has war ended leaving the victors with such a sense of uncertainty and fear, with such a realization that the future is obscure."

Winston Churchill, the man who led the country to victory in the war, had been forced to retire to the sidelines. In the mood for change, the electorate had rejected Churchill in favor of Labour Party leader Clement Attlee. As one member of the new government noted: "In relation to the task before us after the war, our resources are surely smaller than those of almost any other country."

Polk, both pained and fascinated by the sight of this diminished nation, decided it was a good place from which to study the shifting map of Europe before he began filing stories for the L.A. *Daily News*. Like some avid graduate student, he plunged into the task, reading London's lively array of daily newspapers and regularly attending sessions of Parliament.

Among the most painful aspects of Britain's postwar impoverishment was the necessity to dismantle its empire. A nation that could barely keep itself warm, clothed, or properly fed did not have the wherewithal to maintain far-flung provinces. Yet for generations, Britons had regarded the Mediterranean, the Red Sea, the

Persian Gulf, and adjacent territories as being as much their province as the English Channel. Cyprus (a crown colony), the Sudan (under joint Anglo-Egyptian rule), and Egypt itself, though nominally an independent monarchy since 1922, all continued to have strong ties to the British Empire. Such former British mandates as Iraq, Jordan, and Palestine (under British mandate until 1948) formed an integral part of London's sphere of interest.

The war had shown that the Middle East, with its rich reserves of oil and its strategic position linking Europe, Asia, and Africa, was of paramount importance. Greece's location in the eastern Mediterranean was strategically vital to free passage to the riches of the Gulf. London also viewed Greece as a lifeline to India, Southeast Asia, and even East Africa, all of which still had strong commercial ties with Britain. Churchill had paid a very high price to retain primacy in Greece. In October 1944, over Roosevelt's objections, Churchill had agreed to allow Stalin a free hand in the rest of the Balkans and Eastern Europe (with the exception of Poland and Czechoslovakia, which would not remain exceptions for long) in exchange for British hegemony in Greece. Yugoslavia was to be split fifty-fifty between the Soviets and the Anglo-Americans. It seemed a desperate act, bargaining away so much for so little, but London's investment in Athens was already unreasonably high. "The fundamental assumption of our policy," the new British Foreign Secretary had written in a memorandum to the cabinet, was that "Greece must be retained within the British sphere."

At a time when it was least able to spare them, Britain had sent an expeditionary force to fight the Nazis in Greece. Over 25,000 British and Imperial troops lost their lives on Greek soil. Britain would soon be embroiled in the Greek Civil War, a war between the monarchists and leftists (including various shades of republicans and Communists) which had erupted during the Nazi occupation but whose roots reached back several decades. Like all civil wars, it was a tangled and bloody business, the most dangerous sort of conflict for a third party. Its outcome, however, was of signal importance for the retreating Empire.

Polk found his energy quickening in war-ravaged London. Like all visiting correspondents, he paid a call on the icon of their trade, Edward R. Murrow.

CBS Europe was run from three small rooms across the street from the great Art Deco headquarters of the grande dame of the business, the British Broadcasting Corporation. Before the blitz, it had been one of London's desirable neighborhoods, a sedate area of impressive Georgian and Regency houses, a short walk from Regent's Park. Now, a wash of camouflage green covered the BBC's scarred white façade.

From the CBS offices, Murrow had directed the network's coverage of the Nazi steamroller. Here Murrow had also collected some of the network's most talented reporters, "Murrow's Boys," as they were called. They, too, would become legends for their work during the war.

Polk, who had been listening to Murrow's resonant cadences for years, was not disappointed by the man behind the famous voice. They were just about the same height, though Polk, five years younger than Murrow, was more muscularly built. Both were men who cared about their appearance. Murrow combed his slick black hair almost straight back. His Savile Row suit jacket was off, revealing his trademark suspenders and highlighting the knifelike crease of his trousers. A cigarette was never out of arm's reach.

Polk, less formally dressed in a soft tweed jacket and carefully knotted tie, seemed subdued in the presence of the eminent broadcaster. But they had a lot in common: both were self-made; each was driven to succeed; neither was a compromiser. Their respect for each other was mutual and would grow as their professional lives became entwined.

Murrow took Polk around the office and introduced him to his "boys." William Shirer, short and stocky, stood up to inspect the lanky Texan. Howard K. Smith, still very young, with dark wavy hair and the faint vestige of a Southern accent, had been recruited from the wire services, and Eric Sevareid had been lured away from his print job by Murrow. Sevareid reminded Polk they had met before the war in Paris.

There were others in Murrow's circle that Polk would meet later:

Charles Collingwood, like Smith, a product of both Oxford and
United Press, and Winston Burdett, the courtly, complex Harvard
graduate, covering Rome for CBS. Their voices, their delivery,
their style of writing were diverse. Murrow, in his own words, was
looking for "people who were young and knew what they were
talking about . . . without bothering too much about diction,
phrasemaking, and manner of speaking."

It was a wonderful fraternity. With the exception of Murrow,
they had all learned the ropes of foreign reporting as newspaper
and wire service reporters. "What are your plans?" Murrow asked
Polk. Polk explained that he and Kay would look around Europe
and the Middle East awhile, filing for the L.A. *Daily News* and
writing features for syndication, and then make their way to China.

"Well," said Murrow leaning back, his long legs propped up on
his desk, "keep us in mind."

Polk would see his future CBS colleagues only a handful of times
after that. Mostly they stayed in touch through long telexes and
the telephone. But he had left an impression on them all, most
particularly on Murrow. Murrow liked the ease of the man, the
absence of airs. George came across as a modest man, anxious to
listen and to learn.

"He and Murrow were the same kind of people in a way," Polk's
friend and colleague in the Middle East, NBC's John Donovan,
would later recall. "George was not brash, not the heavy-drinking,
free-spending kind of foreign correspondent. I mean, he went overboard when he had money, giving it away, helping people. But
otherwise, he was a very circumspect man. Without being a Bible
beater or having any strong outward religious life, he was a guy
with a very strong streak of morality. A hardworking, quiet, re-
flective man. He was a man who was essentially extremely polite.
He stood by his guns and had strong convictions. But he wasn't a
John Wayne type. He was the Gary Cooper quiet type. Which is
just what appealed to Murrow."

Howard Smith would remember Polk's looks. "Like a blond Errol
Flynn," he said later. Shirer, however, worried that Polk was perhaps too naïve, especially for the byzantine part of the world he
was headed for. "George was more passionately involved in his

work than most. Once he got to Greece, I wondered if he realized who he was playing against."

It would take a while for them to find out what sort of reporter he was. A measure of Polk's eventual standing at CBS was that three men, Murrow, Smith, and Sevareid, would each later claim to have hired him.

7

Fired up by his meeting with the CBS team in London, Polk traveled to Nuremberg. The War Crimes Tribunal, the Allies' final humiliation of Hitler's closest collaborators in open court, was the most sensational story of its day.

Autumn had an unusual bite all over Europe that year, made all the more bitter by a severe shortage of fuel, affecting both the occupied and the occupiers. Driving in a borrowed jeep along the rolling countryside between Frankfurt and Nuremberg, Polk saw German Tiger tanks converted into makeshift shelters against the bombs and the cold.

At the gates of the devastated medieval city of Nuremberg, he was stopped by smartly dressed MPs. Polk, in a war correspondent's Army fatigues, but lacking credentials to cover the event, pleaded his case.

"Just out of the service myself, Sergeant," he said, "on my first big assignment. Have to get there or lose my job."

Getting past the first set of MPs, he was dispatched to division headquarters. He was just embarked on repeating his tale of woe when the commanding officer interrupted him. "George Polk, what in hell are you doing here?" The officer turned out to be a former *Trib* copy boy, whom Polk had befriended when he was a Dartmouth senior working part-time for the paper. Within minutes, Polk was sitting in the crowded press section, squeezed between CBS man Shirer and Marguerite Higgins of the *Herald Tribune*.

"I could have hit Goering and the other mugs with a gently tossed spitball," Polk wrote his mother, "I sat so close to the twenty-one men in the dock."

Everywhere Polk traveled on the continent he felt looks of envy and resentment. Americans in those postwar years were deemed both the hope of the world and the enemies of the traditional order. Americans had flesh on their bones, while Europeans had the haunted look of the undernourished. Americans drove around in cars, while Europeans dreamed only of owning a bicycle. Americans, Europeans had read in their newspapers, were building remarkable houses for themselves, houses with two or three bathrooms and kitchens where everything was built-in (financed by low-interest loans available to returning GIs). Europeans were shivering in gap-toothed wrecks without plumbing or heat. It often seemed to both Americans and Europeans that the Old World had fought itself back to the Dark Ages.

Polk returned to Paris to find Kay shivering in hat, gloves, and overcoat in an ice-cold hotel room on the Rue de Richelieu. She was also inexplicably distracted. While Polk had been away, she had met a *Herald Tribune* reporter named Russell Hill in Berlin. She had seen him only once, but they had spoken several times by telephone. Kay's reaction to Hill had been immediate. She found herself drawn toward his solidity like a victim of frostbite toward a fire.

As Kay's early passion for Polk began to fade, she had to confront the reality of her husband. He was an emotionally dislocated man who used his physical allure to engage in quick and easy flirtations that reinforced his often flagging self-confidence. His nights were still disturbed by his memories of battle, and the recurring physical pain of his war wounds made him irritable and quick to argue. Kay could not tolerate his infidelities, and she was ill suited to the role of nurse-wife.

As he sensed her pulling away from him, George responded by flirting even more outrageously than before. Quick conquests were his way of salving his bruised pride.

That December, *Newsweek* offered Polk a job as Middle East stringer. Polk agreed to file a weekly three-thousand-word cable for the magazine. He and Murrow had also stayed in touch, and now Murrow asked him to be ready to report on the growing Turkish story for CBS.

The Soviets saw the situation left by the war as a chance to fulfill the age-old Russian ambition for a Mediterranean port. Stalin had begun squeezing the Turks for a Soviet base. The Turks were resisting, but there was no telling how much longer they could hold out. The Greek situation was also heating up, though in 1946 Washington was still only a bit player in what was a drama still dominated by the British.

Cairo was the perfect jumping-off point to cover the Middle East. Tensions between the Arabs and the Jewish settlers who arrived by the boatload from Europe were mounting. A world in transition, it was an ideal location for a fledgling foreign correspondent in a hurry to make his mark.

Cairo was at once decayed and sumptuous. George and Kay set up residence in Shepheard's Hotel, one of those fabled, slightly disreputable places where the foreign press inevitably makes its home.

Life should have been good. Polk's career was at a stage where things were really falling into place. But Kay continued to pull away from him. They quarreled frequently, her temper flaring as often as his. He had intercepted several postcards from Russell Hill. But given his own record of infidelities, he knew he had little right to condemn her. He wanted the marriage to survive. He had been bruised by his parents' divorce and did not want one of his own. And he dreaded being alone.

Searching for distractions, he worked and drank immoderately. He collected new friends. One of them, the iconoclastic writer I. F. Stone, on a Middle East journey, fell under Polk's spell. "He was what we call in America an awfully swell guy," Stone recalled. "Friendly, unpretentious, considerate, honorable. Polk was no radical, but a good reporter with an instinctive sympathy for the underdog and a healthy disrespect for stuffed shirts."

"I cottoned to him right away," NBC's John Donovan said, recalling his first meeting with Polk in Cairo. "He covered for me in cases where I missed shows and all sorts of things. Like almost everyone in Egypt at the time, we thought he was the cat's whiskers, this tall, good-looking Texan."

Cairo's sybaritic excesses were a good escape from a marriage that was shriveling. Before Polk probed beneath the city's deceptive carnival atmosphere, he exulted in it.

The British had superimposed themselves on the Egyptian landscape and on its society. Their starched uniforms swarmed in the narrow streets and cafés. Officially, they were meant only to "advise and counsel," but their control was complete. Egypt was their preserve, a cotton farm for the mills of Lancashire. It had worked thus for decades. What Britain needed, Lord Balfour once said, was "supreme economic and political control in the Middle East, to be exercised in friendly and unostentatious cooperation with the Arabs . . ." For it was its position in the Middle East, its ability to safeguard its oil supplies, that kept Britain among the ranks of the great powers.

Away from the Gezira Sporting Club (from which Egyptians were banned), out of earshot of the clipped accents of Cambridge, life went on as it had for hundreds of thousands of years. It was this Egypt that drew George Polk. He dubbed it the land of PID: poverty, ignorance, and disease. He understood better than most reporters in the field that he was a witness not only to news in the making but to history.

He began to sense that radio and even newsprint could not adequately convey the complexity and significance of what he was seeing. He began to think only a book could give him the space to explore the complexity of the changes under way.

"He was extremely careful about his work," Donovan remembered. "He was the only guy I know who had a system of maps. He took the whole Middle East and studied every corner of it. Which is something most of us never did. I occasionally looked at a map, to check things out, but I didn't have a theater area on my wall, like Eisenhower. George was that careful."

One of the critical stories of the area concerned Jewish efforts to establish a Jewish state. "I don't believe," George wrote his family, "the Anglo-American Commission now en route to the Middle East will decide that Palestine can or should become a Jewish national state. Palestine can't care for even half of the poor, destitute people in Europe who are Jewish refugees. So the Commission would be silly to stir up Arab hostility further by deciding in favor of Zionist hopes."

After a lengthy stay in British-ruled Palestine, however, Polk would see things differently. "He became staunchly pro-Israeli," Donovan noted.

Among his first CBS broadcasts was a report from Suez in early 1946 on the meeting between King Farouk of Egypt and King ibn-Saud of Saudi Arabia. "The Arab League," Polk wrote home, "is beginning to get publicity conscious and that's good for us here. It means simply that we have access to the men who make the news. Last night we went out for a talk off the record with Azzam Pasha, who is Secretary General of the Arab League. Over cups of coffee, sitting on priceless oriental rugs, we learned about the League's plans for the Anglo-American Commission. It was an interesting evening," he concluded, adding a forlorn note: "I just wish Catherine could have been there."

Catherine was increasingly not there. She had her own obligations to fulfill for the L.A. *Daily News*, and she was fulfilling them on her own, rather than in tandem with George, as had been their original plan. Her absences, and the loneliness he felt without her, marred an otherwise satisfying time in his life. His writing was stronger, less mannered. There was greater demand for his work by CBS, by *Newsweek*, and by the syndication.

He was no longer bluffing his way in the world. Soon the entire Middle East was his theater of operations. By the end of January he had scored a major coup for CBS. He and Kay were granted an interview by the Turkish President, Ismet Inonu. It was the first time the world had heard directly from the man who was the latest target of Stalinist extortion. Moscow demanded a joint Soviet-Turkish defense system for the Dardanelles and the Turkish straits. The hard reality behind Stalin's message was Soviet maneuvering to establish a toehold in the eastern Mediterranean.

The Turkish President told the Polks that Turkey would fight to protect her sovereignty and that he thought the United Nations could only function if the United States stood in time of peace for the same things it had supported in war.

Americans had become increasingly aware of Turkey. Newspaper cartoons showed a fat little man with a fez on his head peering with alarm down the double barrel of a Soviet rifle. Turkey was now in Stalin's gunsights, just as Czechoslovakia, Poland, Hungary, and Rumania had been during the previous months. It was too late for Eastern Europe, but this corner of the Mediterranean could still be saved.

That spring of 1946, Americans were stirred by the familiar voice of a wartime hero. Winston Churchill spoke from an unexpected place: the small town of Fulton, Missouri, thousands of miles from where the battle lines of a different kind of war were being drawn. Responding to a personal request of Truman's to address Fulton's Westminster College ("This is a wonderful school in my home state," the President had written the former Prime Minister. "Hope you can do it. I'll introduce you"), Churchill took the opportunity to ring alarms across the American continent.

"Warsaw, Berlin, Prague, Vienna, Budapest, Belgrade, Bucharest, and Sofia, all these famous cities and the populations around them lie in what I must call the Soviet sphere, and all are subject in one form or another, not only to Soviet influence but to a very high and, in many cases, increasing measure of control from Moscow. Athens, Greece, alone, with its immortal glories, is free to decide its future."

Not content to simply alarm and then withdraw, Churchill went on to call for the creation of what sounded very much like an Anglo-American alliance, though he called it a "fraternal association under the United Nations," to stop the Soviet Union's relentless land grab. The old warrior prodded America to see that this peace was only another word for an armed truce.

For Polk, America's growing awareness of the world beyond its borders translated into greater opportunities. Peacetime is not when foreign correspondents make their mark. With his Turkish scoop, he survived another initiation by fire. Polk did a "blind" broadcast, a harrowing experience which involves not hearing New York, not knowing when the host, then usually Robert Trout, John Daly, or Douglas Edwards, spoke the words ". . . and now here is George Polk with that report" in his earphone.

Ankara, the Turkish capital, did not have radio facilities, so Polk broadcast his report via a simple telephone line. Not only did he have to start "blind" at precisely the preappointed second, but he had to get off the air at a prearranged instant. There was no room for mistakes. Somehow, everything worked perfectly, and he even managed to get CBS to pass a transcript on to *Newsweek*. Thus two major American news organizations scooped their competition thanks to George Polk. It was intoxicating stuff for a relative newcomer in the field.

By April 7, 1946, CBS felt he had proven himself sufficiently to make him the long-awaited offer. George Polk was named CBS News Cairo correspondent. He was now finally and officially a member of that closed circle of foreign correspondents he had so long admired. Polk would join Smith, Collingwood, Sevareid, Shirer, and Richard C. Hottelet as one of "Murrow's Boys." Murrow was the man he would emulate in voice and delivery and in adhering to one principle: that fact could never be subordinated to passion or polemic.

"George patterned himself on Murrow," Donovan recalled. "In his view Murrow was a kind of vessel of learning in an empty desert of ignorance. Not just in radio broadcasting but in reporting in general. An awful lot of reporters didn't know anything about anything. Wire service guys would be thrown out of a job in Walla Walla and the next thing you knew they were in the Sudan. And of course Murrow was the scholar, the schoolteacher who had backed into broadcasting in a kind of crazy way. He had a historical approach to the news which was unusual forty years ago."

Polk did CBS's first broadcast from Beirut. He set up cable and phone lines from Haifa and Tel Aviv. His was the first American voice heard live from the Holy Land. In a telegram from Jerusalem dated July 5, 1946, Polk sent an ominous message to anchorman Robert Trout in New York:

> Palestine crisis eased somewhat today as British Army completed first phase of operations against Jews suspected of terrorism and violence. But Zionist countermeasures apparently won't be delayed long. Jewish resistance contact told me this

afternoon of a secret meeting arranged for tonight "someplace in the Jordan Valley, Dead Sea area." Representatives of three Jewish underground forces, Haganah, Irgun Zvai Leumi, and the Stern Gang, planning campaign against British. This decision being withheld temporarily for expected statement of policy for Weizmann and for recommendations of the American and British Zionist groups.

Meanwhile, correspondents covering Palestine still having difficult time sorting fact from fantasy following up Zionist reports of British Army and police atrocities against arrested Jews. Correspondents obtained a list of ten persons allegedly savagely mistreated and requesting the British produce these ten, thus confirming or denying charges. Correspondents unsuccessfully demanding eyewitness reporting.

American foreign correspondents had been drawing fire from British authorities since well before Polk's arrival on the scene. Constantine Poulos, the respected Middle East correspondent for *The Nation* and the Overseas News Agency, had recently been expelled from Palestine by the British. Poulos had disclosed that British authorities were arming Arabs and giving aid and comfort to an Arab terrorist leader named Abdullah Khalil.

Polk's own stormy relationship with British authority in the Middle East began almost as soon as he set up shop for CBS. But while he often provoked the authorities, Polk was gaining the respect and the affection of the hard-nosed pack he traveled with.

On the landmark Allenby Bridge between Jordan and Palestine, a British officer stopped Polk and his two companions, Ted Berkman of ABC News and Gerold Frank of Hearst's International News Service.

"Religious affiliation?" the British officer asked of the three, scrutinizing their press passes. "Atheist," answered Polk, deeply resenting the question, knowing his companions' "religious affiliation" to be Jewish. Relations between the British high command and the American press were tense already, and Polk feared the officer might prevent his colleagues from entering Palestine.

The Englishman glared at Polk but did not risk the humiliation of repeating his question. With a look of disgust, he waved all three Americans through the barrier.

Polk's closest friend in the Middle East press corps was John Donovan, his opposite number at NBC News. A burly Irishman with an outsize appetite for life, for drink, and for good times, Donovan had a soft spot for his reserved CBS competitor. The Irishman was a boon companion for Polk. With his gift for enlivening every minute, Donovan was the perfect foil for the more disciplined and serious Polk.

While George was rapidly proving himself at the network, Kay had given up on her own career as a journalist. She quit writing for the L.A. *Daily News*, out of loyalty, she said, following a disagreement her husband had with its management. She and Polk had finally moved out of Shepheard's Hotel into their own apartment.

For several months Kay tried being a housewife. But she was desperately unhappy. Bored and often lonely, she had not stopped thinking of Russell Hill. Their correspondence had continued unabated.

On an oppressively hot summer evening, Polk climbed the four flights to his home to find his wife packing.

"I'm leaving," she told him simply, her voice calm. "It's no use, George. It's not going to work for us."

He stood for a moment, too stunned to speak. He had never met a woman he found as interesting or as unattainable as his wife. Obsessed by his work, he had missed the point she had been making for months, that she was ready for a break.

"Just like that?" he asked. "You can't leave just like that."

"What's the point, George? We've tried for seven years. It isn't going to get better."

"All right, then," Polk said. "We'll have a party. We'll invite all our friends and tell them this is the way we both want it, that it's a friendly parting. All for the best."

She stared at him as though he were speaking a language she did not understand. Finally, she realized this was his way of saving face. It meant everything for him not to be seen as the one left behind.

"Sure," she answered. "Let's have a party." And that was how the astonished friends of Kay and George Polk, the perfect couple, learned their marriage was over.

The healing would take Polk a long time. He was thirty-three years old and alone again. Along with the loneliness, there was a sense of failure. Months later, when his divorce was final and Kay was already enrolled at Columbia University's Russian Institute, he finally wrote his mother.

"You've asked me about my relations with Catherine. After a very difficult time in breaking emotional ties, I think that we both feel very free and relaxed about the situation. By this I mean that our divorce, which became final in October, has taken both emotionally and legally.

"It has been less easy for me than for her, because I am a sentimental guy. Nevertheless, we are through, completely. In the last few weeks I've found a new and pleasant mental relaxation. I never expect to see her again."

Kay married Russell Hill the following Christmas. She eventually gave birth to four sons and never saw George Polk again.

8

On a blistering September morning in 1946, George Polk stood on the dock at Athens' Piraeus harbor and watched a weary, aged king step ashore to reclaim his kingdom. King George II of the Hellenes, surrounded by courtiers in top hats, did not cut a commanding figure.

George II had spent the war years in exile, first in Cairo, then in a luxury suite in London's genteel Claridge's Hotel. He did not love, nor was he loved by, his countrymen, whom he referred to as "foreigners." In fact, it was the king, of mostly Danish blood, who was foreign. An aloof and remote figure, he had no real interest in Greece, its history, or its most recent struggle. Little real affection or even respect bound together monarch and his subjects. Born and bred to be a king, however, George II was anxious now to resume that occupation. His inheritance was the Glücksburg family's noblesse oblige. His passion was stirred less by statecraft than by international gossip and by his English mistress.*

In the 1930s, when fascism of every shade was fashionable in certain European quarters, King George II had associated himself with Greece's own, though somewhat watered-down, Mussolini, General Joannes Metaxas. Metaxas had shamelessly patterned his Third Hellenic Civilization after Hitler's Third Reich, though the means he used to attain his goal of a paternalistic, authoritarian state were far less brutal than those of his German role model.

At the outbreak of the war, Metaxas and his monarch sought to maintain a precarious neutrality toward both Axis and Allied pow-

* George II was to reign only until 1947, when, upon his death, his brother Paul I succeeded to the Greek throne. Paul I was in turn succeeded by his son, Constantine II, who was deposed by a 1974 referendum which abolished the Greek monarchy.

ers. However, king and dictator alike rejected Italy's ultimatum of October 1940, which constituted a direct challenge to Greek sovereignty. Greece thus entered the war, becoming Britain's only active ally during the winter of 1940–41. As Italian invading forces poured across Greece's northern frontier, monarchists and republicans alike fought bravely to repel the foreign aggressors. Churchill, already sentimentally attached to the Greek monarchy, would never forget Greece's staunch stand against its vastly more powerful enemy during London's "darkest hour."

England was the king's spiritual home; the English were responsible for his family's reign. In 1830, after Greece finally shook off centuries of Ottoman rule and was declared a kingdom, the British Minister in Athens, Sir Edmund Lyons, said that Greek independence was largely a myth. There was room for only two Mediterranean powers: the Russians and the British. "Since Greece can't be Russian," Lyons concluded, "it must be British."

To decorate the Greek throne, London had obliged by finding first a German, Prince Otto of Bavaria, who ruled from 1830 until he was expelled in 1862, then a Dane, George I, followed in turn by his son, Constantine I, father of George II. Winston Churchill, the avid imperialist and scion of the House of Marlborough, successfully pleaded the unloved Glücksburg monarch's case during the war with his friend and wartime ally Franklin Delano Roosevelt.

FDR, not much interested in Greece, referred to its monarch as "Georgie" and characterized him as "dumb." Churchill, convinced that only a monarch, never mind how discredited, could assure Britain's continued influence over Greece, ultimately prevailed over his friend. Churchill's preoccupation with the British-Greek relationship, which verged on the obsessional, had two sources. He deemed a friendly postwar Greece to be essential for London's interests, given Greece's strategic position straddling Britain's imperial sea routes and communications to its supplies of oil in the Persian Gulf. The Prime Minister also regarded Greece as "the cork" on the bottle of Soviet expansion into the Mediterranean. Moreover, Churchill, like so many Englishmen of his class and education, was imbued with a love of the Greek past, the mystique and the glory of Panhellenism.

This bright September morning thus belonged to the squinting monarch in his spanking white naval uniform. A recent plebiscite (held under questionable circumstances) showed that the majority of George II's countrymen wanted him to end his comfortable London exile and return to claim his throne.

For weeks prior to the plebiscite, walls all over Greece had been smeared with the message: "HE IS COMING." Others, more ominous, declared: "HELLENES, DECIDE: IF YOU ARE NOT ROYALIST, YOU ARE COMMUNIST." The Communists had boycotted the parliamentary elections held the previous March, which had laid the groundwork for the plebiscite on the monarchy. The left pronounced the elections inherently unfair since authority was lodged in British hands and in those of London's client Royalist-rightist factions.

With a free hand, the Royalists assured their victory long before the people cast their votes. Armed bands of ultra-right-wing vigilantes disrupted leftist political rallies and threatened entire villages if they did not vote for the Royalists. Leftist excesses of the past probably frightened many more Greeks into the monarchists' arms. Fewer than half of registered Greeks went to the polls. The left's boycott of the March elections assured a Royalist victory and a parliament far to the right of much of Greece. And once a monarchist parliament was in place, plans for a plebiscite on the king's return proceeded apace.

Still, compared with the new regimes in Eastern Europe, which didn't even bother with elections, the Greek parliamentary elections and the subsequent plebiscite on the monarchy were triumphs of democracy. Or so the British, its sponsors, hoped the world would judge it.

Among those journalists who did not see the situation in quite this light was CBS's newly named chief Middle East correspondent, George Polk.

"The real facts are," he reported from Athens in September 1946, "that long before the plebiscite took place, the Army and police had rounded up or scared away all persons known to have anti-monarchist sentiments. Thus the Greek government . . . and the Allied Military Force Observing the Greek Elections were able to proclaim stoutly that the plebiscite was free. It was, but well rigged."

On his second day in Athens, George had a taste of what the Greek authorities thought of freewheeling foreign correspondents. For the first time in his life, George Polk was called a Communist. Athens' right-wing newspapers—*Akropolis*, *Kathimerini*, and *Embros*—conferred that label on him.

"We American reporters who watched the arrival of King George," Polk wrote Howard K. Smith from Cairo on November 7, 1946, "a terrified little man expecting an assassin's bullet any minute, were described as being Communists by several of the most important Greek newspapers. Our names were used in the daily articles and our private affairs (or believed to be private affairs) were bluntly examined. . . . This rabid press attack included charges that we wrote under instruction from our Communist-controlled organizations (CBS, New York *Daily News*, New York *Herald Tribune*, etc.)."

From then on, Polk and a handful of his American colleagues— Homer Bigart, Raymond Daniell, Daniel Thrapp, and Constantine Poulos—saw their names almost daily in articles that claimed the reporters "did terrible things from dawn till dusk but almost unbelievable things from dusk till dawn."

"The Greek government went for me personally," Polk wrote Joseph Phillips of *Newsweek* on October 12, 1946, from Cairo, "and the American press generally, like a ton of bricks. We were described in the Royalist–right-wing newspapers as 'all Communists, writing for the *Daily News* of New York, the *Herald Tribune*, CBS, etc. These reporters are cooperating actively with the instructions issued from their home offices . . . they are accepting propaganda, liquor, and women as bribes.' "

"For a gag," Polk wrote Howard K. Smith, "we called as a body on the most offensive Royalist–right-wing editors and declared their charges falsehoods. We also informed these gentlemen that in America it was customary to tar and feather offending editors. Then in the same body, we called on the Greek Communist Party headquarters (in a hideout) and declared that we were very much enraged because we weren't receiving the services customarily extended to reporters: propaganda, liquor, and women. The sequence was good for a laugh," George concluded, "a laugh amid the ruin and poverty and hopelessness that is Greece today."

On his first working trip to Greece, Polk had not been content to stay within the confines of Athens. Crossing the deep channel that connects the mainland to the Peloponnesus, he visited the ancient city of Corinth, then moved north to Larissa, in central Greece, an area that had been sought by Goths, Huns, Bulgars, and Franks as the most desirable slice of an inhospitable land.

In a borrowed jeep he drove to Salonika, the capital of Macedonia. He was stunned by the rapidly changing landscape, which gave him the feeling that he had passed through several worlds in a very short time. Each landscape brought with it a different history, a separate past: the Classical Greek, the Roman, the Byzantine, and the Turkish. The land was as poor as it was beautiful.

Polk found whole villages deserted. He was stopped repeatedly by armed bands. One group claimed it was searching for a renegade Communist; a second group sought a Royalist. Both gave Polk the same answer as to what they would do if they found one or the other: "Kill him."

Civil war, the long-festering feud between monarchists and republicans, had been rekindled, not abated, by the king's return. This much seemed apparent to Polk.

One of the most disturbing places Polk traveled to was a small island off the eastern Greek coast. Five hundred people had been banished here for the crime of "subversive activities" against the Royalist Prime Minister, Constantine Tsaldaris. One of the five hundred was a senile woman of sixty-five, another a child of two months. Both were charged with "plotting against the security of the state."

Disgusted, Polk reported on CBS:

> The roundup of persons even vaguely suspected of not approving the government and not loving the king seems endless, and the most stupid part is that the roundups are progressive in nature. For example, when the government seizes a whole

village as hostage for nearby "bandit" activity, relatives of the captured persons immediately "take to the hills," as the saying is, to seek revenge or avoid a similar arrest. Thus one person seized by the government for bandit activity, sympathy, or proximity may in turn pull any number of relatives and friends into the hills to oppose the government.

The terror was all the more tragic since Greece was already depleted by the war and the German occupation. About a million Greeks were homeless after the Nazis burned two thousand villages. The country at large was wrecked and disordered. Its harbors and ships and railroad tracks, bridges and telephone lines, were destroyed. All this had been inflicted upon Europe's poorest country.

Still, there had been hope among the ravaged population that out of the brave campaign against the Germans would emerge a country free at long last from foreign domination. But the future's poisoned seeds had been sown in the same resistance that had earned the world's respect. It was a divided movement, the precursor of the bitter civil war to come. On the one side were those pressing for the return of the monarchy and the old institutions that were its foundation. The British, with their concern for maintaining a strong presence in the Mediterranean basin, backed this faction, EDES, at the end of the war.

But it was the other side, ELAS, and its political umbrella, EAM, the National Liberation Front, founded in September 1941, with well-known ties to the Greek Communist Party but *not* itself Communist, which had been the spine of the resistance, constituting 90 percent of the anti-Nazi movement. Although made up primarily of non-Communists who, in a very general way, shared a dream of a new "people's Greece," by the end of the war ELAS was controlled by Communists. During the war, the British, through their Special Operations Executive, the body charged with fomenting resistance in occupied Europe, penetrated both left and right wings of the resistance. By March 1943, Churchill had issued a directive to all British officers in Greece that they were to cooperate where possible with resistance groups prepared to recognize the authority of the king and his government. By this stage of the

Nazi occupation there were very few in the resistance who placed much faith in either King George or in his government in exile. Although the left-wing resistance did not shrink from using terror tactics against the Greek population, it nonetheless enjoyed genuine mass support. The British, however, were determined to shore up the EDES right-wing resistance against the possibility of a left-wing power grab at the war's conclusion.

In October 1944, 6,000 British troops and the remainder of the Royal Greek Army in exile, under the command of Lieutenant General Ronald Scobie, landed in Athens. The British-sponsored government of George Papandreou tried to bring about the peaceful disbanding of the heavily armed ELAS guerrillas. Push came to shove on the streets of Athens in December 1944, however, when police fired into a crowd of pro-ELAS demonstrators. In reprisal, ELAS units attacked police headquarters. Churchill cabled General Scobie that he was to treat Athens as a conquered city and, if necessary, shoot to kill to restore order. Churchill himself flew to Athens on Christmas Eve 1944 in the desperate hope of reconciling the warring factions. But Greek had fired upon Greek, and not even the Churchill magic could make them forget their bitterness.

ELAS refused to cede its hard-fought share of power to what it regarded as the forces of reaction and restoration. The former ELAS fighters and their growing number of sympathizers, terrified at the prospect of the restoration of a right-wing dictatorship, headed for the mountains, soon to begin to organize guerrilla warfare, this time not against a foreign army but against their own countrymen.

In 1946, Greece was not yet Washington's responsibility. America was still primarily an observer from the sidelines. The British, as George Polk discovered in his travels, were stage-managing this round. "I talked with a number of British officers and men scattered around the countryside on military or police missions," he cabled CBS on February 3, 1947. "As always, the British servicemen individually were pleasant guys. A good many of them told me frankly they were appalled by the atrocities being perpetrated by Greek soldiers and policemen on Greek captives. One lieutenant colonel complained that he and other British officers often made full reports of these atrocities to London, but that diplomatic word never came back to Athens to curb these excesses."

RETURNING to his apartment in Cairo, George found it occupied by his seventeen-year-old brother, Bill. "You two boys need each other," their mother had declared, and packed Bill Polk off to Egypt. The younger brother was disappointed by his recent rejection for admission to Princeton University. George, although he never spoke of her again, was still deeply hurt by Kay's departure.

"I'm grown up now, George," were Bill's first words to his older brother. Smiling at the earnest adolescent whose soft features were just beginning to shed their baby fat, George replied, "Oh, I can see that." The two brothers barely knew each other.

It turned out to be an astute move on their mother's part. In a very short time, the two drew close. George, sixteen years his brother's senior, loved having him along, both as a friend and as surrogate son. He had dreaded the prospect of returning to an apartment with a thousand reminders of Kay. Now, suddenly, he had a family.

Young Bill Polk was shocked and repelled by Cairo's contrasts. Streams of beggars followed the two Americans from their front door, their scrawny arms stretched out, their low wails undeterred by rejection. Bill accompanied George everywhere. The older brother preached endlessly to the younger, tried to pass on to him what lessons he had gleaned. With Bill, George could give his idealism free rein. America has to stand for something different than the old colonial powers, he would insist. "We have to stand for decency and for freedom, otherwise we have no right to claim leadership of the free world. We're no better than the Russians otherwise."

Peace, the enticing prospect of the year before, seemed remote by the end of 1946. Palestine again reclaimed the world's attention. George, poring over his maps of the Middle East like a general preparing for a campaign, was determined to end his first year with

CBS in the eye of the storm: Jerusalem. Though only three hundred miles from Cairo, it was not going to be an easy trip.

He cabled CBS New York:

> After battling for days Mideast red tape, suspicion, nationalism, etc., three-hundred-mile trip from Cairo to Jerusalem undoubtedly one of the most difficult in the world today. Palestine entry complicated enough . . . what with bitter triangular British, Arab, Jewish controversy. Unhappy Holy Land is today scene of gunrunning, so-called illegal immigration, and trigger-finger jitters, but traveler hasn't seen anything until he has tried to enter or leave Egypt.
>
> Preparations for driving my car from Cairo to Jerusalem began two weeks ago. I encountered forty-two documents to be made out without counting duplicates or triplicates. Deposit of eight hundred dollars to guarantee I won't sell my car outside Egypt is required. Additionally I had to pay customs officials overtime charges for their trouble.

Polk persevered through the sea of red tape and ran the gauntlet at the border, finally arriving with Bill in time for Christmas Eve in Bethlehem. In the first live broadcast from the Church of the Nativity, Polk reported on CBS:

> The shrine city of Bethlehem is packed today with crowds of Christians celebrating Jesus' birth nineteen and a half centuries ago. There are also many Arabs dressed in flowing robes and turbans who work in the tiny city's mother-of-pearl inlaying industry nearby. . . . There are also Jews here for devotional reasons or just sightseeing. . . .
>
> The past two weeks' truce continues in Palestine and nobody expects trouble over Christmas . . . but the Church of the Nativity is heavily guarded and police are in formation along eight miles between Bethlehem and Jerusalem. . . . Despite today's and tomorrow's peace and remembrance of the Prince of Peace, the Holy Land remains a place of political tensions. . . . Now I would like to take this opportunity to wish my

mother, Adelaide Polk, in Fort Worth, Texas, a Merry Christmas . . . and as the bells ring out in Bethlehem . . .

This line was meant to be Bill Polk's cue to toll the church bells for the benefit of thousands of American listeners. Bill, stunned and embarrassed at his brother's surprise message to their mother, forgot his cue. The bells went unrung. George repeated for the third time: ". . . as the bells ring out in Bethlehem . . ." Bill finally shook off his stupor, grabbed the rope, and pulled. The bells finally rang out in Bethlehem.

Bill Polk may have been embarrassed by his brother's enthusiasm, but the folks at home loved it. "Many, many thanks for your Christmas broadcast," producer Ted Church cabled George. "Show excellent all around." Then, in a highly unusual message from the home office to a correspondent in the field, the cable continued: "This is to let you know the vast appreciation of the entire United States staff of your work of the past twelve months. Cheery greetings from Murrow and seven editors, ten writers, couple dozen newscasters and analysts, all of whom have made much use of the extraordinary, clear material you've sent to New York. Wish you could be home this week. We would like to toast your health and bright future. Have as merry a Christmas as possible . . . Best regards."

By the time Polk returned to Cairo, there was more tangible evidence of how highly esteemed he was in his company's eyes. He received his first raise from CBS News.

9

As 1947 got under way, even optimists were losing hope of achieving a real peace. Britain, paralyzed by the worst blizzards since 1881, teetered on the brink of economic collapse. Greece and Turkey, the sole Balkan lands still free of Moscow's grip, seemed ripe for Soviet penetration.

In 1947, George Polk and his own government were set on a collision course. America was about to abandon its traditional policy against "entangling alliances" and embrace Harry Truman's unlimited support of "free peoples who are resisting attempted subjugation by armed minorities." The first testing ground of Truman's Pax Americana would be the country where Polk was to come into his own as foreign correspondent: Greece.

At first glance, Harry Truman seemed a peculiar choice to lead America toward a new imperial era. But the new President had a subtle understanding of geopolitics. Truman saw that the dream of access to the high seas would lead to Soviet pressure from the Aegean to Gibraltar to the Red Sea.

Truman's view of Soviet intentions had been evolving since he took office in the spring of 1945. That summer, he had boarded a plane for Potsdam to meet with Stalin and Churchill. Like Roosevelt, he was at first somewhat beguiled by Stalin. "A man I can deal with," he commented, likening the Soviet dictator to Boss Pendergast, the Kansas City politician. Besides, he and Stalin could talk farming, both having been raised on the soil. Although there were serious differences between them, the President saw common ground for the two wartime allies to work together after the worst war in the history of mankind.

A year later, Truman put little faith in the Soviets' word. They had violated the Yalta agreement too many times. The Red Army had metamorphosed from an army of liberation into an army of occupation. Poland, Hungary, Bulgaria, Czechoslovakia, Rumania, and the Baltic republics were its permanent garrisons. Truman, an avid poker player, was not going to fold on the next hand.

In fairly short order, Truman and a small handful of powerful allies in the Pentagon, in the State Department, and on Capitol Hill convinced their countrymen that Greece was vital for American security. It was a remarkable achievement.

The sheer remoteness of Greece, as well as America's antipathy to messy European alliances, had historically discouraged anything more than a rudimentary diplomatic connection between the two countries.

During the war, the Joint Chiefs of Staff had made it clear that no American troops could be spared in the Balkans, a strictly "British affair." However, in the postwar period oil became a vital element in the United States' assessment of its future needs. The shortest passage to the oil wells of the Persian Gulf was through Greece's front door, the Mediterranean Sea.

Even before Truman became convinced of the need to protect Greece, Secretary of the Navy James V. Forrestal had determined that America's best interest lay in establishing a military presence in the Mediterranean. In February 1946, a cruiser and two destroyers were baptized the U.S. Naval Force, Mediterranean. The Sixth Fleet was thus born.

The intellectual underpinning of the Truman Doctrine came from George Kennan, the tall, lean, cerebral foreign service officer who had observed and agonized over Soviet conduct for many years as a diplomat stationed in Moscow. In an eight-thousand-word diplomatic cable from Moscow on February 22, 1946, Kennan poured out his frustration and disappointment with Soviet behavior since the war.

What motivated the Soviets, Kennan argued, was "centuries old." "At the bottom of the Kremlin's neurotic view of world affairs is traditional and instinctive Russian sense of insecurity." Marxism, Kennan went on, was not the cause of Soviet expansion, but "its honeyed promises" made traditional Russian instincts "more dangerous and insidious than ever before." Then, in an ominous prediction, the gifted diplomat concluded that "the Soviets consider it necessary that our traditional way of life be destroyed. . . . Soviet power is impervious to mere logic of reason, and it is highly sensitive to the logic of force."

"The Long Telegram" was circulated by Forrestal to Truman and his principal advisers, the omnipresent Clark Clifford, Secretary of State James Byrnes, and Under Secretary Dean Acheson. There were two key points in Kennan's "containment" strategy. First, it was time for the United States to draw the line against Soviet expansionism. Second, Washington must form some sort of alliance, military and economic, with Britain and the other Western powers.

By the spring of 1946, Forrestal's "show the flag on the high seas" policy had borne visible fruit. Early one April morning, the hulking gray mass of the battleship *Missouri* sliced through the still, blue water of Athens' Phaleron Bay. It was an awesome sight for Greeks of all ages who thronged the harbor and waved handkerchiefs. Others boarded small fishing boats and rowed out to greet the great ship. The city of Athens proclaimed President Truman an honorary Athenian, while its mayor presented the *Missouri*'s commander with an urn filled with earth from the Acropolis to be placed on FDR's grave.

Among the first to board the *Missouri*, with measured steps and a dignified nod toward the teeming dock, was a bearish man brimming with self-importance: Constantine Tsaldaris, the Royalist Foreign Minister, who was soon to be Prime Minister. Tsaldaris was breathless with enthusiasm for Athens' imposing visitor on this spring day.

"The *Missouri*," he assured its captain, "represents for the Greek people the faith in those ideals which first saw the light of day in Greece and also a hope for a better future, in which want and fear would completely vanish from the lives of men and nations."

His noble words struck a hollow note among those on that dockside who knew that the genial Tsaldaris was among the more corrupt Athens politicians. Accompanied by a small army of lackeys, he swept away from the ceremonies in a long, shiny black Rolls-

Royce. A motorcycle escort added a touch of twentieth-century pomp.

The extremely precarious balance between the right and the left, which had been imposed by the presence of the Nazi forces on Greek soil, had been tipped. Suddenly, one side had a powerful new ally. As the Athens newspaper *Akropolis* put it: "Around us here and over the Balkans hovers the great Russian shadow. So America comes here to tell us, hold tight, and you may be sure we are with you."

Harry Truman's paramount concern was not the civil war or the idea of Greeks killing Greeks over passionately held views of their country's future. Guerrilla raids or the ascendancy of a corrupt monarchy mattered little to him. For Truman, Greece was but one more skirmish in a much larger war, a global war conducted by another power bent on world conquest. What counted was keeping Greece anti-Communist, using whatever means necessary. In retrospect, this grim specter of Soviet expansion into Greece was more paranoia than fact. At international conferences, the Soviets used the continuing British presence in Greece to counter charges that they were seeking hegemony in Eastern Europe. Privately, however, Foreign Minister Molotov assured his British counterpart, Ernest Bevin, that the Soviets would not press the matter. Significant support for the Greek guerrillas came from a different quarter: Tito's Yugoslavia. Tito's feelings of fellowship toward the Greek left were genuine, though the Yugoslav leader also harbored his own expansionist dreams. To a lesser extent, Bulgaria and Albania were also supplying the guerrillas with small arms and military training, in part from fear of the Royalists' long-term designs on their borders. This aid never amounted to anything near the massive support channeled to Athens by London and, soon, Washington.

The Soviet Union, which showed a startling lack of sympathy toward the guerrillas, sent no substantial aid. Milovan Djilas, Yugoslavia's Vice President during this period, recalls Stalin, in early 1948, pounding his fist on the table and barking irritably: "The Greek guerrillas have no prospect of success at all! What do you think, that Great Britain and the United States, the most powerful state in the world, will permit you to break their line of communication in the Mediterranean Sea! Nonsense. And we have no navy. The uprising in Greece must be stopped," he commanded, "as quickly as possible."

Stalin had gained a free hand in Eastern and Central Europe. The Greek Communists, unlike the Eastern European Communists—with the notable exception of Tito—did not owe their existence to Moscow. They had a solid constituency of their own, boosted by their heroic role during the resistance. The Red Army had not "liberated" Greece. The last thing Stalin wanted was another independent Communist Party. Yugoslavia was trouble enough.

But Washington's entanglement in Greek affairs was growing. That fall, the Truman administration gave substantial credits to the decimated Greek merchant shipping fleet. Shipping had traditionally been that seafaring country's lifeblood. A short-term loan to the Greek government followed.

It was not that Washington was blind to the nature of the Athens regime. In October 1946, the American Embassy in Athens cabled the State Department:

> Lack of leadership is what principally ails this country . . . the five-year Metaxas dictatorship seems to have effectively prevented the rise of a new generation of politicians to take the place of the oldsters who still think in terms of the old struggle between Royalists and republicans and miss the meaning of the developments which World War II and the rise of Russia have brought about. Small men, old men, and men entirely lacking in the sense of realism which the situation requires are what we are having to deal with now. In addition, the king, who has been brought back as a "solution" for the problems which the politicians will not tackle, is the same old muddled, indecisive figure that he always was.

Even though the British still had 6,000 troops garrisoned in Greece, America was meddling more and more in Athenian politics. At the end of 1946, Paul Porter, founder of the distinguished Washington law firm of Arnold and Porter and wartime head of the

Office of Price Administration, was dispatched to Athens as head of an economic mission. Once there, Porter sent a cable directly to President Harry Truman.

"You are aware," Porter began, "of the complete reactionary nature of the present government. But one must work with them, as I have, to understand how incredibly weak, stupid, and venal they really are. Their principal asset is the wide fear in Greece of Communist excesses, yet this was offset by their own policies of violence and exploitation."

At the end of 1946, Tsaldaris traveled to Washington to present his case. For two hours, Under Secretary of State Dean Acheson, his long, tapered fingers restlessly tapping his antique desk, listened to the paunchy Prime Minister. Tsaldaris ticked off a long list of Greek territorial claims on her neighbors. Finally, Acheson could hold his peace no longer.

"I lost my patience with him," Acheson wrote in his memoirs, "and told him what sort of statesmanship it was that frittered away its time and energy on territorial claims, when not only northern Greece but all Greece was headed hell for leather toward total destruction."

Acheson, who found his visitor "a weak, pleasant, but silly man, obsessed with the idea of solving his country's problems by gaining new territory," was relieved when the session was over and he closed the door behind the puffed-up Greek politician. Tsaldaris, who understood he had not made a good impression in Washington, consoled himself with thoughts of his real friends, the British. His first loyalty, he often reminded people, was to London.

Washington thus had no illusions about Tsaldaris or the monarchy he represented. The American Ambassador to Greece, Lincoln MacVeagh, a seasoned professional trying to hold on to his integrity in difficult circumstances—and soon to be succeeded by others who made less effort to do so—had alerted Washington as early as 1941: "What Greece has against George II and his dynasty . . . is their avariciousness and self-absorption at the expense of the country."

In spite of ample warnings, the Truman administration failed to use economic and political leverage to pressure Greek politicians to moderate their policies. It chose the quicker and more expedient route of massively backing a regime its own people found repellent, supposedly in the interest of "world peace." It was not the last time Washington was to strike this Faustian bargain. Woodrow Wilson's successors in the White House proved no more estimable players of the imperialist game than the tired empire whose place they were about to take.

On February 24, 1947, Lord Inverchapel, the British Ambassador to Washington, arrived at the State Department with a "blue piece of paper," the trade name for an urgent message from His Majesty's government to the new Secretary of State, George C. Marshall.

A diplomat of the old school, veteran of Moscow and Shanghai, Inverchapel was the perfect messenger of the Empire's distress. An elegant, world-weary man, Inverchapel had been among the first to predict the Cold War. Dean Acheson, with whom he most frequently dealt at the State Department, found him a genuine eccentric, a brilliant, complex, and difficult man.

Lord Inverchapel's news that morning, delivered to the unflappable Marshall, was neither good nor unexpected. Couched in the refined euphemisms of diplomatic language, it simply confirmed what had been rumored for months.

After six years of war and the loss of overseas monetary holdings, London faced intolerable financial pressures. What empire was left would be liquidated. London could no longer afford to bolster either the Greek or the Turkish government with men or sterling. Lord Inverchapel, the consummate servant of the Empire, was ringing its death knell.

Acheson already had compiled a detailed report on the consequences of American failure to pick up where London was leaving off in the eastern Mediterranean. Acheson and Marshall agreed that the security of Greece and Turkey was of vital concern to Washington and that only the United States had the means to preserve those nations' independence.

The day after Inverchapel's forlorn mission, Secretary of State Marshall met with the President and the Secretaries of War and the Navy. They all concurred that funds and authority were needed from Congress to prop up the two endangered Mediterranean lands. There was no discussion of why those countries were vital to America's security, or even whether the Soviets were a real threat in the region.

The men who had witnessed Munich and experienced the even deeper humiliation of Pearl Harbor were not going to be caught unprepared again.

Congress, with its conservative Republican majority, remained the last hurdle before massive aid could be dispatched to Greece and, to a lesser extent, Turkey. Truman wasted no time in summoning congressional leaders to the Oval Office. Acheson captured the high drama of the moment in his memoirs. "I knew," he wrote of the meeting on February 26, 1947, "we were met at Armageddon . . ." Secretary Marshall, however, was not nearly so pumped up. He gave a flat statement summarizing the State Department's recommendations.

Acheson, who had been feverishly preparing for this moment, was crestfallen. "These Congressmen had no conception of what challenged them," he wrote. "It was my task to bring it home. Both my superiors, equally perturbed, gave me the floor. Never have I spoken under such a pressing sense that the issue was up to me alone. No time was left for measured appraisal."

Measured appraisal was not what Acheson delivered to the majority and minority leaders of the Senate, the ranking members of the Senate Foreign Relations Committee, the Speaker of the House, and the ranking members of the House Committee on Foreign Affairs. In the past eighteen months, Acheson told them, Soviet pressure on the Black Sea straits, on Iran, and on northern Greece had brought the Balkans to the point where a Russian breakthrough might open three continents to Soviet penetration.

"Like apples in a barrel infected by one rotten one," Acheson intoned, "the corruption of Greece would infect Iran and all to the east. It would also carry infection to Africa through Asia Minor and Egypt, and to Europe through Italy and France, already threatened by the strongest domestic Communist parties in Western Europe. . . . These are the stakes that British withdrawal from the eastern Mediterranean offers to an eager and ruthless opponent," he concluded. It was the first articulation of what would, in another context, be called the domino theory.

Arthur Vandenberg, the powerful chairman of the Senate Foreign Relations Committee, during the war the most influential of the congressional isolationists, a man of vaulting ambition and transparent vanity, was first to comment.

"Mr. President," Vandenberg pronounced in a solemn voice, "if you will say that to the Congress and the country, I will support you and I believe that most of its members will do the same."

By March 12, President Truman was ready to do just that. The first draft of his historic speech was prepared by Loy Henderson, the State Department's specialist in the area then referred to as the Near East. Clark Clifford, special counsel to the President, saw a dual opportunity in the speech, and shaped it to reflect two concerns. Clifford wanted the President to project himself as a decisive leader and emerge from FDR's shadow. He also saw a chance for the country to finally take a hard line against Communism.

Looking invigorated, as he always did once he had made up his mind, Harry Truman stepped up to the podium to address a joint session of Congress on March 12. Peering through his thick spectacles, he delivered one of the most controversial speeches made by a President in this century.

Truman began by saying that the gravity of the world situation affected American security. But, he said, he would focus on only one potential flash point: Greece and Turkey. The Greek government, the President revealed, had made a formal appeal to the United States for assistance, along with a request for the assignment of American administrators, economists, and technicians to ensure that aid given would be used effectively. The Greek mission, Truman added, would include American military personnel. The Greek Army, he said, needed supplies and equipment to restore the authority of the government. Only the United States could supply this help. Truman said he had considered asking the United Nations to intercede, but could see no way to achieve such an intercession.

In truth, the President was moving his country outside the principle of collective security, outside the framework of the United Nations. Nor did he mention that the government Washington would be backing was both monarchist and reactionary. Though he mentioned Athens' "mistakes" and "extreme measures," Truman said nothing of the repressive practices which had driven thousands of Greeks into the hills to fight as guerrillas.

The task before Truman was much simpler than it would have been two decades later. Greece, for all its troubles, was a world away. There were no cameras to expose the ravaged faces of hunger, the broken bodies of those held captive on barren islands merely on suspicion of Communist activity. No pictures captured Athens' well-nourished politicians in their Rolls-Royces, speeding past children with their begging bowls. Our new clients were utter strangers.

In the years and decades to come, the Truman Doctrine would enable successive American policy makers to intervene on behalf of "free peoples resisting armed minorities." The road from Athens ultimately led to Saigon.

Clifford afterward said that the tone of urgency in the Truman Doctrine reflected the temper of those times. "We had to meet Senator Vandenberg's strategy for getting the aid package through Congress," he explained. Vandenberg's prescription: "Scare the hell out of Congress." Clifford also wanted to "send a signal to Stalin."

Truman asked for $400 million—worth thirteen times that in 1990 dollars—for the first year of the bill's duration. It was a huge amount of foreign aid for a country that had recently faced astronomical war bills. But his message had hit its mark. Senators and congressmen on both sides of the aisle sprang to their feet and applauded when Truman finished. Despite Truman's rousing speech, several weeks of fierce debate followed before the Greek-Turkish Aid Act passed the House by a vote of 287–107 and the Senate by 67 to 23. The polls never showed overwhelming popular support for this massive aid package.

The soul searching began almost immediately. Secretary Marshall, a measured, careful man, was in Moscow for a Foreign Ministers' conference. He found the speech too flamboyant and disturbingly anti-Communist. Though Truman never once mentioned the Soviet Union by name, there was no question that Moscow was the target of his doctrine.

When Marshall cabled Washington his fears, he was told the President saw no alternative course. Truman felt he could not get congressional approval without raising the specter of global Communism.

Walter Lippmann, America's leading commentator, was also alarmed that the doctrine would both intensify and institutionalize the Cold War. Lippmann had no trouble with the aid to Greece and Turkey. But he felt Washington should press the Greek government to embrace not only far rightists but also the guerrillas who had legitimate grievances. In his "Today and Tomorrow" column of March 15, 1947, Lippmann wrote that the Russians should be warned to steer clear of Greek affairs.

Lippmann also was distressed by the President's sweeping rhetoric. Better to announce, he continued in the same column, "not a global policy, but an American Middle East policy. . . . To address the Soviet Union directly and to say that, in view of the pressure on Greece and Turkey, we are reinforcing them, that our object is to stop the invasion of Greece. . . . The advantage of adopting a precise Middle East policy is that it can be controlled for the purpose of maintaining order. . . . A vague global policy, which sounds like the tocsin of an ideological crusade, has no limits."

10

Khartoum, Istanbul, Jerusalem, Tel Aviv, Cairo, Damascus, Baghdad, Athens—those were George Polk's datelines in the early months of 1947. Suddenly CBS could not get enough out of him. There were days when his voice or his cables were on every newscast.

Arriving in Tel Aviv in early February, longing for a good night's sleep after weeks without, he was roused by the harsh sound of a 3 a.m. telephone call.

"CBS New York," the fuzzy voice announced. "Have you heard the latest?" the man on the distant news desk asked, apparently oblivious to the time (it was early evening in New York).

"No. Actually, I've been asleep for a little while," Polk answered wearily.

"The Iran-Iraq petroleum pipeline has been cut in two places. . . . How soon can you get on the air with it?"

By now sitting bolt upright, notebook in hand, Polk said, "Give me half an hour. But first give me the story. No way I'll find anybody at this end awake to brief me."

The deskman dictated the story, which Polk then broadcast with a Palestine dateline. It was a measure of his growing authority that CBS needed Polk's voice to tell a story the correspondent knew nothing about.

Though physically draining, the job was getting easier. Polk was spending the few hours he had free each day on his private project. He had started compiling material for a book on the Middle East. Print in those days had a legitimacy that broadcasting still lacked. Everywhere he traveled, he collected material he could not use on the air. In two days in Khartoum he wrote twelve thousand words on the Sudan. He dreamed of finishing his book during a Nieman year at Harvard.

Back at his house in Cairo, he was just in time to see his brother off. Bill was going to travel on his own through the Middle East before returning home. He had been accepted for admission to Harvard the following fall. George was alone again in the big house, weighed down by memories, and he hated it.

"I'm let down," he wrote his mother. "All the sparkle of this house has gone with Bill. Really hated to see him go. But I've always hated to be left behind." The brothers had formed a strong unit. "Almost every day he was here," George wrote, "he made me gasp mentally over his intelligence and common sense and decency. I liked the guy a lot . . . even though I was a severe taskmaster for him. All I ever had to do was threaten to cut him off from the table and its groaning weight of food . . . and Bill was putty in my fingers."

"I'd like to take a vacation of a couple of months with you all," he wrote his family, "in Texas, California, and then work for a while in CBS headquarters. Of course, if my book gets written and sells, well, I might give up radio for magazine and book work . . . but who knows."

He knew from Murrow, who had experienced reentry problems himself after his years abroad, that it wasn't a good idea for a foreign correspondent to stay away too long. You lost touch if you did.

As head of public affairs programming for CBS, Murrow was general over an army of correspondents, stringers, newswriters, and editors. "A larger news staff than the Associated Press," it was said. Radio was how the nation got its breaking news. For the American public it was a habit acquired in wartime which television would not supplant for many years.

The issues CBS was covering in those postwar years were more complex than the straightforward movement of armies and high-level meetings of Allied commanders, the stories that had launched the careers of Murrow, Collingwood, Shirer, Smith, Sevareid, and the others. The climate in which reporters operated was also changing.

In March 1947, President Truman responded to right-wing Republican charges of vulnerability to leftist subversion in his administration (including Republican House Speaker Joseph W. Martin's call to end "boring from within by subversionists high up in the government"). He issued Executive Order 9835, thereby establishing a Federal Employee Loyalty Program. Coming on the heels of Truman's anti-Communist speech to Congress, it helped legitimize the intolerance that was taking hold of the country. The order required a loyalty investigation of every person entering civilian employment in the federal government. It made department and agency heads personally responsible for assuring that "disloyal" persons were eliminated from the federal payroll.

The standard for banning employment, as set forth in Truman's order, "shall be that on all the evidence, reasonable grounds exist for belief that the person involved is disloyal to the Government of the United States." All civilian employees of the government, however remote from national security matters, were to be listed with the FBI for a check of their names against its records and fingerprint files. Any derogatory information (regardless of the source) would require an investigation of the person named. Nothing ever had to be proved; a rumor or innuendo of insufficient patriotism or leftist tendencies would have the force of fact.

Like the Truman Doctrine, the Loyalty Boards were a departure for the country, which now placed national security above the rights of the individual. There had been intimations, however, of the coming trend. In 1934 the House Un-American Activities Committee was born under the gavel of John W. McCormack. At its inception, the far right was the committee's preoccupation, but within three years Communist organizations became its target. Espionage was its sole concern in the 1930s, soon to include "Communistic" activities under FDR's New Deal. In 1945, the committee expanded its charter in an ominous move. Chairman John S. Wood tried to get a law through Congress under which radio stations across the land would be forced to disclose each commentator's place of birth, nationality, and political affiliation. The measure failed, but not before making a change in the country's vocabulary.

"Un-American" had come to mean only one thing: Communist.

Within weeks, the State Department allowed a team of congressional investigators, led by a Republican anti-Communist vigilante named Robert E. Lee, to ransack the department's loyalty files. The investigators left Foggy Bottom carrying information on 108 past, present, and prospective State Department employees. The material included all manner of gossip, rumor, and unconfirmed allegations from unnamed sources. When the team requested another screening of the department several months later, it was informed that only 57 of the original 108 employees were still on the payroll. There is no record of what happened to the others, whether they had been dismissed or left of their own volition, responding to "the temper of the times."

The news business could no longer insulate itself from the rising climate of fear. On March 31, 1947, William Shirer made his final report on CBS. The brilliant reporter, who had covered the war from Berlin and was soon to write the definitive history of the Third Reich, had lost both his sponsor and his time slot. Shirer claimed the reasons were political: his implacable opposition to the Truman Doctrine. The correspondent, who among all of "Murrow's Boys" was deemed closest to their mentor in intellectual stature, had been an outspoken critic of the Truman Doctrine. "I worked for nine years under Nazi censorship," Shirer commented bitterly, "and would hate to see that come to us."

Shirer was not alone at CBS in thinking the Truman Doctrine was hasty and ill conceived. Joseph Harsch from CBS's Washington bureau commented, "The path to greatness should not start in the mire of Greek politics." Howard K. Smith in London called the Athens government "the worst bunch I have seen at work anywhere. . . . The cruelty of its Nazi-trained police have forced honest men into the mountains. . . . It seems to believe it needs no policy, except when the trough of foreign funds runs low, to shout, 'Communist,' and President Truman will send more."

There was just enough ambiguity about Shirer's departure for the network to deflect the critics' charge that it caved in to government pressure. CBS president William Paley pointed to Shirer's dismal ratings. But the fact remained that Shirer had gone on the air and criticized the Truman Doctrine and the support the United States was providing the Athens government.

In July, CBS announced the resignation of Ed Murrow as vice president and director of public affairs (the equivalent of CBS News president today). Murrow said he hated his job as an executive, claimed he'd done a miserable job at it. Those who had worked under him disagreed. Murrow's one failing, they said, had been his inability to fire people, especially those he liked. The Shirer episode was more than he could stomach. The network's dry press release said Murrow would be resuming his former duties.

Davidson Taylor, a quiet, studious man, more an academic than an executive, was pulled from the programming job he loved and made the new head of news. Correspondents in the field were disheartened. Ed Murrow had been running interference for all of them, keeping them sheltered from the importunings of sponsors and executives. Given the new national mood, they would need even more protection now.

George Polk wrote his family:

I'm a little afraid of the office politics behind the move. I'm a little afraid the move may mean a more conservative line at CBS, which is going through some difficult times recently. Ed Murrow has returned to the air, but there's more to it than that. I'm sorry to have Ed out of an executive job because I think the USA desperately needs some executives who aren't just money-mad. Ed was well started on the wonderful kind of experimental programs American news reporting so desperately needs . . . at least in my judgment.

His "Review of the News," blasting newspapers for distortion and suppression and outright lying, was truly enlightened journalism. I think Ed proved too capable and forthright and decent a guy to play in big business. Thus he's back on the air at $250,000 a year instead of $50,000 as CBS VP. Most of us overseas are concerned over what will happen in radio news, now that foreign news interest seems to be waning and export trade is dropping and the USA seems jittery about an imminent depression.

Polk saw other signs that American interest in foreign news was waning. Some weeks later, in September 1947, Polk received a letter from Harry Kern, his *Newsweek* editor. For the past year, in addition to his regular CBS reporting duties, George had been filing brief, exclusive items for the magazine on the Palestinian conflict, the birth of the Arab League, and the struggle by the British to retain their fragile foothold in the Middle East. Kern now informed him of "the unhappy news that we are obliged to cut down somewhat on our foreign news . . . most American papers and magazines are doing something of the sort since interest in foreign news is at a low ebb in this country, and we are devoting more attention to the coverage of domestic events." Kern was anxious to keep Polk on the payroll, however, and offered him a retainer of $25 a week, a 50 percent cut. "I am extremely sorry to do this," the *Newsweek* editor wrote Polk, "because I have found your material of great interest and help, especially the long backgrounders, and I know that you put a good deal of work into it. I hope that after the first of the year we might be able to go back to the old basis, although there is no guarantee that such will be the case."

Around this time, Polk's cousin, Bill Price, a reporter for the New York *Daily News*, wrote him about the disturbing currents back home. "I presume you realize how hard it is to evaluate what's really going on over your way. The forces crying 'Red' were never stronger than they are now, and despite the dribblings of actual factual reporting coming out of places like Greece, the smoke screen is a dense one."

Ironically, America was reverting to its former island mentality at the very moment its leaders were undertaking the responsibility for "free peoples everywhere." The flames of anti-Communism had been fanned to sell the administration's new foreign policy. The people, however, never passionate about the rest of the world, now began to look for signs of the "Red menace" in their neighborhoods.

"It seems," Ed Murrow wrote an English friend sometime later, "the only way to induce action in this country is through the creation of fear and hysteria."

Early the following year, a House committee requested the federal records of the director of the National Bureau of Standards.

President Truman, getting wind that Dr. Edward U. Condon had become the latest victim of the innuendo campaign, finally awoke to the dangers of a witch hunt. He directed all government offices to keep personnel files in the strictest confidence.

Truman's belated resolve backfired. An ambitious thirty-four-year-old California Republican congressman named Richard Nixon saw his opportunity. Assured that in the present climate facts did not have the same power as accusations, no matter how wild, Nixon flatly stated that the Democrats were responsible for "the unimpeded growth of the Communist conspiracy in the United States." It was only the beginning.

11

George Polk was not about to shape his reporting to suit anybody's notion of national security. With or without Ed Murrow's protection, he was not going to be any more gentle with Washington than with its number one ally: London.

By the summer of 1947, he was back in Palestine, battling British officers to get inside the Latrun detention camp. He and a few other correspondents ignored the British guards ("Those in Palestine," Polk wrote, "are the worst of an otherwise nice race") and entered the gates where Jews were detained. Once inside,

we ran like rabbits to the forbidden area and forced our way into places where we could talk to the prisoners. The British guards raged but had to telephone headquarters for instructions on how to handle us. While this went on, we learned that many of the Jews were held at Latrun for upwards of four years without a warrant, without a trial, without the right to appear in court. Many of them didn't know why they were in Latrun, possibly mistaken identity. We broke the story along with pictures and almost got our visas and press passes lifted. We had a hell of a battle with the High Commissioner by letter. When he refused to see us, we wrote stories about stuffed shirts that occasioned a plea from the British Embassy in Washington for cooperation in Palestine to make us happier, and thereby less likely to write poisonous stories about dastardly Britishers and fascist-like British foreign policy.

Shortly after this incident, Polk was involved in a dustup that focused official British attention on the troublesome American correspondent. Sir Henry Gurney, Chief Palestine Secretary, called a news conference in the High Commissioner's palace. The temperature was over a hundred on this summer day, but Sir Henry was all spit and polish and carefully knotted cravat. He began by commenting ruefully on the lack of proper attire worn by the ladies and gentlemen of the press, most of whom were in shirtsleeves.

At the conclusion of the press conference, which the correspondents had been requesting for many months, George Polk, the only reporter in coat and tie, rose to his feet. "I would just like to take this opportunity, Sir Henry, on behalf of my colleagues and myself," Polk began, amused by the baffled expressions on his friends' faces, "to thank you for taking the time to meet with us today to explain to us your government's policies. However"—Polk paused dramatically, taking in the steamy room, crowded with veteran correspondents—"for most of us this is not the first press conference we've attended. In fact, some of us have been fairly regular visitors at the White House, 10 Downing Street, the Palais Chautemps, and other places. So we'd like to suggest to you most respectfully that this is not colonial Nigeria . . . where a government official can successfully play pukka-pukka sahib."

Polk was no longer smiling. Sir Henry turned on his heel and wordlessly strode out of the conference room. The next day the Palestine *Post* ran a front-page picture captioned: "British Prime Minister Meets Press." The photograph showed Prime Minister Clement Attlee, sweltering in the record heat of the London summer, dressed only in shirtsleeves.

But for all his nerve and flair, Polk, now almost thirty-four, was growing weary of the suitcase life, the endless late-night queries from New York, the cycle of crises in the Middle East.

His views on Palestine had also evolved in the last year. He wrote his family:

> As I'm writing, the light has been fading slightly here in this lovely land. By glancing up from this desk in the Eden Hotel, Jerusalem, I can see the deep purple of the Transjor-

danian hills and above the pink twilight of the great Syrian desert. The atmosphere is crystal clear and cool still . . . such is Palestine's climate.

Every time I come here, I see again how Jews here are different from Jews any other place in the world. Here the Jews are tough, resourceful, unafraid people who feel at home. There is none of the uncertainty or obsequiousness that I've known in Jewish communities elsewhere. Here the Jew doesn't fear the Arab . . . in fact he wants his friendship. In most cases, this suits the Arab fine, because if there is one thing the Arabs understand it is strength. And the Jews here are tough and capable. More intelligent and well-trained underground armies do not exist than the Haganah and Irgun Zvai Leumi. The sheer truth is that the Jews here haven't anything to fear . . . because they are strong enough to look out for their own interest. I hope for a strong pro-Jewish recommendation from the UN Committee . . . and then for prompt United Nations implementation of such recommendations.

Before returning to his base in Cairo, Polk planned to have a look at the British-run internment camps for Jews on Cyprus. "I felt," he wrote home, "these 12,000 unfortunates had simply exchanged a German concentration camp for a British detention place."

The United Nations was about to take up the question of Palestine, and Polk thought the camps would become "a hot political issue in New York." As commercial flights were scarce, Polk accepted a lift aboard a private charter, piloted by a former RAF flier.

We were about three thousand feet on a bright and beautiful day, flying over the rugged hills that are about fifty miles inland from the Mediterranean along the Palestine-Lebanese border, when both engines of the twin-engined Cessna died.

With that Stevens [the British pilot] shouted at me to take over and he jumped back to the tank to work on the booster pump. Of course, by this time the plane was well on its way down, both props windmilling and vertical speed indicator showing about 1,000 feet down per minute . . . I turned sharply toward the sea, looking for a nice smooth beach or a field of wheat. . . . We were at about 1,500 feet . . . with the hills around us actually higher than we were. . . . Stevens was working madly at the booster and eventually did get the engine going . . . but something was wrong. . . . I began a dead engine, forced landing approach and kept watching the air speed indicator and wondering what the Cessna's stalling speed was. Fortunately, when we were close to the ground both engines caught full on for a brief burst. . . . That killed our vertical speed from about 1,000 to 500 . . . and then we were down.

There was a god-awful sound when we hit, and about a second or two after touching down the left wing hooked a tree. . . . I'm not sure of the next few seconds but apparently my head went through the cockpit window . . . after withdrawing it from the hole, I got out somewhat hastily. I know I was only thinking of fire. In the South Pacific I think I can truly say I was only afraid of fire. . . . I had cuts on my forehead and both cheeks . . . apparently from the ragged edges of glass as my head went through the shatterproof greenhouse . . . and somehow I had connected my nose with something very hard. . . . My nose was pushed over to the left, just lying very flat under my left eye.

Rescued by two British soldiers guarding the Lebanese-Palestinian frontier, Polk was eventually driven to Tel Aviv.

A British RAF doctor said I could do no better than to go straight to the Jewish Assutah Hospital. And he was entirely right. The whole thing worked like a dream. . . . Skillful, smooth, but high pressure first aid, two shots for shock and tetanus, then into a bed that looked as though it had been ready all day, piled high with blankets and warmed with electric pads.

I had a careful going-over by a brilliant Czech plastic surgeon named Dr. Wodak, a calm, quiet little man who could play a grandfather in a family movie. . . . But in the operating room he's a stern guy, no foolishness and abrupt orders that keep assistants hopping. He promises me that the cuts on my cheeks will not be detected by "a Leica photograph made at one meter and blown up vun hundred times." The nose, and I give you my word, he disassembled completely and then put back together. He threatens there may be a hint of a broken contour. . . . He also believes I had a slight concussion, but "it is nussing."

In July 1947, the week Murrow relinquished his corporate duties to resume his broadcast career in New York (though he did not actually go back on the air until that fall), Polk left Cairo, still his base, and flew to the northern Greek port of Salonika. Polk found the city "battered and grim, the men and women looking far older than their years. The children are scrawny. Everyone is thin and tired. But," he wrote his family, "I like the Greeks very much. In fact, coming here from Egypt makes every day a delight in human relationships. The Greeks have dignity and color and strength. As a cable from Howard K. Smith put it, 'Welcome Back to Civilization.' "

Though exhausted from the tensions of the civil war, its nerves shattered from guerrilla hit-and-run operations just beyond its city limits, Salonika still appealed more to Polk than Athens. On July 21 he wrote his family:

I dislike that regime so much that being in that lovely city is a tear at the emotions. If you've been hearing any of my numerous broadcasts, I've been letting King Paul [who succeeded his brother George upon the monarch's death earlier that year] and his regime have it right between the eyes. It's fascist and below the belt in every way. On top of that, our Mr. Dwight P. Griswold, the new American Aid Administrator, is an unmitigated jerk. In fact, after his first twenty-minute press conference, we all got together and argued how to handle the story. Most of us agreed to go easy on him for a week or so, in hopes he might learn something. Of course he's hardly to blame because he's just a lame duck former Nebraska governor. And nobody else would have the Greek aid job. So, the problem was not that of getting a good man, but one of getting any man to go to Athens. Griswold's conference was the most appalling I've ever sat through. His assistants are equally bad.

I feel a very critical and definitive broadcast coming up on the subject. . . . It appears we're going to pour money down Athens' hole for any of the government rats to get at.

As much as he privately despised the Royalist regime and its new American mentors, Polk's reporting maintained a remarkably dispassionate tone. For the most part, he let the facts, and not his emotions, tell the story.

He could see that, with the onset of the Truman Doctrine, whatever happened in Greece would have profound implications for his own country. Greece was not just another overseas brush fire. Since Truman's rousing address, it had become America's crisis.

He was also working himself into exhaustion. Each night, Polk's voice was heard for two minutes live on Richard C. Hottelet's network newscast. After sleeping for only three or four hours, Polk broadcast on Robert Trout's early-morning show and on a later broadcast anchored by Douglas Edwards.

While in Greece, he managed to write a piece for *The New Republic*, as well as a long piece for *Newsweek*. *Harper's* commissioned him to do an analysis of America's growing involvement in Greece.

Polk was the sort of reporter who not only could withstand pressures in the field to toe a certain line, but also could stand up to his own editors, for many reporters a tougher battle. He wrote home in July 1947:

One thing I'm very pleased about. I played down the great battle of Konitsa . . . despite New York's urging to give the story everything it could possibly stand. [The battle was a guerrilla attack staged from Konitsa, a town near the Albanian border, with the purpose of setting up a rebel government there.] The pressure from New York was strong, because the AP was filing lavish guff on what wasn't going on. But I prevailed on New York . . . and even Bob Trout played the story down. We drifted along that way for a week. Then the Greek Army General Staff spokesman called a press conference and complained about the civilian Greek government's "exaggerated" communiqués on the Konitsa affair. . . . I felt good because it was all ammunition with which to attack the German collaborator administration of Greek Prime Minister Maximos.

American officials in both Athens and Washington preferred Maximos, an elderly Populist (Royalist) banker, "to the stupidity" of Tsaldaris and as a "more moderate and cooperative" personality, according to Ambassador Lincoln MacVeagh. It was the American Ambassador who engineered his elevation to the prime ministership in January 1947, seeing the choice of Maximos over Tsaldaris as the lesser of two evils.

"But," Polk closed his letter home, "somehow my sleep is troubled by the faces of the children and their thin bodies and their big eyes. . . . I haven't met a Greek yet who can earn his daily keep if he isn't in government or the black market. For those with money, Greece is a lovely place."

His real reason for flying to Salonika that summer he kept very much to himself. Polk had made only this passing reference when he wrote to his family in late June: "I'm looking forward to the trip as an interesting experience, plus possible contacts with some guerrilla bands."

In fact, Polk had been preparing for over a year to penetrate northern Greece, reach the guerrillas, and finally let the American public hear the other side of the Greek story. None of the dozen or so American correspondents roving the region had yet done substantial reporting on the Communist forces. None had spent any time with them. Thus the American public had only the skimpiest knowledge of the men who called themselves the Democratic Army. Their leader was General Markos, a former trade union official, who had been one of the leaders of the ELAS left-wing resistance.

In October 1946, with Greek politics moving swiftly to the right, Markos led his men back to the mountains from where they had successfully fought the Wehrmacht two years earlier. Markos, a militant former tobacco worker from Smyrna, committed to an armed uprising against the right-wing government in Athens, led a growing army of fellow leftists, gathering for the past year in refugee camps across the Yugoslav, Bulgarian, and Albanian borders. Greece's left was bitterly divided, however, between Markos' rural-based insurrectionists and its Athens-based politicians, headed by Nikos Zachariades, who was dithering around in hopes of getting a position in the established government. For until 1947 the Greek Communists were still a legally recognized political party.

However, by July 1947 the U.S. Embassy in Athens had decided on the "necessity" of outlawing the Greek Communist Party, the KKE, and arresting its leaders. Right-wing reprisals and harsh measures imposed by the government of the Royalist Constantine Tsaldaris forced thousands of leftists and Communists to flee towns and cities, joining forces with Markos. His mountain bands grew fiercer, their attacks on villages more frequent and increasingly more violent. The guerrillas managed to cut many areas off from official control. By December 1947 the Markos-led insurgency was operating in full force. His hit-and-run tactics put him at a great advantage over the regular Greek Army. Throughout 1947 and 1948, the so-called Democratic Army could move at will over much of mainland Greece. They had bases in the Communist countries behind the northern frontiers of Greece—Albania, Bulgaria, and Yugoslavia—which provided them with arms, aid, and sanctuary.

That much was known. George Polk did not think it extraordinary to want to learn more about the guerrillas' motives and their dreams for their country. He thought that was his job.

Polk had a source who he hoped would connect him with the guerrillas. He had befriended Floyd A. Spencer in Cairo in 1945. Spencer was an older man, an urbane and witty student of the region, who had been prowling the Middle East since the 1920s.

Spencer spoke Arabic and Greek and he worked in U.S. Army intelligence. He was one of those rare agents who felt comfortable with reporters. Polk's curiosity stimulated him.

Much later, Lieutenant Colonel Spencer would say of George Polk, "I not only liked him, I admired him. Outside of the fact that he was a good friend whose gay, fey, aloof spirit and elfin charm I shall always remember, he was the kind of writer and broadcaster, and the kind of American, we can ill afford to lose. Particularly," Spencer emphasized, "now that we are pouring millions of dollars into an area with no demonstrable results. It will be the George Polks and only they who can tell us what is happening and how to get results, let alone save money."

Spencer loved his beat as much as Polk loved his. He had been to the mountains, talked to the guerrillas, knew the shadowy underworld of Salonika harbor. He was a patriot and anti-Communist and did not think he had to prove that to anybody. He hated zealotry in defense of any cause.

Spencer and Polk spent a lot of evenings together in Khartoum and Cairo, in quiet off-the-record discussions. Between 1945 and 1947, Spencer told Polk whatever he knew of the Greek situation, the guerrillas, and how best to approach them. Not only did he trust Polk; he thought it important that the reporter be armed with as much information as possible.

It was not unusual in those more innocent times, before Watergate and Vietnam hardened relations between government and media, for this sort of friendship to develop. "I was very close to the military attachés in Egypt and in Greece," John Donovan recalled, "because I had served as an intelligence officer there and I used to go in and chat. I wasn't turning in anyone. But I talked generally about politics, and what was happening, and everything else. I was very sympathetic to my country's policies at that time. I didn't want the Communists to take over. I don't think George did either."

On July 4, 1947, during Independence Day festivities at the home of Jefferson Patterson, the American chargé d'affaires in Cairo, Spencer and Polk met for the last time. It was a noisy, informal affair, diplomats mingling with British officers and Egyptian dignitaries in flowing robes.

Polk arrived late. Spotting Spencer, he strode over to the older man's side. "Congratulations," Polk said, for Spencer had been named security and policy review officer at the Pentagon and would soon be heading home to Washington.

"I'm off to Greece in a week," Polk told his friend. "I want to make some contacts in Salonika. Can you help?"

"This time," Spencer later wrote Ed Murrow, "I judged he was ready to go to Salonika and dig in . . . I got down to cases."

"The guerrillas," Spencer told Polk, "use little boats called caïques to ship arms from Salonika to the mainland north of Mount Olympus. . . . When you reach Salonika, go to Thodoros' tavern on the waterfront, next to the Mediterranean Hotel, the official British military billet. Thodoros, when he's not drunk, knows a great deal. But if you go in alone, be careful. You stand out like a sore thumb with your blond hair and those brilliant blue eyes. You won't even brown out very well. Besides, you don't speak Greek and you won't find many in there who speak English. You need somebody who speaks Greek to go with you. But again, be doubly careful who you use as interpreter. Know his background, reputation, affiliations.

"You've got to go at this slowly . . . it all takes time. But Thodoros knows ships and sailors in Salonika harbor. He's done time on the sea himself, and his joint is just to the taste and conveniently located for the patronage of mates, masters, sailors from the little caïques that load and unload just across the street from Thodoros'. Being what he is, and canny to boot, you might need to spend some time with him. Cigarettes and khakis help. Time and patience win good contacts here. Gendarmes, informers, black marketeers all come into Thodoros'. You can learn what goes on and has gone on in Salonika."

Spencer then told Polk what he had already stressed in their previous conversations. "Ninety percent of the city police, special security, and gendarmes in Salonika are unregenerate and unpurged reactionaries . . . the same types who worked all the way through the German occupation . . . Vicars of Bray in spades. Informers working for them are the same types. Unofficial triggermen, bravos, and assorted bullies also swim in this water. You must take precautions," he warned. "And keep a lookout for another interesting character who comes into Thodoros'. Captain Bobby, they call him. Never knew his real name, not wise to pry. He's a sort of harbor liaison between the small ships and the port control, registry of ships. He knows all the ships that for reasons of convenience don't register. I found Captain Bobby interesting enough to give hard money to, about the only one.

"There's another man, further back in the market area, a small street near the old churches, who stands out in front of a tavern turning a spit, if he has not drunk or grieved himself to death. He sports a white mustache and is an Epirote [from Epirus in the northwestern corner of Greece]. He will tell you about his share of sorrow, and when he has finished moaning and lifts his head off the table, he will introduce you casually to the characters who come into his shop. From him you can get to various groups of refugees and agents who live in the nearby and more outlying areas . . . he knows the taverns and the resorts.

"The people who can be reached through these leads know most everything that happens in Salonika. But it takes time and great luck. And, George," his friend finished, "I know you'll be careful."

There is no record of Polk having followed Floyd Spencer's advice. He never spoke or wrote home about his contacts, not even to Ed Murrow. It is unlikely, however, given his appetite for this story, that he would fail to follow up on his most trusted source's advice.

No matter how carefully he proceeded, in the twilight atmosphere of the Salonika waterfront, George Polk's movements would have been immediately observed by those he could pay off to keep his confidence, and others who were better paid elsewhere. The trouble was, there was really no way to get a fix on a man's loyalties in that murky place. Colonel Spencer had the best of intentions in urging Polk to pay a call on Thodoros, the all-knowing tavernkeeper. But Spencer, for all his field experience, did not know that the man, whose real name was Theodoros Ksingakos, was a police agent.

12

He spotted her the minute he boarded the TAE flight from Salonika to Athens: the dark-haired stewardess in animated conversation with a passenger at the rear of the plane. Polk could hardly wait for the stunning hostess to reach his seat.

"Hi," he said in his soft Texas way.

"Hello," she answered in a lilting English, softened by French and Greek shadings. "May I get you something?" she asked, with an impudent smile and a playfulness he found irresistible.

"You could tell me who you are," he said, "and where I can find you."

She laughed and moved on.

Polk was determined. He had only a week left in Athens before he was due back in Cairo. He waited for her to leave the airport and followed her taxi home. He called on her later that evening, bringing flowers, already the suitor. She answered the doorbell of her fashionable Kolonaki apartment, thick white cream smeared all over her face. Their spontaneous laughter broke the ice.

For the next few days, they were together whenever he wasn't filing or interviewing. There was a sweetness and an innocence about her that melted his natural reserve. With her, Polk felt a peacefulness, a sense of well-being he had rarely experienced.

Rea Cocconis did not challenge Polk the way Kay had. She was in awe of the lives he had led, impressed by his larger-than-life Americanness.

Polk fell in love that late-summer week, not only with Rea but with her father, with whom she shared the apartment. Matthew Cocconis was a small, soft-spoken man with wispy white hair and features blurred by age and sadness. Like other Greeks lacking the rapaciousness to profit from their own countrymen's misfortunes, the once wealthy businessman had very little left after the war. During the German occupation he had traded a fine home, a palace almost, off Constitution Square, for several barrels of olive oil. You couldn't eat a fine home and he had two daughters and a wife to look after. Soon after the war, his wife, still young, left him for a rich Egyptian merchant, taking their elder daughter with her to Alexandria. Rea chose to stay with the well-loved father she called Baba.

Baba had raised her, taught her French and English as well as Arabic. They had no money, so she worked for the Greek national airline. But father and daughter alike had a natural elegance, a dignity that was not defined by money.

Baba, who had always wanted a son, and Polk, who had lost his own father so many years before, were delighted to have found each other. The three of them rapidly forged a family. Polk saw a way out of his loneliness. The two lovers, children of divorce and dislocation, did not mind knowing so little about each other.

They were married in a civil ceremony attended only by Rea's father and a newspaperman named George Weller, one of the tribe of roving foreign correspondents whom Polk was forever encountering in trouble spots around the Middle East and who happened to be in Athens at the time. George Drossos, a Greek journalist and, unbeknownst to Polk, a part-time Royalist agent, served as their Greek witness.

But politics was not on George Polk's mind on that golden September morning.

The couple planned to live in Athens. CBS had no objection to Polk's folding up the Cairo operation. The story had shifted to Greece. His new father-in-law offered to move to his country house to make room for Polk in the Kolonaki apartment. Housed in a six-story gray stucco building on Skoufa Street, a narrow passage off Kolonaki Square, under the slopes of Lycabettus, the apartment offered an exquisite glimpse of the Acropolis. The people in Polk's new neighborhood dressed well and seemed to have recovered rapidly from the war.

Polk returned to Cairo in late September to pack his belongings. He wrote his brother:

I returned here and did a relatively routine broadcast on Egypt's grandiose dreams of an Empire, and on its poverty, ignorance, and disease. This touched off *Akhbar El Yom*, the government paper, into a diatribe against me, "a British whore." The paper also gave its account of what I said, all of it dreamed up. So I'm battling Arabs around the Middle East. Before I left Jerusalem, I was getting about two telephone threats a day, of assassination. Now, I've had a couple here in Cairo. So I'm packing a rod night and day.

Death threats had become an occupational hazard for George Polk. They weren't to be taken lightly, but they were nothing to run away from either.

Polk was again energized by plans for the future. The foreign correspondent's pace after his depleting war injuries had always been an act of sheer will on his part. But now he had something other than willpower as a source of energy. He had happiness.

More and more now, his thoughts were about going home. He was anxious to introduce Rea to his family and to his country. But he wanted to delve deeper into the Greek story first. Finally he asked for and received from CBS (which had just promoted him again, adding the lofty title of Assistant Director of European News to his name) permission to take a leave of absence, sometime in 1948, to write his book on the Middle East.

"I'm not interested in doing a quickie book," he wrote his CBS colleague George Herman. "I want something solid and readable, something that can shoot at a general audience while simultaneously being a carefully written reference book."

He had proved himself in the world of radio; he still longed for the level of recognition which academia and the printed word could confer. He reactivated his application to Harvard for a Nieman Fellowship.

Polk again wrote his old mentor, Walter Lippmann, asking for his support with the Harvard board. In the three years since he began his travels in the Middle East, he had kept Lippmann apprised of his movements. In letters marked by a tone of high respect, Polk shared his views on the region with the great Washington eminence.

Polk wrote Lippmann on November 21, 1947, from Istanbul:

As you know, the Iranian Government has just rejected an Oil Treaty with Russia . . . without drawing much political fire from the Kremlin. Further to illustrate what is rather a puzzling situation here on Soviet policy, the Arab Communist Party of Palestine and the Jewish Communist Party of Palestine recently have become embroiled in savage controversy. This has led some diplomats and military intelligence agents in the Middle East to conclude that Moscow is not giving its supporters a very carefully explained or integrated policy line these days. . . . During the last six months I have been asking many observers here why there has been this apparent change in Soviet activity. Frankly I have not gotten any very satisfactory answers. One guess has been that the Russians are concentrating on Europe. . . . Incidentally, if I might suggest a reporter's analysis of the situation here, I believe our program in Greece is doomed to failure as the policy is now being implemented. I have tried to explain my ideas in the December issue of *Harper's* . . .

Two weeks later, Lippmann wrote back:

I am very much interested in your letter and I am grateful to you for taking all the trouble to write me at such length. It is full of most interesting news and observations. I wouldn't undertake to make a serious guess as to why Soviet action in the Middle East has diminished in recent times, though I am fairly certain that one factor in it is the show of American military strength in the eastern Mediterranean. The Russians understand that kind of thing, perhaps even better than our own people, and they know that when we show our strength in the eastern Mediterranean, we mean that they mustn't make

Adelaide Roe in 1907, five years before her marriage to George Washington Polk

George Polk, Sr., in 1908, wearing his Virginia Military Institute cadet's uniform

The wedding of George and Adelaide Polk in December 1912

George Polk, Sr., with his son George and daughter Adelaide in 1918 when George was five years old

Edgehill Manor, the Polk family home in Fort Worth, Texas, where George Polk spent his childhood and adolescence

Interior scene of Edgehill Manor

George Polk at the
Virginia Military
Institute, Lexington,
Virginia

George Polk and his cousins
Jack Scruby and William A.
Price at a California mine
where Scruby was working in
1938

George's first wife, Kay
Phillips Polk, at the time of
their courtship

An official U.S. Navy photograph of George Polk in flying gear, on November 30, 1943, after accepting a Presidential Unit citation for his detachment's role in the Battle of the Solomons. One third of his unit did not survive that battle

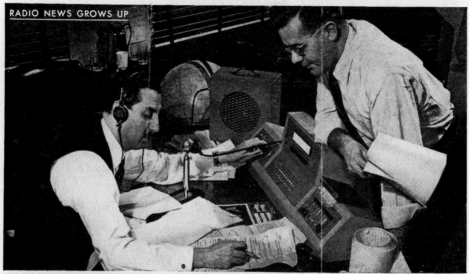

RADIO NEWS GROWS UP

WITH THIS TWO-WAY RADIOTELEPHONE—THE NEWSROOM STAFF CALL IT "TROUT'S PIANO"—BOB MAKES INSTANT CONTACT WITH HIS OVERSEAS ASSOCIATES

TWENTY-TWO FOR TROUT

Ace correspondents feed him on-the-spot reports for his newscast

To get the news, complete and concise, listeners dial CBS for Robert Trout with The News Till Now. Because his reports have the vivid first-hand reality they seek, radio-wise thousands make tuning in Trout at 6:45 EST each weekday a habit. To give his news this graphic authenticity, Trout turns to his team of twenty-two top-rank correspondents in U. S. and world news centers for on-the-spot reports of the news as it is made.

Who are these men? What are their qualifications? As a group they are young, brilliant, educated, well versed in their nation and their world. Averaging up their ages and achievements would reveal this composite: a man of 34, with 10½ years' reporting experience, most of it in the U. S., the balance in four or more foreign countries.

These twenty-two, together with the facilities of the five leading news services, provide Trout and his editors with the substance for complete, objective newscasts of the sort postwar Americans want.

CAMPBELL SOUP COMPANY

BOB EVANS, veteran newsman and expert on national affairs, is Trout's exclusive full-time correspondent in Washington, D. C.

SOME OF TROUT'S WORLD-WIDE NEWS TEAM

H. K. SMITH: LONDON · DOWNS: NEW YORK · COSTELLO: TOKYO · ADAMS: WHITE HOUSE · POLK: CAIRO

LESUEUR: U. N. · BECK: LOS ANGELES · DALY: NEW YORK · HOTTELET: ROVING · HOLLES: CHICAGO

A newspaper and magazine advertisement for CBS News' crack team of foreign correspondents

Edward R. Murrow, center, and William Shirer, at right, in a Paris sidewalk café; man at left is unidentified

Edward R. Murrow and William Shirer broadcasting for CBS News

Howard K. Smith, still in uniform shortly after he joined CBS News

George Polk in his Cairo apartment poring over a map of the Middle East in 1947

George and his younger brother, William Polk, and Zaki, Polk's Egyptian manservant, in the garden of Polk's home in Cairo in 1946

Polk on a trip to a village in the Vardar Valley, Greece, in 1947

Polk and his colleague Dick
Mowrer in Athens, 1947

Polk and his closest friend, John Donovan, relaxing (with Donovan's boxer) at Pantiles Pension, where they both often stayed, in Jerusalem, 1946

Polk with Clifton Daniel of the New York *Times* at Payne Field, Cairo

Polk with his friends John Donovan of NBC, at left, and Homer Bigart of the *Herald Tribune*, center, covering Palestine in 1946. It was Bigart who ultimately reached and interviewed the elusive General Markos, blamed by the Royalists for George Polk's murder. Bigart dedicated that interview to the memory of his friend George Polk

Polk and a group of reporters, including George Weller of the Chicago *Daily News* at left, who was Polk's best man in his wedding to Rea, on the terrace of the Hotel Grande Bretagne, Athens, 1947

NBC and CBS correspondents Donovan and Polk share a microphone and a lantern during a Christmas broadcast from Bethlehem on December 25, 1946

Polk with Fred Sparks of ABC and *Collier's* magazine at Ioannina, Greece, in February 1948

Adelaide Roe Polk and her son George in Istanbul in March 1948, during her final visit with her son before his murder

George and Rea Cocconis Polk in Athens

Rea Polk in a Greek folk costume
around the time of her wedding in
September 1947

Rea Polk on her wedding day

George Polk the year before his murder

any moves which could precipitate a war in that part of the world where they are peculiarly vulnerable. However, as you say, we must expect a renewal of pressure in the Middle East later in the year.

"I have done everything I can legitimately do or that would be of any effect to secure you the Nieman," Lippmann concluded. "I hope to see you when you get back here. Be sure to let me know."

Though Polk was continuing to cover the whole of the Middle East from his new Athens base, it was the Greek story that absorbed him now.

"Your work from Cairo is very good," George Herman cabled Polk. "Your work from Palestine was some stuff. But your cables from Athens have been some of your best work. Excellent. At the last minute we managed to wrap the whole program around your cable . . . also used it on 'The Weekly News Review,' and Charles Collingwood used parts on his eleven p.m. Your other Athens cables were all part of what looks from here like exceptional stuff. Bravo."

It was more than Polk's particular sensibility and his fearlessness about stating unpleasant truths that informed his reporting on Greece. "From his wife and her family, George got a window into the machinations of the Greek government, the corruption of the society, everything that was going on, that a lot of us who did not have access to the information did not have," John Donovan noted.

Polk's broadcasts, of one, two, or sometimes three minutes' duration, dispassionate in tone and content, were not the right forum for his mounting personal revulsion toward the greedy and ruthless dictatorship which had become Washington's Cold War protectorate. A magazine piece was a more appropriate venue.

Polk tended to view the world through a fairly unclouded American prism. It was not a vision that ultimately served him well in the opaque place he now called home. His British colleague Ken Matthews of the BBC noted of the former fighter pilot: "Polk's journalistic objectives assumed for him as concrete a shape as enemy aeroplanes. But he could not, was not perhaps imaginatively equipped, to view the Greek scene through other than American eyes. The Greece of the monarchy, the hierarchical structure of

Greek society, clashed with some dim, unformulated preconceptions of the democratic ideal. And the inefficiency and corruption he detected in the Athens administration appeared . . . to be tainted with a double shame."

Polk's view, surprisingly, was shared by Winston Churchill. Churchill, once so insistent that the Greek monarchy be preserved, both as the best guarantor of stability and as a safeguard of links to the British Empire, was himself repelled by developments in Athens. Reading reports of the Royalists' brutal treatment of the Communist opposition in late 1947, the former Prime Minister wrote to a high Foreign Office official in London: "We have not of course the same responsibility as we had in those days, but when we remember how many islands there are in which people can be put until things blow over, it seems to me very unwise for the present Greek government to carry out mass executions of this character and it almost reduces us to the Communist level."

While Washington remained silent, Churchill decided to approach Greek Queen Frederika, who owed so much to his efforts on behalf of the Glücksburg dynasty. To his complaints about "mass executions," Queen Frederika coolly replied with a question of her own. "Don't you believe in the law?" Churchill answered, "Yes, of course." Whereupon the queen pointed out that all the men executed had been "properly tried and convicted."

Churchill, trying another approach, said it was bad propaganda for Greece. The queen answered haughtily, "There are two countries in the world which are simply terrible at propaganda. One is yours, Mr. Churchill, and the other is mine."

Harper's proved an excellent forum for George Polk's observations. It was his first long piece, and it set off shock waves when it appeared in print in December 1947. The article transformed his name into a notable byline, one of those names people in Washington and New York wove into dinner-table conversations when discussing the Truman Doctrine. His new level of influence in Washington and New York also changed his standing in Athens, from simply another irritating reporter into a dangerous man.

Under the headline "Greece Puts Us to the Test," Polk wrote:

On June 30, 1948, the Greek Army will be the single properly functioning organ of the Greek government. The present official American policy has nurtured this military monster, and on that date it will be turned loose in the Balkans. The American aid program was only a stop-gap measure; it carried an official limitation to June 30, 1948, the end of the American fiscal year. But after only a few months on the Greek scene, the United States has become increasingly entangled in the Greek problem, present and future. . . .

If American assistance is terminated (at the end of the fiscal year) this money and manpower consuming military force will be unleashed upon a country unable to feed her people, furnish her material needs, or meet her daily expenditures. Lacking political and economic stability, but having a well-equipped army, Greece will invite the appearance of a Strong Man . . . from either the Right or the Left. . . .

Strangely enough, two such men have names beginning with the same letter, Z. Right-wing Napoleon Zervas, a fifty-seven-year-old soldier, professional gambler, and unscrupulous politician. No longer sporting the full beard and picturesque uniforms of his earlier days, Zervas today affects dark suits and an air of respectability. But his activities, public and private, are even more sinister than when he participated in four pre-war Greek political revolutions. As Minister of Public Order in a recent Royalist cabinet he directed a ruthless campaign against the opponents of the government, no matter what their political convictions. A secret official American document has referred to Zervas's "dictatorial and fascist tendencies" as being "at variance with the ideals of American democracy." In and out of government, he is backed by the British-organized Greek gendarmerie force, which still includes many officers and men who did police duty for the Germans during the Occupation. . . .

The most likely candidate for the position of strong man on the left is Nikos Zachariades, who, unlike Napoleon Zervas, is a man of brains rather than brawn. A fanatically faithful

Party member and described as the most brilliant student ever to attend the Moscow School of Oriental Studies, Zachariades is secretary-general of the Greek Communist Party. Although he is the acknowledged mastermind of Greek Communist activity, Zachariades has been in hiding during the past year. He has had his share of prisons; at forty-four he has spent nearly ten years in concentration camps, beginning in Greece under the Metaxas dictatorship. . . . The Germans transferred him from Greece to Dachau, where he was released by American forces. . . .

But a leftist or a Communist dictatorship is exactly what the American aid program was originally designed to prevent. Not that the alternative of a Right or Fascist regime would be any better. Either of these extreme governments soon might seek diversion from internal Greek troubles by striking across frontiers into Western-supported Turkey, or into Soviet satellite Balkan nations. Such an event could undoubtedly start another war. For this reason, Greece today is far more important than her small area and population otherwise would indicate.

. . . Greece's pre-war problems, complicated by wartime destruction, would be severe enough if Greece's economy could be bent dynamically to the task of solving the nation's crisis. But almost the exact opposite is true. . . . Thirty-five families dominate the country financially . . . exerting control or influence through interlocking directorates. . . . These thirty-five families are the ruling clique of the two percent of the Greek people who are well enough off to live well. . . .

Although Greece is poverty-stricken nationally, Athens' stores are stuffed with luxury items. I asked an Athens jeweler, who had asked $200 for a watch selling for only $25 retail in Switzerland, why he hoarded. He explained that nobody in Greece believed in the future, everybody wanted to make small investments and large profits, and it was anybody's guess when persons with money would have to flee. As a result he had to be ready to liquidate his business overnight and transfer his capital to a foreign country in the form of a small cargo of convertible items in British gold sovereigns or in American dollars. Meanwhile those with money are putting poverty-stricken Greece through a commercial wringer of astounding proportions. The wringer squeezes buyers of both luxury items and everyday necessities. . . . Capital is restricted to a tiny group in the country. By official favoritism, permission to import is limited principally to the same group. . . . What before the war was a system designed to make the wealthy wealthier, now has become a system designed to squeeze from the country every penny possible as quickly as possible.

For example, consider the Liberty ships which the United States presented to Greece for re-creating the Greek merchant marine. After obtaining the ships, the Greek government promptly sold them to private Greek owners at extremely low prices. Today most of those ships fly the Panamanian flag. Some are netting upwards of $200,000 a year in profits for their owners. Most of the profits are carefully tucked away in private accounts in foreign banks. . . .

The arrival of the American Aid Mission, headed by Dwight P. Griswold, has not greatly eased the internal insecurity of the country. . . . With civil war raging, with wild inflation, and with fantastic increases in the cost of living, a reasonable expectation might be that the Greek government would welcome any and all relief assistance. But relief often impinges upon the money-making methods of the wealthy two percent, so official restrictions block as much philanthropic aid as possible. Today, large stocks of UNRRA supplies are still lying unused in Greek warehouses. Release of these stocks might shake the carefully rigged price levels of rice, clothing, shoes, beds, medicines, and other items. . . . Only after months of battle did CARE succeed in getting release of six thousand gift packages of clothing, food, and vitamins. Greek government officials used every excuse to prevent distribution of the packages, but American press and radio stories caused so much comment that they finally forced a release. . . .

While on a trip to civil war areas along the Greek-Yugoslav frontier recently, I asked a villager if my leather jacket would be safe in my parked jeep. "Of course," the villager replied, "all the crooks in Greece are in the government."

. . . On the basis of likely return, the $300,000,000 American aid program, as it now stands, is a poor investment. It is either vastly too much or vastly too little.

The Griswold Mission understood that the Royalist-Populist party of Constantine Tsaldaris—plus hangers-on such as Zervas—were stimulating instead of curing Greece's civil strife. . . . Anyone daring to criticize governmental policies earns a one-way ticket to a barren Aegean island, without benefit of warrant, court action, or right of bail. . . .

In conclusion, George Polk raised some hard questions for Washington policy makers:

1. Is the United States program preparatory for fighting the Russians? If so, is Greece to serve as a Western allied military base? (Many military experts believe Greece would become untenable the first day of an East-West conflict.) 2. Or is the American investment aimed at attempting to deal a severe setback to Greek Communism, thereby striking a demonstrative blow at European Communism? 3. Or is the American aid program a test of Soviet reaction rather than just a project simply concerned with Greece? 4. Or what?

Within the next few months answers to some or all of these questions must be found. Collectively, they and our methods of dealing with the Greek problem constitute a dramatic test for American foreign policy in action. Certainly, no matter what happens, the United States is now learning both that the treadmill of Balkan affairs is easier to board than abandon, and that the treadmill cannot be ridden half on and half off.

It was a tough piece, one that named names and cited cases. Polk described Constantine Tsaldaris and Napoleon Zervas, the two most powerful and dangerous men in Greece, in the most uncompromising terms. In the government-controlled press of Athens, neither man was accustomed to seeing his name used in anything but a flattering context. Polk was hitting them where it hurt most: threatening their lifeblood, American aid dollars.

Polk's article was not a revelation to either the State Department or the White House. At the end of 1946, economic envoy Paul Porter had sent similar cables to President Truman. However, Porter's cables, stamped "Secret" or "Confidential," were meant for a vastly more limited audience than the readership of *Harper's*. And Truman had already made up his mind that he would back the Royalist Greek government no matter how, in Dean Acheson's words, "incredibly weak, stupid, and venal." Truman was playing for global stakes. The American public, however, could be swayed by a reporter's powerful evidence.

Earlier in 1947, Acting Secretary of State Dean Acheson had written in a restricted cable to Chargé Karl Rankin:

> Department concerned about small amount of foreign exchange and taxation to be returned to Greek government from earnings of Liberty ships purchased from U.S. . . . U.S. government's primary reason for selling these ships is to aid Greek recovery and substantially greater foreign exchange and taxation receipt than those contemplated should accrue to Greek government. Failure to do so would adversely affect U.S. public opinion towards Greece. Suggest you discuss with Greek government possibility of increasing substantially such receipts. . . . Please report to Department earliest possible.

Acheson's concern with U.S. public opinion was echoed by Rankin in a letter to Tsaldaris on April 12, 1947, regarding another of George Polk's charges: that the United Nations Relief and Rehabilitation Administration aid was being withheld from the people it was meant to reach. The chargé refers to an upcoming UNRRA report that is

> rather critical of the Greek government particularly with reference to the following four points. 1. Under the pretext of military hostilities, numerous villages have been deprived of UNRRA food, though investigation revealed that no guerrillas

were in the neighborhood. 2. UNRRA motor vehicles are being used by the Greek military forces. 3. Supplies and equipment remain undistributed in warehouses and at dockside. 4. Plans have not been made for the use of road building and other public works equipment. . . . The Greek government will, of course, realize the unfortunate impression that such allegations could make upon the American public . . .

Thus key American officials cast the Greek problem largely in public relations terms. American public opinion had to be managed; real attempts at solving Greece's problems seemed of secondary importance. An obstinately straightforward reporter like Polk was increasingly seen as the enemy of both Greece and his own country's foreign policy.

Late in 1947, in another show of growing self-assertiveness, Polk terminated his association of several years with *Newsweek*. In a letter to his editor, which some of Polk's colleagues later said ought to be made every reporter's Hippocratic oath, he wrote *Newsweek* editor Harry Kern:

This is a letter that should have been written long ago. But it's been delayed, let's face it, by avarice, my own avarice. Further, this letter pivots on the date January 1, 1948. On that date, as you may remember in your last letter to me about part-time reporters for *Newsweek*, you indicated that I might be in for a raise of pay.

However, Harry, before that date, in fact upon receipt of this letter, I wish to terminate my connection with *Newsweek*. No, I'm not taking any other job, there's been no change in my status necessitating such a termination; and I think you've been very liberal, courteous, and pleasant with me.

Yet, I must tell you frankly that I've wrestled for weeks with my convictions versus what I regard as *Newsweek*'s lack of objectivity. Bluntly, Harry, I don't like the job *Newsweek* is doing. I don't think the book is balanced; I don't think the book is enlightened; I don't like the innuendoes that seem to me to have become *Newsweek*'s stock in trade; I don't agree with the magazine's editorial thinking; and most of all I resent the manner in which *Newsweek* labels a product as "significant," but which I regard as often significantly distorted. . . .

Of course, I know that a letter like this could draw charges that I'm a Communist, but I'll stand on my past, present, and future work to refute such a possible charge. Actually, that is one of the charges I make against *Newsweek*—too free use of that word. Even more specifically, what I'm trying to do is to make an argument for the need for objectivity in reporting . . . not just telling a story with all the facts readily available; instead, I think the word requires going out and getting every available fact before even attempting to write a balanced story.

Naturally, when a person writes an editorial, he is entitled to give his own ideas on a situation—what's good and what's bad. But *Newsweek* labels very little copy "editorial."

Another point that you may raise is that I've been out of the United States for more than two years and that I can have no real conception of the anti-labor feeling and anti-Red hysteria. Perhaps I can't. But I think a man or a publication should resist the impulse to drift with popular pressure just because it's easy. . . . My feeling now is that *Newsweek* is doing anything except resisting the impulse to drift with public feelings; this, in turn, in my opinion, is stimulating further insecurity, thereby making us, as a nation, less likely to decide correct, well-balanced, realistic policies.

While his letter was making its slow way to *Newsweek* in New York, a letter from Harry Kern informing Polk the magazine had decided to terminate its contract with him was on its way to Athens. Budget cutting was the reason cited for the move. But then nothing was ever spelled out, nothing was ever clear-cut in those years of fear and suspicion.

13

George Polk's attack on the Greek right drew a swift counterattack. In late December, CBS president Frank Stanton was hand-delivered a letter bearing the gold-and-blue crest of the Royal Greek Embassy. Inside was a letter from the Ambassador to Washington, Vassili Dendramis, a close personal friend of Constantine Tsaldaris, who was then Foreign Minister.

"Several statements in the [*Harper's*] article representing facts are either totally unfounded or grossly exaggerated," the ambassador wrote. He denied that all of the one hundred Liberty ships sold by the United States to Greece had been transferred to Panamanian or other foreign registry. He further denounced as a lie Polk's charge that American aid money had gone into luxury goods or deposits in foreign banks.

"I would not deny," Ambassador Dendramis added, "that a few unscrupulous individuals succeeded in evading governmental controls (principally owing to the Government's reluctance to suspend constitutional guarantees) and arranged through private channels to send capital abroad. But," he went on, "this is the only grain of truth in Mr. Polk's grossly exaggerated report . . . [which] constitutes a complete distortion of the truth. . . . and I would very much appreciate it if you could find your way to calling Mr. Polk's attention to his obligations under the moral code of his profession."

Stanton scribbled "Discuss handling" on the angry letter's margin and sent it immediately to Dave Taylor, the head of news. Having sounded out Ed Murrow and Don Hollenbeck, the two broadcasters who regularly exchanged phone and cable messages with Polk,

Taylor composed a response to be sent over Frank Stanton's signature:

> Mr. Polk is a veteran reporter, well acquainted with the territory he is covering, and we have found him to be accurate and reliable in reporting for CBS. Our own editors, of course, did not review his article in *Harper's*, but we feel that his character would have led him to follow the same high standards of reporting which he has shown in his broadcasting for us. Since there seems to be direct contradiction between his version and your version of the flag flown by the Liberty ships, and so great a variance on the figures on Greece's import expenditures, we are sending Mr. Polk a copy of your letter with a request for further information.
>
> We feel that if any defense of the *Harper's* article is necessary, it should come directly from the author, who is in a position to recheck his sources of information on the spot.

It was a staunch defense by the network of one of CBS's key correspondents. The Greek government was not accustomed to such a firm line from its American benefactors, especially on the subject of mere news reporters.

As for Polk, he was only too pleased to answer the ambassador's charges. In a letter to Stanton, he wrote:

> Frankly, I am somewhat amused that Mr. Dendramis should protest to CBS for what appeared in *Harper's Magazine*. I believe the reason is relatively simple. The ambassador knows that a letter to *Harper's* would be published, thus allowing me to answer in print. So, to avoid having me answer publicly, the ambassador chose to work from behind the scenes. Also, I'm convinced he's hopeful that his protest may be used against me in CBS assignments.

What mattered to Polk was that in the prevailing climate CBS stood foursquare behind him. In a lengthy report circulated among CBS management, Polk proceeded to outline the poisonous relations between Tsaldaris and his allies and the more independent-minded American reporters in Athens:

My case is mild compared with the attacks being made against other outspoken reporters on the scene. The Ministry of Foreign Affairs has just written to the *Christian Science Monitor* (with its strict rules regarding alcohol consumption) complaining that their correspondent in Greece, Constantine Hadjiargyris, is guilty of using offensive language in dealing with Greek officials and is also guilty of drunkenness at interviews. Knowing Hadjiargyris as well as I do, I know this charge is a lie.

Another correspondent who has drawn Greek government fire is Ray Daniell of the New York *Times*. He arrived in Greece unaccompanied by his wife and, when his articles proved displeasing to the right-wing politicians, they spread malicious slander about Daniell. In one evening at the Hotel Grande Bretagne bar, three professional Royalist touts told me that Daniell was living with a notorious prostitute. Also a lie.

Yet another reporter who has provoked the Greeks is Homer Bigart, of the New York *Herald Tribune*. At the moment, being a newcomer in Greece, Bigart is getting the "treatment" that others of us already have had. In particular, he is being denounced by name as a Communist; he is ridiculed for "looking at things upside down"; he is being refused interviews by persons he needs to see for news purposes . . . such as Tsaldaris. . . .

The pattern of the attack on the other American correspondents here is clever, public denunciation plus official obfuscation. There is nothing so tangible as censorship or blunt refusal to allow a reporter to visit the civil war areas; instead there is a clever plan of making news work as difficult as possible for critical correspondents. . . . Removal of such correspondents may be even more important in the future than at present. The right wants to keep adverse criticism at a minimum; that is easiest by keeping bad publicity as small as possible. The right wing is preparing "dynamic policies" for establishing a veiled Royalist dictatorship in Greece. . . . Behind this scheme is the conviction that the United States is committed to continuing aid to Greece no matter what happens in Athens.

As a covering letter accompanying Polk's memorandum, Ed Murrow penned the following note: "For the past several months I have watched Polk's stuff very carefully and have frequently queried him, either by cable or phone, on material for my own show. I have come to regard him as one of the most careful, able correspondents in the whole CBS organization."

The passage of time did not appear to soften the impact of the *Harper's* article. It would rankle the Tsaldaris regime and its American friends for many months. Several weeks after the ambassador's letter, the Greek Minister of Public Information in the United States, Nicholas Lelis, asked for CBS airtime to try to rebut Polk's charges. CBS agreed, provided Polk replied in the same broadcast.

"I would set aside the argument that a right-wing official must necessarily be 'objectionable,' " Lelis said on CBS. "Just before this confusing postwar era, weren't rightists in general classified as patriots, and wasn't patriotism considered a noble ideal?

"But to call in a stroke 'semi-fascist' a government of the people, elected in elections termed fair, free, and just by 1,500 foreign and American observers, seems to me truly objectionable. I am sure," Mr. Lelis ventured, "Mr. Polk, whose sincere interest in Greece is well known, did not mean to brand thus a representative government controlled by a parliament, elected by the free votes of the Greek people."

(In his cable, Polk had noted: "I might cite the New York *Times* correspondent Raymond Daniell, who wrote, 'Greece has the appearance of democracy, but the appearance is pretty deceptive.' ")

In closing the broadcast, anchorman Larry Lesueur felt compelled to comment: "Now, finally, taking up one misapprehension about correspondent Polk's remarks, it must be pointed out that he doesn't object to the ministers because they are right-wing. He objects because he says they are extreme right-wingers, extremists whose supporters have publicly called for martial law and a mass arrest of all liberals. Correspondent Polk," the anchorman added, drawing from his own memory, "a wartime Navy fighter pilot twice wounded over Guadalcanal, admits of no political bias, except against the extremism which had already led officials of the American government to say they are not entirely satisfied with all aspects of the Greek government."

If the Greek right wing got a cool reception at CBS News, it could rely on a vastly more sympathetic hearing from members of the U.S. Embassy in Athens. A war of nerves had been fought for some time between American reporters and senior American diplomats, who invariably identified far more with the Greek right than with their own country's recalcitrant press.

Many inside the embassy felt that the press should serve as an arm of Washington's foreign policy. This conviction was shared by some high officials in Washington, notably the influential Secretary of the Navy, James Forrestal, who thought that reporters had a patriotic duty not to probe their own government's motives too vigorously.

Early in 1948, Homer Bigart, the Pulitzer Prize–winning reporter for the New York *Herald Tribune*, arrived in Athens to cover the civil war. Bigart had little use for diplomats, and they had little use for him. In Athens he got a taste of what he would later experience in Saigon: an American Embassy that identified with its host country's corrupt government.

It did not take Bigart long to receive his first summons from Chargé Karl Rankin, the ranking American diplomat in Athens (Lincoln MacVeagh had been transferred to Portugal). Rankin, Wisconsin-born and Princeton- and Heidelberg-educated, was a large, solemn, self-important man. He had gotten to know the Greek monarchy during its wartime Cairo exile, where he was posted at the time. Like the Royalists, Rankin loathed Communists of any stripe.

At a time when America's brightest diplomats were being gradually eliminated from the foreign service for insufficient anti-Communist fervor, Rankin rose rapidly in the ranks. No one in Athens or on Capitol Hill could question his Red-hating zeal.

On this January morning, Rankin was all silky-smooth diplomacy with the rough-hewn Bigart. The chargé inquired in a soft, even voice why Bigart had referred to Vice Premier Tsaldaris (at whose request Rankin had summoned the reporter in the first place) as the leader of "the extreme right."

"Isn't there a danger in this appellation, Mr. Bigart, coming from a reporter as well known as yourself, in one of our country's leading newspapers?" the chargé wondered. "Might it not be construed as representing American opinion in Athens? Your inference that Mr. Tsaldaris is trying to set up a 'rightist police state' and to get rid of Sophoulis [the Liberal Prime Minister] could also harm the chance of further aid to Greece. Could it not?"

Bigart said he was not after stopping aid to Greece.

"I hold no brief for Tsaldaris," Rankin continued. "He can be a difficult man. But, Mr. Bigart, he happens to be the undisputed leader of by far the largest party in Greece. . . . And so far as setting up a rightist police state, well, I've heard nothing to suggest that Tsaldaris favored such a step. Democracy," Rankin intoned, "is a tender plant under the conditions that obtain in Greece today. On the one hand, we Americans are driven by military and economic necessity to urge upon the Greeks drastic measures, many of which only a dictatorship could fully implement. On the other hand, we must press them constantly to observe democratic forms and to maintain a maximum of freedom and tolerance. We cannot push them too far or the whole thing could collapse.

"In view of this delicate situation," Rankin coaxed the still-silent reporter, "I'm sure you will understand the danger of your sort of reporting."

"What do you regard," Bigart asked, "as America's number one priority here?"

"Well, a number of position papers have been issued from Washington on this subject. But, offhand, I would say that restoring public order is our first task. With task number two being increasing productivity. Naturally," the diplomat continued, "we are interested in encouraging reforms . . . but the question of cutting off aid to Greece to achieve that end cannot be lightly discussed. So

far, Mr. Bigart, we have not lost a single country where the Red
Army is not in occupation."

The two men were not speaking the same language. It was plain
to Bigart that, for Rankin, the crux of the matter had to do with
the larger issue of not allowing Greece to slip into the "Red fold."
Anything else was superfluous, a waste of the diplomat's time.

Rankin was tireless in his attempts to "reform" the members of
the press. The week following his sermon to Bigart, he faced Constantine Hadjiargyris. Correspondent for the *Christian Science Monitor* and stringer for both CBS and the *Herald Tribune*, Hadjiargyris
was permanently suspect as a result of the moderate politics of his
stepfather, Prime Minister Themistocles Sophoulis, and his own
leftist activities in the Greek Navy during the war. His impressive
intellect and sharp insights into Greek politics made him a favorite
of both Polk and Bigart.

Only the protection of Hadjiargyris' aged but still revered (by
reformists) stepfather kept him free and, possibly, alive. But the
Royalists never tired of their attempts to defame the Greek reporter.

In the latest incident, Hadjiargyris' editors in Boston had been
informed, by a letter bearing the Foreign Ministry's coat of arms,
of his "drunkenness" in the presence of the powerful Under Secretary for Foreign Affairs, Panayotis Pipinelis. As Hadjiargyris
faced Karl Rankin that morning, he feared his job was on the line.

"The fate of your country," Rankin began in his most priestly
tone, "depends very much on public opinion. Therefore, as correspondent for an American newspaper you have a particular responsibility."

"Yes, I agree with you," Hadjiargyris replied, "but a factual
report on Greek conditions at the moment would present a dis-
heartening picture, a picture of government inefficiency, intrigue,
and corruption."

"But this is not the full picture," Rankin interrupted. "Production
is up, much has been achieved in agriculture. A credible record of
reconstruction, however slow. I think it fair these things should be
mentioned in any honest effort to present the Greek picture," Rankin chided, missing the irony of an American's lecture on Greece

to a Greek. Rankin would be in Peking in a year's time, while Hadji had but one city, Athens.

In a secret diplomatic cable that accompanied Rankin's transcripts of these conversations with the foreign correspondents, the chargé noted: "Whether or not informal talks such as these will have any beneficial results on the reporting of these correspondents remains to be seen."

No one in the State Department could fault Rankin for not doing his part to mold the news from Athens. The trouble was, the seasoned American correspondents were not buying Rankin's style of chamber-of-commerce reporting.

The following month, in a confidential memo to Rankin, embassy press spokesman George Edman wrote of that day's press conference: "May I point out that the only correspondent to question the statement issued jointly by AMAG [American Mission for Aid to Greece] and the Embassy, which said 'There is no country in Europe where a greater degree of press freedom may be found than in Greece,' is Homer Bigart. Bigart also called my attention to the fact that the Communist press is not permitted in Greece whereas it is permitted in Italy." The memo concluded with what seemed like a veiled threat: "Concerning Bigart, I'm wondering if the pieces are not beginning to fall into place."

In yet another confidential memo from Rankin, this one to Secretary of State Marshall, the chargé wrote:

> I have the honor to report that biased, fragmentary, and hostile reporting of certain American correspondents has continued with results both in Greece and the United States prejudicial to American policy and interests.
>
> Reports of American press correspondents are accorded great prominence in Greece, and those vehemently critical of the current regime not only deeply offend local opinion and undermine Greek confidence in their political and military leaders, but also cast doubt on America's intentions towards Greece.
>
> Perhaps most important, they tend to restrain responsible

Greek officials from taking necessary action for fear of further alienating opinion in the United States as created through the misinterpretations of local correspondents of influential American newspapers.

In the spring of 1948, with martial law in force, mass arrests of suspected leftists and executions of Communists and would-be Communists continued unabated. Even so, Rankin bemoaned the Greek right's excessive "restraint." "In the United States," Rankin cabled, "as the Department will have noted, biased and unfavorable reporting from Greece has directly affected the editorial policy of several leading newspapers, the New York *Herald Tribune*, the Baltimore *Sun*, and the Washington *Post*, among others, all of which have recently featured strongly worded editorials attacking the current Greek regime and American policy in Greece."

The New York *Times* was notably absent from Rankin's list of sinners, as its reporter was spoon-fed by the right wing. A. C. Sedgwick, the *Times*'s man in Athens, married to a Greek with strong Royalist connections, was, in the words of Harrison Salisbury, his respected colleague on the newspaper, "an embarrassment."

"In these critical times," Rankin wrote, as if oblivious to the ideals of the country he served, "one wonders whether we can afford the luxury not only of our recognized yellow press but also of such serious examples of irresponsibility among the correspondents of our most respected newspapers and agencies. That publishers and editors so often accept without question and editorialize upon the most arrant nonsense sent in by their own representatives may reflect lack of knowledge of all the facts."

In February, George Polk's friend and colleague Howard K. Smith returned to London after several weeks in Prague. On and off the air, Smith described a nightmare in the making: Communist militiamen marching through the graceful, cobblestoned streets of the Czech capital, a submachine-gun station at each corner. Smith left Prague because he could no longer broadcast from there. "The spectacular part is over," Smith told CBS's listeners. "The ugly, quiet part has begun."

It was yet another watershed: the Communist coup that swept Czechoslovakia into the steel grip of totalitarianism. This had been no backward fascist state, but an evolved if fragile democracy in the heart of Europe, a recent victim of Nazi brutality.

In the early-morning hours of March 10, Jan Masaryk, Foreign Minister of the new Communist government of Czechoslovakia, "fell" from a window of Czernin Palace. Masaryk was found at sunrise, spread-eagled in the palace courtyard, barefoot, half naked, his face dirty and contorted with fright.

"They say he committed suicide," Ed Murrow reported that evening. Jan Masaryk had been Murrow's friend of many years. "I don't know. Jan Masaryk was a man of great faith and great courage. . . ." Murrow seemed to be reliving the cruel days of 1938, of Munich, as he spoke into the microphone in a barely controlled voice. "Somehow this reporter finds it difficult to imagine him flinging himself from a third-floor window. . . . A gun, perhaps poison, or a leap from a greater height would have been more convincing."

Masaryk took with him any faint hope of reasoned communication between East and West. By staying at his post as Foreign Minister long after many other prominent Social Democrats and moderates had fled, he had attempted to bridge the divide. He thought he could exercise a moderating influence on the hotheads. He died for that naïve dream. George Polk, like Ed Murrow, had known and been dazzled by the Czech's quicksilver charm. Polk had called on him in Prague in late 1947. Masaryk, unafraid of what reporters would write, liked their irreverent company.

Walter Lippmann commented that the Prague coup and mounting pressures elsewhere "were clearly strategical actions planned by military men in anticipation of war."

Writing in early March to the commander of the Sixth Fleet in the Mediterranean, Admiral Forrest Sherman, Lippmann expressed the anxiety of those times. "We cannot any longer afford to wage a diplomatic and indirect military war against the Soviet Empire all over Europe and Asia.

"Instead of dissipating its strength through global containment, the United States should concentrate on a few critical areas,"

Lippmann advised. "Build up Japan so that the Soviets would have to keep a big army in Siberia, divide the Arab world in order to maintain Western influence.

"Even war is preferable to being paralyzed all over the world with no prospect of a decision and only the prospect of indefinite and unlimited entanglement." The columnist noted for cool reasoning called for immediate mobilization.

James Forrestal's hour had come. His call for a beefed-up military now got a respectful response.

It was the beginning of the most critical period of Harry Truman's presidency. But the President's advisers also sensed political opportunity. Truman faced a tough reelection campaign. Clark Clifford, the shrewdest of political operatives, penned this campaign memo: "The worse matters get, up to a fairly certain point . . . the more there is sense of crisis. In times of crisis, the American citizen tends to back up his President."

Appearing before Congress on March 17, Truman asked for the restoration of the draft. The same day, Britain, France, Belgium, the Netherlands, and Luxembourg signed a fifty-year collective defense treaty. NATO (which was called NAT until after the Korean War, when it gained its final O) was born. In short order, Congress passed $4 billion in Marshall Plan aid for Europe.

The press fueled the crisis atmosphere. "The atmosphere in Washington," the Alsop brothers reported in mid-March 1947, "is no longer postwar. It is a prewar atmosphere." "Where next?" asked a Washington *Post* headline. The paper showed a map of Europe with the areas under Soviet domination shaded. Arrows of alarm pointed to Italy, France, Finland, and Austria. Largely ignorant of the prevailing geopolitics—not understanding, for example, that Harry Truman never held out much hope for an independent Czechoslovakia—many Americans feared war was imminent.

By late March, Germany, where the forces of East and West were face-to-face, was the focal point of the growing tensions. Since the war, the Western allies and the Soviets had been bickering about conflicting aims for the defeated Reich, disagreeing on reparations, control of the Ruhr, and what levels of industrialization the decimated land should be permitted. By the end of March, the

Four Power government of Germany crumbled under the weight of argument and overheated rhetoric.

Berlin was the West's most vulnerable outpost and the perfect place for a showdown. The Soviet authorities announced that, effective April 1, all Americans passing through the Soviet zone by highway or by rail en route to Berlin would have to be checked by Soviet guards for their identity and affiliation. With the exception of military and government personnel, the baggage of American car and train passengers would also be searched. General Lucius Clay, the feisty, jut-jawed commander, interpreted the move as a Soviet effort to drive the Americans out of Berlin and eventually out of Europe.

Clay urged Washington to reject the Soviet order. "Any weakness on our part," Clay informed his superiors, "will lose us prestige important now. If Soviets mean war, we will only defer the next provocation for a few days." The White House approved the general's tough-it-out line.

Like most bold strokes, the general's plan began modestly. He ordered a small-scale airlift to carry food in Air Force transports from Wiesbaden near Frankfurt to Tempelhof Airport in the American sector of Berlin. The Berlin Airlift was under way.

It did not come to war. By June, C-47 military transports, bearing four thousand tons of food and fuel, roared over the wreckage of Berlin, landing every three minutes and forty-three seconds at Tempelhof. It was a powerful sight, tangible proof of Washington's determination to hold tight to what was left to hold.

A surge of patriotism and pride coursed through the American heartland, and Harry Truman's electoral stock began to rise.

In Athens, American diplomats, already predisposed to a tough Cold War stance, drew encouragement from Washington's blunt words and deeds. Their season, too, had arrived.

14

George Polk would not reduce the complexity of the story he was covering to fit the current definition of an East-West struggle. Savoring his gadfly role, he delighted more than ever in pricking inflated national institutions. His newest target was not American intervention in Greece, but one of its unexpected proponents: the Pulitzer Prize–winning playwright Maxwell Anderson.

Anderson, author of *What Price Glory?*, *Key Largo*, *Anne of the Thousand Days*, and many other Broadway hits, arrived in Greece as a "visiting fireman" in November 1947. Every foreign correspondent who cares about his beat fears this particular species. The "instant expert" generally stays five or perhaps ten days in a remote war zone. He then files authoritative pieces that result in resident correspondents receiving unwelcome queries from home. Why, the home office demands, are we not reporting what so-and-so says is the real story?

When the visiting fireman is a respected and highly successful man of American letters and comes up with a different truth than the correspondent's, there is the potential, in a politically volatile atmosphere, for real trouble. Such was the case of the playwright vs. CBS's man in the field in early 1948.

The New York *Herald Tribune* had commissioned the popular playwright, in Athens for the production of his play *Joan of Lorraine*, to share his impressions of the Greek situation with its readers.

It did not take Anderson long to arrive at the source of all of Greece's troubles: Communism. He further wrote that he was surprised at how little criticism he heard of the rightist regime during his stay in Athens. "Although many people agree they don't have a perfect government, they think it wiser to make do with what they have, rather than to insist on immediate reform."

Anderson had bought the most expedient view of Greece's troubles, the view put out by both the State Department and the embassy. It provoked a hot retort from George Polk.

On "CBS Views the Press," a journalism review that regularly criticized the way the press covered events, Polk spoke out against Maxwell Anderson:

> The principal charge I have against Mr. Anderson is his lack of reporting balance. By directing so much attention in his articles to the Communist problem, he suggests indirectly that there are no other problems. Actually, in the opinion of most reporters who have worked in Greece, the Communist problem exists principally because Greece is destitute, maladministered, and the population is hopelessly hungry. On only one point do Mr. Anderson's fictional writings qualify from the news standpoint: he has painted Communists as black as they are Red. However, this viewpoint sounds rather emotional, since he fails completely to explain that Greek government "outright injustice" has converted more Greeks than Moscow's agents could.

Don Hollenbeck, the hollow-faced, chain-smoking anchorman of "CBS Views the Press," understood that most of his listeners would likely agree with Anderson's devil theory of Communism and be troubled or worse by Polk's more complicated version. In his velvet voice, Hollenbeck, himself a constant target of Red baiting, felt compelled to explain: "George Polk agrees that the Reds are up to no good, that they are making use of every possible tactic to win Greece over, and that the way the present government operates is one of the strongest points in the Communists' favor."

In describing the Greek situation, playwright Anderson further wrote that the people to whom he talked discounted stories about terror, arrests, executions without trial, and the exiling of liberals. To this, Polk replied in a tone of contempt: "Apparently Mr. Anderson does not know that the government arrested and held in detention camps upwards of thirty thousand persons, without warrants, court action, or the right to bail." Polk went on to describe a recent prison visit. "Conditions are appalling, and political detainees, many of them ill and almost starving, cringed at the approach of the jailers, and told me their stories in whispers."

It was hard to tell that Maxwell Anderson was reporting from the same country when he wrote, in yet another dispatch: "What is happening here in Greece is typical of what happens when a dictatorship attacks a democracy. The dictatorship moves fast, and its propaganda is excellent. The democracy, made up of various factions, moves slowly, is reluctant to enter a war, and has no propaganda. But only twice in all Greece, where I have talked freely with countless people, have I heard the Communists defended, and not once have I heard the present government attacked and accused of outright injustice, except by an actor in an Athenian theater, himself a Communist."

George Polk's reply to this was blunt. "I have made a survey of my own and this survey brought the unanimous comment that the articles belonged in the realm of simple fiction rather than fact."

Don Hollenbeck closed "CBS Views the Press" with a sharp dig. "The tag line to the entire Anderson series is the fact reported by the playwright that his arrival in Greece was widely reported in the newspapers, and that in some quarters he was suspected of being Communist. There certainly can't be any misconception now."

The distinguished dramatist's reports left a bitter taste in Polk's mouth. They spoke volumes about the hardening of lines back home. Was there any room for reason amid such steely dogmatism? As Polk, Ray Daniell, and Hadjiargyris sat one night in the marble-and-gilt splendor of the Hotel Grande Bretagne bar, the reporters' favorite watering hole, they slipped slowly into despondency. All three toyed idly with the idea of leaving journalism, which seemed headed toward an emphasis on sensationalism and propaganda.

As if by deus ex machina, a bellhop appeared with an envelope for Polk from Don Hollenbeck (the Grande Bretagne was the correspondents' mail drop). It contained a transcript of the broadcast on the Polk-Anderson exchange of views.

"I read the whole thing to the group," Polk wrote Hollenbeck. "It restored our faith . . . well, almost restored it! Anyway, kudos on the slick job of dissection. In fact, Ray Daniell is not going to resign from the *Times*. He's not going to take up lobster fishing off Maine. Hadji said to hell with the public relations job he's been offered. . . . And I basked in the glory of having had CBS do a job that practically no other news organization (legitimate, anyway) would have done. Frankly, I don't see how you get away with such a script."

Hollenbeck's courage inspired Polk to fire off one of his lengthy situationers on Greece. He sent copies to William Shirer and Drew Pearson, both of whom made use of Polk's material as background in their own commentaries. Polk did not ask for attribution for these reports; it was enough that they provided a platform for his views. His byline was becoming less important than getting the real story on Greece, as he saw it, to the widest possible audience.

With mounting anger, Polk wrote Hollenbeck on February 5, 1948: "I'd like to tear the lid off the stupidity here. After all, under terms of the American-Greek aid program, American correspondents are officially guaranteed press privileges." He went on to describe his troubles getting a travel permit to Salonika. "After five days of battling, I've given up on Greek military and airline accommodations (although they've been available to other travelers and some planes even have gone north with less than a full load). . . . We are falling flat on our fannies here . . . doing worse than the British did, and inheriting all the dislike created by wars, rumor of war, and general hopelessness. But the question is: how do you get off the treadmill? I don't know. This is the only story I've ever covered for which I have no positive plan on improving things. I'm just not sure if the situation can be improved; the cards are all stacked against us."

In closing, he wrote Hollenbeck, whom Polk knew only by his

voice and integrity: "I hope I get to know you personally sometime this year, if and when I get back to America."*

In the spring of 1948, George Polk felt a responsibility for hitting hard and often on subjects that most other reporters skirted carefully. But he still maintained a remarkable evenhandedness in his reporting, as in this January 1948 broadcast.

Communist strategies here in Greece have at least two clear objectives. The first is to keep the Greek Army off balance by widely scattered attacks. The second objective of the Communist-led Greek guerrillas is to bleed Greek economic strength. This is accomplished by stopping any reconstruction, by preventing the planting and harvesting of crops, by looting and burning villages, and by forcing more and more peaceful Greeks to become new refugees. . . .

This week, from a secret radio transmitter came the first message from the newly organized all-Communist guerrilla Greek government of Prime Minister Markos. . . . The radiomen listening so intently were members of Greek guerrilla bands, those Communist-led Greek guerrillas that have ravaged and looted and burned and killed pretty much at will throughout Greece for more than a year.

The message ordered the guerrillas to strike again . . . attack undefended villages, seize supplies, impress or kill any able-bodied men, blow up bridges, plant mines on highways.

Yes, such a message has been a routine message for more than six months for the Communist-led guerrillas. But this week something new has been added. The wily, hard-hitting

---

* George Polk and Don Hollenbeck, bonded in their aversion to "the temper of the times," would never meet. Hollenbeck continued his controversial broadcast for many years. The fire from the right grew hotter and more personal. Finally, his critics, notably in the Hearst papers, impugned his honesty, day after day questioned his morality. They wore him down. Isolated at CBS, suffering from bleeding ulcers, Hollenbeck committed suicide in June 1954, one of the casualties of an era littered with shattered lives.

Not even his death stilled Hollenbeck's critics, however. For the day after he was found gassed in his apartment, Jack O'Brian, columnist for the Hearst papers, wrote: "Suicide does not remove from the record the peculiar history of leftist slanting of news indulged consistently by CBS. Hollenbeck was typical of CBS newsmen. He hewed to its incipient pink line without deviation."

rebel chieftain called General Markos has a new title. He has become Prime Minister Markos.

Thus, this week unhappy Greeks have two governments. One is the government most of us regard as the official government; its headquarters are here in Athens . . . with the active support of the United States to the tune of an aid program of some 350 million dollars.

In fact, Americans are now so numerous here that practically every large café in Athens today prints its bill of fare in both Greek and English . . . a lot of shops are putting up little signs which say, "Please Come In. We Speak English." Our presence here is explained by the Truman Doctrine and Congress's vote of aid for Greece. That was last spring. Since our arrival, unfortunately, things here have not improved. In fact, they have greatly worsened. The Greek government continues to deal with everything from the point of view of the most painless political expediency. At the same time, American policy here has been anything but dynamic.

Out of this confusion, only the Greek Communists have benefited. They are dynamic. They have a plan. They look ahead.

No Western reporter had yet penetrated General Markos' mountain stronghold, but most dreamed of an exclusive interview from rebel headquarters. The longer Markos held out, the more mysterious he became, the more his romantic image as King of the Mountain was enhanced. Polk and his colleagues knew little about the man. They had seen his pictures on "Wanted" posters in Athens. They knew he favored loose, brigandish dress, rather than a uniform, and carried a walking stick instead of a gun. By the end of 1947, Markos' rebels—*andartes*, as they were called in Greek—had used hit-and-run operations to capture four-fifths of Greece.

General Markos was not of the Communist Party hierarchy. Born in Smyrna, a tobacco worker by trade, he had spent time in prisons for his implacable allegiance to the Communist cause. His reputation in the year since America became embroiled in the Greek Civil War had been greatly embellished, now that he was defying

Washington as well as Athens. American arms began arriving by the boatload in Piraeus in the autumn of 1947. American administrators were planted inside the Athens ministries. American officers were slogging in the field with the Greek forces, now better equipped and in better fighting shape than ever before. And still this former tobacco worker and his horde of irregulars, operating from bases inside Albania, Bulgaria, and Yugoslavia, eluded the reach of the superpower.

By early spring 1948, Polk was already a target of right-wing surveillance. In March, while he and Rea were on a trip to Egypt, a visitor called at the Polks' Skoufa Street apartment. The Polks' maid, Despina Vroutsis, took careful note of the man's appearance.

Most of George and Rea's friends, with the exception of Hadjiargyris and Rea's relatives, were American or British. The only exception was Mary Cawadias Barber, stringer for *Time* magazine and wife of Stephen Barber, British correspondent for the *Sunday News Chronicle*. She was Greek-born, but seemed more English than the English. Mary's loyalties were strictly with London.

Despina, a young country girl, was thus unaccustomed to her own countrymen calling and would recall this visitor. He was of medium height and slim build. He had fair hair, slicked back to reveal a receding hairline. The Greek man had a small, neat mustache and was nattily dressed in a well-cut, mustard-colored suit. He also had a letter that he insisted he would deliver only into George Polk's hands. The letter, he said, was from England. He gave an English name that Despina could not remember. The visitor's own name, though he did not leave it, was Michael Kourtessis.

Kourtessis knew the Polks were out of the country. He was part of Greece's omniscient invisible government. A labyrinth of Royalist security forces, legal and paralegal, its many twisted branches included gendarmes, military men, and their political allies, like Tsaldaris, who were really only their pawns. Despite its parliamentary-monarchist façade, Greece in 1948 was, beneath the surface, almost as much under military control as it would later openly be under the Colonels in the 1960s and 1970s.

Michael Kourtessis, the fair-haired Greek in the mustard suit, was a member of a secret right-wing organization headquartered in the port of Piraeus, after which the group's front organization was named. The government-controlled and -operated port authority was the political base of Constantine Tsaldaris, the ultra-right-wing head of the Populist (Royalist) Party and also Foreign Minister at the time. (Both the U.S. Embassy in Athens under Ambassador Lincoln MacVeagh and the State Department found Tsaldaris' views and policies too blatantly right-wing for their taste and worked hard to have him removed from his position as Prime Minister in 1947.) Most members of the secret organization, as well as its legal front, the OLP (Organization of the Port of Piraeus), had been members of the Security Battalions, the extreme right-wing forces used by the Wehrmacht to "maintain order" and dispose of Greece's Jewish population during the occupation.

The head of the OLP was a member of parliament, a close friend of Tsaldaris, and a scion of a well-known military family named Yenimatas. Kourtessis, George Polk's nattily dressed caller, practiced no particular profession but was generally available for "special assignments." He was described by the people who knew him best as "capable of anything" and "very dangerous." Men like Kourtessis made possible the existence of front men like Foreign Minister Tsaldaris.

In her memoirs of life in Greece, *It's Greek to Me*, Willie Etheridge, the wife of the Louisville newspaper publisher and U.S. envoy to Greece, Mark Etheridge, vividly captured the flavor of the frivolous insularity of the politicians who operated in Athens during the civil war.

I sat next to Mr. Tsaldaris at an elaborate dinner given by His Excellency, as we say in diplomatic circles, for the Danish Minister and Mrs. Hubert de Wickfeld, a dinner that began with molds of pressed chicken and moved on through soup, meat, vegetables, salad, and two desserts, the first a fancy soufflé, and the second the inevitable oranges, except these were peeled and sliced and soaked in kirsch, and somewhere along this parade of food Mr. Tsaldaris invited me to go with him and Mrs. Tsaldaris after dinner to a policemen's benefit ball in Piraeus.

We were whisked there in a long, brand-new, black Buick, one of eight Buicks the government had purchased with some recently acquired cash, furnishing more ammunition to the circles that claim the present Greek regime is stupid and corrupt. Ahead of us streaked two motorcycle cops with their sirens wide open.

"My husband is very popular," exclaimed Mrs. Tsaldaris. "The committee for the ball sent these escorts to show us the way."

At the entrance to the hall where the ball was in full swing, a welcoming committee awaited us. They flung open the door of the Buick before the chauffeur could reach it, clicked their heels, shook our hands. Mrs. Tsaldaris sailed into the hall like a Labor Day float.

The dancing stopped. The crowd moved back, forming an aisle down which Mrs. Tsaldaris and Mr. Tsaldaris and the welcoming committee paraded. There was clapping. Mrs. Tsaldaris smiled and bowed first to the right and then to the left. "My husband is very popular," she called to me over her shoulder. "The people like him tremendously."

Later there was folk dancing and Mrs. Tsaldaris and Napoleon Zervas, who had been a leader of the most active Right Wing guerrilla group and was now Minister of Public Order, led a select group in an intricate figure. Strutting with high steps around the circle, tossing her head, rhythmically swinging her svelte hips, Mrs. Tsaldaris held at arm's length above her a handkerchief to which General Zervas clung while he hopped, skipped, slid, twisted, twirled, and twitched like a hooked fish at the end of a taut line. . . . Mr. Tsaldaris was also in the dance, but his short, stout figure did not cavort as wildly as General Zervas; nor did his partner prance as spiritedly as did Mrs. Tsaldaris. Yet as the dancers, perspiring and puffing, returned to the table for honored guests, Mrs. Tsaldaris exclaimed happily, "Hear the people applauding? My husband is extremely popular."

In the Piraeus underworld, Constantine Tsaldaris was indeed extremely popular. The head of the Royalist Party, he was like a party boss; he kept lucrative contracts, subsidies, and jobs flowing to his vast network of right-wing thugs and henchmen such as Kourtessis. These were the men who kept him in office. His wife's exclamations notwithstanding, he could not count on his people's love to maintain him in power. He had done much for himself and his men, but very little for the average Greek citizen. He lavishly subsidized the newspapers that hailed him as a democrat, while turning a blind eye to the country's desperate need for reconstruction.

A confidential memorandum, dated May 7, 1948, from embassy press spokesman Edman, a zealous anti-Communist himself, to Rankin reads: "The attacks made on the Liberals by the Rightist press are similar in pattern to the attacks that were made in countries that now find themselves behind the Iron Curtain. . . . I wonder if the Rightist press should not be warned that it is doing exactly what the Commies want it to do? . . . In my opinion Tsaldaris is the person to speak to his friends on the Right. I have been told in confidence that he is responsible for the Government subsidy granted *Eleftheria, Embros, Akropolis, Ethnikon, Kyrix*, and a sixth paper the name of which I am not sure. This subsidy was granted following the wage increase given to newspaper employees and as a sort of a sop . . ." What Edman calls a "sop" sounds like a simple bribe.

Tsaldaris was run by a group of Army officers who were far less known to American diplomats than the Foreign Minister. Even less familiar with Athens' real power center were the eminent American public servants who, from their State Department and White House East Wing offices, ultimately assured the Greek right's survival.

"We had made a policy decision to support Greece," Clark Clifford, one of those public servants, recalled. "After that we trusted our own people on the ground to carry out our policy."

Athens' hidden government first emerged during the German occupation. The founders were two groups of Royalist military officers whose aim was to resist the penetration of the armed forces by republican officers and to prepare the way for the restoration of the monarchy after the war. The officers soon established close ties with the dreaded X, a Royalist terrorist group headed by Colonel George Grivas. The conspirators formed a close alliance with the British, united as they were in their zealous anti-Communist and pro-Royalist sentiments. In 1944, following the Wehrmacht's retreat from Greek soil, London provided the right wing with massive help in snuffing out leftist opposition.

In December 1944, ELAS (National Popular Liberation Army), the leftist anti-German resistance, had made a precipitous grab for postwar power. Afraid that they would soon lose their political gains under the new pro-British setup, ELAS staged a mass demonstration on the streets of Athens.

Churchill cabled his commander in the field: "Do not hesitate to act as if you were in a conquered city where a local rebellion is in progress. We have to hold and dominate Athens with bloodshed if necessary."

Fighting did in fact break out. The rebels refused to disperse, and a shot, whose origin has since been disputed, was fired. Although the British lost 237 troops, there is no precise figure on the thousands of Greeks killed on the streets of Athens in December 1944. It was not an equal fight. The left did not muster anywhere near the amount of foreign support that the right had. Churchill afterward paid tribute to Stalin's restraint for "adhering strictly and faithfully to our agreement of October [1944] and in all the long weeks of fighting the Communists in the streets of Athens not one word of reproach came from *Pravda* or *Izvestia*."

After the leftist massacre, which the Greeks call *Dekemvriana*, the right wing gained a comfortable position in all the security forces. These were run from Athens, but had tentacles reaching into every town and village. Through the legal channels of the country's military apparatus, the officers controlled the courts, the press, the Palace, the police, and the gendarmerie.

According to a four-page secret briefing paper found among the papers of General "Wild Bill" Donovan, Greece's foreign policy was also in "military league" hands, in the person of the Permanent Under Secretary for Foreign Affairs, Panayotis Pipinelis. Known as the "political brains" of the league, Pipinelis (the man who had accused Hadjiargyris of drunkenness) was the principal adviser to Constantine Tsaldaris.

An estimated 200,000 Greeks served the league through the secret terrorist organization X. Both the police and the gendarmerie in the countryside were league-controlled. A vast network of intelligence officers reporting to the 2nd Bureau of Counterespionage under the General Staff honeycombed the security forces. Though the Populist Party was its mainstay, the league could count on the reluctant neutrality of the Liberals and leftists who feared the consequences of challenging such a well-armed and highly organized group.

Though its reach was unlimited, its name was never even uttered by members of the emasculated opposition center or left-of-center parties. No newspaper would print its name.

It was the civil war, of course, that had greatly enhanced the military's power. Measures against Communist fifth columnists were intensified all over Greece. Those same measures, arrests without trial, court-martials, summary executions, and martial law, were convenient in dealing with those perceived as being remotely anti-Royalist or anti-militarist.

By 1948 the Greek Army was the only government institution with any cohesion. The impact of American dollars and advisers, combined with the driving force of their own zealous anti-Communism and the support of the Athenian bourgeoisie, made the military the uncontested authority in that part of Greece not under guerrilla control.

The military league was more than an organization, it was a state of mind. Its key tenet was that only officers, or politicians run by officers, were fit to govern the country. The British and their American successors not only tolerated but nurtured this mentality and helped create a monster beyond their control.

In a secret memorandum to the newly appointed Ambassador to Athens, Henry Grady, dated October 22, 1948, Karl Rankin summed up how little leverage the new superpower saw itself as having.

"We are committed morally and practically to see Greece through at any cost. This country is in effect our instrument . . . one which we are shaping to use in the furtherance of our foreign policy. In speaking of 'Greek responsibility,' we must not forget that these are matters of detail. The overriding responsibilities are ours."

This message of unlimited and uncritical support was delivered by Washington's representatives to their grateful Greek clients. The words did not fall on deaf ears.

15

George Polk, increasingly outspoken in his views, seemed oblivious to his powerful enemies. As it happened, some were in his own profession and had lines to the invisible intelligence operations in Greece. *Time* magazine's two correspondents on the scene, Robert Low and Mary Barber, called for an even deeper American commitment in the civil war.

On January 12, 1948, Low painted Greece's troubles in the most heroic colors and called it "the warmest front in the world's Cold War. . . . All of Greece like little Konitsa (near the Albanian frontier) is besieged by Communism. The larger siege must be lifted and Greece must be made safe. This the Truman Doctrine has stated. It would take more than a dash up a mule track by hardy Greek soldiers to achieve this end."

With a typical *Time* magazine flourish, he described General Markos' mustache as "taking up where Stalin's left off." Not only was Henry Luce's magazine unswervingly anti-Communist; its correspondent Low, whose lifestyle was conspicuously more comfortable than his colleagues', worked at least part-time for the newly formed CIA. Low never had trouble finding a place on planes or jeeps to the war zone.

Some of the good fellowship that existed between intelligence agents and reporters in the field was a residue of World War II. A good many of General "Wild Bill" Donovan's operatives in the Office of Strategic Services, the CIA's precursor, had been journalists. For these reporters, the conflict had been clear-cut: fascism vs. democracy. Once the common enemy had been vanquished, they faced a more complex world. Still, the relationship between the press and the intelligence community was an easy one, based on unspoken understandings. But accepting money from the CIA, as Low did, would have caused scandal even then.

Among British journalists the borders between government and the press were sometimes even hazier. In a 1948 conversation on this subject with Prime Minister Clement Attlee's liaison to MI6, London's overseas intelligence network, New York *Times* columnist Cyrus Sulzberger wrote: "I needled [Hector McNeil] about the way British intelligence employed newspapermen. He said, 'Oh, no, we only hire them in the Middle East.'"

Mary Barber, a shrewd and enigmatic figure, was Low's Athens stringer. She, too, was well connected with both the Greek royal family and its ultra-right-wing politicians. For Mrs. Barber, Constantine Tsaldaris was "a cozy bear of a man . . . someone you could have a nice chat with." Mary Barber's closest friend in the press corps was A. C. Sedgwick of the New York *Times*. He was married to a Greek Royalist, and George Polk and other journalists were appalled by his toadying for the right. The American Embassy in Athens, however, was immensely grateful to Sedgwick for getting its version of events on the pages of the New York *Times*.

To Ed Murrow, Polk wrote:

Sedgwick's return to Greece this fall baffled a number of persons. Following Ray Daniell's trip to Athens last spring, Sedgwick was recalled in what we all understood to be disgrace. The sharp contrast between Sedgwick's copy and Daniell's certainly was conspicuous. Following complaints on Sedgwick's work, he was ordered to the U.S., and Daniell was informed a new man, Dana Adams Schmidt, would take over in Athens. Schmidt came to Greece and did a good, objective job of reporting, one that conflicted in most particulars with what Sedgwick had been writing. . . . But then suddenly Schmidt was shifted to Cairo and Sedgwick [related by marriage to the Sulzberger family, publishers of the *Times*] returned to Athens. There was no explanation but apparently the New York *Times* is not using much of his copy.

Mary Barber, who along with her British husband, Steve, often socialized with George and Rea, never confronted Polk with her skepticism about his kind of reporting. She would later say that Polk "did not really understand Greece, nor what was at stake in the civil war." She had no great love for American reporters like Homer Bigart and George Polk, who, in her words, "threw their weight about a bit."

The British, Mrs. Barber's adopted people, were beyond reproach. With hundreds of years of practice in dealing with subject peoples, the British did not "throw their weight about." Among her good friends while she worked for *Time* magazine was Nigel Clive, an MI6 man in Athens. Clive's right-wing views were a subject of comment even among his colleagues in an agency not known for sympathy toward the left. Clive's wife, Maria, also Greek, did not hide her feelings that any reporter who wished to visit Markos and the Communists was a traitor. From her point of view, you simply couldn't be respectful toward both sides in a civil war.

Clive and Sir Charles Wickham, the chief of the British Police Mission in Greece, were among Mrs. Barber's closest companions in Athens. The man Mrs. Barber describes in her memoirs as her first love was Frank Macaskie, a former British Army officer in Greece who became the correspondent for *The London Times* there. Macaskie, on special assignment to British intelligence, shared Mrs. Barber's suspicion of George Polk.

In general, Englishmen like Macaskie, Clive, and Wickham were deeply resentful of the waning days of the British Empire. Their most conspicuous attitude toward America was one of condescension.

Though Britain had been bled white by the war and could no longer afford the luxury of far-flung dominions, in its view it had the expertise, the civil servants, the diplomats, the spies, and the policemen to do the job that the Yanks, lacking all experience in these matters, would now finance.

The Mediterranean, these staunch imperialists held, must remain a British theater of operations. It was a mentality that would suffuse British Foreign Office and MI6 thinking until the Suez catastrophe ended all such illusions.

Feelings of innate British superiority vis-à-vis the rough-hewn new arrivals had to do with more than just centuries of imperial service and experience. It was also tied up with culture and education. British operatives and officers like Clive, Macaskie, and Wickham arrived in the land of the Elgin marbles fresh from Oxford and Cambridge, Pindar and Pericles buzzing in their heads. Their backpacks were stuffed not with detective thrillers but with well-thumbed volumes of classical poetry and archaeology.

What did the new imperialists, the Americans, know of avenging Byron's memory? They only wanted to change everything, and fast. They came with their dollars, their jeeps, their naïveté, and their impatience, and in British eyes, they understood nothing about this ancient civilization.

In her memoirs, *Xenia*, Mary Barber reveals this condescension in the following scene after a flight to Athens in 1947: " 'Was that the Acropolis?' my American fellow passenger asked as we disembarked, and when I said it was, he muttered, 'My goodness, the Greeks sure need our help. It looks in real bad shape.' I wanted to laugh, and to explain that part of the beauty of the Acropolis today was that it was old and 'in bad shape.' Greece, I knew, was receiving generous U.S. aid and needed it badly, but the Acropolis, well, that was all right and had been for many years."

Sedgwick, Mary Barber, and Frank Macaskie, though journalists, were known to fellow reporters to be as hostile to Polk's persistent criticism of the Greek government, to his "dangerously misplaced righteousness," as were Karl Rankin, Constantine Tsaldaris, and scores of other, less visible people on the right.

In February, George Polk left behind the warm, sunny days of Athens and again flew to bitter-cold Salonika. He toured battlegrounds that skirted the Albanian frontier and filed pieces about the civil war, now in its third year.

As was often the case when Polk reported from remote spots without adequate phone lines, Douglas Edwards read his cable on the "CBS News Roundup," on February 11, 1948:

> We've just received a cable from CBS correspondent George Polk which is very reminiscent of the kind of dispatches sent

in from the front of World War II. Polk is in the north with the Greek Army and he reports from somewhere on the frontier . . . that the first campaign planned by the Greeks in collaboration with American military advisers is drawing to a successful close.

Two Greek divisions around a place called Nestorion are mopping up in the mountainous territory in an area formerly a stronghold of the Greek Communist-led guerrillas. Three thousand Greek Army troops, observed by the American advisers, have broken up the guerrilla formation at Nestorion and probably have perpetrated an attack on the town in an attempt by the guerrillas to seize it as a headquarters for General Markos' rebel regime.

George Polk says that during the campaign he has watched the guerrilla force flee from Greece into the Soviet satellite nation of Albania. The Greek Army stopped two or three miles inside Greek territory, to avoid an international incident. The campaign, Polk says, has been bitter with cold and snow and frostbite common among Greek troops. The brightest feature has been American chow, the same combat rations that were issued the American Army in the field.

Our correspondent says that lower-ranking officers, plus a few select Greek Army commanders, seem worthy of leading a Greek Army that actually has a will to fight, but apparently the Greek General Staff is unwilling to incur the necessary personnel losses in order to really crush the guerrillas, and on the whole, so far, the government forces have been losing the civil war.

Polk returned to Athens in late February, exhausted from the grueling trip north. One morning, preoccupied with plans for his mother's imminent arrival in the Middle East, he answered the doorbell of his Skoufa Street apartment. Polk, whose office was across the hall from the front door, faced a man dressed in the worn, coarse clothes of a Greek tradesman. Something about the man's intensity made Polk understand he had something other than selling on his mind. Stepping inside, the Greek spoke in good English.

"I have come from the Party. We have heard of your interest in visiting General Markos. We are prepared to take you there. But of course it will take time to arrange."

Polk did not commit himself. Nor did he discourage the "tradesman." He said he was about to go to Istanbul, to meet his mother. "We can renew contact when I return."

"Be careful, George," Hadjiargyris later warned.

"This is not my first contact with a Communist," Polk confided to his Greek friend.

"George, be careful. And please," he implored, "don't tell me about such contacts in the future. It can only be used against me."

Polk took this contact seriously enough to tell CBS's Istanbul stringer, Leo Hochstetter, about it. "Tell Howard K. Smith I'm getting close to the other side," Polk said, as Hochstetter was headed for London. He also wrote his brother, Bill, that he seemed to be making progress on his Markos story.

On February 27, George and Rea flew to Istanbul to meet Adelaide Polk. When they had parted in 1945, George had been en route to the Far East, in pursuit of a different life, with a different wife. But the Mediterranean, the Middle East, and Greece had waylaid him as it had so many other travelers. Polk had expected to make his career in the Orient, the place where he started in the business. Cairo, Jerusalem, and finally Athens had come at him with too great a rush. He had all but forgotten Peking and Shanghai, which at the time were swept up in their own convulsions.

In her stylish navy blue suit and wide-brimmed hat, Adelaide Polk looked wonderful to her son. The three years' absence had been kinder to mother than to son. She found George considerably aged, scarred by his many accidents, with a look of deep fatigue around the eyes. But she banished all dark thoughts on this day. She wanted to savor each moment with her adored eldest child.

Now a widow with a job as a school librarian and a life of her own, she still brought out the best in Polk. Her unwavering belief in him had been one of his greatest sources of strength. There is something good in everyone, something to be learned from each, she always insisted. I never met a boring person, she used to tell him. There was so much of her in him: her innate generosity, her curiosity about her fellow man. She, who once had wealth and social position and lost them both, like her son cared little for either.

Looking at her tall, well-built son, she exclaimed, "George, I feel like the dove that has given birth to the eagle."

On her first trip overseas, she wanted to taste every exotic detail of the Middle East. By her second day in Istanbul, she was knocking back glasses of ouzo, the powerful anise-based liqueur favored by the Greeks.

Adelaide fell in love with her pretty and eager-to-please daughter-in-law, and ended up feeling sorry for Rea. Polk's wartime malaria flared up again, causing him fatigue and pain. He was more or less resigned to the nightmares, but the new bout of malaria drained him of energy and his temper flared at the slightest provocation. His mother could see the strains on the new marriage.

In Athens, each evening Adelaide and Rea accompanied Polk to the cable office where he sent his dispatches to CBS. His mother was appalled at the primitive conditions of the "studio." It was a tiny room a few blocks from home; he had covered the walls with Army blankets for soundproofing. The room was always either too cold or too hot.

Polk wrote more and more stories about the Greek people, "little-guy stories" he called them, avoiding weighty official pronouncements, Greek or American. Polk had found his own voice. He no longer emulated the sonorous tones of Murrow, the hard-bitten style of John Donovan of NBC, or the statesmanlike pronouncements of Lippmann. His was an unselfconscious style, conversational, without straining for folksiness. Without a trace of zealotry, he was never reluctant to express a definite point of view.

I'd like to tell you about Private Yannis Papadopoulos. Yanni is a thoroughly nice guy, twenty-eight, married, and a good soldier. His family lives here in Athens. Mrs. Papadopoulos and their two children, Dimitri and Maria, live in a fourth-floor attic room in an Athens slum. They do not have running water, nor electric lights, nor central heating, nor adequate clothing, nor medical care. They're typical of a lot of civilians.

Because her husband is a soldier, Mrs. Papadopoulos receives nine dollars a month as living expenses for herself and her two children. But life is hard on Yanni, too. In the field he receives five dollars a month. . . . On his last leave from the civil war areas, Yanni suggested that they sell their last family heirloom, a small silver frame that holds the picture of Yanni's grandfather. . . .

I saw Yanni not long after he had returned to the war zone. This time he was with an advanced scouting unit of the Fifteenth Mountain Division, someplace near the Albanian-Yugoslav border. When I arrived at Yanni's company headquarters, everybody was just lining up for chow. Much of it was U.S. Army chow, food that has come to Greece as part of the three-hundred-and-fifty-million-dollar American aid program. Yanni and his fellow soldiers like U.S. Army food . . . with one very definite exception. Greeks don't eat corn the way we do. They hate corn, canned or on the ear. So here's a tip for Washington's military masterminds . . . don't ship any more canned corn to Greece. Yanni told me confidentially that even his little pack mule refused to eat canned corn.

But Greek soldiers are happy about other American supplies. These include big two-and-a-half-ton trucks, jeeps, machine guns, and planes. . . . But Greek soldiers do not have dynamic leaders. In fact, the Greek military high command appears almost as bad as the Greek government. Both are shot through with favoritism, inefficiency, and corruption. The result? The Greek Army has been losing the civil war progressively, losing it to the Communist-led Greek guerrillas.

For example, while I was in the embattled northern areas, a Greek Army unit made a drive through guerrilla-held territory. Visiting the area, I saw vacant villages, looted buildings, burned warehouses, untilled fields. The inhabitants had long since fled before the Communist threat . . . fled to already overcrowded refugee centers in the larger towns. So the Greek

Army drive was important. Pursuit of the Communist-led guerrillas continued for three days. Then, just as the guerrillas were almost surrounded, and to the utter amazement of the American tactical advisers, the Greek high command called off the drive. No reason was given. But a good guess is that the necessary final assault would have caused a number of Greek Army casualties. And no Greek Army commander wants to leave himself open to political charges because of personnel losses.

This, then, is a fair cross section of the Greek problem. My friend Yanni is ready to fight his country's enemies. He wants to win and go home. Yet some of his officers lack the offensive spirit necessary for winning. . . . This is George Polk in Athens.

Adelaide stayed for a month in Athens, at the Grande Bretagne, where Churchill, too, had stayed and which currently housed the British Police Mission. A part of her feared for her exceptional son. "My man-child is a giant in these parts," she wrote home of her son. "It really frightens me how all the world thinks him great here. I feel as though I am the mother of Achilles Polk. . . . He strives for the ultimate, the top, and thus he is tense and hard pressed. Ed Murrow told me in New York, 'George is magnificent, so thorough, so informed, so well rounded.' "

On the first anniversary of the Truman Doctrine, Polk filed a report guaranteed to displease both Athens and Washington:

Just a year ago today, our President announced the Truman Doctrine for the eastern Mediterranean. That doctrine was supposed to combat Communism and prevent Soviet penetration here. Today, the United States has made an official report on the past year's accomplishments. Frankly, these accomplishments are not many.

The civil war continues between the Greek Army and the Communist-led guerrillas. According to today's official American report on Greece, the Royalist Greek Army has lacked offensive spirit during the fall and winter. Stated another way, the Communists have been winning the war here in Greece. Actually, that is about all that can be said on American accomplishments here. That isn't a very good promise for the future.

In the spring of 1948, the world's attention shifted from the Balkans to Palestine. There, Arabs and Jews were locked in combat, while London, whose mandate was due to expire on May 15, attempted to extricate its troops with whatever dignity the British could muster.

Polk, impatient by late March to plunge back into that story, bid his mother a lighthearted goodbye in Alexandria, Egypt, where they were visiting Rea's mother. "I said goodbye to him early one morning, for I knew I was going back to America soon. But we planned to see each other in late June in America," Adelaide wrote in her journal. "Personally," she wrote on March 6 from Athens, "I would prefer him to be more of the common clay."

In her final letter home from Athens on March 10, Polk's mother wrote: "Let me repeat my psalm of thanksgiving for my children, and friends . . . let me say I am indeed blessed among women. George seems much better . . . his 'third nose' is pretty good, not as beautiful as his second nose (Australian) nor his first (the one he was born with), but I thank God he is alive and safe and HAS a nose . . . he looks thin but eats well, is highly tense and worked out . . . he seems NOT to be able to rest nor let down . . . I feel it most imperative for him to have a quiet lazy summer at or near a beach."

Polk reached Jerusalem in late March. Douglas Edwards read the following, based on a cable sent by Polk from Palestine:

Polk has just made a hectic trip across the Holy Land by car, talking his way past suspicious guards at both Jewish and Arab roadblocks, drawing scattered shots from unknown marksmen, and trying to convince the British Mandate forces a reporter has a right to be cruising about the country under such conditions.

Our correspondent says one unusual road hazard is steel-sheeted trucks driven by both Arabs and Jews. These ten-ton monsters race along the roads, the drivers peering through slit windows, and woe to anybody who gets in their way. . . .

In anticipation of an intensified battle of roads, the Jewish Defense Force, Haganah, is undergoing special convoy task force training. If the British military withdraws from most of Palestine, as now scheduled for May 15, Polk says the Haganah will attempt to win and hold the road connections from Tel Aviv to Jerusalem. The Zionists consider this link vital.

In Jerusalem, Polk shared a hotel room with John Donovan, his old friend and NBC competitor. "He looks like hell," Polk wrote his brother, "as do all the reporters . . . just walking cases of jitters. The shooting and bombing never stops and those guys look ten years older than when I last saw them. Five correspondents have been killed or wounded in three months. The tragedy of it all is almost unbelievable."

On April 17, Polk was back in Athens. "You are a Communist," the anonymous voice on the telephone hissed in Greek-accented English. "Take care. We will kill you."

Though he had received death threats before, in Cairo and in Palestine, Polk was sufficiently shaken to summon Hadjiargyris to his apartment.

"In Greece these threats do not usually materialize," the Greek journalist reassured him. "My stepfather gets them from his right-wing opponents all the time."

"I'll wait and see if they call again."

16

The letter with the New York postmark was delivered to George Polk's Skoufa Street address at the end of April.

Polk read the letter with quickening pulse. It was from an employee of the Chase Bank in New York, not a friend. It was one of those letters reporters with reputations for tough-mindedness sometimes receive out of the blue, the unsolicited and unexpected reward for brave reporting. The stuff of a major scoop.

The letter contained the piece of information Polk had been looking for, the missing evidence that would enable him to "tie the can," as he wrote Murrow, to the regime that he held in such profound contempt.

Constantine Tsaldaris, the head of the Royalist Party, the most powerful politician in Athens, the Foreign Minister who had gone begging to Washington for more aid, with promises of economic austerity in return, had broken his own country's law. At a time when Greece was desperately trying to prevent the flow of currency out of the country—indeed, it was a crime to send money out—Tsaldaris had just deposited $25,000 in a personal account at the Chase Bank. In 1948, $25,000 was a large sum of money, $325,000 in 1989 dollars. From a public servant of a bankrupt country living off American foreign aid, it was an obscene sum.

"It would have been extremely difficult for us to go back to Congress," Clark Clifford noted forty years later, when told of the letter's contents, "and ask for more money for Greece had this information come to light."

The implications of the letter he held raced through Polk's mind. Outrage in Washington. An embarrassed State Department, which had just renewed its request for congressional funding of the Truman Doctrine. A vindication, finally, of all Polk had warned against. The demise, surely, of this comic-opera politician and the thugs who backed him.

Polk did not tell any of his colleagues, not even the trusted Hadjiargyris, about his letter. Its contents were too explosive. But he had to tell somebody. He could not contain its news for weeks without getting some kind of reaction and perhaps counsel on how to proceed. Someone else had to share his outrage and his excitement.

Polk settled on two Americans in Athens whom he trusted implicitly. He confided the story of the $25,000 deposit to Melvin Johnson, the director of CARE in Greece, and to Homer Davis, the head of the American College in Athens. Self-contained men who did not frequent the company of the small clique of Athens correspondents, they kept their own counsel. They could also perhaps share Polk's revulsion and his hope that, with this evidence, he could precipitate the end of a demeaning relationship between Washington and the Greek oligarchy.

Polk also told his wife, who had a different reaction. Rather than delight in Polk's journalistic good fortune, Rea instantly sensed danger. From her point of view, they began to live with a ticking time bomb the day they received the letter with the New York postmark.

Being the sort of reporter he was, however, Polk felt duty-bound to confront Tsaldaris himself with the information. It was one of the most basic tenets of his trade: get the man's reaction to so devastating a charge of misconduct. Ed Murrow would have expected that of him.

Polk was not going to report the Tsaldaris story until he reached New York. But he was going to nail down as much as he could of it in Athens. On this story, in this climate, operating according to the highest standards of his trade proved to be a fatal miscalculation.

On Monday, May 3, 1948, Polk made one of his many trips to the office of Nicholas Baltatzis-Mavrocordatos, the Under Secretary of State for Press and Information, and requested an audience with Foreign Minister Tsaldaris. "It's urgent," Polk said. "As you know,

I'm shortly returning to the States and I have received information which is important to Mr. Tsaldaris."

This time, Polk was not kept waiting for long.

The interview between the portly Foreign Minister and the tall, spare American began well enough. Tsaldaris was courtly and formal. Over little cups of thick Greek coffee he said he hoped Polk had been well treated by his country, and would honor it with his presence again soon.

Polk thanked the Foreign Minister and expressed his fondness for the country. Then he asked about Mr. Tsaldaris' American bank account. The meeting fell apart. Polk was playing by rules incomprehensible to Tsaldaris and the powerful men who backed him. These were not public servants in the American sense. They saw themselves as accountable to no one but their own military and political allies. Polk did not recognize the power and pervasiveness of the network that supported the Foreign Minister.

George Polk saw only the burlesque figure of the Foreign Minister stammering protests against the irresponsibility of this charge and its dire consequences for the civil war. He saw only the grasping man, evading as always the real issue, ducking behind the ready-made phrases of the Red Scare. Polk lost his temper.

"This will finish you, Mr. Tsaldaris!" he shouted at the Greek, who must have understood that in fact it could.

An irrepressible and, under the circumstances, dangerous streak of self-righteousness motivated the reporter. Perhaps, too, the physical pain that never really left him made him less cautious than another man might have been. He was fed up and he was going home.

"I'm going to blow this story sky high when I get home," he threatened the Foreign Minister, who knew from his intimate friend Ambassador Dendramis in Washington that Polk was a rising star. A lot of people would be listening to Polk.

Later, Rea said only, "I am surprised he lived for three days after that interview."

17

For several decades, speculation and controversy have surrounded the subject of George Polk's last days. Some pieces of evidence that have recently surfaced eluded investigators at the time, or were ignored by them.

In particular, there are three crucial reports, which for political reasons were suppressed in the 1940s and 1950s and which remained unavailable for later investigations. The first is an eleven-page report filed by Colonel James Kellis, dated July 22, 1948, and addressed to General "Wild Bill" Donovan. The other two reports were prepared by Lambros Antoniou, Kellis' informant in the Populist Party and the Piraeus right-wing underground. These were sent to Colonel Kellis. Further crucial evidence comes from the personal diary of Mrs. Waide Condon, the wife of the USIS officer called upon to identify George Polk's body. Mrs. Condon herself spent the week following the murder looking after Polk's widow and recorded both Rea's and her own experiences at the time. Though important witnesses, the Condons were never questioned by authorities. A portrait of a murder conspiracy emerges from the evidence these sources provide.

Sometime between Tuesday, May 4, and Thursday, May 6, Michael Kourtessis, henchman of the Piraeus right-wing underground, flew from Athens to Salonika. Kourtessis was a "lieutenant" of a Royalist member of parliament named Yenimatas, who also had ties to British intelligence. Kourtessis had the previous week successfully delivered a letter into Polk's hands. The letter offered a possible contact with Markos, but the offer was apparently not firm enough for Polk to alert his home office or anyone else about a possible interview with Markos.

The letter was just enough of an enticement so that the next time they met, Kourtessis would not be a stranger to Polk.

Kourtessis' Piraeus group, very much like X, the better-known Royalist terrorist underground, held secret meetings and drew its members from Piraeus longshoremen and the government services, such as the military police, among the most powerful security organizations in Greece. All members were supporters of Tsaldaris. Many were former members of the Security Battalions. A substantial portion of the Security Battalions had been assimilated into the various right-wing security forces. Many also were recruited as agents of the British. In the words of one Scotland Yardsman doing duty in Athens: "All the best chaps in Greece were in the Security Battalions." Yenimatas, the head of Kourtessis' front organization, recruited by the British during the war, made no secret of his continued ties to London.

Kourtessis did not travel to Salonika alone. Accompanying him was his friend and political ally of many years, the chief of security in Salonika, Major Nicholas Mouscoundis. One of the country's best-known and most feared policemen, Mouscoundis had a reputation as the most skilled of the many Communist hunters in the land. He was personally credited with breaking the back of the Communist terror organization OPLA, the left-wing counterpart of X. Legend had it that Mouscoundis accomplished this by tricking one suspect into believing he was about to be roasted alive. At the last moment, the man decided to talk.

Like Yenimatas, Mouscoundis was a stranger to American officials in Greece, but he was very close to the British. For the previous three years Mouscoundis had worked in tandem with the British Police Mission in Salonika. The Greek anti-Communist warrior had formed a particularly close relationship with one member of the Scotland Yard team stationed there to train and supervise the Greek police: Colonel Thomas Martin.

On Thursday, May 6, the day before Polk's flight to Salonika, Colonel Stacy, also of the British Police Mission in Salonika, officially informed Mouscoundis of news the Greek was already expecting. An important Communist with a group of ten assassins and saboteurs was expected in Salonika within the next few days.

Colonel Stacy alerted Mouscoundis that the assassins were on an "important job." Security should be even tighter than normal.

Two days later, Colonel Martin alerted Salonika police chief Apostolos Xanthopoulos that an important, unnamed Communist had arrived in Salonika and again warned of possible trouble. Neither the ten saboteurs and assassins nor the "important Communist" ever in fact appeared in Salonika.

It was not altogether unusual for the British Police Mission to alert Greek security to events on the Greeks' own turf. The British had a well-deserved reputation for having the best intelligence on all groups in Greece. The Mission, dispatched to Greece by Foreign Minister Ernest Bevin in 1945, had evolved to far greater scope than its original mandate of training, organizing, and equipping Greek policemen. "The instruments of British policy in Greece today," said *The New Statesman and Nation* on February 1, 1947, "are the Police, Army and Economic Missions. Their directives and policies are carried out by Greek police chiefs and Ministers of Supply who seek to sustain the fiction that the policies which they enunciate are their own . . . the position of the British Missions is strong since it is to Anglo-American aid alone that Greece looks for her economic rehabilitation."

The role of the British Police and Military Missions as "instruments of British policy" in Greece continued well past the commitment of American aid in 1947. Britain had the expertise, the colonial experience, and the infrastructure to retain an influence it deemed a vital part of her foreign policy: a strong presence in the Mediterranean. After 1947, London and Washington were meant to ride the Greek horse together, but America conspicuously lacked what Britain excelled in: experience. Most American diplomats and intelligence agents in their early days in Greece deferred to their more seasoned British colleagues and looked to them for leadership. British troops remained in Greece until 1954.

The pervasive influence of the British Police Mission in Greece can in part be attributed to the man under whose command the fifty Scotland Yard agents served. Heading the Mission was Sir Charles Wickham, whose six-foot-two frame and majestic bearing gave the impression of a far younger man than his close to seventy years. Wickham was a product of Harrow and the Royal Military College at Sandhurst. On Wickham's team were some of the London Metropolitan Police Force's most senior officers. The much decorated Sir Charles had previously served the Empire with distinction in Ulster, where he was also police chief, as well as in Siberia and South Africa.

One area where Sir Charles was less than energetic was the purging of ultra-right-wing former Nazi collaborators from the Greek police and gendarmerie, though the British had promised to do this under the 1945 Treaty of Varkiza (the agreement following the so-called Battle of Athens in December 1944, under which the leftist ELAS guerrillas were to disarm and cede control of three-fourths of Greece in exchange for promises of legal recognition, free elections, freedom from prosecution for combatants, as well as the purge of Axis collaborators from the police and military. The agreement was honored mostly in the breach). In its February 1, 1947, article, *The New Statesman and Nation* reported: "After one and a half years' work by the British Military and Police Missions . . . Greece remains the one country in Europe, outside Spain, whose Army contains in positions of authority a greater number of ex pro-Nazis and collaborators than those identified with the Resistance."

How precisely did it happen that Sir Charles Wickham, holder of the French Légion d'Honneur and the Order of the Crown of Italy, member of the exclusive Army and Navy Club on London's austere Pall Mall, became entangled with a bunch of Royalist roughnecks whose trade was murder? The answer is as old as the Acropolis: political expediency.

A group like X and its many offshoots, such as the Organization of the Port of Piraeus, received large grants from the nervous wealthy of Athens. They had the most to lose from widespread public anger and from the prospect of a leftist or even a centrist government. These currents—anti-Communist, monarchist, nationalist, and capitalist—fostered an alliance between army and police and politicians like Tsaldaris, who had thugs to do their dirty work.

The military and police had been in the forefront of the official campaign against Communism. Their men were the primary targets of Communist reprisals. Leftist guerrillas commonly executed captured policemen. Many members of the military and police belonged to X, as did five hundred gendarmes in Salonika alone.

More or less passively observing these unsavory alliances were the British Military and Police Missions. Sharing an anti-leftist bias, they did little to restrain the excesses of their Greek proxies. Some of them, in fact, could be just as cold-blooded.

Nor did the British have any illusions about the men they were keeping in power. They did not feel, however, that they had the luxury of choice. In many ways the British had nurtured these underworld figures from the start. The British had backed Napoleon Zervas, the head of the EDES right-wing guerrillas (dissolved during 1944), during both the occupation and the civil war. Zervas, one of the targets of Polk's *Harper's* article, the same Zervas who had danced that acrobatic jig with Mrs. Tsaldaris, made no secret of his fascist tendencies.

C. M. Woodhouse, the British commander of the Allied Military Mission in Greece, called Zervas "a questionable character" but "ours."

Constantine Tsaldaris' loyalty to London superseded his more tenuous connection to Washington. A secret telegram from British Ambassador Clifford Norton to the Foreign Office on May 8, 1948, makes that plain: "Tsaldaris knows he is disliked by the Americans and indicated that his first loyalty is still to Great Britain."

British diplomats, unlike their American colleagues, were at least clear-eyed about the dangers of such alliances. A year before Polk's murder, Sir Reginald Leeper, British Ambassador in Athens at the time, cabled: "The right is the only guarantee of a pro-British foreign policy in Greece. . . . But the real problem . . . is not only that their leaders are very second-rate . . . but also that they are controlled by forces outside their party."

18

Room 25 of Salonika's Astoria Hotel was a room like thousands of others in second-class hotels around the world, impersonal and meager. A building of no particular architectural distinction, the Astoria had several dozen rooms favored by the overnight trade to Salonika. The rooms were stale with human traffic, providing only beds and the barest necessities. Americans, particularly visiting journalists, preferred the more picturesque Mediterranean Hotel on the bay.

George Polk was not staying at the Astoria by choice. The military information officer at the Salonika airport had booked the room for him when Polk found that his plane could not continue on to Kavalla that day because the Kavalla airport was closed. The Astoria Hotel's usual clientele consisted primarily of Greek officers. Unlike at other hotels in the security-tight city of Salonika, the Astoria's front door was left open all night to accommodate their comings and goings.

Room 25 featured a narrow bed and a small desk facing a window looking out on Agias Sofias Street. Just around the corner, but out of sight, was the great curving bay which lapped the city with its remarkable blue water.

Polk had not come to Salonika to keep an appointment. He was there really by chance, or so he thought. Being the sort of reporter he was, he made the most of the diversion in his itinerary. He asked anybody with an inside track—diplomats, military men, and colleagues—for contacts to the Communists. Salonika was a good place for that, the first stop on the underground railroad to the mountains.

Sometime during Polk's two-day stay in the Astoria, Kourtessis or one of his men made contact with him. By 9:30 a.m. on Saturday, Polk had made appointments for both Saturday and Sunday evenings, appointments he told no one about but whose existence was indicated by his turning down other invitations.

Polk left a meeting with Gerald Drew of the United Nations Special Committee on the Balkans at 8:15 p.m., Saturday, May 8. He told Rupert Prohme of the USIS that he was busy both Saturday and Sunday evenings but was free to have dinner with him on Monday night. Someone had asked Polk to save both nights, perhaps to leave room in case the plans misfired Saturday night; possibly also to prevent anyone from raising an alarm too soon.

Polk had made a lunch date with an old friend, Waide Condon, of the embassy in Athens, for Monday. He was clearly not expecting to make the long, hazardous trek to the mountains before then, for as Homer Bigart found out from personal experience a few weeks later, such a trip takes at least a week. He was not expecting much at all really, as he made plain in his last letter to Ed Murrow. He had also asked Rea to join him in Kavalla in the middle of the following week.

On Saturday evening, over a dinner of lobster and peas, he met the conspirators. He must have thought they were Communists, but in fact they were in the pay of the Royalists. As a subsequent secret investigation revealed, Kourtessis earlier that week had picked the men, the place, even the menu, which was chosen to suit an American's tastes. Evidence also indicates that Kourtessis returned to Salonika a few days after the crime and then melted back into the impenetrable shelter of the Piraeus underworld.

Between them, Kourtessis and Mouscoundis had a large pool of killers to choose from. A Greek Communist looked no different from a Greek Royalist. The deception was made easier by the fact that many security policemen either had themselves once been on the other side or had a brother or a cousin who had "gone to the mountains." That is in the nature of a civil war.

As for the killers, all they needed to know of Polk was that he was hell-bent on getting to the Communists. There was no need for any of them to know the American reporter had information that would expose the leader of their party for what he was: crooked, selfish, and stupid. It was enough for them to have been told that Polk wanted to give the Communists, their loathed enemies, the chance to tell their version of the Greek Civil War to America. As MI6 agent Nigel Clive said: "If a Greek soldier knew Polk was on his way to see the Communists, well, that's what they had guns in their hands for." They also had orders from the highest authority to proceed with the job.

The assassins also had to speak English, as Polk's Greek was nonexistent. The American had to be made to feel at ease, for he was a tall, strapping man, short-tempered and combative. Polk, clearly relaxed, consumed nearly three pounds of lobster at dinner. He had a few drinks. The precise location of the dinner has never been traced, but it had to have been in a private home. No one was to see the diners together. No one did.

Polk was not a heavy drinker, so they could not get him drunk enough to carry out their prearranged execution. Instead, as the conspirators were later to boast, they laced his drink with a reliable soporific.

At eleven o'clock, George was seen back in the Astoria. As was his habit, he undressed, put on his pajamas, and sat down at his typewriter, his hedge against loneliness in a claustrophobic hotel room. He wrote two letters. Neither letter ever reached its destination. The first was to Edward R. Murrow, and would later be used as a key piece of evidence, proof of Polk's fixed appointment with the guerrillas. A careful reading proves the opposite. He wrote Murrow:

> I wanted to get up to date on conditions here. Frankly one of my reasons for coming north has been to get into some kind of direct, really businesslike contact with the Markos government crowd. Since 1946, I've not had a contact with the Greek Communist Party that I believed was a real contact. Lots of persons have presented themselves to me claiming to speak authoritatively, but I think they were all phonies. So, with a contact through a contact, *I'd like to get in touch with persons who count.* If necessary, I'll go outside Salonika, to any other town or village "they" may designate. Most of us have done

an awful lot of talking and writing about the objectives of the Markos gang, and yet few of us have really factual information. I've worked since December on getting to Markos' headquarters . . . even blindfolded, if necessary. I'd like to put Markos on the air from his secret radio station. *I've offered to let them write the script on every word Markos says while I'll just give him cues* and do the translating. Then, when I come "outside" I'll be able to tell any story I care to. (I suspect the real hitch is that Markos' "secret" radio station is Radio Tirana or Radio Belgrade.)

The conspirators had succeeded in their masquerade. Polk was convinced that for the first time he was on the trail of "the real thing." But it is equally clear that he thought the process had only just begun. He had made them "an offer"; he was waiting for Markos' response. It would take some time for the details to be ironed out, for mutual confidence to be established.

The Greek government would use this unsent letter as their only solid proof that Polk was on his way to the mountains. They would also seize upon Polk's hyperbolic phrase, "even blindfolded, if necessary." When Polk's inert and bloated body was finally fished out of Salonika Bay, officials alleged, he was wearing a blindfold.

The other letter, still in his typewriter, was a chatty account of his activities to his mother. When shown the letter (which she was not allowed to keep), Adelaide thought it sounded as if he was just killing time, as he often did when he wrote her from strange places. It had no particular news to relate. He was counting the days until he went home. Polk, who always mailed letters the minute he finished them, no matter what the time of day, did not finish this one.

There was no sign of a struggle. By the time Polk's assassins came for him, the soporific must have taken effect. As he was dressed in pajamas, they grabbed his tweed sports coat, his khaki pants, shoes, and socks. Two men were required to carry Polk's inert body out of the room, but they did not have far to go. For this was one of the Astoria's desirable features: deep but compact laundry baskets on wheels full of clean or used laundry, scattered on every floor and available at all hours to accommodate the military clientele's erratic traffic. Within seconds they dropped Polk's body into a conveniently parked basket and pushed it the few steps to the small, old-fashioned elevator.

The killers blundered here. For though they carried Polk away in his pajamas, they failed to take his shaving kit or any of the tools a reporter would bring on a story. Polk, a fastidious man, would never leave on an overnight journey without at least his razor and probably a few other items. Nor would he set off for the biggest story of his life without his typewriter and his camera. His captors left all of this behind.

With piles of linen covering George Polk's motionless body, the men walked out of the Astoria into the quiet of a Salonika side street.

There, in the shelter of the alley behind the hotel, they quickly stripped him of his pajamas and dressed him in the shirt and trousers they had brought along. (The pajamas had to be disposed of by the killers. The cover story manufactured to account for them was one of the few flaws in an otherwise nearly flawless crime.)

Then one of them fired a single bullet at point-blank range, probably with the use of a silencer, into the back of Polk's slumped head.

Again the murderers erred. In too great haste, the executioner fired the fatal shot before they had put Polk's sports coat on. His shirt was both bloodstained and bullet-burned, but his sports coat was unmarked. Only one man, Waide Condon, called on to identify his friend's body, would make note of this oversight.

The men bound Polk's hands and feet with thick rope. They left enough space between his wrists and ankles, perhaps six or seven inches, to make it easy to carry his body the short way to the bay.

There was no one there to witness the assassins hauling the bleeding body across Nikis Street, unlit and deserted at this hour. Slowly and carefully they moved down the three or four narrow steps to the quay, then quickly heaved the body into the water, eerily quiet after midnight. George Polk was still breathing, though unconscious, when his own weight dragged him under the still surface.

19

On Monday, May 10, just before noon, a postman reached into the mailbox next to the White Tower, the last remnant of the ancient wall that once surrounded Salonika, and found the evidence around which the Greek government would build its murder case. It was an envelope addressed: "To 3d, the Third, Police Station, Salonika." The handwriting was rough.

Police chief Apostolos Xanthopoulos, to whom the postman personally delivered the envelope, found that it held George Polk's war correspondent's identification card and a Pan Am pocket calendar for the year 1948.

On May 12, the Associated Press Athens correspondent, Socrates Chakales, a Greek reporter with firm right-wing sympathies, punched this cable out on the world wire service:

> George Polk missing from hotel room in Salonika since last Sunday. Police saying Polk making effort to contact guerrillas. Press Minister confirmed this, adding not unusual for American correspondents to be out of contact for a week. American Information Service officer in Athens said Polk planning to make direct contact with guerrilla forces. From Salonika, American Consulate and Greek military security officials are searching northern Greece for Polk. Security officials began investigation several days ago after Salonika police received by mail U.S. war correspondent's credentials.

Minutes later, CBS's Dave Taylor sent his own uneasy query to the Foreign Press Section of the Greek Foreign Ministry in Athens:

"Can you tell us anything further? How and where is Mrs. George Polk?"

Mrs. George Polk was already in Salonika. Following her husband's telegram of the previous Saturday, she had booked herself on a flight to Kavalla, where he had told her to meet him. Her flight, like his, was diverted from Kavalla, with its still-flooded airfield, to Salonika.

It was the first time since they met that her husband had failed to meet her plane.

Deciding to check at the hotel where Polk had been staying, she took a taxi to the Astoria. She was stunned by the state of her husband's room. Polk's typewriter, without which he seldom moved, sat on the little desk, with an unfinished letter to his mother still in it. His razor, toothbrush, and toothpaste were scattered on the bathroom shelf, but oddly his pajamas were not on the door hook. The narrow bed was tightly made.

Rea felt panic tighten in her chest. She would not allow that feeling to take root. She dropped her small bag and began to plan for her husband's imminent return. He will need some hot water for a shave, she informed the desk clerk. Please have some sent up. He nodded laconically and told her once more that Polk had not been seen since Saturday night.

She had to keep moving, keep ducking the dark thoughts. She walked the short distance to the American Consulate in search of a familiar face and some reassuring words. Waide Condon was there to supply both. A tall, avuncular figure with horn-rimmed glasses and a thick salt-and-pepper mustache, the former Salt Lake City publisher turned USIS officer in Athens greeted her warmly.

"Don't you worry, Mrs. Polk." He smiled and patted her hand. "I've known your husband since Washington days, and I know as well as you do he knows how to look after himself. Probably got that big interview he's been working so hard for. The big scoop he's going to take home with him."

"Yes. I'm sure that's what happened," Rea said, relieved to be in the company of an American official who did not seem to regard her husband with any hostility.

Condon had been recruited by USIS to smooth relations between the embassy and the American press corps. It was a shrewd choice. A man of proven anti-Communist sentiments, he also had good relations with many of the reporters. Unlike Karl Rankin, he did not regard newspeople as dangerous.

"But he said to meet him on Wednesday," Rea began, her fears resurfacing.

"Well, he stood me up, too," Condon said evenly. "We had a lunch date here on Monday, and I haven't heard from him in three days. That means he's on that story."

"But I don't understand why his typewriter is still on the table with a half-written letter to his mother still in it. That's just not like George. He wouldn't think of going anywhere without his typewriter. And, Mr. Condon"—Rea's voice broke—"George has a habit of writing letters late in the night, and no matter whether it's two or three in the morning he goes out and mails them. . . . And why didn't he take his razor or his toothbrush?"

"A typewriter can be a bulky thing, you know. Now, why don't you leave a note for him and come home with me and meet my wife, Geneal. Have some dinner with us. We've got our fourteen-year-old son, Michael, here, too."

Rea shook her head. "I want to wait for him in the hotel. He might be back any minute," she said, wild hope momentarily supplanting despair.

By now Condon was also worried, though he would continue to soothe Rea's fears for three more days.

Rea was struggling to convince herself that Polk had left this hotel room abruptly on the trail of a big story, possibly the exclusive interview with General Markos he had been so eager to arrange. She did not want the consulate or anyone to interfere with her husband's pursuit of the story. On her first night in the Astoria, she received a call from Gregory Staktopoulos, who asked to interview her on the subject of Polk's disappearance. She put him off. Gregory Staktopoulos was one of the few Greek reporters in Salonika with a strong command of English. In his late thirties, Staktopoulos had once been a diligent, if unimaginative, student at the prestigious Anatolia College, an American institution set in the gentle hills behind Salonika. Greg, as he was called by his American teachers, was a scholarship student amidst the sons of Salonika's privileged families. The only son of a widow from Turkish-occupied Smyrna, he knew he would eventually have to support his mother and two sisters. His brother had been killed in World War I.

Staktopoulos had spent approximately five minutes in George Polk's company. AP reporter Helen Mamas had introduced them on the evening of May 7. Mamas, a Greek-American from Worcester, Massachusetts, relied on the ever-helpful Greg Staktopoulos to keep her apprised of anything he filed for Reuters, the British news agency, which was his other employer.

He had not, however, accepted her invitation to join the group of reporters avidly listening to the CBS correspondent at the bar of the Mediterranean Hotel. The man known to his teachers at Anatolia College as "such a good boy" never took a drink.

Now his paper had assigned him to cover the story of George Polk's disappearance.

More and more agitated, Rea left Waide Condon's office to look for Helen Mamas at the Mediterranean Hotel, where she had been told a UN conference on child abduction was in session. Though Rea found Mamas' views affected by her right-wing journalist fiancé, she remembered her as warm and friendly. Polk had introduced the two women to each other in Athens.

Also covering the UN meeting was the courteous and carefully dressed reporter from *Makedonia*. "My friend and competitor, Gregory Staktopoulos," Helen Mamas introduced him to Rea. Staktopoulos asked about her husband. Rea had already put him off once, but it had been easier on the telephone.

"He has only just gone to Kavalla," Rea lied to the reporter, half wishing to convince herself, half wanting to safeguard what she hoped was Polk's exclusive. "There is really nothing to report. He hasn't disappeared. He hasn't gone to the mountains." She declined his repeated requests for an interview.

Rea returned to the Astoria and found the room untouched. Polk had not returned. Keeping hope alive was becoming a greater act of will than she could muster. Before fleeing again from the dismal place, she wrote a note: "I have just gone out for coffee. Please stay in the room and don't ring up or see anyone before you see me. *It's important.*"

She had to alert him to the police suspicions that he had been "to the other side." He had to have an explanation ready about how he had spent the last few days. She knew how much this story meant to him. She would do everything to make sure the authorities didn't prevent him from getting it out.

In the early-morning hours of May 13, she had finally drifted off to a restless sleep when the door of Room 25 was suddenly flung open.

"Security!" three men barked at her, flipping on the bright ceiling light. Sitting bolt upright, Rea froze.

"You know where he is," one of the men insisted.

"Tell us what you know. He left a message for you, didn't he?" Rea could not find her voice.

"No, nothing," she whispered finally. "I know nothing." They searched the room and, finding nothing, left Rea shaking in silent convulsions.

Having lived through the occupation and now several rounds of civil war, she felt she could recognize Greek police, even out of uniform, and she was convinced these men were police.

The following day, Don Matchan, the young reporter who had last seen Polk in the bar of the Mediterranean on Saturday night, called on Rea. He told her there were new rumors around town. "Somebody's put out the word that George had a nervous breakdown."

Rea, listening intently, nodded. "He was not in good shape physically, it's true. Before he left he said to me, 'This time I'm not going to stop any bullets, honey.' Still . . ." She shook her head.

"Well, the other story going around is that he shot himself," Matchan said, avoiding the woman's eyes.

"Impossible," Rea blurted out without a moment's pause. "A lie. George would never do that."

"No, of course not," Matchan agreed hastily.

On Friday, May 14, Raleigh Gibson, the consul general, sent this telegram to Secretary of State Marshall:

George Polk CBS correspondent still missing. All government organizations searching northern Greece. Greek official opinion is that Polk endeavoring to contact Markos. Mrs. Polk in Salonika, requested consulate to take no further action for time being.

Rea's days were now spent in a trancelike state, as rumors about Polk swirled and as her terror at the prospect of more nighttime intruders mounted. Yet she dared not change hotels, for the Astoria was where Polk was last seen, and to where he might return.

At daybreak on Sunday morning, Mr. and Mrs. Waide Condon were awakened by shrill cries beneath their window in the American Consulate building on the bay. The cries were not of alarm but of shock and horror.

"*Ine enas pnigmenos!*" someone shouted down below. "It's a drowned man!" A body, with only the head visible, bobbed gently on the surface. A fisherman tried to lift it into his little boat, but it was much too heavy. Finally, he tied a rope around the corpse's right arm and, with agonizing effort, rowed his way back to shore.

The binoculars of the harbormaster, George Tzirides, had been trained on the fisherman ever since he spotted something on the water's surface. Very little that happened in the bay escaped Tzirides' binoculars during the civil war. Now he signaled the fisherman to pull up alongside the harbormaster's dock. Soon Tzirides ordered a half dozen men to wade into the shallow, murky water and tug the bloated body to shore.

"Call Mouscoundis," Tzirides instructed one of his men. It was clear to him this was a case for Salonika's security chief.

To the Americans, several stories above the harbor, still oblivious to the gruesome scene unfolding in the water below, the voices had the violent edge of swearing.

Giving up on sleep, the Condons got up, and Geneal went to make coffee. Then the telephone rang. "Major Nicholas Mouscoundis calling. Mr. Condon, George Polk has been found dead. His body just washed ashore at the wharf in front of the British Consulate." The Greek spoke matter-of-factly. "The corpse was tied to a rowboat and towed to the harbor. He has been shot. We understand he was a friend of yours. We would like you to come to the morgue and identify the body."

"So that's what all those cries were about. They found George's body right under our window." Geneal Condon gasped. Waide threw on some clothes and left for the Salonika city morgue for one of the most dispiriting tasks any human being can be called on to perform. Condon would never be able to obliterate the memory of his friend's partially decomposed body.

The coroner, oblivious to Condon's pain, made him wait until they pumped out the contents of George's stomach to find out what he had last eaten and when. Lobster and peas, concluded Dr. Constantine Eliakis, consumed less than an hour before he was killed. But Condon barely heard. He rushed from the awful yellow room with its inhuman stench, to be sick in the coroner's bathroom.

"Death from drowning," Dr. Eliakis was saying crisply when Condon returned to the stainless-steel table. Shot fired by small-caliber revolver or pistol, point-blank range at back of head, but still breathing when thrown into the bay seven days before. . . . No sign of struggle. . . . Robbery ruled out. All of Polk's valuables, including several hundred dollars in traveler's checks, thirty dollars in drachmas, a gold wedding ring inscribed "Rea Cocconis 9.11.47," and keys, were still in his pocket. . . . Deposits of cuttlefish eggs on the soles of his shoes and the folds of the rope showed the body had been motionless on the sandy bottom of the harbor for at least one week.

Dr. Eliakis immediately wrote an eleven-page autopsy report. Quite unusually, the report referred not only to the condition of the corpse but to the specifics of the crime, impossible to have deduced from the autopsy itself.

The crime, the report noted, "took place in a rowboat. . . . The victim was fired upon first, then bound . . . because there were no signs of a preceding struggle." Thus the autopsy itself did its part in establishing the official version of the murder of George Polk.

The report, dated May 16, 1948, was, in the words of Consul General Raleigh Gibson, "considered by the Greek officials and the officials of the British Police Mission in Salonika to be scientifically correct." This is the first official mention of the British Police Mission's involvement in the case.

Subsequently, not a step in the murder investigation would be taken by either Greek or American officials without British supervision. Nor would any American official question this acute interest on the part of London's officers in the field. It was their turf, after all; they had the expertise and the background.

Mouscoundis later asked Condon to break the news of her husband's death to Rea Polk. Condon refused.

A stranger, a policeman barely feigning sympathy and sorrow, informed Rea she was now a widow. Overcome by anger and grief, Rea told him to get out of her room. Then, exhausted from seven days of torturous anxiety, she collapsed into a state that was neither sleep nor wakefulness. Later, she could not recall how she had spent the first hours after the policeman's visit.

Raleigh Gibson sent word to George Polk's employer, CBS News, via the State Department: "Please inform the Columbia Broadcasting System George Polk's body washed ashore in Salonika Bay. Foul play indicated. Further details to follow."

It was three o'clock in the morning on May 17 when the telephone rang in the St. Louis home of Adelaide Polk's sister. Adelaide picked it up, for she had been sleeping on the living-room couch next to the phone for seven days, ever since George was reported missing.

The voice at the other end of the line was that of CBS correspondent George Herman. He was no longer trying to sound upbeat. She knew immediately what he had to tell her. "They have found George, Mrs. Polk. I'm sorry, but he is dead."

There was nothing more to say. The terrible details would wait. She wanted as much as he did to get off the phone fast. She wanted to be finished with her crying before daybreak so she could start making plans to return to Athens.

Polk had long ago told her he wanted to be buried wherever he died. She would lay him to rest in Athens, where he had found some happiness. She wanted him out of Salonika.

20

———

Major Mouscoundis wasted no time in compiling a three-page confidential report, which he made available to American officials. "Mrs. Polk arrived in Salonika on the 12th of May," the report stated. "She expressed no alarm over the disappearance of Mr. Polk, letting it be known as late as the morning of the 16th that Mr. Polk would return safely from his interview with General Markos."

Further on in the police report, Mouscoundis alleged: "The chief of police in Athens stated to a confidential informant that Mr. Polk quarreled with his wife on the evening of his departure from Athens, and that two of her relatives are members of the Communist Party . . ."

"Among the facts of the case are the following: Polk's arms and legs were tied prior to the murder. His legs were loosely tied, allowing him sufficient movement to take only short steps. During the 1944 disorders in Greece, the Communists had their prisoners tied similarly. . . ."

Those among his colleagues who knew George Polk even slightly found this the most preposterous "fact" of all. Polk, a man of proven courage, eternally wary, was not a man to let anyone bind his ankles, loosely or otherwise, without a fierce struggle.

Like an incantation, the police began to repeat this point over and over. George Polk's was a "Communist-style murder."

"Mr. Polk was shot at the base of the cranium, the occipital bond, and the bullet emerged from his head at the left nasal cavity. Similar method of execution was employed by the Communists in Greece against German collaborators, thus ensuring death and conserving ammunition."

The next day, the news was splashed across the front pages of many of the world's major newspapers. In those overheated, suspicious times, each article revealed much about its author, and something about the publication.

A. C. Sedgwick of the New York *Times*, called the "unofficial spokesman of the Greek right" by his colleagues, advanced the official version even further, writing:

> The police also stated, in reply to questions from the United States, British, and local authorities, that they had received information that Mr. Polk was on his way to make contact with the guerrillas. Mr. Polk left Athens a little more than a week ago, having kept the purpose of his visit to Salonika a secret. However, friends said that they had gathered from conversations with him that he intended to visit the headquarters of the guerrilla chief, Gen. Markos Vafiades, "for a story" and that he thought Salonika the best place from which to start. This morning, before the news of his death became known, the Athens press reporting his absence voiced the opinion that he had gone to report on bandit activity from the bandit side. . . . A late message from Salonika to this correspondent suggested that perhaps Mr. Polk had not been able to prove his good faith to the Communists with whom he had made contact and that, suspicious of his errand, they had killed him.

Time reduced the murder of a respected American journalist to a typically pithy formulation: "After two years as chief Middle East correspondent for CBS, he was ready to go home. But first he wanted a feather in his cap: an interview with Communist guerrilla chief Markos."

Newsweek, on the other hand, displayed a balance that seems almost brazen given the political climate of those times.

> At first Greek police pictured Polk's death as accidental; finally gave out details that spelled murder. Then they sought to picture Polk as a victim of a Communist death trap while

en route via the underground to get an interview with Gen. Markos, leader of the Communist-backed Greek guerrillas now fighting the Athens regime. But behind him George Polk left evidence disputing this theory.

Polk, like such reporters as Homer Bigart of the New York *Herald Tribune*, . . . had seen much to find fault with in Greek officialdom. For broadcasting and writing the news as he saw it, Polk, like Bigart, . . . had been smeared as a Red himself by the right-wing, pro-government press . . . had found his work hampered by red tape, intimidation, and obstruction by Athens officials. In talks with his colleagues in Greece, in letters to his younger brother, William Polk, and to Drew Pearson and numerous other newsmen in the States, George Polk left a record of death threats he had received. None, from the evidence, were from the left.

On May 17, one day after George Polk's body was retrieved from Salonika Bay, Ed Murrow's listeners were startled by the very personal grief which shaded every word of his broadcast:

And now this reporter would attempt to say something about George Polk. He is dead. His body, hands and feet tied with twine, a bullet hole in his head, was taken from Salonika harbor yesterday. He had been missing for one week.

George Polk had been for more than two years the chief Middle East correspondent for the Columbia Broadcasting System. It is believed that he had gone from Athens to Salonika for the purpose of arranging an interview with the guerrilla leader, General Markos, although precise information on this point is lacking. The police in Salonika have said that they are hunting for "suspected Communists" with whom Mr. Polk might have been in contact in his efforts to interview the guerrilla leader. According to the Associated Press, twenty or more Communists have been questioned. The record does not show that any non-Communists have been questioned. The Premier of Greece has ordered the entire police force of the country to uncover details of the murder. One leading government spokesman, who declined to allow the use of his name, stated, "We are one thousand percent sure it was the work of Communists." He offered no support for this statement.

Polk, in common with many other good American correspondents, was not popular with the Greek government. Such men as Raymond Daniell of the New York *Times*, Seymour Freidin of the New York *Herald Tribune*, Robert Vermilion of the United Press, Homer Bigart of the *Herald Tribune*, and Constantine Hadjiargyris of the *Christian Science Monitor* have all been attacked either openly or by indirection as Communists or "pinks." This is a device that is frequently used in Europe and is not altogether unknown in this country.

As far back as February 3, George Polk, in a private letter, said there were a number of vague hints that "somebody is likely to get hurt." But he was inclined to think then that it was more likely that correspondents writing material critical of the present regime in Athens might be framed on some black market charge as an excuse to expel them from the country.

There is nothing in the record to show that Polk feared physical violence, either from the Communists or from the right-wing government forces. Indeed, his whole record shows that he didn't fear anything. This was a reporter who had worked in half a dozen capitals and flown both fighters and bombers for the Navy during the war, was wounded in the Solomons and decorated for bravery.

George Polk had that honesty and integrity, the reverence for fact and indifference to criticism, which gave him the respect of the men in his trade.

Since this reporter returned to broadcasting nine months ago, much of the material about the Middle East, and particularly about Greece, carried on this program came from Polk. Invariably it was clean, hard copy, well documented. And his stories stood up, every last one of them. He spared neither the corruption, inefficiency, and petty political maneuvering of the Greek government, nor the vacillation of American foreign policy, nor the atrocities, committed by the Communists. What happened he reported, without fear and in language that all could understand.

And now that he is dead, the question is not whether he might have had cause to fear the Greek government or the Communists. The question is: Who killed him? And that would seem to be a matter with which our government might concern itself with full vigor.

Certain it is that you have lost one of the ablest, most conscientious and courageous reporters who has ever served you.

21

The great promenade along the bay was filled each evening with Salonikans out for their accustomed stroll. For an hour or so they abandoned their multigenerational dwellings and went to Nikis Street to peer into the luxury hotels, the restaurants, and the consulates flying the flags of the great powers—the British, the American, and the French.

Waide and Geneal Condon and their son Michael wove their way among the promenaders. It was the day Polk's body had surfaced and the Condons were physically and emotionally depleted. The family settled in the ornate comfort of the Majestic Hotel's dining room. Finished with a meal of seafood, Waide leaned back to savor his cup of strong Greek coffee and tried to block out thoughts of his friend under the coroner's scalpel.

"Good evening, Mr. and Mrs. Condon," a dark-suited Greek bent down and whispered. "I am instructed to tell you to please leave this restaurant by the back door."

"What the hell . . . ?" Condon looked up. "We're Americans and we're not about to leave till we're good and ready. And then we'll leave the way we came in. By the front door. No matter who you are."

An angry flush spread up from his throat as he returned to his coffee and pretended to ignore the Greek who stood quietly beside his chair.

"I am a security agent," the man answered evenly, as if that were explanation enough. "We know who you are and I have been directed to advise you that you are in danger if you leave by the front door."

"What the hell is this all about?" Condon roared again, now

causing heads to turn. "At least you can tell me what this is about."

"It is because you are now involved in the Polk case," the agent whispered. "You were called to identify the body and that makes you a material witness."

"Where is Mrs. Polk?" Geneal Condon asked suddenly, realizing that if they were in danger, surely the widow was at far greater risk.

"I really can't say." The man sounded a bit less patient now. They were asking for more than he was instructed to deal with.

"Who is looking after her? Who is with her?" Mrs. Condon demanded.

"She is at her hotel and in the company of newspaper people," he said irritably. "But I suggest you heed my warning now, and leave by the back door." Then he was gone.

The Condons sat motionless for a time. How had they become entangled in a murder that left them stunned and horrified but that they had nothing to do with? For that was the agent's meaning, that they themselves were somehow guilty by association. But of what crime?

Moving like the blind, but suddenly feeling exposed, the three Americans made their way out of the restaurant, by the back exit.

"I'm going to find that poor girl," Geneal Condon, a woman of unusual spirit and courage, announced once they were outside. "What if it were Pat, Waide?" she asked her husband, referring to their own daughter, who was roughly Rea's age.

Tying a scarf around her hair, Geneal followed the dark back streets from the Majestic to the Astoria. She found Rea still in Room 25, but not alone.

"Leave me alone, leave me alone," the young widow moaned into her pillow while a dozen reporters crowded around her. "Leave me alone. I've told you everything I know," she sobbed. They wrote down every word she uttered.

"Get out of here!" Mrs. Condon shouted at them. "All of you. This minute. Why are you torturing this poor girl with her husband lying dead in the morgue? If you don't clear out in just one minute I am going to call the American Consul and the police and between them they will clear you out!" She was shouting at the top of her lungs, and the Salonika newspapermen, who had never seen an American woman in this state before, were temporarily stunned. Then they left.

"I am Geneal Condon," she said softly, turning to Rea. "Waide's wife. He was a friend of your husband and I've come to look after you." Moved by the young woman's youth and vulnerability, she put her arms around her.

Rea now spilled out all her pain and her darkest suspicions to this kind, unexpected visitor. "Please don't leave me. You are the first person to show any kindness since . . ."

"I won't leave you for a minute, dear," Geneal said.

To distract Rea, Geneal told her about her own family in Utah. About her daughter, who was Rea's age and had recently given birth to Geneal's first grandchild. Rea said her husband's family was from Texas, which brought back thoughts of George and fresh sobs.

"I will talk to you because you are so kind. But I will never talk to anyone else," Rea finally said, anger supplanting pain. "They can threaten to kill me, I won't say a word to them," she insisted, spitting out the word "them."

"I will never repeat anything you tell me," Geneal replied. "Not a word. If I am asked, I shall say, 'I don't know any more than you know; Rea has not told me anything more.' "

Until her death more than thirty years later, Geneal Condon revealed her new friend's confidences only to her husband and to her diary.

"The Communists did not kill him," Rea said after a while with icy calm. "He would only have put Markos on the air and let him tell his side of the story to the world." Rea, physically and emotionally exhausted, soon fell into a deep sleep, her first in over a week. Geneal spent the night in a chair by Rea's bed.

The next morning a Greek newspaper was delivered. It carried the banner headline: "REA POLK SAYS HER HUSBAND WAS INSANE."

"Oh my God!" Rea screamed. "Those lying bastards. I never said anything like that."

"Well, can you think of what you said that might have led them to that conclusion?" Geneal asked.

"They asked me everything about George. How I met him. How long we had been married. Was it a happy marriage? I didn't think any of it was their business, but I just wanted them to get out, so I answered all of them. Then they asked me if George had a bad temper. I said, 'Yes, he did. He got mad at me lots of times.' . . . Oh," she moaned in sudden comprehension. "I was speaking English, for the Americans. But there were many Greeks, some French among them, you see. They must have looked up 'mad' . . . found 'insane' . . ." Geneal was already on the telephone, urging her husband to demand a retraction from the newspaper and to send a telegram to Rea's father and mother.

A knock at the door jolted both women. "Major Mouscoundis," the man announced himself. He came bearing George's gold watch and wallet with all its contents and to ask Rea a few more questions. "All I know," Rea replied, "is that he was going to see Markos and someone killed him before he could get there." But Rea had a question of her own. What happened to the telephone and address book and the notepad, as much fixtures on George's person as his wristwatch? The major shook his head. They were gone.

After he left, Rea turned to Geneal. "Do you see what I mean? The Communists couldn't have killed him. They could have used everything in his pockets. They need money to buy food and guns. All they need to do is step over the border and buy them in Bulgaria. They need every drachma they can get their hands on."

Geneal Condon, fresh from the American heartland, her anti-Communism as bred in her bones as her patriotism, was troubled and confused. The longer she stayed with Rea, the more convinced she became that the widow, young and naïve as she was, was probably correct in her assumption that the right and not the left had murdered her husband.

"And his pajamas are gone," Rea blurted out suddenly, as though grasping the final piece of missing evidence. "George would never leave his razor behind and take his pajamas. Geneal," she said, her voice dropping to one decibel above a whisper, "he was murdered in this room. He was killed right here. Not shot, because there wasn't any blood, and somebody might have heard, but it happened here. They had to destroy his pajamas, which told a tale . . . that's why they haven't been found."

After four nights with Rea, Geneal decided the widow was in stable enough condition to be left on her own for a night. Besides, Mrs. Condon missed her husband and son. "I'll be fine," Rea assured her as she was leaving. "I'll just write some letters to George's sisters and then go to sleep."

Before Rea was allowed to return to Athens with her husband's coffin, she faced hours of grueling questioning by Major Mouscoundis. The widow held her ground, stubbornly refusing to sign any document claiming that Polk fell into a Communist trap.

In frustration and anger, Mouscoundis bellowed at her, "We will never allow a person to lower the government of Greece by writing against it. Never."

The newspapers faithfully reflected the government's hostility toward the widow. In an article a few weeks later, the right-wing paper *Phos* stated: "It has been ascertained that Polk had a quarrel with his wife prior to his departure for Salonika. Mrs. Polk's indifference is unexplained. She did not worry when told her husband disappeared or when the body was found. She spoke without much sympathy and said her husband became 'mad' due to neurasthenia from wounds he received in a plane crash in Palestine. Among his friends, police are due to question Mr. Hadjiargyris, correspondent for the *Christian Science Monitor*, to whom Polk entrusted his office."

On May 17, following a briefing by Commander Gordon of the British Police Mission in Salonika, Frank Macaskie filed a short piece for *The Times* of London. "Polk is known to have expressed a desire to visit the headquarters of the Communist rebels, and some disinterested foreign experts believe that he may have done this and been murdered afterwards by Communists for reasons of security. The truth of the matter will probably never be known."

Even on the chaotic Greek scene, for a reporter to conclude, one day after his colleague's body was retrieved from the bay, that Polk's killers would never be found is a staggering piece of defeatism.

That same week, a different version of the Polk murder was broadcast by Don Hollenbeck. On "CBS Views the Press," Hollenbeck regretted the absence from Greece of Homer Bigart, in Belgrade, Hollenbeck noted, attempting from there to arrange the Markos interview George Polk had failed to achieve.

> In absenting himself from Greece at this particular time, Mr. Bigart has lost touch with one of the most important stories to come out of Greece recently: "Who Killed George Polk? And Why?"
>
> Knowing Homer Bigart's devotion to the truth, one misses his reports on a story where the truth is so difficult to isolate. . . .
>
> George Polk did not die to become a martyr or a rallying cry for any politician of whatever complexion. George Polk died because he was trying to find out the truth. In this case, he had indicated he wanted to get an interview with the leader of the Greek guerrilla forces; as he had told a friend, we've had lots of secondhand reports about what those people are doing, and he'd like to get the facts for himself. If the facts had been critical of the Communists, George Polk would have so reported them. If the facts had been critical of the Greek government, George Polk would have so reported them. He was an apologist for nobody.
>
> The survival of truth and the free flow of news are at stake. In these days when more and more obstacles are put in the paths of reporters who are trying to learn the truth, and to communicate that truth to readers and listeners, the murder of a good reporter is more than the death of one man. It is the murder of truth, and truth is having enough trouble surviving these days.

To Hollenbeck and his CBS colleagues the murder was a death in the family. John Donovan, the feisty Irishman who covered the Middle East for NBC, returned to New York to press CBS into action.

Ed Murrow, prone to dark moods, had rarely seemed so embittered. A letter to Murrow from Polk's colleague Ray Daniell did not help. Daniell wrote:

It was a little like old times to hear your voice on the phone last night. At this distance, of course, it is difficult to form an intelligent opinion about Polk's death. However, there is one thought which I can't escape. That is, that if he were really going to try to make contact with Markos, it seems to me that there would be little motive for the rebel conducting officers to murder him. On the other hand, if he had made contact with the rebels and the X-ists or the other right-wing groups discovered it, they would be very likely to liquidate him . . . I think there is little chance of anything coming of the government investigation.

Howard K. Smith and Eric Sevareid immediately volunteered to fly to Athens on behalf of CBS, to begin an independent investigation. CBS turned both down, saying their friendship with Polk would color their objectivity. Winston Burdett, CBS Rome correspondent, who did not personally know Polk, and a member of his bureau, Peter Tomkins, were dispatched instead.

Burdett, a Harvard-educated New Yorker, was a careful and thorough reporter, a talented, albeit troubled, figure. It would be years before CBS News and the rest of the world would learn the heavy freight Burdett was carrying in those days.

In 1955, subpoenaed by the Senate Internal Security Subcommittee, Burdett admitted under tough interrogation that he had been a member of the Communist Party from 1937 until 1942. He revealed to the world and to his stunned colleagues that he had engaged in espionage activities during the early war years. Married at the time to an Italian partisan and Communist Party member named Leah Schiavi, by 1948 he had severed all connections to the Party.

Burdett had more than the usual cause for disenchantment with Communism. He had recently been forced to confront the fact that his wife had in all likelihood been assassinated by Russian agents in northern Iran. While there on a Party mission, Leah had accidentally discovered a Soviet training camp for Communist guerrillas.

During Burdett's agonizing session under the hot television lights of the Eastland committee, the CBS reporter revealed the names of other pro-Soviet correspondents, including his CBS colleague Alexander Kendrick.

"I have learned to understand what Joseph Stalin stood for," Howard K. Smith later noted, "but I can't for the life of me figure out Winston."

CBS's Peter Tomkins, a former OSS agent with mettle to match his healthy appetite for life, was unencumbered by ideology and burning with outrage at a colleague's brutal death.

Tomkins had an idea. He would maneuver an interview with the guerrillas. Trained in the cloak-and-dagger arts during his OSS days, he would make his way to the mountains through Albania, see Markos, and come out alive, proving to all the world that the Communists were not in the business of murdering American reporters. Burdett balked. "It's too dangerous," he said. Nothing came of Tomkins' plan.

Homer Bigart was the reporter to finally realize the dream of reaching Markos. It was fitting that it was Bigart, who called George Polk "a kindred spirit, a loner like me," who succeeded where so many had failed. The two men practiced the same tough-minded journalism, shunning the pack mentality of many in their profession, unafraid of arousing the ire of the powerful men they covered. Bigart, who would soon be awarded his second Pulitzer Prize, was, like Polk, the eternal outsider.

Without fanfare, Bigart made it to Markos' mountain hideaway later that summer. "George's murder opened the door to Markos for me," Bigart later said. But reality, as so often happens, did not match the fantasy. The result of the moment so deeply yearned for by George Polk and so many correspondents was ultimately disappointing.

Before leaving Belgrade, where the guerrillas reached Bigart with Markos' invitation, for the perilous mountain journey, Bigart wrote George Polk's brother, Bill, this note:

> I am leaving tomorrow for Greece, hoping to get the story your brother went after and to find out if the guerrillas can shed any light on the murder. If I have any luck, I hope that

the stories I send will be regarded as a sort of personal memorial to George, who never forgot there were two sides to every story and who gave his life trying to get "the other side."

Bigart filed three pieces describing his harrowing journey, in the company of Communist guides, over Yugoslav territory into war-torn northern Greece and his conversation with General Markos. In an open field he faced the legendary renegade surrounded by his guerrillas and discovered that none of them spoke much English. The interview for which one man had allegedly died was hardly the stuff of a major scoop.

Neither Markos nor any of his lieutenants seemed to know anything about Polk's murder, though they made ample propaganda use out of it on their radio broadcasts. They were convinced it was the Greek right who was responsible.

Though Bigart's articles were more interesting for their vivid descriptions of the hardships of guerrilla life than for anything Markos had to say, his newspaper, the respected *Herald Tribune*, nevertheless found them too controversial to print. The *Tribune* sat on his cables for weeks, afraid that publication would cause too great a stir. Finally, the paper was shamed into publication. "By then," Bigart later commented, "I was too disgusted with the *Trib* to read the articles."

"I could see the hatred on all the Greek faces when I returned to Athens from the mountains," Bigart recalled. "In their eyes, I had betrayed them."

Under instructions from Secretary of State George Marshall, the American government put Bigart under twenty-four-hour guard in Athens. The State Department was not about to risk another American casualty. Though he had been with the people who allegedly murdered his colleague, Bigart was never questioned by any of the scores of investigators on the Polk case as to what he had learned from the "bandits."

Without warning or explanation, Peter Tomkins was removed from the Polk investigation shortly after he entered Greece. CBS replaced him with John Secondari, the son of a prominent Italian right-wing politician, who was also on the CBS Rome bureau staff.

Secondari was better known for his own ultra-rightist views than for his reporting skills. His animal energy was in almost absurd contrast to Burdett's wan elegance.

Secondari accepted as gospel whatever the Greek investigators fed him. Burdett, though a veteran newsman, also showed a desire to accept the official story at face value.

While CBS had been putting together its team, another group of journalists was drawing up its own plans. Walter Lippmann, the preeminent man of the establishment, the columnist with access to kings, queens, and prime ministers, counselor and critic of presidents, rallied some of his more distinguished colleagues to the task at hand. Lippmann had known Polk, occasionally acting as mentor to the younger man. As the unofficial elder of their mutual trade, he also felt a certain responsibility.

From his imposing Tudor-style house on Washington's Woodley Road, he had little trouble persuading William Paley of CBS, James Reston of the New York *Times*, syndicated columnist Marquis Childs, Joseph Harsch of CBS, Ernest Lindley of *Newsweek*, and Eugene Meyer, publisher of the Washington *Post*, among others, to join his cause. On May 21, 1948, these respected figures of American journalism formed the Overseas Writers Special Committee to Inquire into the Murder of George Polk. Notably absent was Polk's friend and celebrated gadfly of the powerful, Drew Pearson.

These pundits and executives, some of whom had perhaps supped too often at the tables of the powerful men they or their staffs purported to cover, comprised the grandees of the Washington–New York journalistic establishment. Supremely pragmatic men, they thought and wrote on a global scale. The "little guy" whom George Polk made his frequent subject was not among their themes. The Cold War, the East-West chess game, that was the stuff of their conversations and columns. Of the group, only Marquis Childs was something of an exception. Not only did he write about George Polk's murder, but he did so with remarkable balance.

In his May 19 syndicated column entitled "Why Was George Polk Murdered?" Childs wrote:

The murder of George Polk is like a sudden lightning flash in the murky atmosphere of that troubled country. It deserves the fullest investigation which should have the backing of the Government of the United States. I saw George Polk in Athens last fall. He was one of the three or four really able correspondents in Greece. In the midst of the intrigues of Athens, he kept his eyes on the main goal, to give the American people the whole story regardless of who might be hurt or offended. . . .

That is why the first attempt to put the blame on the Communists, with whom he was supposed to be trying to make a contact . . . must not be taken at its face value. That is too easy and the regime in Athens should be made to understand that that is too easy. . . .

It is because of such reporters as Polk and others that the network has achieved its high standards of news coverage. Edward Murrow of CBS, in several able discussions of the Greek tangle in recent months, gave full credit to Polk for digging out the background and the facts. Until recently there were several American correspondents in Greece interested in getting more than the routine news and not at all interested in sending out merely the government point of view. . . . Today only Hadjiargyris of the *Christian Science Monitor* is left. . . . We need more than ever today the kind of reporting George Polk was doing in Athens. It is possible that Polk was killed in an effort to establish contact with the Communists. . . . But the circumstances surrounding his death as reported from Salonika do not make it sound that way.

I have lost a gallant and loyal friend. I last saw him at a wedding party when he was about to marry a charming Greek girl. He was very gay and very happy. We have all lost a man who believed in freedom and in truth and it is a loss we can ill afford.

It did not, however, occur to Walter Lippmann to make Polk the subject of one of his columns. In a revealing entry in his journal for 1950, Lippmann scribbled during a trip to Greece: "Saw the

King, the Prime Minister, et cetera, the usual people." If George Polk was an eternal outsider, Walter Lippmann and the men he gathered together to "inquire into" Polk's murder were preeminently insiders.

Their first stop was in keeping with their credo of working from the inside. The upright and solemn former general of the army, Secretary of State Marshall, received Lippmann and several other members of their newly formed committee. If the secretary had any doubts about the impact of the assassination in Salonika, the sight of this imposing delegation dispelled them. Lippmann spoke for the group. Could their team see State Department data and cables bearing on the Polk murder? Lippmann inquired. Secretary Marshall saw no reason why not. In fact, he had already put William Baxter, assistant chief of the department's Division of Greek, Turkish, and Iranian Affairs, in charge of the matter. "In Athens," he continued, "Chargé d'Affaires Karl Rankin will report on the Greek investigation's progress. In addition, Oliver Marcy and George Edman, secretaries in the embassy, have been assigned to follow the case. The embassy," Marshall declared, "has already put pressure on the Greeks to proceed with the investigation."

What Marshall did not announce was that Robert Driscoll and Christian Freer, of the CIA's Athens station, had been given the job of intermediaries between American and Greek officials. All information on the murder would be filtered through agents Driscoll and Freer.

Marshall further assured his visitors that he would look into the possibility of conducting a secret American investigation, independent of the official Greek one. He said that the Greek officials seemed anxious to please, but he noted grimly, "Pleasure is not what we are after. Information is."

Marshall then asked, "Have any of you formulated your own theories as to motive for the murder?"

"We are keeping an open mind, Mr. Secretary," Lippmann replied. "We have no theories," he said, thus missing the first of many opportunities to weigh in on the side of something other than diplomatic niceties for his murdered colleague.

"What strikes me," Marshall mused, "is that no attempt was made to conceal the body. It seems that care was taken that the body would be found. It would have been so easy for the murderer to have tied a stone to it and sunk it permanently."

Silence greeted this probing line of thought. None among the committee found reason to distrust the Greeks' rush to conclude that this was a "typical Communist-style execution." Not one of the eminent group noted that the corpse served a double purpose: it rid Athens of a dangerous irritant and at the same time provided vivid proof of Communist brutality.

In a show of good faith, the secretary picked up the latest cable he had received from Rankin in Athens. Scanning it, he summarized its contents: "The Greek Attorney General is studying statements made by Rea Polk and Helen Mamas of the AP. In addition to the Communist angle, Rankin feels the right wing is not a likely prospect because the murder was committed in a typical Communist way. The right wing's murder technique is different, he says. There is the possibility of a love triangle, which would involve Rea Polk. Or, lastly, professional jealousy might have been the motive."

Marshall then looked up from the cable. "The Greek Attorney General seems puzzled by something else. Why didn't Polk's best friend in Greece, the *Christian Science Monitor* man, Hadjiargyris, go to Salonika himself to console the widow?

"Rankin says it's clear officials want to believe the murder was not committed by anyone from the right wing. But Rankin is equally certain they wouldn't suppress any information leading in that direction. It seems that the gendarmerie and the local police have dropped all else to work on this case. The British police," the Secretary of State concluded, "are also investigating the case actively. It seems that Sir Charles Wickham also rules out the possibility of the right wing covering up information. Sir Charles tells Rankin the murder might take some time to solve, however, since it's a political crime."

Before closing this congenial meeting, the secretary and the members of the Lippmann committee agreed that if any other groups approached the Department of State wishing to pursue the investigation, Marshall would advise them that the Lippmann committee was already on the case.

Four days before Marshall received this distinguished delegation, Sir Charles Wickham made a trip from Athens to Salonika, described as "extraordinary" by embassy secretary Oliver Marcy in a cable to the department stamped "Secret." "During which," Marcy wrote, "Wickham had a two-hour conference with his Mission personnel allegedly on the Polk case. Thereafter the Greeks are reported to have asked the British whether they (the Greeks) were on the right track in the Polk case in believing that the Communists had perpetrated the murder. Sir Charles is reported to have replied that they were, and to have implied that an important Communist named Vasvanas was involved."

This Greece, the Greece of terrorists of the far left and far right and their powerful mentors, was a foreign place to Walter Lippmann and his fellow committee members. With the exception of a brief trip to Greece by Ernest Lindley, no member of the committee ever visited the scene of the crime. Too many other obligations kept them from undertaking the gritty job of investigating a murder that would necessarily lead them into some of the darker corners of a country they knew only as a pawn in the East-West chess game. They needed a man they could entrust with that high-risk job, a man who traveled in their circles, who would have instant access to "the King, the Prime Minister, and the usual people." A man of consequence, like themselves.

General "Wild Bill" Donovan, Lippmann's choice, seemed an inspired one for the job of counsel and chief investigator. Donovan, the founder of the wartime Office of Strategic Services, was the country's most decorated civilian. He was a man of polished surface, with a high reputation as a master in the dark arts of espionage, and he still possessed his own network of carefully cultivated contacts throughout Europe.

A second-generation Irish Catholic from Buffalo, New York, Donovan, like Lippmann, was a socially conscious man, avid for the company of the highborn and the powerful.

"We felt Donovan would have more access than anybody," Joseph Harsch would later recall. "Lippmann had complete trust in him. We were satisfied he gave us all he knew. He dispelled this nagging suspicion we originally had that the Greeks were not doing everything. . . ."

The former war hero had some time on his hands in 1948. While still head of the OSS, he had hatched the plan for the postwar CIA (whose austere lobby is still dominated by a larger-than-life marble statue of Donovan). President Truman, however, suspicious of Donovan's ambitions and his spreading power base, cut him out of the Agency and retired him in 1946. Since then, Donovan had been practicing law with the blue-chip New York firm bearing his name, Donovan and Leisure. He had not lost his appetite for adventure, however; his love of the cloak-and-dagger game was to be lifelong. Donovan, according to his protégé William vanden Heuvel, "never met a war he didn't love."

Nor did he ever really cut the ties to the Agency, which he regarded as his own child. Lawrence Houston, a tall, spare, affable product of the University of Virginia who had drawn up the legislation for the CIA and for decades acted as its chief counsel, was used to Donovan's 3 a.m. phone calls. "Did I wake you, Larry?" the general would ask. And before Houston had a chance to answer, he would give him his latest idea for waging the secret war against Communist infiltration. It fell to Houston to absorb these late-night shocks, as Frank Wisner, the CIA's secret-operations man, irritated with Donovan's constant kibitzing, had ceased taking Donovan's calls.

Donovan's greatest passion was clandestine operations. He was fascinated by the CIA's newly formed and blandly named Office of Policy Coordination, set up in 1948 for such operations. A man of action, he was grateful for Lippmann's call and the chance to come in from the cold world of corporate law.

"The CIA continued to rely on him," his law partner James Withrow recalled. "And Donovan would do anything the CIA asked. That was his first loyalty." Donovan, whose devil theory of Communism would only grow more obsessive with the years, was studying Russian around this time. "You've got to know your enemy," he advised Bill vanden Heuvel.

Over lunch in the chapel-like hush of Washington's Metropolitan Club, "Walter" and "Bill" raised their crystal tumblers to toast their new partnership. They agreed that the Polk case was charged with troublesome implications for both Lippmann's profession and one of the linchpins of America's Cold War foreign policy: unlimited support for Greece.

"I will choose my own man, Walter," Donovan announced in his rich baritone. "Someone I can trust enough to leave behind in Greece."

Did it occur to Walter Lippmann that Donovan's first loyalty would surely not be to the journalists, certainly not to George Polk's memory, but to the world he had nurtured into existence, the secret world of intelligence?

Though Donovan was no longer officially connected to the CIA, "his boys," the agents he had recruited for the OSS, were then, or would soon be, occupying the Agency's upper reaches. Richard Helms, Allen Dulles, William Colby, and William Casey were among them. They revered Donovan as only soldiers can revere a commanding officer.

In 1948, Secretary of Defense James Forrestal, the iciest of Washington's legion of Cold Warriors, invited Donovan to serve on a secret committee dealing with issues of the most delicate nature for the country's security. Donovan was joined by Dr. Vannevar Bush, who had worked on the first atomic bomb, and the first CIA director, Admiral Sidney Souers, to study problems of defense against an unconventional attack. "Wild Bill" Donovan was cleared to read top secret CIA material. All but officially, the old spymaster was back.

22

George Marshall would look back on his career and point to one country on the map with uncharacteristic pride: Greece. He liked to think his efforts on behalf of Greece in its most troubled hour had been its salvation. Queen Frederika, the thirty-year-old Greek monarch who was the granddaughter of the German Kaiser, was one reason for the secretary's special interest in Athens (the consort of King Paul I, she ascended to the throne in 1947 upon the death of George II). At Churchill's behest, Frederika had sought out Marshall in late 1947. "Talk to him," Churchill advised, "as one soldier to another." The advice paid off. Frederika made a very convincing plea for continued infusions of American aid. The young queen and the elder statesman began a correspondence that would span many years.

Marshall already had a convert in President Truman, who also felt aid to Greece was a critical part of Washington's Cold War strategy. But in 1948 President Truman's attention was splintered. East-West relations had reached another crisis point in Berlin. The Czechoslovakian crisis had shocked the country, and spurred the birth of the NATO military alliance. Roosevelt's dream of postwar harmony among the victorious allies was proving to be more dream than vision.

Above all, Truman was preoccupied that spring with the agonizing birth pangs of the state of Israel. Greece was no longer the top priority. "We had made a policy decision on Greece," Clark Clifford noted. "It was the responsibility of competent people to make sure that policy was carried out. We knew that the Greek people had been badly served by their leaders," Clifford recalled, "yet the fact that we had made our decision to help them was a great morale booster to them. Without our intervention they would have fallen to the Soviets. We felt our choices were between freedom and tyranny, decency and ugliness."

By the end of May 1948, however, the American involvement in Athens was becoming a controversial issue. Two weeks after the discovery of George Polk's body, the story of the murdered CBS man was still major news.

Drew Pearson was the most relentless in keeping the Polk story alive. His "Washington Merry-Go-Round" column was required reading in the nation's capital. On May 23 he took on the Greek government:

> Evidence points to the probability that rightist forces within the government were responsible for Polk's murder. Only the Greek government had access to his broadcasts. Only they knew how critical he had been of Greek rightist attempts to sabotage the American reconstruction program. The Greek guerrillas had everything to gain from the interview with Polk. The Greek government did not want him in Greece and did everything to get him out.

At Lake Success, New York, where the UN was meeting, the Standing Committee of the United Nations Correspondents, representing three hundred newspaper and radio correspondents, resolved that the unsolved murder of George Polk "is a threat to the successful work of all other correspondents." The UN press corps went on to state that "Mr. Polk's death arouses special concern because his unbiased reporting is known to have produced threats against him."

The New York Newspaper Guild called for the appointment of a joint commission of correspondents and members of the U.S. government to investigate. Polk's brother, Bill, and his cousin William Price joined this group of working newspeople, which included such foreign correspondents as Homer Bigart, John Donovan, and Constantine Poulos.

When members of this newly formed group, calling itself the Newsmen's Commission to Investigate the Murder of George Polk, called on Lippmann, they received a distinctly lukewarm greeting. Bill Polk requested that the columnist issue a statement indicating there was no conflict between the Lippmann committee and theirs. Lippmann, without giving reasons, declined to do so. His refusal was tantamount to preventing the Newsmen's Commission from gaining access to officials in either Athens or Washington. Could there be a joint statement of general aims or a joint memorial statement? Again the answer was no. The Newsmen's Commission, a genuine grass-roots effort, was thus crippled in its infancy.

John Donovan had no faith in the official investigation. "George had evidence," Donovan insisted in a 1982 interview. "He told me he had the goods on Tsaldaris. As soon as he got back to New York he was going to destroy him. They had to get rid of George." It was not what officials or news executives wanted to hear.

With each day's passage, Donovan felt that the chances of catching the real killers were diminishing. But his undisguised impatience was becoming a liability from NBC's point of view. The network stopped giving him assignments. There was no talk of sending him back to the Middle East, his turf for a number of years.

When John Donovan finally got his hearing, the worst suspicions of an increasingly paranoid man materialized. "You are going to have to resign from that committee," his executives told him. "All they're trying to do is prove that the Greek government murdered Polk."

"I happen to think they're right," Donovan answered. "And no, I'm not going to resign."

Three days later, the twenty-eight-year-old correspondent received a call from a low-level news executive. NBC, Donovan was told, was over budget and had to cut back on its Middle East coverage. It was the end of Donovan's broadcast career.

And after a while even Murrow was cut off from the investigation, asked to hand over his own Polk file to CBS. The Polk case was deemed to be an executive matter, placed in the hands of network president Frank Stanton.

At the networks and elsewhere in New York, the whispering campaign had begun. The Newsmen's Commission was too left-wing. William Price was unexpectedly moved by his paper, the

Daily News, from covering the UN to the police beat, traditionally a rookie's territory. He was often followed by agents of the FBI, which, under Hoover, equated dissent with treason. Price found that his career in mainstream journalism, like Donovan's, was over.

The Newsmen's Commission's fund-raising efforts dried up. While Eugene Meyer, the millionaire publisher of the Washington *Post*, was having no trouble raising thousands of dollars to finance General Donovan's numerous trips to Greece, the Newsmen were hard pressed to come up with several hundred dollars to send a single reporter.

Their only full-time staffer, a young Vassar graduate named Shana Agar, soon to be Shana Alexander, continued to answer their mail and their phones after there was no money left to pay her. John Donovan and his boxer were often her only companions in the bare single room which was the commission's headquarters.

A well-placed rumor here, a deftly dropped innuendo there, and suddenly reporters of solid reputation, honorably pursuing the question of who murdered an esteemed colleague, found that their motives were suspect. Yet the Newsmen had powerful, or at least prestigious, backing. Reached in Havana, Ernest Hemingway cabled them: "Delighted to sign appeal you sent. Been trying to arrange my affairs to enable head team but unworkable. If I could speak Greek I would go anyway but un-Greeking on such a cold trail I believe honestly would not be worth the sacrifice involved. But happiest if you use my name anyway. I back your fight. Please explain to Bill Polk and wish him luck."

Bill Polk, out of Harvard for the summer, decided he would not return to school the following fall. Harvard suddenly seemed irrelevant. "I kept thinking: What would George want me to do? What would George be doing in my place? The answer was: everything."

The nineteen-year-old Polk knocked on doors on Capitol Hill, looking for congressional backing for an investigation. He found unexpected support from Massachusetts senator Henry Cabot Lodge, who said that as a former newsman himself he felt a responsibility toward the dead reporter. The Republican senator promised to put pressure on the State Department to keep the heat on Athens. He also entered a great deal of material related to the case in the *Congressional Record*. Unlike the networks, Lodge agreed to back the commission if it ever made it to Greece.

Congressmen Claude Pepper and Wayne Morse (from Florida and Oregon, respectively) were also supportive. Morse said he thought it was a disgrace that, after almost a month, so little had been done to find the killers. Both agreed to pressure the State Department. There was little point, Bill Polk was told, in approaching the President. As Congressman George Sadowski of Michigan put it: "You'd just put him on the spot, son, asking him to investigate his own doctrine."

Under Secretary of State Robert Lovett was all smooth reassurance in his answer to Senator Lodge's query on what was being done to solve the Polk murder. "American officials involved have reported that the investigation is being 'efficiently handled.' That it is 'thorough and vigorous' and that it will be impartial. American correspondents who wish to observe on the spot the measures being taken to apprehend the authors of the crime are being given the full support and assistance of American and Greek officials."

In answer to Lodge's question regarding what protection had been extended George Polk by the Greek government, Lovett sounded an unintentionally ironic note: "It may safely be presumed that Polk would have seriously objected to surveillance or the assignment of a bodyguard had the Greek authorities made any such proposal."

By the end of May, the voices demanding justice in the case had begun to worry the Department of State.

"Polk murder has caused strong reaction from individual congressmen, newspapermen, and journalist groups," Secretary Marshall cabled the U.S. Embassy in Athens.

> Some express distrust of Greek willingness or ability to carry out thorough investigation. Almost all suggest independent U.S. investigation in order to certify to U.S. public that facts are not being concealed for local Greek reasons.
>
> In view of public interest and department's desire to take all appropriate measures to uncover responsibility for murder

of U.S. citizen, department wishes U.S. citizen with technical knowledge of police methods to follow the case working in closest cooperation with Greek police and British Police Mission.

Frederick Ayer, Jr., presently AMAG security officer, possesses necessary qualifications and in addition is on the spot and has firsthand knowledge of Greece. Unless you perceive objections because of local circumstances unknown to department, Ayer is instructed to relinquish all duties with AMAG and devote full time to following the investigation of the Polk case, reporting to the department frequently. . . . Department assumes Greek government, in light of recent announcements that any groups wishing to investigate would be welcome, will not object to this arrangement. Embassy should make appropriate respresentations explaining Ayer assignments and reasons for our wish that he be given all official facilities to report facts to department.

It should be made clear that this represents no, repeat no, lack of confidence in competence of Greek investigation but will permit department to answer criticism and inquiries in U.S. with more authority.

The Greek government, whose approval the State Department so anxiously sought, wasted no time in giving it unequivocally to this particular appointee. From their point of view and from that of many American officials, Frederick Ayer was highly qualified for the job. His anti-Communism was as deep-seated as that of the man who recommended him for assignment to Greece, FBI director J. Edgar Hoover. Ayer, nephew of General George Patton, was a Harvard graduate who served as a counterintelligence specialist on General Eisenhower's staff before joining the FBI. His field of expertise was the investigation of Communist fifth column infiltration. Though he never officially left the FBI, he was assigned the job of undercover security agent in Athens, in violation of the FBI's charter. Ayer was a favorite of the extreme right wing both in Athens and in his home state of Massachusetts, where he later sought public office.

Among his first steps on being assigned to the Polk case was to hire one of his underground contacts to serve as his aide. Memos Papadopoulos was devoted both to Ayer and to his parent organization, the right-wing terrorist underground X.

The same week General Marshall enlisted Ayer's services to monitor the Greek investigation, General Donovan chose his own man to accompany him to Greece. Lieutenant Colonel James Kellis, a former OSS operative, was the sort of man any commanding officer would want on his team.

Kellis was a self-contained man, trained in all the deadly intricacies of infiltration and guerrilla warfare. He was also a genuine war hero, the stuff of OSS lore.

"But you'd never hear about it from him," his lifelong friend Congressman John Blatnik, a former OSS agent himself, said. "Kellis was a quiet man. Never one to talk about his exploits or his great war record. Or to show much feeling at all." His own family was unaware of Kellis' breathtaking exploits behind enemy lines in Greece and later in China. Born in Alexandria, Egypt, of Greek parents, Kellis was orphaned at a young age and raised by an American uncle. Kellis, who would join the CIA in the 1950s, had been a close friend of William Casey since they both served in the OSS together.

Donovan could have chosen from among hundreds of his loyal OSS veterans, but Kellis was his first choice. If anyone could sort out truth from fabrication, it was the stolid Greek-American with the computerlike memory. Kellis knew the country, knew the language, knew its labyrinthian politics. Kellis also had an unblemished reputation for fair play.

At the time the general's call reached him, Kellis was serving in the Pentagon as an Air Force intelligence officer. He was excited at the prospect of serving his former commanding officer and relished the idea of getting away from his desk and back into the field.

Within a day, Donovan arranged to have Kellis released from Pentagon duty. He asked Kellis, however, to tell no one about the nature of his new assignment.

It would not stay a secret for long. Kellis' phone at the Pentagon rang again the next day. "Colonel Kellis," the caller said, "my name is Jack Anderson and I work for Drew Pearson. I understand that you are going to Greece to investigate the murder of George Polk for General Donovan."

"Where did you hear that?" Kellis, unaccustomed to having his cover blown, was aghast.

"We have our ways," Anderson said, giving the oldest answer in the book for such questions.

"Well, Mr. Anderson," Kellis said in a resigned voice, "I'll give you a little background on this, but I would appreciate it very much if you cooperated with us."

Anderson said he felt sure Pearson would agree to the deal. Kellis explained that his former commanding officer in the OSS had asked for his help to ensure "a thorough, impartial, and penetrating investigation" of the Polk murder.

"Mr. Anderson," Kellis stressed, "I believe it is in the interest of the newspaper profession that this investigation be conducted quietly. And since my orders are not official for this assignment, I'd appreciate it if nothing was printed about it."

Jack Anderson gave his word and kept it. On May 31, before leaving for Greece, Kellis called the newsman to thank him.

Others would not be so discreet. Even before he left town, Colonel Kellis was the subject of heavy cable traffic between the Greek Embassy in Washington and the Athens Foreign Office, Constantine Tsaldaris' domain. Having applied for a visa to travel to Greece, Kellis was puzzled by the embassy's too long silence. Days went by and he still had no word from the Greeks.

Finally, an impatient General Donovan called Ambassador Vassili Dendramis. What was holding up the colonel's visa? he asked. "It seems there is some concern," the ambassador explained, "about Colonel Kellis' background. The time the colonel spent during the war with ELAS, the left-wing resistance forces," Dendramis tried to explain. "We are concerned about his safety in Greece."

Donovan, appalled that one of his most gifted agents would be deemed a figure of suspicion, told the ambassador it was in his country's best interest that Kellis be immediately granted a visa.

Kellis' visa, like most of Donovan's requests, was granted. The last day before Kellis' departure from Washington, however, the Greek Ambassador placed a call to the State Department and tried to cancel Kellis' travel permit. The department informed Dendramis it was too late.

On June 5, Secretary Marshall sent his own cable to the American Embassy in Athens: "Lippmann committee planning to send to Greece Lieutenant Colonel James Kellis, formerly OSS and presently on active duty with the Air Force in Washington. In attempting to keep Kellis trip secret, committee hopes to keep any mention of his visit out of the newspapers and requests embassy officers to treat this information confidentially."

By the time Colonel Kellis landed in Athens, however, there were very few Greeks or Americans concerned with the Polk investigation who were not fully briefed on the former resistance hero, the first significant threat to the Greek government's control of the investigation.

23

U p the dusty, winding road from the Salonika city morgue to the airfield where George Polk had arrived a few weeks before, Rea Polk's car followed the flatbed truck that carried her husband's coffin.

When Rea heard the wheels of the TAE flight finally whir into the belly of the plane, she felt a wave of relief. She was leaving the hated place forever.

When the plane landed at Athens, relief was supplanted by bitter fact. She had her life to lead now, without George.

Her husband's Stars and Stripes–draped coffin would lie in state in the small Anglican chapel not far from the Parthenon. Rea did not want the funeral to take place until Adelaide Polk arrived several days later. She made it quite clear she wanted no official Greek presence at her husband's funeral.

Costas and Aileen Hadjiargyris were at the airport waiting. Since they were the Polks' closest friends, Rea was not surprised to see them. Her father, she assumed, must have let them know the time of her arrival. She was somewhat startled, however, to see Stephen and Mary Barber standing there, Mary holding a small bouquet. But Rea was glad to see them, too, glad for any compassionate faces. In the car, she told her friend Aileen she could not bear to go back to the Skoufa Street apartment, not just yet. Could she stay with the Hadjiargyrises? Of course. They would be more than happy to have her.

Mary Barber, however, insisted that Rea stay with them. Too tired to protest, Rea agreed.

Upon reaching the Barbers' home in Athens' Patissia quarter, Stephen Barber quickly excused himself and his wife went straight

for the telephone, as Rea and Hadjiargyris would later recall.
"There is no need to worry, Sir Charles," Mary said into the re-
ceiver. "Stephen is on his way and should be with you at the Grande
Bretagne." Though Rea seemed anxious only for the company of
Aileen Hadjiargyris, Mary Barber devoted much of her time over
the next few weeks to Rea. Mrs. Barber also spent a great deal of
time on the telephone to Sir Charles Wickham. Of the British Police
Mission chief, Mary Barber notes in her own memoirs that "I saw
quite a lot of him." During Rea's stay, Stephen Barber shuttled
between the British Police Mission headquarters at the Grande
Bretagne and their house in Skoufa.

Hadjiargyris and his wife were mystified by "the sudden show
of friendship" the Barbers extended to them as well. Relations
between the *Christian Science Monitor* man with his well-known anti-
Royalist politics and the Barbers had hitherto been strictly businesslike. "My impression," Hadjiargyris wrote Bill Polk later,
"from the general attitude of the Barbers was that they probably
wished to find out how much my wife and I knew about them and
the entire case. This impression is valid also as regards the attitude
of the Barbers toward Rea Polk. Sir Charles," Hadji noted, "shared
the interest of the Barbers in some way which remains undefined
to me."

Mary Barber would later describe Hadjiargyris as "shifty and
always complaining. We tried to warn Polk about him." But for
the three weeks following George Polk's murder the Barbers had
a seemingly inexhaustible appetite for the Hadjiargyrises' company,
as they did for Rea's.

Rea's father, Polk's devoted Matthew Cocconis, was staying in
the Skoufa Street flat. He had the key to Polk's office, which still
held all of Polk's files, including those containing two critical pieces
of evidence: the letter with the New York postmark informing Polk
of Tsaldaris' $25,000 bank deposit, and Kourtessis' hand-delivered
letter. Anyone wishing to gain access to these files would have to
have both Rea's and her father's confidence. Unlike the job of
removing a notebook from the pocket of a corpse, this assignment
called for someone whose English was expert enough to quickly
locate two letters among scores of other documents. Polk was known

to be an efficient organizer of his files. He was writing a book and kept everything.

On May 20, Hadjiargyris pressed Rea to return to the Skoufa Street flat to supervise a police search. As was always the case during those days, Mary Barber was with her. Hadjiargyris was also present and recalled the Greek policemen being at sea with the vast collection of papers, carbons of CBS scripts, letters home, and letters to friends. The policemen copied down the strange names of his correspondents and at one point one of them asked Rea if "Dearest Family" was a man or woman. The search lasted from early afternoon until evening. Rea pronounced all of Polk's files accounted for. The police did not at this point remove anything from the apartment.

The next day, Mary Barber suggested to Rea that perhaps she ought to retrieve those documents which were relevant to her immigration to the United States. Mary offered to help. Rea accepted her offer, and sent Mary to Skoufa Street to find her personal files, birth certificate, marriage license, and the like. Rea remembers Mary presenting her with her personal documents the following day. That evening, Winston Burdett and John Secondari arrived at Polk's apartment to conduct their own search of their colleague's files. They were looking for any clues to the murder in his correspondence. It was Burdett who noticed that George's correspondence file ended on February 5, 1948. The March, April, and May files, accounted for the previous day, were now missing.*

Adelaide Polk arrived in Athens late that evening and was met at the airport by Burdett and Secondari. Among their first pieces of news to her was the discovery of her son's missing papers, which the CBS men immediately suspected held critical clues to the crime. She, too, was shocked at the news. Mrs. Polk insisted they immediately alert the authorities. She then asked Hadjiargyris to help her conduct her own search. "Why don't you take George's cor-

---

* Following the hardcover publication of the book, Mary Barber Henderson informed the publisher that she is "certain that [she] never removed . . . documents giving clues to the murder." She said, "If [she] went to Polk's office it could possibly have been to fetch personal documents such as Rea's birth certificate and marriage license—though [she does] not recall doing so and [points out that] Rea's father, who had the key to Polk's office, which was in his flat, could surely himself have brought these papers to Rea."

respondence and the CBS files to your own apartment," Mrs. Polk suggested, "and go through them yourself, make sure the missing papers are not in there someplace." Hadjiargyris, only too aware that he was a likely candidate for the role of scapegoat, declined. "I have made a habit of never being alone in George's office. I keep my hands visible at all times." Mrs. Polk, new to this climate, looked puzzled. Wasn't he her son's best friend in Greece? Surely he could not be suspected of his murder!

In the end, Rea returned to the apartment and, going through the files yet again, confirmed that three months of correspondence was missing. She also confirmed that the files had been taken since her last search two days before.

They buried her husband the following day, May 22, 1948. George Polk was laid to rest in the stately white marble Cocconis family vault. Rea's mother-in-law couldn't understand why the young woman was so adamant about keeping all Greek officials away from the last rites. In the end, the government prevailed, however. "The Greek government," Adelaide Polk wrote her family on May 23, her third day in Athens, three days which saw a dizzying number of events unfold in her son's murder investigation, "feels George's death is 'a blot on their honor' and begged to be allowed to pay for and conduct the funeral. Rea in her great grief and bitterness against the Greeks would not hear of it. Indeed, she insisted on a small, almost secret funeral at 8 a.m. Saturday. Mr. Edman, the press attaché at the American Embassy and Mr. Ka-vanides of the Ministry of Information and I discussed the matter and finally decided it was best to let the Greek government at least attend the funeral. This was done and actually the government took over the funeral in the most beautiful manner."

Rea was not even allowed to pay for the flowers. Gorgeous wreaths from the important ministers surrounded George Polk's coffin. Adelaide Polk, her features grimly set in her private grief, was supported by George Kavanides, the same man who had approved Polk's trip to Salonika. "It is an honor to bury George Polk as one of our own heroes," he told Adelaide Polk. Rea wept openly as the coffin disappeared beneath mounds of new earth and leaned on Mary Barber's arm. Chargé Karl Rankin, Minister of Justice

George Melas, and Minister of Public Order Constantine Rendis stood in solemn silence, just behind the two women.

Rea and Adelaide Polk would not be allowed a decent interval for their grief, however. "Five police were here yesterday until 10 p.m.," Mrs. Polk wrote her family on May 25, "going through George's papers. They are seeking any clue, a name, a telephone number, a coded message. Of course they weren't actually police, but have heavy titles, Magistrate, etc. They took off the files of George's correspondence to CBS and four huge envelopes of material from Iran, Iraq, the Middle East.

"The government is trying to pin the crime on the Communists, whom George attacked severely here. They say they MUST find the criminal at once. . . . However, as yet nothing has been found after the Feb. 5th file of letters. . . .

"Rea insists on going to America and to college there," Mrs. Polk noted, baffled by her daughter-in-law's ardent wish to leave her homeland. "Nothing can dissuade her." The ubiquitous Mary Barber was helping Rea fill out applications to Columbia University.

Adelaide Polk was a fast learner. After only five days in Athens, Mrs. Polk had reached the conclusion that "some Communist will confess to the crime . . . probably under duress. But I am not supposed to conjecture. So discount and don't talk about it. Most people think differently as to the criminal, and of course the men who did it aren't the ones who planned it, but hired hands, they think."

During Frederick Ayer's first trip to Salonika he met with Colonel Thomas Martin, who, in Consul General Raleigh Gibson's words, "is this Englishman who is following every move Mouscoundis makes." The British colonel and the FBI man found common ground in both their anti-Communism and their devotion to the Greek right.

If Major Mouscoundis was Colonel Martin's man, that seemed to have been good enough to recommend him to Ayer, who boasts in his memoirs:

I somehow succeeded in having the Minister of Justice and the Minister of Public Order jointly sign a paper stating that

Major Mouscoundis was in sole and exclusive charge of the investigation, that no one was to obstruct him, and that the forces of all the other organizations were to be put at his disposal. I also saw to it that the document in question was reprinted in the daily press and read on the radio.

Ayer, largely ignorant of the tangled web which tied Mouscoundis to both the British and an ultra-right-wing faction of the Populist Party, was deeply impressed by the apparent zeal with which Mouscoundis attacked the murder investigation. In his first police report on the case, Mouscoundis wrote:

> Police got in touch with American Legation. . . . Notices sent to other districts of Greece for information on Polk. Efforts to find traces of Polk, who showed desire to meet Markos. His wife showed no worry over disappearance. Full investigation begun noon May 17. Three hundred police, including 70 detectives from 15 police stations, were sent out exclusively on the Polk case. Over 30 cars and motorcycles were put at disposal of the police working on the investigation. Work of this police detail was supplemented by 500 undercover agents who were particularly interested because of the 25,000-drachma reward.
>
> Over 200 suspects were examined for their movements before, during, and after the crime. Remains found in stomach indicate he ate in a seafood restaurant. Police tried to find out where the rope was bought. Questioned 600 boatmen and restricted them so that they could not leave. Also investigated boats that left and arrived in the harbor during those days.
>
> Polk's picture was circulated to all newspapers in order to get people who had seen him to come forth with some information. . . .

This impressive catalogue of police activities continues for nine pages and offers this conclusion: "Police believe that the plot was organized by the Communist Party, not by a Greek mind. The police cannot prove this, but fully believe that they are on the right track and know what they are looking for."

Despite this remarkable flurry of activity, despite the total involvement of the country's preeminent Communist hunter, Mouscoundis, the man who broke up the dreaded Communist terrorist organization OPLA, not a single clue was turned up, not even which restaurants served lobster on the night of the murder (a fact that would take Colonel Kellis one day in Salonika to pin down).

Most remarkably, with the exception of a handful of American journalists and diplomats and one unfortunate Greek reporter named Staktopoulos, no one in Salonika recalled seeing the tall, blond American.

Sir Charles Wickham had put Colonel Martin in charge of the day-to-day "investigation." Martin and Mouscoundis, with three years of riding in double harness behind them, formed a unit. The Greek and British monarchies had few tougher or more zealous servants than these two policemen, the tall, lean Englishman and the short, balding Greek.

And yet, in Sir Charles's monthly report to the Foreign Office marked "Secret," there is not a word about British Police Mission preoccupation with the murder. "The murder at Salonika," Wickham wrote in his May report, "of G. W. Polk, representative of the Columbia Broadcasting System, caused quite a stir both here and in the U.S.A. The fact that he left behind a letter to a friend in Italy in which he stated that he intended to try to get an interview with Markos led to many conjectures as to the motive for the murder. In spite of intensive inquiries in Salonika and Athens, the police and gendarmerie have been unable, so far, to obtain any information regarding the crime."

His Majesty's consul general in Salonika cabled news of the murder to the Foreign Office, with this telling footnote: "Greek authorities believe Polk had been in touch with local Communists. Mysterious. One must hope that the Communists did it."

The official American interest in the case was more overt and increasing. Cables from the State Department to the embassy daily drove home the point: A suspect must be found. As Colonel Kellis later noted, had there been a Communist on whom some suspicion could have been pinned, Mouscoundis would not have wasted any time.

When Consul Gibson mentioned to Colonel Martin the State Department's displeasure at the lack of progress, the British policeman informed him, as Gibson reported to the Secretary of State, that "the interest of the police had not slackened, but Martin hoped that the information obtained by the interrogation of Hadjiargyris and Rea Polk would give some new leads to follow. If not, the police investigation would slacken. Martin stated that he was keeping the police active, but new leads were essential, otherwise they could not be kept occupied."

"The Americans," Sir Charles Wickham later told Hadjiargyris, "wanted blood at any price. And they got it."

Lacking a likely Communist suspect, the authorities cast some of those closest to George Polk in the role of possible conspirators. The investigators began to construct a murder case which would incriminate the dead man's widow and his closest friend, deemed to be enemies of the regime. Both Rea and Hadjiargyris had been too vocal in their suspicions regarding the right wing. Hadjiargyris backed up his with reports he shared with his colleagues of George Polk's rightist death threats. Hadjiàrgyris also had an incriminating record as an anti-Royalist, pro-leftist activist. As a sailor in the Royal Greek Navy in 1943, he helped to organize a mutiny aboard a naval vessel. He had been court-martialed and imprisoned for his part in the mutiny.

Neither the American Embassy in Athens nor the two CBS men, Burdett and Secondari, resisted the official attempt to incriminate Rea and Hadjiargyris. Quite the contrary; they became its enthusiastic proponents.

The widow was the first suspect. Police chief John Panopoulos began a series of interrogations in Athens, often lasting from early morning until late evening. Major Mouscoundis had already questioned Rea in Salonika, shortly after Polk's body was found. "Isn't it true," Mouscoundis had pressed her, "that you had a lover who swore to kill your husband? Or maybe you yourself organized the murder out of jealousy of another woman?" Anger and loathing fortified Rea with a strength that she did not know she possessed.

The twenty-year-old woman, alone for the first time in her life, proved surprisingly resistant to police interrogation tactics.

Getting nowhere with the "love triangle" motive, Mouscoundis had reverted to his original plan. "They are trying to break me down," Rea confided to Waide and Geneal Condon. "They want me to sign a paper admitting I believe the Communists killed George. I don't know how much longer I can stand it."

In the time-honored tradition of all police states, the Greek officials attempted to isolate Rea, to convince her she was hated by her own countrymen, in order to undermine whatever resistance she still offered. The Royalist-controlled press echoed the police line, portraying Rea as a "bad" Greek, not a patriot, not even a good wife.

Her father and her mother-in-law, though absorbed in their own grief, were Rea's main sources of support, apart from the ever-present Mary Barber.

Winston Burdett offered no protection to either Rea or Hadjiargyris against the Greek government's smear campaign. Not speaking a word of Greek, the CBS correspondent seemed to rely heavily on Fred Ayer for his information. Burdett seemed all too willing to believe the worst of Polk's widow, cabling CBS that Rea "has shown callousness and a spirit of opportunism hardly befitting a bereaved widow." The CBS correspondent does not cite any examples of this behavior, however.

Paraphrasing Royalist press reports, Ayer cabled the Secretary of State on June 5 that Hadjiargyris was "a noted skirt chaser . . . and according to KKE [Greek Communist Party] informant he is 'our best propaganda specialist and one of our two or three best espionage agents.' "

Consul Raleigh Gibson informed the State Department, on May 28, that Burdett and Secondari were "very good men and that all evidence points to the fact that the authorities accept them as coworkers."

On June 2, Ayer cabled Marshall that "Burdett and Secondari have strongly urged Minister of Public Order Rendis and Chief of Police Evert to question thoroughly, under arrest if necessary, *Christian Science Monitor* correspondent Hadjiargyris and Rea Polk."

And in a confidential memo from the embassy in Athens to the State Department on the subject of "Attitude of U.S. Press Toward Greece," embassy secretary Robert Miner states:

CBS correspondents express satisfaction with Greek efforts to solve murder. CBS men felt their fellow U.S. correspondents are giving distorted view of the situation in Greece. They are amazed that certain of their colleagues with excellent reputations had fallen into the trap of biased reporting with only bad things being reported. Burdett and Secondari attribute much of this to the diabolically clever and reasonable-sounding Hadji, who has implanted an attitude of hostility in them.

CBS correspondents are definitely of the opinion that Hadji knows a "great deal more" in the Polk case than he is telling. They feel the only way to get more information out of Hadji is to put him through "an old-fashioned third degree."

The CBS men even earned kudos from the CIA. In a memorandum for the director of Central Intelligence from Athens station chief Robert Driscoll, dated June 8, the two reporters are singled out for doing an excellent job of reporting on the case. "Burdett and Secondari believe that the Salonika police are doing all that is possible. They cite numerous examples of painstaking work and all-out efforts to solve the crime. Mouscoundis, in charge of the actual investigation in Salonika, is considered a first-rate detective. Authorities," the secret memo goes on, "are still groping blindly and seizing on every straw. Hadji, who declined police protection, and Polk's widow will be interrogated soon, partly on the insistence of Burdett and Secondari. They will probably not be arrested." Indeed, the prospect of Hadji's arrest had already been the subject of troubled exchanges between the American Embassy and the State Department.

On May 19, Chargé Rankin, then still the ranking American diplomat in Greece, had sent the Secretary of State a cable marked both "Secret" and "Urgent." "Constantine Hadjiargyris, stepson of Prime Minister Sophoulis and local correspondent for the *Christian*

Science Monitor, is being shadowed re the Polk case and may possibly be arrested shortly."

What seemed to suit the embassy's own inclinations, however, alarmed the State Department. On May 20, Secretary Marshall, using uncharacteristically blunt language, sent Rankin this message, also marked "Secret":

> In view *unfounded suspicions* raised by Polk killing, arrest of Hadjiargyris would have disastrous repercussions in U.S. press in absence of incontrovertible evidence of his complicity with Communists or murder.
>
> Department is aware of Hadjiargyris's background and his dubious relations with U.S. correspondents in Greece. Presumably Greek authorities now suspect he served as Polk liaison with Communist underground and also resent his story about Polk's receipt of rightist threats. However, an honest appraisal of his dispatches from Athens in the past few months shows them to be among fairest and most informed and objective emanating from Greece. They show an intelligent and sympathetic understanding of Greek government's problems and are by no, repeat no, conceivable interpretation pro-Communist. Please discuss this with appropriate Greek authorities.

The secretary's message is less fair-minded than it would appear at first reading. Marshall's "unfounded suspicions" refers to questions about right-wing involvement in the Polk murder. Calling these questions unfounded and implying that they are a problem rather than a possibility to be considered in effect tips the case away from a real, honest-to-goodness investigation at the very outset. If it was not the right, then by definition the murder had to have been committed by the left. By defining Hadjiargyris' reporting as unbiased, not "pro-Communist," the secretary indicates that a correspondent's politics is the determining factor in establishing his guilt or innocence. Marshall thus openly acknowledges the Polk murder to be not simply a crime against an American journalist. The Secretary of State establishes it for what it clearly represented for the American government: a political cause célèbre, with truth relegated to play a subordinate position to the greater demands of Washington's foreign policy. Thus, inadvertently perhaps, Secretary Marshall confirmed the Mouscoundis-Martin-Wickham line on the murder.

With the police interrogating him almost daily, Hadjiargyris took steps to avoid the fate of his friend. In a shrewdly calculated move, he claimed his life was in danger and asked the Athens police for protection. Once under official protection, his chances of falling victim to an official assassination were greatly reduced. Taking a page out of Polk's book, he wrote to many influential Americans, alerting them to his plight. Marquis Childs, Drew Pearson, and Walter Lippmann, as well as his editors at the *Christian Science Monitor*, were kept fully informed of his treatment by the authorities.

"I do not discount the possibility of being murdered," he wrote Ray Daniell of the New York *Times* on May 25, "by either side so long as the murder can be organized in an untraceable manner. But I think, and in this all my Greek friends who know their way around this country agree, that the main danger is of getting framed. It would be easy to produce false witnesses or forged documents to prove anything they cared to prove against me. The only thing that might possibly stop them is the fact that Sophoulis [his stepfather] is still Prime Minister. But for how long? And will they be stopped even by that? Their hate against me is at this moment phenomenal."

The ardently anti-Communist Ayer was not content with the level of harassment applied to Hadjiargyris and Rea: "Information needed from Hadji to help lead to a solution of the case will be prevented by the very observance of democratic police and judicial methods which Greece has been condemned for not observing."

The Greek Civil War was waged almost as much in the pages of Greece's newspapers as in the forbidding Grammos Mountains in the north. The Greek right-wing press, an organ of Foreign Minister Tsaldaris' Populist (Royalist) Party, continued its daily barrage against Hadjiargyris, accusing him of withholding information and of being anti-Greek—the same sins Ayer attributed to him.

But the Communist press was also finding a rich store of propaganda material in the case. On May 30, Markos Radio announced:

> Polk's murder was planned by the American Secret Service in Athens and by Greek security police and was carried out by Salonika General Security. Polk was baited under the following circumstances: It was known to both the Greek monarchists and the Americans that Polk came to Greece with the intention of meeting General Markos. Such a meeting would undoubtedly result in the revelation of the true state of affairs in Greece, which the monarchists try to conceal so awkwardly.
>
> No sooner did Polk arrive in Athens than he was contacted by two men who told him that they could take him to Markos and that he should go to Salonika on May 8. There he was abducted by Mouscoundis . . . near the Luxembourg nightclub . . . and put in a rowboat and shot in the back of the neck. . . . The monarchists and the Americans would then claim that he went to Free Greece and was murdered there by the Democratic Army. But a proverb says, "The clever bird is caught by its beak." The monarchists failed to hide Polk's body, which some days after was washed ashore, provoking an international scandal.

Propaganda of any stripe is, by definition, crude. This one suffers primarily from lack of a plausible motive for the murder. There was simply no record of the monarchists shooting reporters for the crime of attempting to reach Markos.

Hadjiargyris, who did not know who killed his friend, still knew too much. He knew from Polk himself about the right-wing death threats. He had also observed the Barbers' close relationship with Sir Charles Wickham, especially after Polk's death when they insisted on keeping Rea close to them. Hadjiargyris also insisted that, aside from family members, the Barbers were the only ones who had access to the Polk apartment the day the critical files disappeared.

What the authorities feared was that Hadjiargyris, linked from the very beginning to Polk, eventually would take the stand and tell all he knew of the murder. There was no way a court could fail to call him to testify. The important thing was to discredit him first. His word on anything had to be suspect.

It is not difficult to find other reasons for the right wing's fury toward Hadjiargyris. He had been employed by two of the monarchy's most hated critics: Homer Bigart and George Polk. His most unpardonable sin, however, was that he remained objective in his coverage of the civil war.

There are only so many ways to destroy a man's reputation. One is by charging him with loose living, immoral conduct. The other, in 1948, was to hint that he was a leftist. At that time, the vaguest leftist connection could cost a man his job, friends, and position. Smear campaigns were routine in Greece, where suspicions and intrigues were a by-product of the civil war.*

Both Hadjiargyris and Rea, whose early rage at the Greek right had been too vocal, now read in the Greek newspapers lurid and totally fictitious accounts of their immoral behavior and alleged Party connections. Karl Rankin, Raleigh Gibson, and Fred Ayer were cheerful purveyors to Washington of any right-wing rumors floated about them, no matter how outlandish.

In mid-June, in his regular weekly cable to the Secretary of State, Ayer wrote:

> Following from highly placed Salonika Communist contact, Ayer informed crime not planned or committed in Salonika but probably on orders and through an agent of Cominform.
> Rea Polk certainly played a part. Hadji probably did. . . . Rea known to have belonged to the KKE and also active for Party in Egypt. Strong rumors exist that she is today a highly placed agent.

In a cable dated June 23, Ayer claimed to possess hard information confirming Rea's role as a KKE courier while she posed as

---

* Many years later, Hadjiargyris did in fact join the Communist Party of Greece, the KKE, and, for a while, was editor of a Communist newspaper. According to Leon Karapanayotis, publisher of *Ta Nea*, the largest-circulation afternoon paper in Greece: "He was hounded into the Party by years of official harassment."

an airline stewardess. Ayer made a special point of asking Marshall not to show this information to the Lippmann committee.

Nor was Ayer above employing the same tactics the Greek interrogators had been using on the young widow. "If you want to leave before your American visa expires, point the finger at the Communists," Ayer offered. "The gate will miraculously open for you."

The FBI agent had managed to persuade the embassy to withhold her travel permit. In his memoirs, *Yankee G-Man*, Ayer savors Rea's desperate pleas to be allowed to leave. "On a Sunday morning Rea called me at my so-called apartment and asked if she could come to see me that noontime. I told her she could not, as I was planning to go to the beach and have a rest for the first time in many days. When could I see her then? How about six o'clock this evening? I must admit," Ayer writes, "that Rea had a very pleasant voice and seemed satisfied at the prospect." Ayer, it seems, had begun to believe the officially floated rumors of the widow's immoral conduct.

"Rea was on time and dressed to conquer. Admittedly black was the motif but there are blacks and blacks. The dress was gauzy and not overly opaque, the hat was black, broad and flattering, the gloves of black kid and elbow length. The perfume was less than subtle and the smile when it returned was practiced and lovely. . . . I told her that I was perfectly aware of why she felt she had to get to the United States, inasmuch as I was the one who had arranged the orders that she should not leave."

Ayer, amused by his little game of cat and mouse with the young widow, made plain that in this matter the Americans were as one with the Greek officials she so deeply loathed. "I told her that the only condition she must meet in order to leave was that she should go to Salonika, submit to interrogation by the chief of the gendarmerie (Mouscoundis) and satisfy that astute man that she was telling the truth and all she knew. She promised me she would and made her graceful departure, leaving in her wake a tantalizing scent."

For Adelaide Polk, her grief in Athens, with its daily reminders of George, was compounded by confusion. She did not understand why "Win" Burdett, so kind and thoughtful toward her, was so hostile toward Costa, as she called Hadjiargyris. Nor could she fathom her daughter-in-law's passionate hatred of her own country.

Her aim was to ensure that nothing marred the memory of her son. But she was no longer sure whom to trust and whom to fear. She, who believed there was good in each living being, found Athens' atmosphere of distrust unbearable. She wrote her children on June 4:

> I am longing to get home . . . it is too full of grief here . . . and I have done what I came for . . . shown my love and my interest and have seen the end of things. Now I no longer mind seeing my and George's friends. . . . Rea was at the cemetery again today, arranging fresh flowers. We go out there every few days. It isn't far and each time after a storm of grief I feel calmer and more at peace. The nearby Parthenon gives me strength in its serene beauty.

In surveying her son's work, she felt a surge of pride:

> I become astounded at the colossal amount of work he did. His correspondence with the great and the near great of the world is in itself amazing. His files for *Newsweek* are enormous. . . . His articles, his writings, his letters, and his broadcasts, as well as the immense amount of work he had to do to send out his long cables and scripts . . . really it's the most re- markable thing. His work looms up as almost impossible. And with it all the dozens of books he read and marked and studied. It's all stupendous. Mr. Cocconis said he often worked 18 and 19 hours a day. And then he traveled so much. Amazing! And he was my child. . . . Such a life. And, I might add, such a death.

24

General Donovan landed at Hellenikon Airport in Athens on June 10, 1948. His trip aboard the TWA Skymaster had taken two days, with stops in Newfoundland, the Azores, Shannon, Paris, Geneva, and Rome preceding the landing in Athens.

Donovan had not wasted a moment of his time in flight. He had read all the secret briefing papers prepared by his former agents— "his boys," he liked to call them—on Greece and on what made this case worthy of the general's particular gifts. Warriors from the heroic days of the OSS, his agents had since moved over to the fledgling CIA. By now Donovan knew who all the players in the Polk case were. From his unmatched CIA sources he had learned about the tangled web of legal, paralegal, and illegal security services that ran the country America had chosen to save from the fearful Antichrist.

The struggle at hand had to do with everything this man held dear. It had to do with the right of a man to make himself into anything he chose. Donovan, the son of an Irish Catholic railroad worker from Buffalo, had achieved that. He called Churchill his friend along with scores of cardinals, kings, Rothschilds, Roosevelts, and Astors. You couldn't do that in a Communist country. It had also to do with worshipping the God you chose, which Donovan did with a passionate Irish mysticism. It had something to do with living well, extremely well, in big, fine houses, and flying on rich men's planes and sailing on their yachts. All of which Donovan did with equal gusto. "Fortune favors the audacious," he had scribbled in his schoolboy's notebook. He had transformed the aphorism into a way of life.

Among the papers Donovan had committed to memory during his long transatlantic journey was one signed simply "A."* "Do not put on file and do not forward in any way whatever. Simply destroy this whole letter," were A's instructions to him. But Donovan, who himself never put anything in writing, did not destroy either that letter or many others pertaining to the case. No doubt he meant to in due course, but when he was quite suddenly felled by a powerful stroke in 1958, he left a good many such papers behind.

A provided Donovan with comforting reading. There was nothing in A's memorandum to shake Donovan's fervent hope and firmly held conviction that the murder was indeed a Communist job.

In his letter, A wrote:

P. told his mother in March 1948 that he had discovered another link in the chain to Gen. Markos. The mother says she repeated this to no one.

No reliable information about possible rift between P. and wife. Dan Thrapp, United Press, wrote officials (from Rome) saying he and P. had discussed at length the feasibility of seeing Gen. Markos. Thrapp opposed the step because of danger; earlier, though, he had made advances and met an individual in Sal . . . who was a link in a chain to Gen. Markos. . . . Important: Hadji: first arrested for Communist activities in 1931. Known to security police since then as Communist with various types of activities. Directly responsible for mutiny aboard naval vessel in 1943; preached straight Communist line. Later involved in mutinous activities in Middle East. Still later, started to work quietly selling his views to Western reporters. Noted as skirt chaser, on intimate terms with female employees of UNRRA.

No witness to date stated that P. ever definitely said any-

---

* "A" does not identify himself in the memorandum other than by this initial. Nor does this initial appear as a signature on any other papers relevant to the case. One plausible deduction is that "A" is Frederick Ayer. However, Ayer was in Athens during this period and the memorandum carried a Washington dateline. It is clear from the full text of the memorandum that "A" is someone who had been a member of the OSS and continued to be part of the postwar intelligence network.

thing concerning threats from Right, or from Govt. or from any quarter. Mrs. P.'s belief regarding such threats was based on hearsay from Hadji.

Opinion of U.S., British, and Greek officials having contact with Mrs. P. is that she is callous, not overly moral, and an opportunist. Hadji is extremely clever, wily, and resourceful. According to the chief of police, he is "much more highly placed in the KKE and much more dangerous than you would think."

The language A uses to describe Hadjiargyris is remarkably similar to that used by the Greek right in its many diatribes against Polk's friend and colleague. It was not only ideological paranoia that fueled both the anonymous author of this briefing paper and the man for whom it was prepared. Through the eyes of men trained in subversion and clandestine operations, it is possible to see the Polk murder as an insidious plot to drive a wrench into the fragile Greek-American alliance.

Years later, Donovan would confide to William vanden Heuvel how he saw his role in the Polk case. "I forced the Greeks to get a trial going. And I outmaneuvered the Communists, by beating them to a legitimate attack on the extreme right."

Winston Burdett, John Secondari, and Fred Ayer stood waiting on the tarmac when the general strode across, trailed by his soft-spoken aide, Colonel Kellis. "Even after a twenty-eight-hour flight he was mentally alert," Ayer later marveled. "He had thoroughly studied all the material on the case and asked questions which were not only apposite but penetrating. I don't believe that he was thoroughly satisfied by the manner in which we were handling the case. But at least he did not report that we were trying to cover up an assassination by agents of the Greek government."

Between his arrival at three-fifteen in the afternoon and one-thirty the following morning, Donovan managed to interview Minister of Public Order Constantine Rendis, Hadjiargyris, Ayer, and Burdett. A few hours later he was up and on his way, with Kellis and the two CBS men in tow, to catch a Salonika-bound flight. Consul Raleigh Gibson received the investigators at the Salonika airport. Again keeping a pace that exhausted the younger members of his entourage, Donovan saw the Attorney General, Christos Moustakis, and the chief of police, Apostolos Xanthopoulos, before lunch. No murder, the police chief boasted, had gone unsolved in this city since 1936.

At two o'clock, Donovan and his party moved on to the Olympus Naoussa, the restaurant where George Polk had dined with friends and colleagues shortly before he died. Colonel Thomas Martin and Commander Gordon of the British Police Mission were waiting for the Americans. Donovan and Kellis were both impressed by the Englishmen's grasp of the case and its many intricacies.

Returning to the airport to catch the last flight to Athens, the group was met by Ayer and a short, square-shaped man whose melancholic air belied his reputation as Greece's toughest cop. "Major Nicholas Mouscoundis at your service." The British-trained officer inclined his head before the general.

"Ah, yes." Donovan smiled in recognition. Ayer and Burdett had told him what an exceptionally thorough job the major, charged with the investigation, was doing. It was only bad luck that he had not yet come up with a trace of the killers. "I shall leave Greece in two days' time, on Sunday, Major. But I will be returning in one month," Donovan said, "at which time I hope this case will be solved."

The major bowed in silence. He did not need to be reminded. The Mediterranean policeman saw before him not so much a man as the living embodiment of his small country's many debts to its benefactors across the sea.

Back in Athens, the general received many former OSS warriors, come to pay their respects and offer their services. One of these was an OSS veteran named Lambros Antoniou.

The general had lunch with Rea and Adelaide Polk, charming both of them with his gallant attentions and flawless courtesy. "General Donovan's presence," wrote the trusting Adelaide Polk to CBS News executive Davidson Taylor on June 12, "is a wonderful influence."

Later that day, Donovan met with the aged and frail Prime Minister, Themistocles Sophoulis, and, responding to Ayer and

Burdett's urging, demanded to know why Polk's widow and his best friend, Hadjiargyris, had been so gently dealt with. "I am speaking frankly to you about your stepson, sir," Donovan confided, "because I know you to be an honest man. Nothing should prevent a searching interrogation of these two witnesses. They should both be in police hands, not entrusted to the Ministry of Justice, ill equipped as it is to conduct a real interrogation."

The Prime Minister gave his word. A tough interrogation of both Rea and Hadjiargyris would take place.

That night, the general dined alone with Sir Charles Wickham. Physically, culturally, and philosophically, the two men were well matched. The sixty-nine-year-old Scotland Yard veteran would provide General Donovan with counsel on the Polk case on each of his subsequent trips to Greece. There would be no need to discuss the sordid details of the case. It was sufficient that each saw the real problem as one of managing a potential crisis. Both knew that the regime they were backing in Athens was corrupt. Still, the Cold Warriors agreed, they were keeping the "Bolshies" at bay.

Donovan's next meeting revealed a side his agents revered: he was loyal to his own. Facing the Greek Foreign Minister, Donovan lost his temper.

"Are you aware, General," Foreign Minister Tsaldaris inquired, "that the man you have appointed to this investigation, Colonel Kellis, has a rather questionable war record?"

"I am fully aware," the general answered, in a voice as cold and sharp as a stiletto, "of Colonel Kellis' record of bravery while fighting alongside ELAS guerrillas. He was one of my best men, Mr. Tsaldaris. I am not equally certain, however," Donovan added, glacial blue eyes flashing, "of your own war record."

The general turned on his heel and left the Foreign Minister groping for a retort. Just over a month before, George Polk had stormed out of Tsaldaris' office in similarly high dudgeon.

The story of the brief exchange between Donovan and Tsaldaris quickly made the rounds in the hothouse world of the Athens American community, enhancing Donovan's already lustrous reputation.

Karl Rankin, ever sensitive to the pulse of the Greek right, cabled

Marshall on June 14: "Tsaldaris has queried embassy regarding Kellis, including his alleged erstwhile ELAS liaison activities and the fact that he is remaining here after Donovan's departure. The matter," the chargé noted ominously, "is liable to cause an unfortunate impression."

Through the distorted lens of Cold War politics, a genuine war hero's record was suddenly a matter of embarrassment to his own country's officials. The dubious past of their new clients, however, seemed not to give the Americans a moment's pause.

Before returning to New York, General Donovan—accompanied by Colonel Kellis—visited the man who, along with Constantine Tsaldaris, had been George Polk's most dangerous enemy: Napoleon Zervas. Polk, in his *Harper's* article, had described Zervas as "a short, fat, powerfully built man who needs glasses but likes to be seen without them . . . a fifty-seven-year-old soldier, professional gambler, and unscrupulous politician . . . his activities . . . are even more sinister than when he participated in four pre-war Greek political revolutions. . . . In and out of government he is backed by the British-organized Greek gendarmerie force, which still includes many officers and men who did police duty for the Germans during the Occupation."

Zervas offered to put his "intelligence network" at the disposal of Donovan and Kellis. Nothing ever materialized of that proffered help. Did Donovan allow himself to think for a moment that with "help" from this quarter he would ever get near the truth? More importantly, did he want to?

In his secret report to Marshall regarding Donovan's first visit, Ayer said the general was "satisfied police were doing an efficient and thorough job, especially in Salonika." The general also reassured Ayer, Burdett, and Secondari that he had no intention of allowing other investigators from among Polk's colleagues to come to Greece.

Ayer closed his report of June 13 on a somewhat defensive note. "No criticism of this work is justifiable," he wrote. "Col. Martin of the British Police Mission agrees."

The investigators—Mouscoundis, Burdett (for the CBS man was accepted by the official investigators as one of their own), Ayer, and Kellis—had only one month before General Donovan's return, one month in which to produce a suspect. Donovan had given them a deadline, and Donovan was not a man any of them relished disappointing. Six weeks after the murder, the sad truth was that they did not have a single hard lead.

Rea Polk would shortly be scratched off their list of potential suspects. Nor could the half dozen energetic investigators trap the hated Hadjiargyris. "I have never tried to handle a man," Ayer wrote of Hadjiargyris, "who was so quick mentally and so utterly aggravating. I was uncomfortably aware that he was more devious than I, and more than a match for me in any game of question and answer." John Secondari, Burdett's hotheaded partner, losing all sight of the fact that he was employed by CBS News and not the Salonika police department, told Ayer, "I still think the SOB Costa is in on it somewhere. I'm sure he's not telling the truth. He's too damned smug. He knows that nobody dares throw him in jail or rough him up because he's Old So-and-so's stepson and represents the Majesty of the American Press. You know what I'd like to do? I'd like to take a few shots at him in the street at night, just close enough to knock his hat off. Then, when he was damned good and scared, I'd like to kidnap him for just a little while and have a heart-to-heart talk. I bet I'd find out what I wanted to know."

On June 26, Rea traveled to Salonika and submitted to a final session with Major Mouscoundis. Unsmiling and under pressure from the masters he served, Greek, British, and American, Mouscoundis was not looking for information this time. He knew he had everything Rea had to give by now. At her insistence, she had even taken a lie detector test.

Lies having no basis in fact could not be silenced by fact. Like most, and this is the police state's strongest asset, Rea had a limited capacity to absorb hate. She was ready now to do what he asked of her. She signed a sworn statement prepared for her by the major stating that she believed her husband was murdered by the Communists.

Mouscoundis told Ayer, "It is a sincere change of opinion on her part. She did not say this only because we wished her to. She truly believes it. She agrees that if the government would have done it, the body would not have been found, the identification card never sent."

He went on with some satisfaction to inform Ayer that Rea also said she disliked Hadjiargyris. Regrettably, she could provide no concrete evidence against him.

Rea's sudden animosity toward her husband's friend was prompted by something Mouscoundis told her. "Your friend," he said of the Greek reporter, "tells us you slept with a British officer on the night of May 8." May 8 was the night George Polk was murdered. Rea, no longer sure of who or what to believe, would never again trust Hadjiargyris.

Suddenly, Ayer, who days before had been certain of Rea's ties to the Party and of her role as a Communist courier while she worked as a stewardess, wrote Marshall that the charges against her were "not definite enough to justify action." They had what they wanted from her. They could call off the smear campaign. If her reputation in her native land had been permanently damaged, write it off as another casualty of war.

Still, the FBI agent was not convinced Rea should be let loose on an unsuspecting American public. "Permanent presence of Rea in U.S. with access to all press," Ayer advised, "must be weighed against temporary blast" officials would suffer for denying her the right to leave Greece.

Thus it was clear that it had never been Rea's guilt that kept her on the list of police suspects, but her potential to do harm to Greece and to America's unconditional support of the Greek right.

Later that same week Rea was finally allowed to leave her homeland for an uncertain future in America. Before boarding her American military transport, she spat on the soil of Greece, a very Greek gesture of contempt.

Awaiting Rea in New York was a young man of medium height and the serene, even features of a seminarian. William E. Colby, former OSS agent and future director of Central Intelligence, was General Donovan's trusted aide. Colby and his wife, Barbara, befriended Rea, who badly needed friends in New York. Trained in all aspects of espionage and counterinsurgency, Colby spent many hours interrogating the young woman about all she knew of her husband's murder. Rea confided to him her reasons for suspecting the right wing of responsibility for her husband's murder. But Colby was Donovan's man, and though Donovan's mandate was from the Lippmann committee, none of the statements Rea gave Colby ever reached even the Lippmann committee, let alone the greater American press.

The twenty-year-old widow would never again see her closest companion during the weeks following her husband's death. On September 17, 1948, Mary Barber did, however, send Rea Polk a message. It was more a warning than a message, really. Mrs. Barber, visiting Greece after her departure shortly after Rea's own, called on Rea's father in Athens. "Tell Rea not to mix herself in the Polk case anymore. The Minister of Justice has shown me a transcript of her CBS broadcast on the murder [CBS Report Number 3 on the Murder of George Polk, September 9, 1948]. For her own good, she must not get any further involved," Mrs. Barber advised him, strange counsel from a reporter. "If she does, they will throw her out of America, for they will think she is a Communist. Tell your daughter to be careful."

Though Rea and Hadjiargyris had been harassed and vilified, ultimately they had enough Americans concerned with their welfare to keep Greek officials from charging them with murder. What Major Mouscoundis needed was a suspect who had no defenses. He needed someone who was virtually alone in the world. A suspect without resources and without a sympathetic profile was required for the role of scapegoat.

Mouscoundis was about to find just such a suspect. But there was a man in his way. His name was John Panopoulos, a Greek policeman like Mouscoundis, but an honest one. Panopoulos, who worked for the Ministry of Public Order as chief of the Athens town police, was in nobody's pocket. Unlike Mouscoundis, he did not owe his job to the British. Having once helped to capture the would-be assassin of the country's well-loved republican reformist Prime Minister, Eleutherios Venizelos, he was also protected by legend. Panopoulos thought he smelled a rat in the Polk case. Early on, he began to document the peculiar British obsession with an American citizen, both before and after his murder.

Panopoulos' methodical policeman's mind continued to return to three days:

May 6: Two days after Polk put in his request for a permit to travel north, Colonel Stacy of the British Police Mission alerted the Salonika police that ten Communists would soon arrive in the town to commit acts of sabotage.

May 8: Colonel Martin of the British Police Mission informed Salonika police chief Apostolos Xanthopoulos that Communist agents were already in Salonika to prepare for an act or acts of terrorism. (At this stage Polk's body had not surfaced, though he had disappeared the day before.) As was soon to be clear, the only known act of terrorism in security-obsessed Salonika that week was the murder of the American reporter.

May 20: Sir Charles Wickham called on Xanthopoulos, discussed the Polk case for three hours, and then returned to Athens. Panopoulos also knew that it was Colonel Martin who made sure that Mouscoundis was put in charge of the murder investigation.

But Panopoulos could not make any significant advance beyond these facts. He still hoped that General Donovan would be sympathetic to his observations regarding the British preoccupation with the case. Panopoulos' own boss, Minister of Public Order Constantine Rendis, was a realist. Though a Liberal and thus not a member of the Royalist Party, he was a politician nonetheless, and fanatically anti-Communist at that. Rendis was not the man to follow Panopoulos' troubling speculations regarding the crime.

Vaios Papastathopoulos, a security agent who was Panopoulos' aide on the Polk investigation, recalls the day all of his boss's files on the case were removed from Panopoulos' hands. It was around mid-July when a group of Americans, strangers to Papastathopoulos, arrived to inform the stolid Greek policeman that his findings "weren't in Greece's interest," since Athens' staunch ally, Great Britain, was implicated.

Panopoulos, who died of a heart attack in 1957, retreated into the silence of a duty-bound public servant. But he was sufficiently convinced of his case to outline to General Donovan the sequence of the movements of key British figures just before and after Polk's murder. A reasonable man, Panopoulos worried about his own position, and asked the American not to inform Minister Rendis, his boss, of his continued suspicions. He need not have been so anxious. There is no record of Donovan ever discussing Panopoulos' suspicions with any officials, Greek or American.

With renewed urgency in the wake of General Donovan's visit, Mouscoundis plunged into his mock investigation. His preferred candidates for harassment were still newsmen. In this, Mouscoundis was confident of the full support of the American Embassy. Next to receive the Mouscoundis treatment was United Press correspondent Daniel Thrapp. Thrapp made the mistake of confiding to his Rome colleague Winston Burdett before the latter's departure for Greece that he knew a man or two in Salonika who might have been contacts for Polk. Thrapp had been a friend of Polk's while serving in Athens. The two men had talked idly of the mythical Markos interview, in the way all reporters around the Grande Bretagne bar did. Thrapp, moreover, was known to Mouscoundis from his numerous trips to Salonika. Mouscoundis, who needed a name as urgently as a bloodhound needs a scent, was determined to get the name of a Salonika contact out of the UP man.

Thrapp knew the stakes were deadly. A naturally wary man, he resisted all attempts to get him to return to Greece. He also refused to give information to the U.S. Embassy in Rome or an emissary sent from Athens. He understood that a seemingly harmless drop of a name could lead to major trouble.

A month or so before George Polk was lured to his death, Thrapp was in Salonika. One evening, two Greeks came to his hotel room with an offer the UP man could barely make out. They looked hardened enough to be foot soldiers of either side. Thrapp, reluctant to be left alone with them, led the two to a small tobacconist's shop around the corner. "What are they telling me?" he asked the English-speaking shopkeeper.

"They are Communists!" the clerk whispered, terror in his voice. He might as well have said, "They are lepers!"

Thrapp, who did not trust them as the genuine article, told the two men to go away, he wasn't interested. But he was never sure afterward if the men had been sent by Mouscoundis to bait him or if they had in fact come "from the mountains." Unlike Polk, Thrapp was not prepared to take a chance.

In a letter to Clifford L. Day, the London bureau chief of UP, Thrapp voiced his disgust with the tone of the investigation:

> I hold no open sesame to George Polk's death. No one but a couple of bird-brains like Winnie Burdett and his secondary fellow Junior G-Man Secondari would suggest that I do. . . . I never met Secondari until he came lurking around in early June with a lot of bughouse ideas about secret plots and clues and other movie paraphernalia. They all have some idea that I and I alone can solve the Polk killing. Everything I know you could write on the back of a postage stamp. . . . I cannot reveal the name of this guy in Salonika or his address or anything else about him for two very good reasons: It would get a lot of other people in a jam if I did so. These people would have to be brought in because I could not tell of this bird's background without telling who told me so. I cannot throw a bunch of people who have been of very great help to me to the wolves simply in the (completely baseless) hope that it would put someone on the track of Polk's murderers.
>
> . . . Burdett says, "Thrapp spent quite a lot of time in Salonika building up his contacts." I spent a lot of time there trying to build up some contacts, but the result mostly was nil, for the same reason it was nil for Polk and a lot of other guys who tried the same thing.
>
> Polk and I discussed it once over lightly, neither letting the other know what he was really talking about. It was too good a story to share. I had little idea of Polk's plans and have in fact learned more about them from the subsequent investigation than I knew when I left Greece.

The investigators ignored Thrapp's energetic disclaimers. In fact, lacking other leads to follow, they deemed Thrapp sufficiently important to send General Donovan to Rome. (The resourceful general was able to combine the trip with a papal audience.)

After a pleasant hour with the young foreign correspondent, Donovan emerged satisfied that Thrapp knew little or nothing about the case. Thrapp later said Donovan didn't seem to have the facts of the case down, and didn't ask him the right questions about the reporters' customary contacts in Salonika.

Thus June passed, as had May before, uselessly, with Greek investigators and their American supporters chasing after people whose only crime was their politics. And all the while Greek and American officials hinted that the real villain behind the crime was the American press.

"The Attorney General and Major Mouscoundis," Raleigh Gibson cabled the Secretary of State on June 28, "had both planned to interrogate Hadjiargyris in Salonika but through fear of criticism from the American correspondents in Athens as well as from American columnists they changed their plans. . . .

"With regard to the crime having been committed by the extreme right, or an individual connected with it," Gibson continued, "it is believed that the Communists would have taken advantage of this and publicized it. There is no doubt that the Communist intelligence set-up is an efficient one in northern Greece and that the Communists must know, or are in a position to find out, who committed the murder."

The consul general's remarkable faith in Communist infiltration of Salonika under martial law is not matched by his faith in the right wing's penetration of Communist forces. This is all the more startling given the fact that the right was the ruling power and boasted a daily haul of Communist prisoners.

Lieutenant Colonel James G. L. Kellis had been in Greece less than two weeks when he realized that something was terribly wrong about this nearly two-month-long farce they called an investigation.

25

It was a question of police incompetence, Colonel Kellis told himself at first. Plus the fact that it was a political murder, the toughest for any cop to tackle. Nicholas Mouscoundis seemed to be giving it his best shot anyway. Little by little, however, Kellis observed too many "clues" that didn't add up, too many people too feverishly pursued with no result in the end. Other clues, clues that showed a glimmer of promise, Mouscoundis dropped in haste. Kellis' unease grew daily, for it was equally apparent to him that Mouscoundis was a shrewd professional, a man with brilliant survival instincts in the quicksand of Greek politics. Kellis took his time drawing conclusions about people. He was a slow-moving man who gave away almost nothing.

He had first thought of Mouscoundis as a colleague, a partner in solving this awful crime. We are going to do this, we are talking to so-and-so, his early letters to Donovan read. It seemed to be a joint Kellis-Mouscoundis effort.

But after a while, Jim Kellis realized he was really quite alone in his determination to solve this murder. It seemed to Kellis that nobody else in Greece wanted to get to the bottom of it. What he did not realize was that there were very few people in Washington who were interested in a genuine investigation either.

When he arrived, Kellis had been just as convinced as any of the other American officials on the scene that George Polk died at the hands of Communists. But Kellis was a different sort of investigator than Burdett, Ayer, or even Donovan. He did not shape his investigation to anybody's political requirements. He simply assumed he was there to get at the truth.

Donovan, he thought, picked him from among all his other comrades because he was best qualified to handle the job. Kellis was not an innocent. But, like the murdered man, he was incapable of subordinating truth to any cause, no matter how compelling. Thus, like Polk, Kellis was a dangerous man in Greece in the summer of 1948.

Unlike the other Americans on the scene, Kellis spoke Greek. It was much tougher for Major Mouscoundis to mislead him. Burdett, Ayer, and the rest could not travel and move about freely without an officially sanctioned interpreter. Their Americanness glowed like fluorescent paint.

Kellis' facility with the language gave him great freedom, and his short, square frame, curly black hair, and deep-set dark eyes made it easy for him to blend in with a Greek crowd. He could work like a real investigator, not a visiting dignitary whose every move is warily observed. And he was practiced in going underground. He had planted bombs not far from Salonika during the German occupation. He knew how to ease a Greek's natural suspicion and turn it into trust. He was one of them, really. With his low-key persuasion, and money as a lubricant, Kellis could get people to talk.

It was little things at first, things he could attribute to sloppy fieldwork. Like Mouscoundis making nothing of the fact that Polk was bound with rope uncommon in Salonika, a type imported from the Middle East. And why hadn't the police checked on which restaurants served lobster on the night of the murder, since the autopsy revealed almost three pounds of lobster in the dead man's stomach? It only cost Kellis ten dollars to bribe the orchestra leader of the Café Luxembourg to find out that lobster had been served there on the night of Polk's disappearance. But when Kellis showed him the photograph of Polk he always carried in his pocket, the orchestra leader only shook his head.

When he tried to talk to the Astoria Hotel staff, neither trust nor money cut through the sullen fear he read in their faces. Most of them had already spent sufficient time in police custody to want nothing more to do with the case. "They are afraid of something,"

Kellis wrote Donovan on July 22. "Only through intimate and daily contact could anybody get the truth out of these people." Kellis would not be permitted the luxury of that sort of time.

Major Mouscoundis continued to insist on the accuracy of the British-supplied intelligence regarding Communist terrorists in Salonika around the time of the murder. Kellis' own evidence cast serious doubt on this. Mouscoundis claimed that Colonel Evangelos Vasvanas, one of Salonika's better-known Communists, a folk hero to some, had slipped into town the weekend of George Polk's murder. Vasvanas had managed somehow to elude the Greek security forces, but, with dramatic flourish, Mouscoundis described the capture of five other Communist guerrillas. Mouscoundis elaborated on how their Communist chief, a Captain Menolas, had been wounded in the hand during the skirmish. Kellis asked to interview him. He was not taking anything for granted anymore. Not since he overheard the major say to one of his subordinates, "Be careful what you say in front of Colonel Kellis. He understands Greek."

"During the War," Kellis wrote Donovan on June 28, "I participated in sabotage. I have some knowledge of material used in this type of work, the planning required, the transmission of messages to undertake sabotage, etc., etc. I do not believe, as the police do, that this group, which was captured on May 21, entered Salonika to cause sabotage for the purpose of interrupting the Polk investigation."

Two policemen, Mouscoundis' men, sat in on Kellis' interview with the jailed Communist. The captive was tense and guarded. But Kellis knew what questions to ask. Menolas' story of his capture, under Kellis' grilling, did not correspond to Mouscoundis'. Nor did Kellis notice a wound on either of Menolas' hands.

As proof that Communist saboteurs had been dispatched to Salonika, Mouscoundis showed Kellis two messages "intercepted" by the Greek National Army. "Markos orders Macedonian headquarters to intensify sabotage in Salonika in order to impede the Polk investigation and place it in a position of secondary importance. Signed, Papas, Director of General Security."

Kellis flew to Athens the next day to verify that the intelligence had come from the Greek General Staff communications division.

A careful search of messages received and intercepted during that period confirmed Kellis' hunch. "Papas" was a phony.

Kellis finally confronted Mouscoundis. "You're not playing straight with me, Major. You're covering up something."

Mouscoundis replied lamely, "Colonel, don't press me. There are questions of national interest involved here. I have my orders. I have only a few years of my career left," Mouscoundis pleaded. "I do not wish to lose my pension."

But who has given you your orders, Kellis asked. Who is putting this pressure on you? Mouscoundis simply shook his head. For the first time, Kellis had a sense that he was dealing with a very frightened man.

The Salonika waterfront apartment of Raleigh Gibson, a small haven of Anglo-Americana, was where British and American officials met to drink and gossip. The dapper, bald Gibson, toward the end of a long and unspectacular career as a foreign service officer, possessed an unlimited supply of PX scotch and a wife who loved to entertain. The Gibsons' parties were convivial gatherings where liquor and the too quick intimacy of men and women serving in remote and dangerous places prompted flowing conversation and exchanges of confidences.

It was at one of these parties that Colonel Kellis met Captain Victor Rich of the British Army's Infantry Brigade. Captain Rich was too low in rank to have been privy to all the discussions and strategies of more senior officers, but his position as intelligence officer kept him well informed.

Captain Rich had a few drinks under his belt when he confided to Kellis, "Don't listen to what the Greek police are telling you. Polk was killed not far from the place where he was found. They didn't kill him in Athens because they didn't want a police shake-up down there."

Kellis, who committed to memory every word the British captain uttered, maintained his usual impassive expression. "Can we talk tomorrow morning?" he asked the British officer.

"Sure," Rich replied, "come to my office."

Kellis was at the British Military Mission headquarters on Nikis Street early the next morning. He found a different man from the one he talked to the night before. "I talked too much, Colonel," Rich began, his voice remote, his features impenetrable. "I am sorry. But I cannot discuss this matter further."

"Rich knows something," Kellis wrote General Donovan, "but is not at freedom to discuss it." Kellis' brush with the truth was the first of many such enticing moments, usually involving British military officers with ties to the intelligence services, who had been, in the words of the historian of British intelligence, Nigel West, "reminded of their duty under the Official Secrets Act."*

Discouraged by Captain Rich's abrupt change of heart, Kellis tried another Englishman he had met at Gibson's home. "From Rich's office," Kellis wrote Donovan, "I visited Captain Stacey† of the Salonika Balkan Counter Intelligence Section." Stacey, though again a low-ranking officer, seemed less afraid of the consequences of speaking his mind than Rich.

"Captain Stacey discussed the police theory of the crime," Kellis writes, "and told me that he did not agree with them. Stacey pointed out that the person the police accused of participating in or organizing the crime, Vasvanas, came in and out of Salonika by land and Stacey claimed to have followed his moves while in the city. He doubts Vasvanas' connection to the crime.

"Many British officers connected to intelligence and counterin-

---

* Nearly three decades later, George Polk's cousin, Baltimore *Sun* foreign correspondent Jefferson Price, met a former British Army officer of Greek ancestry. Over a Hong Kong poker table, the retired officer learned of Price's connection to the dead man. Gregory S., like Victor Rich, knew something about the case and, he, too, "talked too much." Price, excited at the proximity of something like a solution to the decades-old mystery, engraved three words on his memory: British Police Mission.

When, on this author's behalf, Price attempted to pin the officer down, he was rebuked: "Jeff," Gregory S. wrote on February 27, 1988, in a registered, special delivery letter from his home in Hong Kong, "I advise you to read carefully the following away from the fantasies of your memory. Some useful information for you: When you met me in Hong Kong and we talked about the Polk case, I informed you what I read continually in the Greek press. Some of them have reason to believe that the British Mission was involved in order to embarrass the USA."

Gregory S.'s own memory is faulty in a letter whose aggressive tone seems intended less for an old poker pal than for the record. While the Greek press has over the years alluded to possible involvement of British and American intelligence agencies in the Polk murder, there has never been any serious examination of the role played by the British Police Mission. Gregory S.'s poker table information was too vital for Jefferson Price to allow his memory to play tricks on him.

† Not to be confused with Colonel Stacy of the British Police Mission in Salonika.

telligence (mostly in covert capacities)," Kellis goes on, "would let drop a cryptic remark that the police are faking. On two occasions these men pointed the finger at the Greek Military Police."

Like a slow-stirring but implacable guard dog, Kellis now moved deliberately forward, following tracks without regard to danger to himself or to the sacred cause of Greek-American relations. He stopped checking in with Major Mouscoundis. The Greek policeman had, in Kellis' eyes, been transformed from investigator to suspect.

The day after his conversations with Captains Rich and Stacey, Kellis made a secret trip to the place from where Mouscoundis said Vasvanas had embarked. Eleftherohorion, a fishing port near Salonika, was honeycombed with gendarmes and security forces, in all but name a Greek National Army stronghold. "If any caïque," Kellis wrote Donovan, "usually fishing in this area, and I estimate there to be about fifty, was involved in the crime, I believe that the gendarmerie would have discovered it long ago."

There was more than the evidence Kellis had amassed thus far to refute Mouscoundis' theory of Communist saboteurs arriving by caïque to murder George Polk. There were also George Polk's movements in his final days, which made a lie of the official version of his murder. It was not his fixed appointment with a Markos agent that prompted Polk to send this telegram to his wife: "Decided remain Astoria Hotel Salonika because United Nations story upshaping on child abduction. Perhaps continuing Kavalla Monday or Tuesday then returning Athens. Don't forget," Polk had urged his wife, "advise me here any word Nieman Fellowship."

Mouscoundis claimed this telegram was simply a ploy, a cover for Polk's real movements. There was no real news coming out of the UN committee on child abduction, he had assured Kellis. But Kellis, in characteristic style, called on the headquarters of the UN Special Committee on the Balkans (UNSCOB) and discovered that a press release, number 80, had been issued the day of Polk's telegram, announcing "a common realization that the task was urgent and that practical measures should be undertaken as soon as possible. A meeting was called for the following morning."

"I don't know," Kellis wrote Donovan, "if Mouscoundis checked the papers or press release no. 80 of UNSCOB."

Why, Kellis wondered, had Polk called on Randoll Coate, the British information officer, known to have solid contacts with the Communists from his resistance days, and asked him for help with contacts? He had already made the same request of Colonel "Ace" Miller. To Mouscoundis these were all cover moves. "They are trying to present Polk as a mysteriously acting person," Kellis wrote Donovan. For him this picture of Polk simply didn't fit with everything else he had pieced together about the man.

"The police theory is that Mr. Polk already had a contact with the Communists prior to his departure from Athens and also had a rendezvous at Salonika. If such a rendezvous existed," Kellis posed the crucial question, "why should he manifest himself at the plane until 12 noon Thursday for Kavalla? Why should he ask three Americans, one British, and two Greeks if they knew of a way to get him in contact with the Communists?"

In the eyes of the Greek right, Kellis was permanently tainted as a result of his OSS undercover days fighting the Germans alongside the ELAS guerrillas (though during the resistance ELAS was not Communist but represented a wide spectrum of leftist and centrist views). This same experience with the resistance gave Kellis an appreciation of the ELAS guerrillas' mentality. "They are at least wise in one thing," he wrote Donovan, " 'the conspiratorial way.' They know when to keep their mouth shut and they always maintain strict secrecy in their operation." Polk, to Kellis' mind, did not comport himself like a man who is party to a top secret rendezvous. "Wouldn't Polk's hunt for a contact arouse the organs of the police?" Kellis wondered.

Mouscoundis had an explanation ready for Polk's continued search for a "contact" even while he already had a road map to the guerrillas. "The police claim that this was just another method of covering Polk's actions, of possibly looking for another way, in case his regular contact failed. This is so much nonsense to me, and I refuse to believe that policemen with so many years of experience can believe in such a childish explanation.

"My belief," Kellis concluded, "and it is supported by the facts, is that the late Mr. George Polk did not make a contact with a bona fide Communist, if at all, until at least 8:15 p.m. Saturday May 8th. Between 8:15 and midnight he probably met someone. For anyone," wrote Kellis after weeks of stalking the security-infested port city, "to commit such a crime in Salonika with such speed and still two months later the police to be unable to uncover the murderers makes me wonder."

In his final letter to Donovan from Greece, on July 22, Kellis inadvertently presented the conspirators with an unexpected gift. The colonel listed people who "supposedly knew something or are involved in the crime." Among them were the Salonika military police (with no particular members specified), Stefanakis, the chief of Salonika political security, George Drossos, the Greek liaison officer with UNSCOB, Kavanides of the Ministry of Information (who approved Polk's travel plans to Salonika), Lieutenant Colonel Papas of the Athens gendarmerie, Lieutenant Georgandas of the Greek General Staff intelligence division, Mr. Limberopoulos of UNSCOB, and, finally, Gregory Staktopoulos, Greek newspaperman. Of all the names and organizations on Kellis' list only one was ever pursued by the Greek investigators. For only one could be pursued without threatening the rickety structure of the official version of the murder: Gregory Staktopoulos.

In a CIA memorandum written by Kellis on December 3, 1953,* the colonel wrote: "Gen. Donovan reviewed very carefully all of the ten suspects that I had submitted to him in my confidential report and *asked the Greek Chief Investigator (Mouscoundis) to concentrate on one, a Greek newspaperman . . .*"

Thus, willy-nilly, Kellis, as zealous a crusader for truth as George Polk, advanced the cause of the cover-up by providing a list of "suspects." It is also clear from Kellis' report that it was Donovan who handpicked Gregory Staktopoulos, who fit the profile of the scapegoat perfectly.

Unlike "Wild Bill" Donovan's other CIA briefing papers, Kellis' forthright account of July 22, 1948, could not have given the chief much pleasure.

* It was finally declassified on May 31, 1978, though the version released then contained many deletions made for "security" reasons.

Whoever committed this crime [wrote Kellis] has power, the facility of mobility, protection, and expert direction.

During my stay with Mouscoundis I realized that this man certainly had a good control over the Communist situation in Salonika. Only a few high-ranking Communists were not discovered as yet and I doubt that Polk could have managed to get in contact with them in such a short time. . . .

The police attribute this crime to Col. Vasvanas, the Communist leader of Pierra, who was in Salonika May 4–9. Despite the fact that Captain Stacey, who is reputed to have the best penetration of the Communists in Salonika, excludes this possibility. How did Polk manage to get in contact with him?

One fact that we should consider at this moment: Certain American newsmen are being followed by organs of the government in Greece. This is certain. Particularly when Polk asked indiscreetly for ways of meeting the Communists, at least in one instance in the presence of a Greek official, is it possible that he was shadowed by security officials?

Kellis closed his letter of July 22 to his commanding officer with his most damaging information:

Information has been received to the effect that Tsaldaris despised Polk for his attacks on him and the right-wing leaders. The article in *Harper's* left a strong impression here.

We hear that Polk had an interview with Tsaldaris prior to his departure for the north in which he threatened Tsaldaris that he would expose him. A letter sent by a friend from New York notifying Polk that Tsaldaris deposited $25,000 with the Chase Bank disappeared. This letter was received by Polk, who related the contents to Mr. M. Johnson of CARE, who in turn related the contents to Dr. Homer Davis. I met Dr. Davis, who is a person of high integrity. *He verified the information for me.*

When Kellis began to share some of his findings with Chargé Rankin in the presence of Sir Charles Wickham, Robert Driscoll and Christian Freer of the CIA, and Fred Ayer of the FBI, their response was dismissive.

"I don't see why you're breaking your back trying to uncover who killed this correspondent," the imperious American chargé said. "If you as a military officer, or I as a diplomat, were killed, none of these people would give a damn."

Kellis, repelled beyond words, walked out of the gathering. He was also certain now that an Anglo-American cover-up of the murder was in place.

The same day, Rankin's telex to Secretary Marshall crackled of crisis. "Freer and Driscoll, who had been following the investigation details for the Embassy, have discussed case with Kellis and report his belief based on little more than personal prejudice. . . . In view of the above situation the Embassy believes the sooner Kellis is removed from the scene the better."

Two days after Kellis sent the general his letter informing him of Polk's confrontation with Tsaldaris, Donovan was in Salonika.

26

The American general smiled. "Major, I want you to be candid with me. Has there been any pressure from your government brought to bear on you in the manner in which you have conducted your investigation?" Mouscoundis, shifting uncomfortably in his seat, shook his head slowly. Burdett and Kellis sat on either side of General Donovan. Also present in the American Consulate conference room was Theodore G. Lambron, a Greek-American medical student, who, though lacking any prior investigative experience, had been engaged by Donovan to assist in the inquiry.

"I have read your last police report," the general pressed on, "and it is not what we would call a police report at all. It is a political argument. I am afraid I shall be forced to say as much publicly, if that is the way the investigation is going, Major," Donovan stated flatly.

"I have done everything from a police angle," Mouscoundis answered, "and I shall continue to do so."

The general shook his head. "The situation is worse than it was during my previous visit. Why have we reached this impasse?"

"We have received information that a Communist leader entered Salonika from the mountains on May 4," the major said, picking up his favorite alibi for inaction, "and disappeared on the night of the murder."

"Major," the general said, his most unforgiving gaze fixed on the Greek, "an arrest is desired."

"I do not like the sound of that," Mouscoundis answered feebly. "It shows no appreciation of our bad luck on this case."

"What about those five terrorists you picked up?" Burdett queried. "Did anything come out of that, Major?"

The major again shook his head despondently.

"It was a phony, Major," Kellis said. "The message you got from Papas at National Security informing you of saboteurs coming to divert you from the Polk case was never sent. Not by National Security anyway. I checked. It was a plant."

"It seems to me," Burdett added, "that you have theories on this crime but they are based on political intelligence, not facts."

"The facts will come as soon as an arrest is made," Mouscoundis said.

"Someone telephoned Polk at his hotel on Saturday night," said Donovan, who had been briefed by Kellis. "Polk then left his room quite suddenly. Who was this person? Has anything been done to try to find this person?"

"We do not know anything about this phone call," the major said, "but we have circulated Mr. Polk's picture as far as Kozani."

Donovan turned to Kellis. "Why don't you share some of your findings with the major? He might find them helpful."

Kellis proceeded to outline for the group the results of his independent investigation. He expressed his own theory that Polk could not have had a solid Communist contact prior to leaving Athens, since all his movements in Salonika contradicted this police theory. He had not in fact intended to travel to Salonika in the first place. Polk, Kellis made plain, had decided to stay on in Salonika to pursue the child abduction story.

"But there was nothing happening on that story," Mouscoundis protested.

"The UN press release," Kellis said, "would seem to contradict that."

"Why should Polk be interested in child abduction," Mouscoundis demanded, irritated because Kellis was confusing his straightforward scenario, "when all he wanted was to reach the mountains?"

No one bothered to answer. Kellis pressed on remorselessly, armed with facts to counter each of Mouscoundis' theories.

After Kellis had given the times and places of each of Polk's appointments during his fateful two days in the city, Donovan again took up the interrogator's role. "I have heard that Randoll Coate, the British information officer in Salonika, is supposed to be the best-informed man in northern Greece on the Communists. I understand he's left town, Major. Did anybody talk to him in time?"

"No," said Mouscoundis. "Does Colonel Kellis rule out the possibility that Polk's actions were a cover for his true purpose?"

"He was an open man," Burdett volunteered, "not the type to camouflage."

"For the sake of the investigation," Donovan pronounced, "I will agree with the major's theory that perhaps Polk was under orders from Athens to behave a certain way while in Salonika."

It was a brief remark, seemingly inconsequential. Its repercussions were enormous. In one smooth stroke, the general shifted his support to the police theory of the crime. It was a theory that hinged on Polk's being in Salonika to keep a rendezvous with Markos. Though there were no facts to support this, Mouscoundis' case against the Communists did not hold up without it. It seemed that Donovan had not registered the compelling logic of Kellis' methodical analysis. Or that he preferred not to follow it. Donovan's aggressive posturing toward Mouscoundis had been a carefully calibrated performance, which he described to William vanden Heuvel as acting as a "legitimate critic of the right."

Mouscoundis, with room to breathe now, had meanwhile asked an aide to phone George Drossos, a prominent right-wing journalist, Greek government observer at the UN Special Committee on the Balkans, and agent of the Tsaldaris regime. Drossos was rumored to have information regarding Coate. Drossos also knew George Polk and, in a bizarre twist of fate, had served as one of his and Rea's witnesses at their wedding.

Within minutes George Drossos stood at the end of the Greek-American conference table and launched yet another theory on who led George Polk to his death.

"I ran into Randoll Coate at the British 10th Infantry Brigade mess the week George disappeared," Drossos began. "Coate is an old friend of mine and a very clever man. He told me Polk called on him on Saturday. He asked the Englishman to put him in contact with the bandits. Coate wanted to see just how serious Polk was, so he told him, 'All right, I can give you an introduction to a cousin of Markos.'

"But Polk wasn't fooled," Drossos continued, "since Coate had already given that name to Stephen Barber, who found it useless. 'I want a real contact,' Polk insisted. Coate could see he was serious about going to the bandits but replied he had no such information. 'Don't worry,' Coate told me, 'I'm sure Polk's with the bandits by now.' "

Drossos helpfully provided two more bits of evidence to support the theory that Polk was in fact en route to the Communists when he was murdered. He claimed to have "by chance" seen a cable from the Greek Consul General in Istanbul stating that Polk had told his CBS colleague in Turkey that he already had a contact who would get him to Markos.

And again "by chance" Drossos happened to have been in Rome in June and talked to Dan Thrapp regarding the Polk case. Thrapp, said Drossos, told him that in his view the crime was "prepared" in Salonika. The UP man asked Drossos if any of Polk's friends had stepped forward with information. If they had not, Thrapp supposedly concluded, it was because they either were involved or were Communists.

In this apparently innocent fashion another man was drawn into the circumference of the investigation. Randoll Coate's misfortune was that his long-overdue transfer from Salonika to Oslo occurred the week following the Polk murder. This coincidence, added to the incriminating facts that Salonika police allegedly found lobster shells in his trash can and that Polk called on him shortly before he disappeared, would cast a shadow over him that lasted his entire professional life.

Coate's biggest problem was that he was not at all convinced of the rightness of the British mission in Greece. An idealist enamored of the classics, he preferred the company of Greeks and journalists to that of his fellow British diplomats. He was not the sort of man the Foreign Office would go out of its way to defend. He was too openly dismissive of the colonial mentality of the likes of Sir Charles Wickham. "I despised our Greek policy," he recalled in 1987, "and I loved the Greek people." Coate, like so many other British diplomats posted to Greece, had a fondness for intelligence gathering and had been reprimanded for excessive dabbling in this field by his superior, A. G. R. Rouse, former chief of the British Information Department in Athens. The suspicions attached to Coate also were later reinforced by a letter (dated May 3, 1949) that Costas Hadjiargyris wrote to Greek Attorney General Panayotis Constantinides alluding to British preoccupation at many levels with the Polk murder, including Coate's alleged role. In an attempt to fight back against his continued harassment at the hands of Greek police, Hadjiargyris went so far as to suggest Coate might have been Polk's contact to the guerrillas and may have been "in the boat at the time of the murder and indeed may have pulled the trigger."

Coate now believes that, in the eyes of Greek (and perhaps some British and American) officials, he had been permanently contaminated by his time with the left-wing ELAS guerrillas during the occupation. Though he admitted to having seen Polk on his last day in Salonika, he also saw nothing remarkable about this. No American journalist would pass through town without calling on him. "The Americans simply didn't have their own contacts," he recalled. "Everybody knew we had them." It is a fact that Raleigh Gibson, the American Consul, called daily on the British Consulate to be briefed on guerrilla activities.

Drossos, having deftly muddied the waters, took his leave of the group. Kellis resumed his attempt to present his case. "Based on all my investigations," Kellis persevered, "I do not believe George Polk had a lead to the Communists until 8 p.m. Saturday. The coroner reported that Polk was killed a half hour after eating that same night. Who in Salonika," Kellis asked, "can commit a crime like this and keep it covered up? Mobility, power, freedom of action," Kellis said, "these are the three things this crime required."

"What, then," Burdett asked, "is your conclusion, Colonel?"

"My conclusion is that if Polk did not have a contact until 8 p.m., the Communists could not have murdered him. They could not do so without orders." Kellis spoke with the quiet authority that came with knowing the enemy's method of operations.

Mouscoundis, again losing ground, mumbled a few words about

the Communists knowing something about the crime nonetheless. Again Donovan dexterously rescued the Greek's sinking ship. "In my opinion," he intoned, "too much attention is being paid to the right or the left committing this crime. More attention should be paid to individuals. Let's keep this case away from politics," said one of the most politically motivated men in the room.

Mouscoundis, seizing the opening, again floated the name of Colonel Vasvanas, the Salonika Communist leader. Vasvanas had been in Salonika, he said, to arrange for saboteurs to come in. Can you prove this in court? Donovan demanded. No, the major conceded, but in my heart I feel it is so.

Burdett finally stirred. "Why have only Communists been examined so far as suspects? What about some other angles?"

General Donovan, who would later tell NBC's John Donovan that CBS employed too many Communists, said, "I know you have your instincts, Major. I know you are following them on this case." He smiled sympathetically. "But I cannot go home to the United States and tell the people that we are relying solely on your instincts."

"I assure you, General," Mouscoundis concluded, "that I am doing my very best. No one can derail this investigation."

The general thanked Mouscoundis and assured him he was placing all his faith in his effort. Kellis spoke not another word. His investigation, his carefully gathered facts, his dozens of interviews, his high-risk trips to godforsaken outposts in search of evidence, all seemed to have already vanished into the ether. What hurt was that it was General "Wild Bill" Donovan who had undercut his work and obscured the facts of the case.

Donovan did not fire Kellis. But he did nothing to stop his removal from the case. The telegram arrived on the very day of this tense meeting of the investigators. It was sent by the general's aide William Colby and said only, "Kellis must return Washington." The decision was attributed to the Secretary of the Air Force, Stuart Symington.

On July 31, after Kellis had already gone, the general sent a telegram to the Lippmann committee: "I believe it is important for

Polk case that Kellis return next week for one month." Let the record show, this message seemed to shout, as did so many of Donovan's terse communications.

Ernest Lindley, the *Newsweek* editor who became Lippmann's unofficial deputy on the case, called Kellis at his Washington home the following week. "The general wants you back in Greece, Colonel," Lindley told him.

Kellis, whose loyalty to his former commanding officer was total, by now understood that this invitation was meaningless. Kellis wrote bitterly to General Donovan on August 5:

> While I was in Greece, Mr. Rankin and Mr. Ayer devoted much effort to have me recalled. Their radiograms, which I consider unfair, biased, and often inaccurate, may reflect on my service record, and I believe that I should no longer associate myself with them and this investigation. If they were as much interested in pressing the investigation as they were in having me recalled from Greece, I have no doubt that the guilty parties would have been found long ago.
>
> In case you feel that I am unduly worried about them, I suggest that you ask the State Department to show you all communications, repeat all, from Salonika and Athens regarding the Polk case and myself. I am sure you would find some of those characters exposed to their true colors.

Lippmann stayed very much aloof from this newest controversy. Yet it is clear from a memorandum he received from Ernest Lindley on July 29 that Lippmann was fully briefed on some of the most disturbing facts of the case. Lindley had taken it upon himself to telephone Kellis upon the latter's return from Greece.

> Col. Kellis said his informant (an officer in the gendarmerie) had come to him Saturday and told him that he had information that the Greek military police in Salonika had committed the murder. Kellis said that Minister of Public Order Rendis had confided to him (confidentially) that he believed the extreme Right had committed the murder. . . . Col. Kellis

said it was very difficult to unearth any information about the case, because of fear on both sides. It was "amazing," however, how many officials told him the Right had committed the murder. . . . Asked whether or not he had any "conclusive" evidence, Col. Kellis said "no," that everyone seems to be afraid to express himself. If they dare to come out openly and express an opinion, their lives are in danger. The Military League is a very powerful and ruthless organization. These people are as bad as the Communists, Col. Kellis said. The Communists in Salonika are too weak to commit such a crime and to cover themselves up so completely, he said. The police in Salonika have a number of ex-Communists who are able to identify most of the Communist leaders at sight. When they find a Communist in Salonika they dispose of him. . . . Kellis said that the people in Salonika are very much afraid to tell what they know, much more reluctant to talk than the people in Athens. Kellis believes there is someone who "put the fear of God into these people" . . . Kellis said he did tell Gen. Donovan about his informer in the gendarmerie, and one or two British officers . . . he believed the gendarmerie officer (Kellis' informant) would divulge the whole story to Donovan, but he wasn't certain about the British. K. said he believed they have instructions to lay off in this case. He said that most of the British he would talk to would drop a cryptic remark, and would give him a lead or a hint, but would never give him the complete story. . . . K. told of meeting a British officer at a cocktail party who pointed out to him that Polk was executed by the Rightists and that the execution was planned, but that they wanted Polk to get out of Athens before the execution was carried through . . .

Kellis said he honestly believes the British must have information in this case. He said the British have been playing at this game of intelligence and counterintelligence in Greece for many years. They have better sources than our people have. . . . Kellis said that one time when he was weighing the evidence one way and the other he called a British intelligence officer in Athens and told him that in his opinion the Right committed the murder. Kellis told the British officer that he would appreciate it if they would at least correct or check him . . . even if they were unable to divulge anything. The officer's answer was, Don't worry, we will correct you. Kellis says that was all they would say . . . but that they hadn't raised any points in opposition to his theory. . . . It is Col. K.'s belief that by pretending ignorance of the discrepancies of the investigation we are becoming silent partners of the crime . . . He said the Greek Government would detect this and it would compromise our integrity.

Walter Lippmann, like the State Department, was more discomfited than outraged by Kellis' forced departure when he was so close to unraveling the conspiracy behind the crime. Nobody in Washington, certainly not the eminent pundit, wanted to take a stand on the case and publicly urge that Kellis return to Greece.

A masterpiece of bureaucratic obfuscation was produced by William Baxter of the State Department's Division of Greek, Turkish, and Iranian Affairs. He wrote Under Secretary Charles E. Bohlen on August 5:

We want the Lippmann committee to understand that any decision with respect to the loan of Col. Kellis' services is within the competence of the Department of Air, which may have technical or legislative limitations which would make it impossible to accede to such a request. We do not want the Air Force to feel that we are urging them to allow Col. Kellis to go again to Greece. On the other hand, we have no objection to his return if the Air Force is willing to give him leave for that purpose.

Mr. Lindley intimated to me that Col. Kellis felt that the Department was not satisfied with his conduct in Greece and would recommend against his return. I explained to Commander Colestock [Kellis' Air Force commander] that our Embassy in Athens, as well as officers of the Department, had pointed out earlier, when Col. Kellis accompanied Gen. Donovan to Greece in July, that any former OSS officer who had worked with ELAS during the war would be suspected by the Greek Government of being unfriendly to the present regime. This does not reflect at all on Col. Kellis personally. . . . On the basis of that and the fact that his continued presence in Greece following the departure of Gen. Donovan might be difficult to explain, the Embassy felt it might be advisable for him to return to Washington at the time of Gen. Donovan's departure.

Never mind, Baxter seemed to be saying, that the colonel was just about to break open the investigation. If his presence in Athens offends our friends there, Kellis must come home. Baxter does not even pretend that the State Department is interested in solving the murder of George Polk. But then neither Donovan nor Lippmann seemed terribly concerned about Kellis' findings either. Each man would keep Kellis' discoveries very much to himself.

In a cable to the Secretary of State marked "Secret" and dispatched from Salonika on August 12, Consul Gibson was far more blunt than Baxter about Kellis' future. "My personal opinion," Gibson advised Marshall, "is that Col. Kellis has lost the confidence of Greek authorities. That he is not *objective*, and that his return would be prejudicial to the investigation." In the Cold War lexicon, the word "objective" had thus assumed a new meaning. It was agreed that Kellis' return would be "prejudicial" to the official investigation.

Despite the best efforts of his own government, Kellis had left his mark on the course of the investigation. Before his departure from Athens he and Donovan paid a call on John Panopoulos, the Athens chief of police, who had himself been shunted aside in favor of Mouscoundis. The major is holding back, Kellis bluntly told Panopoulos and his chief, Minister of Public Order Rendis. It was the first time Minister Rendis learned the Americans were less than satisfied with the investigation's progress. Rendis assured Kellis and Donovan that he would put Panopoulos back on the case. But as for Mouscoundis, the minister noted, "He is in charge because Mr. Ayer wrote to us requesting this. We believed it was your wish, though we never felt he was the right man for this investigation."

Rendis promised Donovan he would send a Colonel Vouklarakis, who until recently had been Mouscoundis' superior in Salonika but had been transferred to Crete, back to Salonika. But all this was just window dressing to allow Donovan to leave Greece with his head held high. "I've given them a big push," he could tell the Lippmann committee. In fact, Mouscoundis was still in charge, and Mouscoundis was no more interested in getting at the truth than Donovan.

When the big break on the crime finally came, Kellis was already back in Washington. On August 10, 1948, two weeks after Kellis' departure, his plant inside the gendarmerie, former OSS agent Lambros Antoniou, finally hit pay dirt. On that day, in a letter hand-carried by his uncle to Kellis in Washington, Antoniou wrote a terse message regarding Michael Kourtessis of the Piraeus right-wing underground. (Kourtessis was the man who, as the Polk's maid, Despina Vroutsis, testified, had called on George Polk several days before his fatal trip and handed him a letter, now missing from his files.) Major Mouscoundis, Antoniou wrote Kellis, had taken Kourtessis to Salonika *days before* and *just after* the murder.

Kellis, still trusting Donovan despite his earlier betrayal, turned Antoniou's letter over to the general. Twelve days later, he received another, more urgent message from Lambros Antoniou:

> What I mentioned cryptically in my first letter I repeat with more certainty now. My informant tells me that Mr. Yenimatas, the president of the Port of Piraeus, a Royalist Deputy, heads an organization of trusted members of the Royalist Party in Piraeus. Their members were formerly enlisted in the Security Battalions and generally politically leaning to the extreme right. Mr. Michael Kourtessis and Mr. Hercules Ksengopoulos are lieutenants of Mr. Yenimatas. They confided to my informant, whom they consider one of their trusted members, that "Polk deserved his fate and that the person who committed the murder is now at Piraeus under police protection."

The informant gathers from their conversation that the person who committed the murder is a member of the Royalist Party and that their organization [the Organization of the Port of Piraeus] knows all the details of the murder.

I repeat that my man is a member of the organization and has their complete confidence.

Michael Kourtessis went to Salonika prior to and after the death of Mr. Polk without any apparent reason. He is a close personal and political friend of Major Mouscoundis and only a few days ago exchanged correspondence. He is . . . capable of anything.

Mr. Yenimatas during the German occupation served as a British agent and still enjoys their confidence.

My man is in contact with these people trying to elicit more information, which we will turn over to Mr. Lambron with the understanding that nothing is turned over to the authorities until we have all the details so as to make it impossible for them to cover it up.

When General Donovan came through he was busy and did not get the full story. However, he mentioned he was coming back soon.

As you know, I do not trust some persons. The danger is great.

I realize that it is not possible to pass all the details of this case in this letter. Remain confident, however, that my information is correct . . .

By then another source had informed General Donovan about Kourtessis' movements before and after the murder as well as his affiliation. In a two-page memorandum dated August 10, 1948, Donovan's new aide Theodore Lambron wrote:

It is said that within the OLP there exists an organization called Constitutional Organization . . . similar to other rightist groups like "X." One of its leading members, Mike Kourtessis, supposedly was taken to Salonika by Mouscoundis five days after the crime and possibly before. Was this looked into?

It is reported that Yenimatas' right-hand man in this undercover rightist organization is a top employee of OLP named Triandaphion . . . another man two days later told our informer that he knows the murderer and he is an OLP member and that he suspects that the police are trailing the murderer now. The above-named Kourtessis fits the description of the man who according to Polk's maid came to Polk's house with a letter for Polk and refused to leave the letter and waited and gave it to him in person. This took place just a few days before Polk's assassination. According to our same informer, the Constitutional Organization of the OLP is recruiting members from both workers (mostly longshoremen) and government services (ESA or Greek military police). ESA officers belong to the CO . . . reputed to hold secret meetings, secret headquarters, and to have prominent advisers especially in the Populist Party.

There is no record either of the Greek police "trailing" the OLP member alleged by Lambron's memo to have been the murderer or of General Donovan doing anything other than filing Lambron's information among his secret papers.

Despite his humiliating treatment by his own government, Kellis remained dogged about solving the Polk murder. On August 10, Kellis wrote Donovan:

I do not expect that much would be accomplished unless you get the complete cooperation of the State Department. If Secretary Marshall believes that the parties involved in this murder should be prosecuted irrespective of their political alignments, positions, etc., this should be made clear to our officials on the spot.

While the investigation was directed against the Left, most State Department officials were cooperative. When I received information that this is a "Rightist crime" and expressed my views, some State Department officials became concerned, to put it mildly.

I would like to respectfully submit a suggestion in regards

to the future conduct of the investigation. Since it appears that generally the Greeks are reluctant in getting involved in this investigation, I believe it should be carried on covertly. There are some people you may contact on a covert basis and finance their independent investigation. It may cost as much as $15,000. Mouscoundis as in the past would follow his line of investigation, while two other contacts (Panopoulos and the gendarmerie) will follow the other leads. Each investigator should act independently without any knowledge of the investigators assigned to other leads. A mail drop or a contact man may collect their information in Athens and relay it to you (Lambron may fit this job) via the TWA pilots, thus avoiding other channels.

When you collect sufficient evidence, this evidence may be submitted to the State Department with a request that the U.S. Embassy in Athens press the arrest and prosecution of the persons involved.

I suspect that although some persons may be willing to talk, they would hesitate to appear as witnesses in court. Preparations should be made to safeguard and evacuate from Greece any key witnesses willing to testify in court.

We might as well face it, the people involved in this crime are powerful and ruthless. In order to expose them, it would require patience, courage, and much support from this side.

It would not have occurred to Kellis that "Wild Bill" Donovan fit neatly into the category of the powerful and the ruthless.

Donovan had already drafted a memorandum on July 31, 1948, addressed to the American Embassy. The document makes clear that Donovan perceived his task largely as a public relations job. His role was to keep the lid on a boiling pot, keeping motives, methods, and evidence entirely to himself.

His high-toned message to the embassy began:

Even though the Greek authorities explore every possibility and use their best efforts, the cold trail and unfavorable circumstance may deny them discovery of the murderer of George Polk.

The compulsory abandonment of the investigation with resultant failure of the Greek and American people to be made aware of the facts collected by the authorities could breed misunderstanding and recrimination between the two countries. In an effort to avoid this danger, it is suggested that in the event that it should appear the investigation is bound to collapse, the following procedure be suggested to the Greek Government in its own interest. 1. That the Government with the approval of the Parliament set up a Royal Commission for the inquiry into the murder of George Polk. 2. That this commission should consist of three of the outstanding members of the Judiciary . . . 3. That the commission so constituted shall be vested with full authority to call and conduct meetings and hearings in camera for the taking of testimony and the transaction of such other matters as the court may determine.

This masterpiece of legal gibberish is nothing less than staggering, given that the author already knew of a highly plausible motive for the murder and was familiar with the police state where it occurred. A Royal Commission to Investigate the Murder of George Polk had a nice ring to it, however.

The embassy shared Donovan's view that this was largely a public relations problem, and thus supported Donovan's proposal for a Royal Commission to investigate a crime that Greece's crack policeman, Mouscoundis, could not seem to solve. Rankin in his cable to the Secretary of State on August 17 said bluntly that the whole plan was a smoke screen to cover up the absence of a real investigation: "During the last 'inspection' of the Polk investigation Donovan suggested the formation of a judicial committee, as a practical means to satisfy American public opinion that Greece is doing all in its power to conduct a thorough and unbiased investigation."

As always, Rankin was energetically pursuing any avenues that led away from the real facts. "The Embassy has been endeavoring to pursue the possibility that Polk may have become involved in a dope or other criminal ring."

Theodore Lambron soon found himself in an impossible position. The embassy that had worked so assiduously to discredit Jim Kellis now turned a wary gaze on the student turned investigator. In a confidential memorandum prepared for Rankin, with a copy sent to CIA station chief Driscoll, embassy secretary Oliver Marcy wrote of Lambron:

> He claims to be an old friend of Donovan's though he apparently did not work for OSS, at least not in Greece. He is allegedly "helping" Donovan, but not, according to him, taking as active a part in the investigation as did Kellis. I have met Lambron and talked with him several times. He appears a cautious individual (at least vis-à-vis the Embassy), not given to expressing his own views, though he has dropped a few remarks about the "unfortunate plight of this country." He has also indicated his relations with the Greek authorities are not too good. A report to Foreign Minister Tsaldaris written by George Drossos described him as sharing Kellis' views on the Polk murder and on the Greek Government.

Like Kellis, Lambron had been given no particular instructions other than to follow the investigation on Donovan's behalf. Unlike Kellis, however, Lambron had no experience, no history, in the subterranean world of Greek politics.

Lambron turned over the explosive facts collected by Lambros Antoniou to the Greek authorities. Only Athens police chief John Panopoulos, nominally back on the case but in reality powerless, gave him an honest response to the new information. "I cannot investigate this further," Lambron quoted Panopoulos, in a letter to Donovan dated August 23, "nor will I put this in a written report." In the same letter to Donovan, Lambron wrote:

> For the record, I will repeat Panopoulos' own story . . . He suspects the British because of their unexplained interest and interference . . . According to Panopoulos, Col. Martin was

the man who convinced Ayer to request that Mouscoundis be placed in charge of the investigation and also that Col. Martin is following every move Mouscoundis makes relative to the Polk case.

Saturday, I saw Consul Gibson who was down from Salonika and he announced to me with an air of accomplishment, "We have this Britisher Martin on Mouscoundis directing every move Mouscoundis makes."

On September 14, 1948, Lambron again wrote Donovan:

One of Consul Gibson's subordinates who dislikes him told me that Gibson . . . is too pro-British to do justice to his position as American Consul. In the course of one of our conversations, Gibson showed interest in knowing to what extent you shared the views of those who considered the British possibly involved in the crime. Naturally, I told him that you wouldn't even discuss the possibility. To this he said that he was very pleased as he feared that all this loose talk might have influenced you.

27

"An arrest is desired." Those were among General Donovan's final words to Major Mouscoundis before leaving Greece following his second inspection tour. The general did not say, "The killers must be found," or "Justice must be served." George Polk's murder, still unsolved and unavenged three months after the event, complicated relations between the two countries. The murder of a reporter, a sideshow in the deadly combat between the Free World and Communism, must not be allowed to occupy center stage.

Mouscoundis' own government, most particularly the head of the Populist Party, Constantine Tsaldaris, was driving home the same message. "Tsaldaris," Donovan's aide Lambron wrote him on September 3, "has complained to the Minister of [Public Order] that he hasn't even arrested anybody." Thus the powerful ally and the crooked politician, each for his own reasons, "desired" an arrest.

Mouscoundis, who bore the ultimate responsibility for the Polk case, was in some ways waging the critical battle of the Greek Civil War. His conduct of the murder investigation was a battle for the confidence and tax dollars of the American public.

Mouscoundis understood that three months after the body of George Polk surfaced American opinion makers needed more than dazzling statistics on how many "suspects" he had hauled in for questioning. Mouscoundis had succeeded in drawing attention away from the real killers, but he still did not have a suspect.

None of the plotters had bargained for the persistent interest shown by a number of Americans in this case. In Greece, where hundreds died of bullet wounds, hunger, or despair each day during the civil war, Polk was just one more combat casualty. But in his own country, Polk's murder raised questions about America's intentions as it carved out its new role in the world. A handful of his colleagues had the power to keep the spotlight of American public opinion on the case.

Ed Murrow, disgusted with the lack of progress, had initiated a series of tough-minded CBS reports on the subject. Over the period of a year, starting on June 19, 1948, some of the network's best-known voices devoted four half-hour prime-time broadcasts to George Polk's murder. Howard K. Smith began the June 19 broadcast:

> An American reporter has been murdered in a foreign country, doing his job. His murder cheapens the lives of American reporters everywhere. It cheapens the life of the truth. . . . All reporters everywhere are vitally concerned in finding the answer to the death of George Polk. The survival of truth and the free flow of news are at stake. . . . The murder of a good reporter is more than the death of one man; it is the murder of truth, and the truth is having enough trouble surviving these days.

In its second half-hour broadcast on the murder, Winston Burdett reported on July 31:

> Ten days ago, General William Donovan and I returned to Athens to follow the police investigation. We found that the Greek police, as far as we could fairly judge, had failed to explore all the political possibilities. Or, more accurately, they had not explored them all with equal zeal and energy. Their major hypothesis was that George Polk was murdered by Communists. The Greek police have devoted 90 percent of their time and effort to exploring the Communist angle and a rather unenthusiastic 10 percent to examining other possibilities.

"This is George Polk," the familiar, haunting voice began the third CBS report on Thursday, September 9. "And now back to the Columbia Broadcasting System."

"That man," CBS news chief Davidson Taylor intoned, "whose voice you heard, is dead . . . murdered in cold blood four months ago today, in Salonika. . . ."

And then a voice American listeners were unaccustomed to hearing, a soft, girlish voice, tinged with a Mediterranean lilt: "This is Rea Polk," she began.

> I'm in the United States now. My husband and I had planned to take the trip to Salonika together. Just the night before my husband left, I decided to remain in Athens, in order to finish packing for the trip to the United States. I have always regretted that decision. I have always felt that if I had gone to Salonika, too, it might never have happened. My husband wanted to go north because he did not know that part of Greece too well. He wanted a last look around, before coming home. That is all he told me of his plans.

Then Murrow picked up the narrative:

> Who it was that George Polk met that night we do not know. None of his friends, none of the persons whom we know he saw in Salonika, has been able to help us on that point. None of the hotel employees seems to remember anyone's having come to visit George or his having gone out in the company of any person. No one seems to know where he ate his last meal. No Salonika waiter or taxi driver remembers him, and he was memorable enough, a striking American figure in a Greek city, tall, blond, blue-eyed, broad-shouldered, thirty-four years old. . . . Tonight, after four months of investigation, the Greek police are up against a blank wall.

By the end of the summer, the State Department, the CIA, and the FBI were all informed of a possible motive for the murder. On August 10, Oliver Marcy of the Athens embassy, more adept in the byways of a bureaucracy than in clandestine affairs, cabled William Baxter of the State Department a personal message:

There is one aspect of the Polk case of which you have probably heard, but which has not yet been set down in writing so far as I know. It is an exceedingly delicate point but one that should be followed up if possible and we hope here that you may be in a position to do so. As you know, the story has circulated that George Polk had a terrific fight with Tsaldaris the day before he left for Salonika. This has been confirmed to me by Rea, among others, who quoted George as having informed Tsaldaris that he "had the goods on him" and was going to "break" his government.

Although no firm information is available as to just exactly what Polk thought he had on Tsaldaris, one of the most persistent stories is that he had discovered that Tsaldaris had shortly before deposited $25,000 in his personal account in the Chase Bank. If this point could be proved or disproved discreetly, it would, needless to say, be very interesting.

Just how one could go about checking the story of course is a matter which we cannot determine. The mere fact of an investigation, if it became known, would obviously make valuable political ammunition for both Tsaldaris' political enemies and the Communists.

If you find it possible to check the story it would be appreciated and the answer might help us in the investigation. If not, it would at least assist in combating some of the rumors which are circulating concerning governmental complicity in the murder.

Though Marcy says nothing about concern that such a revelation might be damaging to Washington, the fact that it might be "political ammunition for . . . the Communists" meant the same thing in the highly charged climate of 1948. Marcy's cable forced the Athens CIA to widen its ring of co-conspirators. A mostly sanitized telex* from CIA agents Freer and Driscoll to the Agency's Washington headquarters, dated August 24, 1948, states:

> Further information through Embassy source indicates lump deposit of $25,000 made to Chase Bank relatively short time before Polk's murder. This information previously sent to Department in a personal letter to Baxter. Attempting to obtain information on [name blanked out] financial status.

An undated cable sent by the State Department to the FBI, which remained classified until June 6, 1988, states:

> Greek Foreign Minister, Deputy Prime Minister and leader of Populist Party who presented Greek case to the UN Security Council is reported to have a large sum of money on deposit in one or more of the banks in New York City. George Polk is rumored to have had knowledge of these deposits. Will the Bureau please endeavor to verify this and inform the Department?

More than forty years after George Polk's murder, these are the only official documents dealing with the motive for the crime that have been released. Two hundred and fourteen other cables relating to the case are still being withheld by the CIA, the State Department, and the FBI under the category of "Security Classified." While American officials worried about how to contain a potentially explosive lead, the Greek investigators were putting into action a plan that would satisfy both governments.

On August 14, at 3:30 in the afternoon, Gregory Staktopoulos stood waiting for the trolley that took him each day to his office at the Salonika newspaper *Makedonia*. Just as the trolley screeched to a stop, two plainclothes officers moved in on the reporter. Staktopoulos and his captors rode in silence to the faceless building that served as the city's security headquarters. The secret policemen refused to answer the stunned reporter's questions.

* When this cable was declassified in 1988 by the CIA as a result of a Freedom of Information suit by this author, all names save Baxter's were deleted.

Once there, Staktopoulos was neither questioned nor processed in the normal fashion. He was simply warehoused in a basement cell, his shoes and all other tokens of dignity appropriated. The long nightmare of Gregory Staktopoulos, chosen as a sacrifice, had begun.

Two days later, Mouscoundis ordered the arrest of Anna Staktopoulos, the reporter's sixty-eight-year-old widowed mother. Later that week his two unmarried sisters were hauled in. No charges were pressed against any of them.

In many ways, Mouscoundis and his puppeteer, Colonel Thomas Martin, back in Salonika after a month's home leave, had chosen their victim well. Staktopoulos was an ideal target. A small-time opportunist, he was an excessively accommodating man, quick to adapt to the wishes of others. He was not the sort whose plight, however unjust, would cause too great a stir.

Whoever ruled this unfortunate corner of the Balkans, Staktopoulos ended up serving. He had once worked for the Germans during the Nazi occupation, as a reporter on one of their propaganda sheets. But when it was the fashion for Salonika reporters to resist the Nazis under EAM's umbrella, he translated English news dispatches for the Communists.

Soon enough, Staktopoulos fell out with the Party. He was not an ideologue. That cause was just a job for a man who supported two sisters and a widowed mother. "Just a reporter who liked to write love letters," as one less than admiring colleague described him.

Then came the English, the new army of occupation, and soon Staktopoulos was writing about the civil war for Reuters, the British wire service. There were rumors around Salonika that he did some free-lance work for the British secret services, but then, in those days, who didn't?

Most recently, he had found a job with a respected and, by local standards, moderate newspaper, *Makedonia*. One of his responsibilities was keeping abreast of foreign correspondents who came to Salonika to cover the war and the activities of the UN Special Committee on the Balkans, which was headquartered in the port city. Thus he had briefly met George Polk the day before Polk disappeared and filed a routine item about the CBS man's presence in town. That, too, would serve Mouscoundis' need for ammunition against him.

Until he was arrested and nobody wanted to have anything more to do with him, he had been well liked. Staktopoulos was not a threat to anybody, he liked to be helpful. He was one of those locals whom foreign correspondents exploit shamelessly in their brief forays into strange places, milking them for all their names, places, and local lore. They all had his name in their notebooks: Bigart, Thrapp, Ed Clark of UP, Ray Daniell of the New York *Times*, and George Polk of CBS. They would wine and dine him when they ended up in Salonika, and then forget about him until the next time.

Mouscoundis let Staktopoulos wallow for days in his subterranean cell, his stockinged feet ice cold from the damp stone beneath them, without telling him why he was there. This is a familiar technique for wearing down the new inmate's resistance. If you make the victim feel perfectly alone, perfectly defenseless, he is much more likely to do your bidding. Staktopoulos, a pliant personality to begin with, could not long withstand total isolation. The British-trained Mouscoundis was applying the sort of technique that was regularly used to great effect, and regularly written about, on the other side of the Iron Curtain in those days.

After several days of seeing only the jailer who brought him food, Staktopoulos was finally brought before Major Mouscoundis. By then the policeman had the piece of evidence that he was sure would break the man who stood before him.

"Your mother's handwriting." Mouscoundis brandished an envelope. "It was she who addressed the envelope with Polk's identification card, which you sent to the Third Police Station, wasn't it?"

Staktopoulos, stunned, did not answer. The allegation was so farfetched, he told himself, they couldn't be serious. But it explained why he was a captive in this house of horrors. And his mother, too, perhaps? What did they mean? That he, a loyal son who had put off marriage to support his mother and two sisters, would drag his mother into something like this? They could not mean this.

"I have a typewriter," was all he could manage to utter. "Why would I ask my mother to do this when I have a typewriter at home?" Mouscoundis did not seem to hear him. He rapped out questions in a rapid-fire monotone, without pausing for breath, without bothering to hear if Staktopoulos had an answer. Staktopoulos' words, in fact, were not relevant to Mouscoundis' performance at all.

The prisoner's long night had begun. It was always at night. Just as he had managed to doze off, his cell door would crash open. "On your feet!" the jailer would bark, and Staktopoulos was marched off to Mouscoundis' office to endure further accusations and interrogation. And for a while he endured. After several days he had lost all sense of day and night. When, after an hour's sleep, the jailer shook him awake and shoved him, staggering, into Mouscoundis' office, only sleep began to matter. He stood slumped under a blinding light in the hours of dawn and still denied he was a Communist, still denied he had led to his death the American reporter he had seen only once in his life. "No one," Major Mouscoundis assured him, "leaves this building alive."

Then they began to use other, more persuasive methods of interrogation. Mouscoundis had help. There was Giorgos Tsonos, who offered Staktopoulos a drink when he was craving one, but then told him it had been laced with cognac. Whatever it was, it made him hallucinate and repeat things that were spoon-fed to him. Tsonos would later provide Staktopoulos a detailed description of Polk, to prepare him for the trial. For Staktopoulos scarcely remembered the American journalist from that chaotic scene at the bar of the Mediterranean Hotel when Helen Mamas had introduced them.

Tsonos and his assistant, Papatsoris, beat him with truncheons and applied electric shocks to the soles of his feet. Forty years later, the scars from those long nights are still visible on his soles. Nor did Staktopoulos ever regain his full hearing after Tsonos' and Papatsoris' blows to his head.

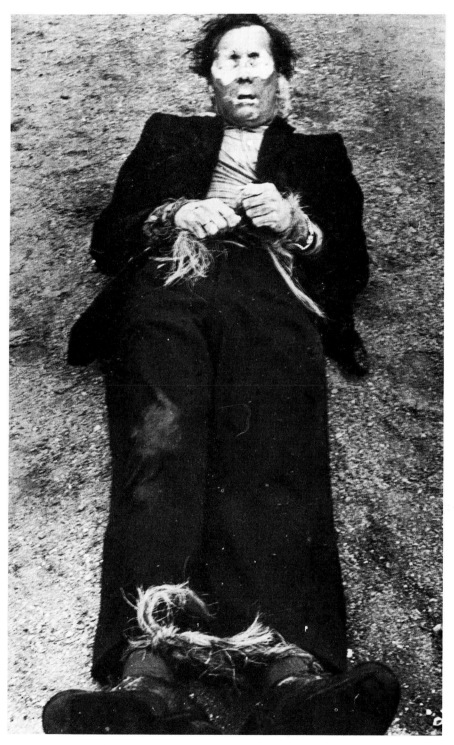

The body of George Polk, photographed just after it had been retrieved from Salonika Bay

Waide Condon, the American diplomat who was called on to identify Polk's remains

Geneal Condon, Waide's wife, who spent several days with Rea Polk following Polk's disappearance

Salonika Bay around the period of Polk's murder. The destroyer in the background served as the Greek monarch's private ship

Salonika Bay and the quay at promenade time in the spring of 1949. A pro-government rally is under way in the square just adjacent to the bay

The post silhouetted against the harbor marks the spot where Polk's body was found

Polk's funeral in Athens. Gendarmes act as pallbearers and Polk's widow is supported by Mary Barber, *Time* magazine stringer. Adelaide Polk follows, with a Greek government official on either side

Adelaide Polk flanked by two Greek government officials at her son's funeral. The Minister of Justice, George Melas, is seen on the right

ΕΥΘΑΛΙΑ Δ. ΚΟΚΚΩΝΗ
ΕΓΕΝΝΗΘΗ ΕΝ ΣΥΡΩ ΤΗ 30 ΙΟΥΝΙΟΥ 1847
ΑΠΕΘΑΝΕ ΕΝ ΑΘΗΝΑΙΣ ΤΗ 5 ΙΟΥΛΙΟΥ 1917

GEORGE W. POLK, LIEUTENANT USN
BORN OCTOBER 17, 1913, FORTWORTH, TEXAS U.S.A.
DIED MAY 8, 1948, SALONICA GREECE

Polk's gold-inscribed white marble tomb in an Athens cemetery

The British-trained Nicholas Mouscoundis, chief of Salonika security police, charged with the Polk murder investigation

Apostolos Xanthopoulos, chief of the Salonika police

Greek Minister of Public Order, Constantine Rendis, center, announcing to the press a "partial solution" to the Polk murder. Rendis claimed that Polk had been slain by Communists in an effort to "discredit the Marshall Plan." He also announced the arrest of Gregory Staktopoulos and his mother as prime suspects

Chargé d'affaires Karl Rankin relaxing with his wife

Walter Lippmann

William Donovan as a
young attorney in 1922

General Donovan alighting from a plane on one of his transatlantic journeys during the time of the Polk investigation

Rea Polk at New York's LaGuardia Airport on April 6, 1949, being interviewed by her brother-in-law, Bill Polk, as he prepared to leave for the Salonika murder trial at which he would represent the Newsmen's Commission

Gregory Staktopoulos testifying at his Salonika trial, April 1949. The jury is seated above

A witness for the prosecution faces the three judges in the Salonika courtroom

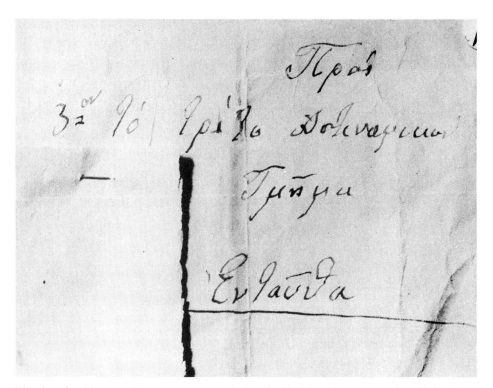

The handwriting on the envelope containing Polk's identification card, which led to the "breaking" of the case

Staktopoulos and his mother, Anna, facing the Salonika court

William Donovan and William Polk during the murder trial

General Donovan chats with CBS's Winston Burdett during the trial

Winston Burdett testifying before the Senate Internal Security Subcommittee regarding his Communist affiliation, June 1955

Gregory Staktopoulos, seated next to his mother, Anna, weeps as he hears the court announce his sentence

"Why me?" he kept asking them, and himself. When the police had taken testimony from the most likely witnesses—waiters, fishermen, and boatmen, as well as many of Polk's colleagues—Greg Staktopoulos was never among them. And now, suddenly, he sat alone in a cell of this damp stone fortress.

Like some voracious bird hacking at his prey, Mouscoundis wore down Staktopoulos' resistance. His torturers alternated between degrading him and offering him another role: that of patriot, a chance to save Greece embarrassment by confessing to the murder. "You are doing this for Greece," Mouscoundis reminded the beaten man.

And from Athens came one of the Big Men. The Minister of Public Order, Constantine Rendis, visited Staktopoulos in the Salonika prison, like some general arriving unexpectedly at the front to bless the lowliest of his foot soldiers. "Your obligations to your country," declared the cabinet minister, "are without end."

"Then why not ask your son to play this role, Mr. Minister?" Staktopoulos whispered. One of Mouscoundis' henchmen answered the prisoner's impudent question with a hard punch to the mouth.

Then began the prisoner's final and most painful ordeal. Making him take off his clothes, Mouscoundis and Tsonos began pulling out, one by one, the little curly black hairs that covered the prisoner's chest and back. Playfully dubbing him "Gorilla," his torturers decided that had been Staktopoulos' Communist *nom de guerre*. Their next step was more gruesome. Tightly binding Staktopoulos' arms and legs with wire from his wrists to his elbows and from his ankles to his knees, they laid him on the floor like a beached whale. After a while the prisoner began to writhe in pain, flipping himself this way and that, futilely seeking relief from his agony. When his wails turned to shrill cries, someone stuffed a rag in his mouth. Then, when the victim no longer cared whether he lived or died just as long as the pain stopped, he heard someone call, "Ether, ether." And then Staktopoulos saw and felt nothing more for a long time.

Finally, when he regained consciousness, they brought in his mother. The sight of her, a gaunt, dispirited captive of two months, extinguished whatever spirit he had left.

An elated Raleigh Gibson cabled the Secretary of State on September 1, two weeks after Staktopoulos' incarceration:

> Attorney General and Major Mouscoundis are optimistic that Staktopoulos will confess his knowledge of the crime when confronted with evidence of his mother's handwriting. Major Mouscoundis has requested two days before confronting him with evidence since he feels Staktopoulos is not ready to break. Local officials consider Staktopoulos the key figure and expect him to confess.

General Donovan was ecstatic at the news. Finally there was movement on the case. Best of all, the man in custody was a Communist agent. Donovan immediately obtained a copy of the only real evidence against the Greek reporter: the envelope containing Polk's identification that Mouscoundis alleged had been addressed to the police by Staktopoulos' mother. Through his assistant William Colby in New York, Donovan dispatched a duplicate to his law firm's trusted graphologist, Klara Goldzieher-Roman.

"It was written," the graphologist's report came back, "by a man who was not over thirty years old, a Greek who attended Greek schools. Although he did go to school he was not a literate man, since he was not used to writing and made one error in spelling and another in the method of writing the address. The error in the address consisted of his writing the number of the police district both as a number '3' and following it by the same thing written out as a word, 'third.' "

Miss Goldzieher-Roman further stated that the man who wrote it "had a very strong constitution, but was in very bad health and that he may well have been wounded."

The graphologist proved remarkably acute in her professional judgment. For in 1977, after a long investigation, Stylianos Papathemiles, Minister for Northern Greece, finally located the man who had actually addressed the envelope that helped convict Staktopoulos. His name was Savas Karamichalis, a young, semi-literate Salonika grocery store owner, whose handwriting absolutely matched that on the envelope. What is more, Karamichalis admitted to having addressed the envelope for his friend Efthemios Bamias, who had stumbled upon the American document on the quay. However innocent their part in the crime, both Bamias and Karamichalis were afraid to speak out at the time.

Once again, as when Colonel Kellis presented him with some unpleasant but undeniable facts, General Donovan turned a blind eye. The conclusions did not support his chosen solution to the crime, and he ignored the graphologist's analysis.

The State Department's cables from Salonika were full of good cheer that September 1948. On September 23, Raleigh Gibson informed Washington:

> Staktopoulos will not be arrested before September 27. He is, however, giving some information now. He states that he knew in March of Polk's plan to visit Markos. He admits that: 1. He joined EAM in 1943. 2. Joined the Communist Party [KKE] in 1944. 3. Attended school for Communist leaders taught by Markos, among others, in 1945. 4. Assigned to a Communist paper in Salonika, where he was in contact with high military and political party leaders (the party at that time legal). He was taught self-defense.

Neither Gibson nor any other American official seemed bothered by the Greek reporter's lengthy incarceration without charge. Nor did they find it peculiar that his "confession" was so slow in coming. Gibson seemed to feel the lack of progress was a result of the police being too soft on the captive. "While I am still of the opinion that Staktopoulos has information needed to solve the case," Gibson had cabled the State Department on September 11, "I am not fully convinced the present method of questioning is effective with an intelligent and clever man."

Desperate, the prisoner reached out to the woman who had introduced him to George Polk, Associated Press reporter Helen Mamas. "You must bring her here," he pleaded with Mouscoundis. "She will clear my name, she will tell you how I came to meet Polk." But Mouscoundis was determined to isolate Staktopoulos from all of his former connections, friends, and colleagues.

"Only I can save you now," the jailer told his captive, as he began to pump the first of several confessions from the beaten man.

In a telegram marked "Urgent and Confidential," Consul Gibson informed Secretary Marshall on October 2 that in "sworn testimony of Gregory Staktopoulos taken by Attorney General and Inquiry Magistrate Staktopoulos gave complete picture of crime and admitted to being an eyewitness and stated that *andarte* Col. Vasvanas was present. He gave the name of the man who fired the shot killing Polk. Complete details will be forwarded."

Helen Mamas, the telex continued, would be cross-examined before Staktopoulos to "clarify certain features of Staktopoulos' statement."

"I am confident," Gibson added, "that the true solution of the case will follow the testimony of Staktopoulos and Mamas. Please do not release the above," the consul urged, "to the Lippmann committee or the press."

And on October 8, Gibson further exulted: "Staktopoulos is considered one of the key men in the Communist Party of northern Greece. George Polk met real Communist contact 1 a.m. Saturday through Staktopoulos, and was told he would be taken to mountains Saturday night and that Staktopoulos would act as interpreter. Staktopoulos is considered to be giving real facts of crime but is endeavoring to picture his part only as interpreter contact. He does not want to give the name of the real contact," Gibson assured his chief, "but Major Mouscoundis is confident that he will secure his name as well as the names of the other key men."

The case which for five months had so troubled politicians, policy makers, and diplomats in Washington and Athens appeared on the brink of a solution that would satisfy them all.

28

"Well, well, Major Mouscoundis," "Wild Bill" Donovan boomed, "you look to be a well-satisfied man." The general, who seemed to fill up the American Consulate's conference room with his presence, extended a firm hand to the smiling Greek officer. It was October 12, six weeks had passed since Donovan's last visit. The major had met the general's deadline.

"With the man we have in custody," Mouscoundis replied with solemn formality, "complete light has been shed on the case. We now know that George Polk was taken in a boat, with Gregory Staktopoulos acting as interpreter. He was then killed in the typical Communist manner," the Greek policeman pronounced.

"Staktopoulos was taken ashore while the others dropped Polk's body overboard. You see that cape?" The major pointed out the consulate window to a finger of land that jutted into the bay. "That is where he was shot, a thousand meters from that bit of land. The boat was then rowed ashore, near a seafront restaurant, which, due to the time of year, is now closed."

"How was it that George Polk was blindfolded and tied up?" asked Winston Burdett, who, as always, accompanied the general on his call.

"Staktopoulos and Polk entered the boat together. They sat together in the boat and were rowed to a point where two other men were picked up. Communists," the major noted reassuringly, "one of whose names we have, the other we do not yet possess. One of the two said to Polk, and Staktopoulos translated, 'We will blindfold you so you cannot see where we are going.' The man whose name we do not yet have then handed the boatman a handkerchief to do the job. After rowing some fifty meters more, the boatman stated that for security reasons Polk's hands and feet would also have to be tied up. Polk voiced no objection to this either. The boatman did the tying. And," the major noted matter-of-factly, "about three minutes later the boatman shot Polk. They searched his body and handed Staktopoulos the identity card, telling him to mail it. They also told him to keep his mouth shut, or else. . . .

"Staktopoulos also admits he was sent from Salonika to Athens to talk Polk into making the trip to the mountains. Polk had a contact in Athens, he says, who prepared him for the trip," the major went on, warming to his tale, which seemed to be having the desired effect. "On the night of August 14, we arrested eight people and searched their homes, including that of Staktopoulos. It was then we found samples of Mrs. Staktopoulos' handwriting. Mrs. Staktopoulos became extremely nervous when we showed her the envelope. Her son also showed immediate reaction on seeing the original envelope. 'Is this the handwriting of anyone familiar to you?' we asked him. 'Don't mention my mother,' he cried out.

"The place where Staktopoulos and Polk had dinner on Saturday night is also known to us. We also know that George Polk paid the bill.

"Staktopoulos has no criminal record, but has been a Communist since 1943. In 1944, he was one of the first journalists on the local Communist paper. In 1945, he was one of the twenty-eight students at a Communist school for instructors in Salonika. Markos taught political economy at that school. He says he fears reprisals for having talked. His home might be blown up, he says.

"Of course, his instructions in this crime came from Vasvanas," said Mouscoundis, as if stating the obvious, "who was here in March with orders for Staktopoulos regarding the Polk trip."

General Donovan, a well-pleased man himself, raised no questions regarding Staktopoulos, Vasvanas, or the claim that an experienced and cautious American reporter allowed himself to be bound hand and foot and blindfolded. Nor did he ask for the name of the restaurant where the two men shared Polk's last meal, or even the name or present location of the boat that had taken Polk to his death.

It was just as well he didn't, as Mouscoundis would not have been able to provide answers. By not pressing the major, Donovan, a trained trial lawyer, gave his stamp of approval to the extraordinary scenario. The general said only that he would return for the trial.

Later that week, the Greek government officially charged Evangelos Vasvanas, Adam Mouzenides, and Gregory and Anna Staktopoulos with the murder of George Polk. Only the latter two were ever apprehended. Mouzenides, like Vasvanas a well-known Salonika Communist, had actually been dead for over a month when Polk arrived in Salonika.

Vasvanas, who lives today in Rumania, was fighting in the mountains at the time, and claims he did not learn of the murder's details until 1965, when a Greek newspaper again took up the case. "Do you know what difficulties we faced at that time?" Vasvanas, who escaped from Greece in 1948, asked an inquiring reporter. "To go down to Salonika, under martial law, kill Polk, and then return . . . it would have been impossible."

The official communiqué, released to the press on October 17 by the Greek government, implicated the Communists in the crime:

> The search made by the authorities in Polk's room at his hotel brought to light the fact that Polk in his letters addressed to persons in the United States came to Salonika for what he believed would be a great success. He desired, as he wrote, to reach Markos' headquarters, "even blindfolded."

Thus Polk's literary license in his letter to Ed Murrow was given a literal interpretation by the Greek police, in their attempt to reconstruct an event that never took place. For there is no mention of a blindfold in the exhaustive eight-page autopsy report filed by the Salonika coroner on May 25, 1948, though this same report gives such minute details as the width and type of rope used to bind George Polk's hands and arms.

By now Staktopoulos had "confessed" to being party to an elaborate conspiracy, involving a series of clandestine meetings in Salonika and Athens with various Communist operatives who prepared to take Polk on his fateful journey. This, in spite of the fact (as Kellis informed Donovan in his letter of July 22) that Polk and other outspoken reporters were trailed by Greek security police.

"Staktopoulos," the communiqué reads, "arrived first at the appointed place on May 8 at 2030 and half an hour later Polk arrived, carrying a soft package in his hands, presumably pajamas, in view of the fact that they were missing from his room.

"After they had their dinner," the communiqué explains, "Polk having eaten lobster, Staktopoulos informed Polk that they would embark in a rowboat, which in the meantime came alongside, their destination the small cape of Karabournaki."

Since the autopsy had revealed that Polk had consumed an extraordinary amount of lobster and peas a half hour before he was shot, the location of the fateful dinner became a crucial part of the investigation. The site of the reporter's final meal was never actually named, however, as Polk did not consume it in the company of the hapless reporter Staktopoulos. Despite their best efforts, investigators could never marshal sufficient corroborative testimony to pinpoint the meal's location.

> Polk accepted that for reasons of security his eyes be covered with a large fisherman's handkerchief and Mouzenides tied his hands and feet with pieces of rope, but in a loose manner, as was also ascertained in the autopsy. When Mouzenides was covering Polk's eyes the latter said, "Even blindfolded I would go where I must go." And when Mouzenides was tying Polk's hands and feet the latter added, "And now we proceed to our destination."

These words, according to the communiqué, "were Polk's last."

It was the communiqué's description of this scene, later repeated in the indictment of the suspects, which most infuriated those who knew the murdered man.

Lieutenant Colonel Floyd Spencer, the Pentagon intelligence officer who two years earlier had been George Polk's first source on the Greek Communists, expressed his outrage in a letter to Lippmann:

He makes statements which sound utterly unlike Polk: "I am willing to reach the place where I must go even blind-folded." This, when he was being blindfolded. And again he remarked seemingly with sangfroid when his feet were being tied: "We are now proceeding to our destination." One is in doubt what to admire more, the unparalleled arrogance of the bumptious little Greek Rightists in seriously presenting this testimony for the consideration of a great and friendly nation, and to its reputable journalists, as an explanation of a still unexplained and brutal murder of a journalist very friendly to the Greek cause, or, on the other hand, the ineffable ef-frontery of the witness who seriously presents such claptrap for consideration.

The communiqué concluded with this statement:

These are the real facts about the murder of the unfortunate Polk, and as to the reasons for which it was committed, Stak-topoulos says exactly these words: "My personal opinion is that Polk's murder was planned by the Cominform and was carried out by the Communist Party of Greece in order to throw the blame on the murder to the Right, thus to defame Greece abroad and to stop the application of the Marshall Plan to Greece, by protest in the United States against Greece, and also to frustrate the military aid to Greece. I know the Greek Communist Party. It cannot do anything, even breathe, unless it receives orders from the Cominform."

"Wild Bill" Donovan couldn't have asked for better than that.

That same week in mid-October, Secretary of State Marshall landed in Greece aboard the *Sacred Cow*, President Truman's per-sonal plane, on a brief fact-finding trip. The visit, of paramount importance to the Greek government, was not marred by a single embarrassing note. So far as Marshall was aware, the Polk case was well on the way to a satisfactory solution.

Within the course of one day, Marshall met with the king and queen (his faithful correspondent), with Prime Minister Sophoulis, who told him, "Greece's fate is in your hands," and with Foreign Minister Tsaldaris and the other members of the cabinet. Throngs of Greeks lined the streets of Athens and shouted, "*Zeto Marshall!*" ("Long live Marshall!") as he passed.

Once inside the American Embassy, however, Marshall found a dispirited group of diplomats. Despite massive American intervention, the civil war was not going well, and the ravaged country's reconstruction effort was faltering. As long as the war continued, Marshall was told, Athens' politicians could hide their inaction and incompetence behind the smoke screen of a state of siege.

Moving on to the U.S. Military Mission, nicknamed the "Temple of Knowledge" by Greeks, the secretary met with British and American commanders. Both groups recommended an increase in the U.S. military presence in Greece. Marshall agreed. Greece, America's *raison d'être* for the Truman Doctrine, would not be abandoned after so massive an intervention.*

Marshall was not much more discerning than his diplomats on site in seeing Greece only through the myopic lens of the Cold War. "What is happening in Greece," Marshall wrote Robert Lovett in the fall of 1948, "is merely an expression in keeping with the local circumstances of the general Soviet or Communist plot."

Back in New York, General Donovan could hardly contain his satisfaction at the outcome of the Polk investigation. Always a favorite of the press, Donovan was now given full credit for moving the Greeks off dead center in the case. Not surprisingly, the State Department did not like the sound of that. On October 27, William Baxter fired off this unusually sharp letter to the general:

---

* It is hard to predict how much deeper America would have been drawn into the Greek Civil War had not unforeseen outside forces crushed the guerrillas in the following years. In the summer of 1949, Tito shocked the world, East and West, by breaking with Stalin and defecting from the ranks of the Communist International. The Yugoslav leader, looking for new friends, had to offer the West some token as a sign of good faith. He did so by closing his borders to Greece, cutting off the guerrillas from their chief source of supplies and sanctuary.

The guerrillas were already hobbled by an internecine struggle between the Stalinist Nikos Zachariades and the "Nationalist" General Markos. Tito's blow proved fatal. The Greek National Army, fortified with $353.6 million worth of American warplanes, ships, mortars, and artillery, and directed by U.S. officers, finally routed the vastly outnumbered rebel bands.

I am somewhat apprehensive at the possible reaction to the paragraph [in the New York *Herald Tribune*] in which you are quoted as saying that before your first trip to Athens, "nothing had been done by the Greek government to inquire into the murder, nothing was done by our Embassy to make representations and nothing was done by the State Department to make inquiry." Several people in the Department have already questioned me about this section of the story and I am certain that Greek officials if they see it will ask for comments. I would appreciate hearing from you as to whether this particular statement was accurately reported by the *Herald Tribune*.

Reflecting the same concern, Lippmann, in a letter to Donovan dated November 1, 1948, asked the general to tone down his self-serving version of events.

Your remarks, as quoted in the *Herald Tribune*, are not literally correct, but I think that all members of our committee are persuaded that there was no vigor in the American action and that the case would have languished but for your intervention. We base that feeling, as much as anything else, on reports both from you and from Lindley, and our own reading of the telegrams.

My personal advice to you is not to write a letter to Baxter, but to tell him orally that while you were not correctly quoted, it would be better for him to drop the subject than to compel you and us to raise a great many questions which have perturbed us all during the course of the inquiry.

In a revealing statement regarding the columnist's own familiarity with the most sordid chapter of the American investigation, Kellis' removal, Lippmann adds: "You probably know that we have rather ugly documentary evidence about Kellis and his recall, and that more than cancels out the minor inaccuracy of your own statement to the reporters."

This is the first indication from Walter Lippmann, who seems generally to be either on a European tour or out of reach at his

Maine retreat during the summer of Kellis' travails with the embassy, that he was in fact fully briefed on that episode. Lippmann the establishment grandee seems to have won out over Lippmann the journalist. Neither he nor any other member of the committee who might have had access to the "ugly documentary evidence" of Kellis' removal saw fit to share it with his readers.

Like Donovan, Lippmann seems all too anxious to get on with the trial of Gregory Staktopoulos. On October 21, he again wrote Donovan: "My general view is that the prospect of an open civil trial may be regarded as marking the accomplishment of the first objective of our committee. Our second is simply to see that the trial is fully reported. After that, our job, it seems to me, will be to pass some sort of judgment on the results."

Lippmann concluded on a self-congratulatory note: "I think it can be said that we have served the American press effectively, in that we have brought the case to a position where the press as a whole through its own correspondents will have an opportunity to deal with the crime."

On October 26, William Baxter cabled the embassy in Athens and the consulate in Salonika that the general was again playing his favorite role of the behind-the-scenes manipulator of events:

> It is evident to [Donovan] that there will be further moves to cast doubt on the bona fides of the Greek Government which will take the form of agitation by Communist-controlled groups to raise money, or to pressure the Lippmann committee to use its funds, for the hiring of legal counsel to defend Staktopoulos. . . . General Donovan realizes that this kind of propaganda campaign should not be allowed to gain any momentum, which he fears possible if interested groups work on Bill Polk, who, he says, "seems to have sold out completely to the Commies."

Donovan had decided that a "way to block this unfortunate contingency might be to arrange for unimpeachable legal counsel to be retained to represent Rea Polk throughout the trial."

Eventually, this "unimpeachable legal counsel" turned out to be the general himself. On March 29, 1949, Donovan persuaded Rea Polk to grant him power of attorney in all her legal matters, including representing her at the murder trial of Gregory Staktopoulos.

Enrolled as an undergraduate at Barnard College since the summer of 1948, Rea was still deemed a threat to Tsaldaris. Given her fragile emotional state, she might yet share her knowledge of her husband's meeting with the Greek Foreign Minister with the press. She needed close watching. Hence Colby's attentions, as well as Mary Barber's message left with Rea's father warning that Rea risked deportation as a Communist if she kept talking about her husband's murder. Later that fall, the twenty-year-old Barnard freshman faced a far more terrifying visitor.

On October 19, returning to her dormitory on the Columbia University campus at 116th Street and Broadway, Rea found a pile of messages, all from the same caller, marked "Urgent." The name chilled her: Athanasios Tsaldaris, the son of the Greek Foreign Minister.

She returned his call and learned he was in town and had "messages from your family." Could she have dinner with him that night at Nino's, a favorite East Side Italian restaurant of his? Having been raised in the same circle of the privileged Athenian bourgeoisie, she knew young Tsaldaris. She was anxious for news of her aged father, alone now in Athens. Rea agreed to have dinner with him.

In the taxi to the restaurant, Tsaldaris told her that he, too, had studied at Columbia. "I taught them more than they taught me," the young Greek, in his mid-twenties, announced. "I find America is like grape juice which may or may not become wine in a hundred years. As to foreign affairs, Americans are like babies. They know nothing about it," concluded the son of the man whose place in Greek politics was largely assured by American aid money.

Midway through their dinner, Tsaldaris lowered his voice. "I am going to tell you something," he began, "and then we'll forget all about it." He then launched into a tirade about how, though the Polk case had been solved in Greece, still people in America refused to believe it. Then he came to the real point of the evening.

"Would you be willing," he urged the widow, "to make a statement saying that you believe in the Greek government's case?"

Caught off guard, Rea began to weep quietly, as she did at any mention of her husband in those early months. Tsaldaris quickly dropped the subject and began to talk of mutual friends in Paris.

After dinner, he suggested they meet a group of his friends in an uptown bar. About ten Greeks, some standing at the bar, some seated, were waiting for them when they arrived. Tsaldaris ordered drinks and led Rea to a quiet table.

"Do you love Greece?" he asked suddenly.

"I love the Greek people," the widow replied.

"Would you be willing to help Greece?" he pressed. "Because the Polk business has hurt Greece very much, you know."

"I don't care," Rea said. "My husband was murdered."

"Your husband," young Tsaldaris stated, "asked for what he got. He wanted to see the Communists. He got what he wanted."

"Please," she pleaded, "please stop talking about this. I can't stand to talk . . . or think about him . . . dead."

"But you have to realize," he said, anger mounting, "he is dead. Dead! Dead! Thousands of Greeks are killed each day. A lot depends on you. But maybe you don't care about Greece anymore? Maybe you care only about America and have given up on your own people . . . since you are not even willing to make a statement saying the case is solved, finished. . . . Maybe"—he lowered his voice, for she was weeping again—"your husband taught you to hate Greece. Then you should say so openly. Then you have an excuse not to help."

"No, no," she protested, "that is not the case."

"Your husband," he interrupted, "would never have forsaken his country. If you do not do this, you will be a traitor to yours."

"My husband loved people everywhere. He always tried to help the people without any power," she said. "But I do not read newspapers. I cannot bear to see any of the stories about this case. It hurts too much."

"But you cannot be indifferent to this. You must make a statement that the Communists killed him, if that is what you think. Or that they didn't kill him. If you feel that way. But if you read the newspapers you will see how obvious it is that the Communists killed him."

Then he added: "Why should we have killed him? There were plenty of other writers who said worse things about Greece."

"I don't care. Just stop. Please," she pleaded. "If only you knew how unhappy I am. If I had a gun," she said, "I would kill myself."

"If you agree to make a statement," he urged, as if he hadn't heard a word she uttered, "I will take you with me to Washington. I have a friend there I can put you in touch with. He can supply you with a fully loaded gun. It is so much easier, though," he said with a sneer, "to jump out of a window. You are so weak. You sicken me. When my brother died, I did not shed a tear. But whenever I go back to Greece and see that bit of land, believe it or not, I cry."

Rea was sobbing now in the back of the taxi that was taking them both back to Columbia. Stepping out of the cab, she turned to him and with what little force was still left her she shouted, "I will never make any statement."

Tsaldaris grabbed her long hair and pulled her back into the taxi. "You need to be shaken, to get your senses back."

"Let me talk to my friends," she pleaded, so he would let her go. "I will see what they think."

"Yes, your friends Bill Polk and Poulos at the Newsmen's Commission. . . . I knew you would talk to them anyway. You know," he said with a leer, "I could write what I like about this meeting. I could say you slept with me or that you said you don't care about Greece anymore . . . anything I want to and could even produce evidence. Poor little Rea," he called after her as she fled from the taxi, "in a way I have so much sympathy for you. In another way you are so ridiculous."

Terrified at her homeland's long reach, Rea turned to a man she regarded as her ally. The next day, October 20, she gave a sworn statement of Tsaldaris' threat to William Colby. Colby dutifully transcribed her words and then sent them off to his boss, General Donovan, who had no intention of letting the unfortunate incident go any further than his filing cabinet.

Rumor of Rea's harassment at the hands of young Tsaldaris

nonetheless reached Bill Baxter at the State Department. The department was as dedicated as the general to keeping unpleasant news regarding its client state from the American public.

On December 9, Baxter sent this "Secret" cable to Oliver Marcy of the Athens embassy: "I assume that the maneuver of Tsaldaris le jeune will leave you as aghast as it did me, for it appears unbelievably *inept*. Please treat the information as highly confidential, since as you will note I learned of it by accident."

"Inept" was the harshest adjective the State Department could find to describe the attempt by its protégé's son to terrorize a widow in mourning.

As for her "friends," the Newsmen's Commission, they kept banging their heads against hard, but invisible, walls. Nor is there any record of Rea telling them of her harassment at young Tsaldaris' hands. The Newsmen's efforts to get involved in the Staktopoulos investigation (rumored since September to be progressing apace) had been stymied, as had their fund-raising. Their appeal to the well-financed Lippmann committee to share some of its funds was rejected.

On October 4, in answer to Newsmen's Commission member Irving Gilman's letter of September 20, Lippmann wrote:

> Our committee does not agree that it is important to get your team to Greece as soon as possible, and in fact believes that it would interfere with the inquiry which is now taking place there. The presence of two American investigating parties in Greece at the same time would only serve those officials who may not wish to pursue this inquiry. As General Donovan is about to go to Greece for the third time, I should consider it most unfortunate if another American investigating team arrived there in the near future.
>
> The murder investigation is carried out persistently and we have no intention of dropping it. In view of the fact that your decision to appoint a team to go to Greece implies that you have reason to think that you could solve the mystery better than the investigators who are already there, I should like to ask you whether you have any clues, contacts, or evidence on

the case which are not in our possession and if you have, whether you will place them at the disposal of General Donovan and our committee.

In the end only two members of the Newsmen's Commission traveled to Greece—Constantine Poulos, who had already been reporting from the region for *The Nation*, and Bill Polk. They arrived only in time for the April 1949 trial of Gregory Staktopoulos for the murder of George Polk. They paid their own way.

29

General "Wild Bill" Donovan, while professing to serve the interests of American journalists, stood like an impenetrable wall between the facts and the reporters and, ultimately, the American public. In his success at controlling the flow of information, Donovan was certainly helped by the temper of the time. Had more journalists with powerful voices exhibited more skepticism and more persistence, Donovan could not have succeeded. In the late 1940s, most reporters, whose stock-in-trade is supposed to be curiosity, exhibited remarkably little of it.

Ed Murrow and a small handful of his colleagues were the exception. They tried to keep the Polk story alive. But even Murrow seemed incapable of taking the leap to the realization that Donovan might not be working for the same side he was. Neither Murrow nor any other member of the New York- and Washington-based establishment press could accept in 1948 that an adversarial relationship between government and press already existed. Only four years had passed since the end of that great patriotic surge which had been the engine of the war effort. Watergate, which would permanently shatter the old trust, was more than two decades away. If Murrow can be faulted for anything in this case, it is a dangerous lack of skepticism. Though he called for truth, he was not sufficiently energetic in its pursuit.

Of all journalists, Walter Lippmann was in the best position to observe the true nature of this investigation. He also possessed the credentials, the clout, and the platform to cry foul. One can only speculate as to the impact a Lippmann column on the sabotaging of Kellis' investigation would have had on the case. But he seemed concerned less with the truth than with staying in the good graces of his establishment "friends," who found him a convenient conduit for spreading their views.

Lippmann sent Staktopoulos' confession, forwarded to him by General Donovan, to an eminent Harvard University professor of criminal law, E. M. Morgan. Morgan's reaction to the Greek reporter's self-incriminating testimony, which would form the backbone of the upcoming trial, was unambiguous. In a letter to Lippmann dated March 17, 1949, Morgan wrote:

> Both Professor Maguire and I read the so-called Confession of Gregory Staktopoulos. I submit the following with his concurrence.
>
> These papers do not contain a confession. The contents are an account of events leading up to the murder of Polk, of the murder itself, and of certain subsequent events . . . at most make him an accessory after the fact. . . . The whole performance cries aloud for cross-examination.
>
> . . . And these pages have mysterious persons who will not reveal their full names and who act in true mystery story fashion. . . . The whole performance impresses me as devised to describe actions prior to the event which are not subject to corroboration or denial by other available witnesses. The conspirators are described either so as to be impossible to identify, or, if identified, to be beyond probability of apprehension or possibly prosecution.
>
> The story of the murder itself is fantastic. Polk might well have consented to be blindfolded by people whom he believed friendly. But no sane person would have consented to be bound hand and foot. There was no explanation for such a precaution given or asked. How any man of common sense could have submitted without requiring at least a plausible excuse is beyond comprehension.
>
> The witness takes good care to put himself where he could not see the shooter. He says, "I heard the whistling sound of a bullet near me." The shot must have been fired from a gun within a foot or two back of him, and unless I am badly misinformed, there could not possibly be a whistling sound

of a bullet at such exceedingly short range. He later refers to this as the "sound of the gun" but says nothing of an explosion, muffled or otherwise.

I do not know what use is to be made of these statements. If they are to be offered against him to show that he had a part in the murder of Polk he cannot very well explain them away. If they are to be used as evidence of the guilt of the persons named therein, particularly of Vasvanas and Mouzenides, they are in my opinion so inherently weak as to be practically worthless unless they are corroborated by other credible evidence.

How much impact would a Lippmann column on this shameful "confession" have had on the Greeks' case? Even with such a persuasive rebuttal in hand, the revered American journalist remained silent.

On April 12, 1949, the trial of Gregory Staktopoulos, his sixty-eight-year-old mother, Anna, and two absent (one presumed dead) Communists for the murder of CBS correspondent George Polk began.

The smell of fresh paint mingled with the sea breeze wafting in from the bay as hundreds of curious residents of Salonika crowded in for the first day of the trial. The bare windows of the courtroom opened on the spot where the body of George Polk had been found almost one year before. A single crude icon of Christ hung just above the prosecutor's chair, the sole bit of decoration in the bare-walled chamber. Overhead, a fan feebly played at stirring the air, soon warmed by hundreds of bodies, sixty of them standing, lining the walls. When a witness unfriendly to the government (there were only two) took the stand, the fan was turned off, the windows shut.

It was in an atmosphere electric with hate that Gregory Staktopoulos and his mother, a faded, ordinary-looking Greek housewife, were led into the dock. The prosecution's job was to depict these two plain Greeks as sworn and dangerous enemies of all the good citizens gathered in the courtroom. Civil war, and the extreme emotions it ignites, had prepared the ground for the case.

One day during the trial, Staktopoulos' own paper, *Makedonia*, published a letter from a Mrs. Sultana Kyriakidou in which she "renounced" two of her own daughters, Margarita and Paraskevoula. They were in the mountains with the guerrillas, according to the mother's letter, and "as agents of the Slavs were seeking to destroy Greece and the Greek race." These kinds of letters appeared each day, as a father turned publicly on a son, a sister on a brother.

There were often compelling reasons for these domestic betrayals. It was frequently a question of being employed or unemployed, having an apartment or being homeless. The authorities controlled professional licenses, business permits, housing, and even the license to operate a bicycle. Persons who had Communists, socialists, left liberals, or progressive republicans among their family or their circle of friends were best advised to make public disavowals.

Five members of the American press sat in a reserved section of the room: Alexander Kendrick and Winston Burdett of CBS, Ed Clark of United Press, Barrett McGurn of the New York *Herald Tribune*, Socrates Chakales of the Associated Press, and, occasionally, A. C. Sedgwick of the New York *Times*. Neither *Newsweek* nor *Time*, whose stringer Mary Barber had left Greece the summer before, covered the proceedings on a day-to-day basis. Compared with the turnout at other political trials staged in Europe around the same time, this was a mere handful of reporters. Two reporters for the American press, Clark and Chakales, had instructions to "hold coverage to a minimum."

America was also represented by the solid bulk of General Donovan, the legendary spymaster, who strode into the little room each morning as though into battle. Next to him sat the young brother of the murdered man, on leave from Harvard University to observe the trial. Bill Polk had lugged a clumsy reel tape recorder with him from New York to tape the proceedings. Only after he returned to New York did Bill Polk realize that General Donovan's persistent pencil tapping on the table had drowned out all other sounds on his recorder.

Hunched next to Polk was the *Nation* correspondent Constantine Poulos, a somber man, no good at disguising what he thought of the proceedings. Poulos' skeptical features were familiar to Greek and American officials, who had fulminated about his dispatches from Greece and the Balkans for the past five years. He and Polk were there not as reporters but as observers for the ill-fated Newsmen's Commission.

Close by, the American Consul, Raleigh Gibson, whispered to his neighbor, British Police Mission commander Gordon, out of uniform for the occasion. Gibson's attention was focused less on the prosecution than on the conduct of the American press.

"Poulos comes with well-known leftist background," Gibson cabled the State Department on April 20. "His actions will bear close watching and careful attention." As for CBS's Kendrick, Gibson wrote: "He assumes with perhaps some justification that any journalist not sold on Greece and the prosecution's case is assumed to be a Communist." Young Polk, Gibson noted, has an attitude of "sullen dissatisfaction . . . Some portion of this is due to the feeling that the trial is 'staged' and that evidence is insufficient to prove George Polk was a victim of a Communist plot."

Police records of the period reveal that the twenty-year-old Polk was under constant surveillance during his stay in Salonika.

The crowd had no trouble identifying the accused. His sharp features and slicked-back hair, his general appearance described in the press as "satanic," had been staring at them for months in their local newspapers. *Time* magazine (without their own reporter on the scene but drawing on wire service dispatches) savored every detail of the prisoner's appearance, describing him as "wearing a grey suit, silk shirt and crepe-soled shoes, looking more like a clothier's model than a working journalist, or a man on trial for murder." The elderly woman who now sat next to him, and who seemed much older than her sixty-eight years, did not fit anybody's image of a hardened co-conspirator. Gregory and Anna Staktopoulos wore the resigned expressions of those in full knowledge on the first day of the trial what the final day would bring. The court itself acknowledged as much. The verdict was preordained.

"Legally, I am required to be on this side of the court," the prosecutor announced on the first day. "Actually, my position is beside the defense. We are on the same side. We agree as to the perpetrators of the crime. The only difference between us is whether or not Gregory Staktopoulos knew that George Polk was to be murdered."

Peering down at the proceedings from a high wooden bench were three judges, solid Royalist elders, loyal to Athens and devoted to the present order of things. Two young women, court stenographers, sat at the foot of this high bench, and sometimes became so engrossed in the proceedings they dropped their pencils to listen.

From the second day of the trial, Staktopoulos' court-appointed defense attorneys voiced their solidarity with the prosecution. "The defense supports the obvious theory that the Greek Communists decided to execute Polk. We agree with the prosecution; there is no doubt that the crime was committed by the Communists."

"Do you have any doubt that the Communists committed this crime?" the three judges periodically asked of witnesses. Few did.

The jury of twelve, selected from lists submitted by merchants, manufacturers, and professional associations and civil lists of business and property taxpayers, was picked in ten minutes.

Attorney General Christos Moustakis read the fifty-page indictment of Anna and Gregory Staktopoulos and the two Communists who were to be tried in absentia. The indictment established the trial's theme; its text attempted to resolve glaring contradictions and inconsistencies which had riddled Staktopoulos' six "confessions." The Greek Communist Party was guilty of more than the murder of an American reporter. The real motive for the murder, according to the indictment, was to slander Greece. Polk was killed because the Communist Party wanted to defame the motherland and thereby cut off United States aid. "There has never in the annals of Greece," Moustakis intoned, "been a murder of a foreign person and especially a correspondent, because hospitality has always been worshipped as a goddess in Greece." The George Polk murder trial was transformed into a patriotic exercise.

According to the indictment, Staktopoulos' only defense was that he was an unwitting dupe of the KKE, the Greek Communist Party. Polk arrived in Salonika to contact a KKE agent who could get him to Markos. Staktopoulos, a KKE agent, contacted Polk and told him he would take him to another agent in town. Polk agreed; the rendezvous with the agent was kept.

"What should I take with me?" Polk asked the agent, according to the indictment. "Pajamas and the absolutely necessary articles for work," he was told. This detail, needed by the prosecution to account for Polk's missing pajamas (which both Rea Polk and her maid recalled Polk packing for his trip), added an unintended note of humor to the trial. For though a man of immaculate habits, Polk was an outdoorsman, at home sleeping under the stars and highly unlikely to bother with pajamas on an arduous mountain trek. Given a choice of taking his shaving kit, typewriter, camera, or pajamas, George Polk would certainly not have opted only for his pajamas.

On the night of the murder, according to the indictment, Polk met Staktopoulos, who took him to the Luxembourg restaurant for dinner. After a meal of lobster and peas, the two men walked to the bay side of the open-air restaurant and stepped into a small boat. At the oars was the exiled director of the KKE's regional office, a former Communist Party deputy in Parliament, forty-seven-year-old Adam Mouzenides. A short time later, the indictment claims, the boat touched land to pick up Evangelos Vasvanas, also exiled from his native Salonika, for "fanatical" Communist activities, and reportedly a political commissar with the guerrillas. With him was an unidentified man.

A few moments later, Staktopoulos was instructed by Mouzenides to inform Polk they would blindfold him. Polk agreed. After another few minutes, Mouzenides said they would have to bind his legs and arms. Polk again agreed. "I was sitting beside him," the indictment quotes Staktopoulos, "happy because I was talking English and helping a colleague, when I heard a shot and Polk slumped forward. I was paralyzed with fear." The conspirators rowed Staktopoulos ashore. Carrying Polk's identification, he was warned to keep quiet before he was let go.

Every other witness in this highly polished performance was meant to confirm this scenario. There were a few gaps, however, which not even the full power of Salonika's multiple security services and the combined imagination of the Anglo-Greek plotters could gloss over.

There were those who, at great personal risk, stubbornly refused to bend the truth to suit the government's need. The manager of the Astoria Hotel, for example, where Staktopoulos was supposed to have met Polk, denied ever seeing Staktopoulos. It was common knowledge that hotel managers in Salonika kept an eye out for foreigners and reported their comings and goings, and their visitors, to the police.

While Mouscoundis had bought the silence of certain of the hotel staff through lengthy incarceration, the manager, a man of unusual personal courage, held his ground. So did the waiters and the owner of the Luxembourg restaurant, who denied seeing either Polk or Staktopoulos on the night of the murder. Staktopoulos, a regular customer, was known to the staff, who certainly would have remembered had he and a tall, blond American dined there on the evening of May 8.

Most others, however, found it in their best interest to play along with the government.

The first witness, Angelos Vlassis, an Athens druggist, claimed to have seen Mouzenides four months after he was pronounced dead by the KKE over their official radio. "I saw Mouzenides," said the little man, standing in front of the high court bench, his hat in hand, "at Canning Place in Athens. He recognized me, but did not stop. I called to him when he was near. I noticed he was growing a mustache."

The prosecution next produced a renegade Communist named Zafiriou. He, too, claimed to have seen Mouzenides. "I am going and wish to say goodbye," the Salonika Party leader allegedly told him in March 1948. "I am going on a mission which is a very difficult and dangerous one," Mouzenides allegedly told Zafiriou as he left guerrilla headquarters on horseback on March 20. "I am sure," the witness helpfully added, "one hundred percent, that he was the organizer."

Zafiriou, who had worked as a factory hand in Moscow from 1933 to 1947, returned to Greece a disappointed Communist. Since then, his chief occupation had been serving as an "expert" on Communism, appearing at various trials, writing "top secret" reports on Communism for the Greek General Staff and for the Greek newspapers. He was portrayed as a high-ranking Party man by the prosecution.

"I wondered," Zafiriou asked out loud during the trial, "was it possible for the Greek Communist Party to give an order for the execution of Polk and to organize the murder? I put my heart on my hand and I said, unhesitatingly, yes."

Neither Staktopoulos' defense nor the jury, which had the right to speak out and often did during the trial, questioned Zafiriou's reliability as a witness.

A wan-looking young girl, long hair lank and complexion prison-sallow, stood before the judges and jury. Her testimony, in a low, mumbled voice, revealed she had been traveling and living for the past year with Mouzenides. The jury of solid Salonika burghers gaped, fascinated at Anna Molyvda, a creature from another world. The stenographers forgot to take notes.

Molyvda claimed to have been with Mouzenides a few days before the murder in Salonika. At a rendezvous between the two high-ranking KKE agents, Vasvanas and Mouzenides, she claimed she overheard the latter say, and here the young girl's mumble was transformed into a ringing proclamation, "The question of the boat has been arranged. I have seen Staktopoulos, and I shall probably see Polk."

The girl uttered those two critical lines as though her life depended on it. She did so with good reason. Though this fact was not mentioned during the trial, Molyvda was in police custody at the time. The charge hanging over her head was frequently punishable by death: harboring a fugitive Communist. Just before she took the stand, the prosecutors quietly revealed that only one of two other Salonika women, named Eufstatiou and Papazoglou, who had been arrested for harboring Mouzenides was still alive, and she had been sentenced to life in prison. The other woman had already been executed. Mouzenides' own wife, Eudoxia, arrested in December in connection with the Polk investigation, had also been executed. Anna Molyvda, Mouzenides' companion, was the dead Eudoxia's sister.

After her testimony, Bill Polk asked to see her privately at police headquarters in Piraeus. Though an appointment was made for him, and Polk flew to Athens to keep it, when he turned up police informed him "a terrible mistake" had been made. Anna Molyvda had been sent out of town the day after Polk's call for an appointment. The Greek Attorney General had already informed Raleigh Gibson that Polk "was to be closely guarded and was not allowed to talk to Anna Molyvda, to Staktopoulos, or to Stylianos Mouzenides [the accused Communist's brother, also a government witness] except by permission of the Attorney General."

General Donovan had better luck seeing Anna Molyvda. When he emerged from his meeting with the young woman, Donovan pronounced himself satisfied with her testimony. Deep religious feelings, Donovan announced, had prompted her sudden revulsion toward Communism.

Stylianos Mouzenides, the guerrilla leader's brother, a stolid family man, once had a successful practice as a Salonika dentist. He told Bill Polk he'd lost most of his patients as a result of his Communist brother. Stylianos was desperately trying to save his family. He publicly denounced his brother and, more important for the government's case, claimed he had received a phone call from him from Salonika in mid-April, bolstering the prosecution's claim that Mouzenides was still alive.

"Do you think your brother is guilty?" Bill Polk asked him after the trial.

The dentist averted his gaze and, with a pained expression, answered, "Yes, I voluntarily denounced him to the police."

Ten years later, in a letter to Associated Press correspondent William Johnson, Stylianos Mouzenides said the police had used third-degree techniques to extract his "voluntary" testimony.

A careworn old man with wispy white hair leaned on his cane and faced the prosecution on the third day of testimony. Life had not been easy for Matthew Cocconis since the murder of his well-loved son-in-law. His daughter had left for a strange land, and his tangles with the police never seemed to end. Day after day, he shuffled off to the Athens police headquarters to face grilling about George Polk's politics and leading questions about his son-in-law's closest Greek friend, Hadjiargyris.

"Why did Polk want to go to the mountains?" a juror asked the old man. "Is there any justice there? Didn't he realize that justice is on our side?" The old man had no answer.

"Did George Polk love the Greek Army?" the prosecutor asked Matthew Cocconis.

The old man sighed deeply and, after hesitating, said, "Yes. He liked it very much," though Polk's father-in-law was all too aware George had called it "a military monster" in his *Harper's* piece.

And when twenty-five-year-old Helen Mamas, the AP correspondent from Worcester, Massachusetts, was called to the stand, the courtroom resounded with the audible clash of two cultures, two approaches to both the law and journalism.

"Since the court indicts Staktopoulos," one of the three judges demanded of her, "what is your opinion?"

"I cannot answer that," Mamas replied, much to the court's displeasure. Everyone else in this trial had opinions and was freely encouraged to express them, so long as they were on the side of the prosecution.

"Have you formed a definite opinion as to which side of the fence Staktopoulos is on?"

"That is up to the court to decide," Mamas rejoined, the first witness not to concur with the prosecution's claim that Staktopoulos was a malicious killer.

"Staktopoulos confessed his presence during the murder. What is your opinion," the judge continued in his attempt to lead her, "particularly when the next day he asked you, 'What news do you have of Polk?' "

"I don't think it's fair to express an opinion."

"You said Staktopoulos represented the opposition," a juror pressed the reporter. "You mean opposition to the country or the Communists?"

"I mean the rival press," she said, and the three judges, the jury, and the public all looked baffled.

"Do you find it natural when there is an official government in Greece," one of the judges asked, "that foreign journalists should try to smuggle themselves into the bandit lines?"

"I don't see why not." The young blond reporter shrugged. "This is the basic work of a reporter." The audience gasped audibly.

Word had spread through Salonika on April 14 that the Prime Minister's stepson, Costas Hadjiargyris, was to testify that day.

The courtroom was even more tightly packed than it had been. On this day they turned off the lone fan and shut the windows tightly. Nor was the "unfriendly witness" offered a chair, as the others had been. By the end of Hadjiargyris' six hours of testimony, he was dripping wet and exhausted.

The Greek journalist described in minute detail the day he and the Barbers went to Rea's apartment, and the circumstances surrounding the disappearance of the files. Nor did the defense or the prosecution press him on why someone would go to such lengths to remove the dead man's papers. It was as though no one even heard the witness, whose testimony was so stubbornly out of step with the rest.

"This trial," the Attorney General, the ranking member of the court, admonished, "is for the purpose of examining before the court all data collected. Wrong or not, all the audience in this court and in the whole world expect to hear from you all you know of the missing correspondence." One of the three judges interrupted. "You were the only friend of the late Polk. This morning a witness said, 'Hadjiargyris is a Communist.' This does not matter to the court. It is sufficient that you tell the truth. It is true, though, that there is a decision accusing you of past Communist activities. Therefore, there is something against you. I appeal to you as a Greek, and ask the truth for the sake of the bloodshed, the defamation, and the slander for which Greece has suffered and is still suffering."

"I am not a Communist," Hadjiargyris interjected uselessly. The court had already been instructed otherwise. "In 1943 I joined EAM and was sent to a concentration camp as a Communist. I was released in 1945. When back in Athens it is true that I contacted all parties to find out the truth of the prevailing conditions . . . why the December insurrection was started, and why so many people were massacred. The Foreign Minister sent me to London as press officer. I returned to Greece as correspondent for the *Christian Science Monitor*. I admit to having made mistakes, but in the long run, my articles have done more good than harm for Greece."

"We do not want political speeches," the Attorney General interrupted him, making it clear who had the right to make political speeches in this remarkably verbose courtroom. "Limit yourself to the subject of the trial. We want to know about the files," he pressed, having just heard the Greek reporter's exhaustive description of how the files disappeared.

"I told you that the file was removed at Rea's request."

"Therefore, you say that the dossier must be asked from Rea or the Barbers?" asked the judge.

"Yes, it cannot be otherwise," Hadjiargyris responded.

"Mrs. Barber testifies that at Rea's request she took the files," the judge interjected, referring to Mary Barber's statement to the authorities made the previous summer, before her departure for London, "but when Rea looked in them she noticed that correspondence was missing."

"I am surprised. Mr. Barber should have been cross-examined with me," Hadjiargyris said.

"You insist that the documents were lost in the hands of the Barbers?" the Attorney General asked.

"Yes."

One of the judges quickly shifted to more solid ground. "When Polk's body was found, what did you cable?"

"That the crime might have been committed either by the KKE or by the right-wing extremists," Hadjiargyris answered.

"Why did Polk stay in your home [on the eve of his trip to Salonika] for so long?" the judge asked, ignoring the witness's answer. "What did you talk about?"

"Nothing about the trip," Hadjiargyris answered.

Turning to Staktopoulos, the judge, in reference to one of Staktopoulos' six confessions, asked, "You went to meet 'Yannis' in Athens. What did he tell you?"

"He said, 'When Polk comes, we will send him up, because Hadjiargyris is interested in this trip.' " The accused, like a well-trained seal, picked up his cue to implicate the man on the witness stand.

"It is a lie," Hadjiargyris answered calmly.

"You had free access to everything in Polk's house," the judge pressed the witness, absurdly jumping from one subject to another. "Did you or did you not? Rea Polk's mother [*sic*] says that when you were asked about the missing file, drops of perspiration fell from your forehead and your anxiety was visible. The concierge said that after the women left the Polk house, you left carrying a yellow dossier." The judge, still bent on drawing Hadjiargyris into the disappearance of the files, stuck to his scenario, glossing over Mrs. Barber's statements regarding the files.

"If I had a parcel," Hadjiargyris answered, "it was Rea's clothing."

"Who killed Polk?" one of the judges, anxious lest the trial slip from its well-rehearsed script, asked the man awaiting this question.

"The Communists," Staktopoulos answered in a voice as clear as a bell, while Hadjiargyris was still on the witness stand.

"Why?" the same judge asked.

"To defame Greece," came the rote-learned reply from the accused.

"Is this your handwriting?" the judge asked Anna Staktopoulos later in the trial, showing the old woman the envelope in which Polk's identification card arrived at police headquarters.

"It doesn't look like it very much." She shrugged. "But it appears that I wrote the address on the envelope."

"Yes, yes!" Her son sprang to his feet. "It is yours."

"I do not remember if I wrote it," came Anna Staktopoulos' weary voice. "But if you say so, then I did write it."

In a gesture toward giving the appearance of a fair trial, Staktopoulos' attorney called on seven friends of the defendant to testify on his behalf. Only one among them answered the call, an American. Not a single Greek friend of the defendant turned up in court. On April 18, Dr. Carl Compton, the dean of Staktopoulos' American-run high school, took the stand. Like Hadjiargyris, Compton seemed as if he were testifying in a different trial. Though given in Greek, his testimony, simple and straightforward, free of political messages or any prompting whatsoever, sounded as though it were spoken in a different language.

Dr. Compton, a soft-spoken, middle-aged man, recalled the defendant as a student. "He was good, not brilliant, faithful in his duties. I remember him well. He was interested in writing and wrote well. He was always quiet and was liked by his teachers.

He was a peaceful and reserved type, not secretive. When this case was brought to court, I talked with friends and their opinion is the same as mine. That is, that he was a calm person and wanted to be of help to others."

"Do you believe him capable of this crime?" Nicholas Vassilikos, one of Staktopoulos' state-chosen attorneys, asked the educator.

"Absolutely not," Compton answered. "There is no doubt in my mind. His character was good and he couldn't change so completely within such a short time."

"Did you hear that Staktopoulos was said to have been among the top-ranking Greek Communist leaders?"

"Well," Dr. Compton replied, "I heard he was interested in EAM, but I did not hear he was a member of the KKE. EAM was patriotic and all young men joined in it, as Staktopoulos did. Later some were slow, others quick, to withdraw."

"Had you heard that he was a fanatic?" the judge asked.

"No. Nothing at all about that," came the unwelcome answer.

At this awkward intersection the presiding judge turned to the only person present who could save the moment.

"Stand up, Staktopoulos. You have heard all of this. What have you to say?"

"I was a Communist," the defendant began his speech. "I declare that Greece is innocent of Polk's blood. I accuse the KKE, the Cominform, and Moscow. I will disclose the obscure persons who committed the crime, and who organized it," Staktopoulos promised. Then, turning toward the members of the American press, he said, "I address myself to my foreign colleagues, and ask them to spread the truth over all the world. That is, that the crime was organized by persons in whose interest it was to do it. I wish my voice could be heard all over the world.

"I thank Dr. Compton. I wish to tell him that Anatolia College does not produce criminals. I wanted to help a colleague. I did not know what those dishonest fellows wanted to do." The man who had been drugged and beaten then launched into a long exposition of his own childhood and his early responsibilities toward his family after the death of both his father and his elder brother.

Embarrassed at his client's often slurred speech, Staktopoulos' state-appointed defense lawyer interjected, "Due to his injury in an automobile accident, he has some difficulty speaking rapidly."

Summarizing his life and career for the court, the defendant sealed his own fate. "If I say that I abandoned the KKE, I will be lying, but I do not agree that all Communists are murderers. For instance, the Party knew that I am not the person to throw a hand grenade or participate in OPLA [the Communist terror organization] . . . but my being crossed off the Party list was fictitious. Here, I must say that the government and the police must be careful," Staktopoulos warned, "because persons such as myself may have been crossed off the list in this way. Churchill, number one enemy of Communism, said that we should be afraid of Communists in disguise, more than of the openly declared ones."

As Staktopoulos wound up his long-winded account of his own duplicity, he asked rhetorically, "Who ordered the murder of Polk? All Communists know, but won't tell. I believe the order was given by the KKE. Mouzenides and Vasvanas had no personal reasons to kill Polk. They did it because they were ordered to. I may add that high-ranking Communists are very careful in carrying out orders. Polk's murder would have stopped aid to Greece and aid from the Marshall Plan. In the security station where I was detained, I awoke and became a Greek," the doomed man proclaimed, closing where the trial had begun. Patriotism was the ultimate virtue, with truth hardly a concern.

In summarizing Staktopoulos' case, his defense attorney called his client guilty, and applauded the prosecution's handling of the case. Rea Polk, proclaimed attorney Vassilikos, "insulted her country and forgot her oath to be present at the trial. She, as a Greek, betrayed the traditions of her country."

Rea Polk's real reason for not being present was not her "un-Greek" sentiments, but her doctor's orders. New York psychiatrist Louise Brush, under whose care she had been for the past year, wrote General Donovan just before the trial: "I think that for her to do so [attend the trial] would produce severe nervous symptoms and might result in suicide."

During the trial, Rea Polk was nonetheless portrayed as a callous, unfeeling woman who cared little about either her motherland or her husband.

Though Rea's name was frequently used as an illustration of a "bad" Greek, one other name was never uttered during the entire ten-day trial—that of Constantine Tsaldaris. Neither the prosecution nor the defense brought up Polk's fateful interview with him or the American reporter's vow to unmask him. Moreover, no mention was made of the letter informing Polk of Tsaldaris' deposit in a New York bank account.

Nor were most of the other crucial figures with information about the case ever called on to testify. Absent from the courtroom were Michael Kourtessis, Major Nicholas Mouscoundis, Colonel Thomas Martin, Sir Charles Wickham, Mary Barber, Colonel James Kellis, Karl Rankin, Christian Freer, Robert Driscoll, Fred Ayer, and Waide and Geneal Condon. The reporter who had actually achieved what the court claimed Polk was attempting did not appear in the Salonika court. Homer Bigart, who dedicated his Markos interview of the previous summer to his friend and colleague George Polk, was never called on to share his assessment of the Communist guerrilla leader's own knowledge of the case. Nor, it is fair to point out, did Bigart or many other concerned journalists turn up at the trial on their own.

It came as a surprise to no one when the verdict was pronounced. On April 21, 1949, CBS News reported the "findings" of the court. "A former Communist newspaperman was sentenced to life imprisonment for complicity in the murder of George Polk," Don Hollenbeck announced on the CBS "World News Roundup." Hollenbeck noted that Staktopoulos' defense did not plan to appeal that decision. The CBS anchorman then turned the program over to the correspondent on the scene, Winston Burdett.

"In the minds of some, there may be doubt as to the exact degree of Staktopoulos' guilt, but there was never any doubt as to the verdict," Burdett reported from Salonika. "What we witnessed in the small arena of that bare courtroom in Salonika was a living miniature of postwar Greece, its passions, its weaknesses, its tragic story. But we also saw a trial, by Greek standards and by Greek rules, a fairly conducted trial. It established most of the facts that it set out to prove in the case of Gregory Staktopoulos." Burdett's conduct throughout the case was contradictory. In retrospect it seems he was burdened by his own concealed history.

Raleigh Gibson echoed Burdett's good feelings about the trial when he told the press, "I have always had confidence that the trial would prove to the world how and by whom George Polk was murdered, and this has been done. The judicial part of the case was prepared with care and efficiency. The trial was one that can be remembered with pride. All judicial officials are to be complimented."

Gibson singled out one name for the highest praise: "The name of Major Mouscoundis must be especially mentioned and he must be complimented for intelligence, diligence, patience, and brilliant work."

General Donovan was equally cheered by the results, and told correspondents, "I attended every session of the trial and found it honestly and efficiently conducted, with fair and full opportunity for the defense to represent itself."

Before leaving Greece, George Polk's brother was finally granted his long-expressed wish to talk to the man convicted of his brother's murder. Bill Polk found Staktopoulos slumped on his cot in a tiny cell inside police headquarters. Two expressionless Greek police officers stood inside the cell's heavy steel door. Polk was accompanied by a man assigned as "interpreter" by the embassy, though Staktopoulos' English was fluent. Nicholas Notsios, an American of Greek origin, had already performed this role for General Donovan during the trial. Bill Polk did not know what Donovan knew about Notsios: that the "interpreter's" real employer was the Central Intelligence Agency.

"Do you think I could have killed your brother?" Staktopoulos looked up at the young man, tears soaking his red-rimmed eyes. Bill Polk, whose own nerves were too frayed for much more, asked to leave the cell.

"Young man," General Donovan said, glaring down at Bill Polk sometime later, "there is a war on. Stop asking these troublesome questions. You'll end up spoiling your chances for a good future."

When the brother of the murdered man obstinately continued with his questions, Donovan could only attribute it to one thing: Bill Polk, Donovan informed the State Department, was a Communist.

"I don't ever want to come to Greece again," Bill Polk scribbled in his journal.

To his cousin Bill Price he wrote:

I have been a target of all eyes since the first day I arrived and have not been able to make a move without being seen and followed. It is a horrible feeling, a sort of spotlight of suspicion. It would be easy to return here if I hated the Greeks. But I don't. It hurts me to see them torn to pieces between two dray horses of the extremes.

Where will telling the truth [about General Donovan] get us? I know that he said in Salonika that it was foolish to talk about a war with Russia, because we are already in it, and might as well start fighting it. I think we had better be ready to hit hard when we do [tell the truth] because I think the old boy can be a vicious enemy and can throw more weight than you or I will ever be able. I don't think we can give him anything more than a few stings which might make him mad enough to really let fly at us. I don't think it's worth it.

Between you and me, I think the old boy knows the full story . . . but, like so many others, saw the trial as a battle against Russia through our respective chess pawns.

I feel a little rotten inside after this trip.

Aftermath

F̲ew of the American journalists
who attended Staktopoulos' trial from the day it opened on April
12 until the day it closed on April 21 were bold enough to voice
their darkest conclusions. Alexander Kendrick of CBS was one who
did: "The job of American correspondents in Greece will be even
harder than before," Kendrick reported on CBS when it was over.
"The hostility of officials will be more pronounced; their news
sources will shy away from them; the interest of the police in their
activities will be more evident; there will be even more attempts to
plant information; and their Greek associates will be even more
afraid to work for and with them."

Still, Kendrick noted that one positive side effect could yet result
from America's participation in this disturbing judicial exercise.
"This trial can erect a red light for American policy makers, make
them ask themselves why they and the Greeks should be afraid of
American correspondents; and whether honesty and integrity in
American reporting are not after all laudable war aims also . . . no
matter what kind of war is being fought."

Ed Murrow, whose own correspondents, Kendrick and Burdett,
were giving him conflicting reports, felt he could do little but formally close CBS's own investigation of the murder of George Polk.
"Those of us who knew George," Murrow said, his voice tinged
with regret and resignation, "and worked with him can never cease
to be concerned about his murder. There is nothing more to say,
except that George Polk was one of those reporters who believed
that 'the pursuit of truth shall set you free, even if you can never
catch up with it.' "

The case would not so easily release its hold on some of the others it touched. On June 21, 1949, Colonel Kellis formally accepted General Donovan's version of the events. "Lacking your legal and investigative experience," Kellis wrote his former commanding officer, who had sent him a copy of Staktopoulos' indictment, "I accept your finding without any hesitation and thus happily close this case."

In reality, letting go did not turn out to be quite so simple. There were too many people with long memories. Kellis was placed under surveillance by the military security agencies he had served with distinction. One day he walked into his office to find a security man going through his trash basket. "Get out," he shouted at the startled agent.

In the mid-1950s, when the ugly currents of hate and suspicion had exhausted themselves and the nation gradually returned to its senses, Kellis was proposed for the position for which he was eminently suited. His entire career and background had prepared him to be CIA station chief in Athens. Christian Freer, the CIA agent who had been Kellis' nemesis during the Polk investigation, vetoed it. "Too biased," Freer said of Kellis. He did not need to elaborate. "Too biased" was code for too liberal, too much of a stickler for those democratic principles to which the Truman Doctrine laid false claim.

Kellis did not get that appointment, but ultimately his distinguished record overwhelmed the objections of those still myopically anti-Communist. He received appointments to sensitive positions. At the outbreak of the Korean War he had been put in charge of CIA operations in both Japan and Korea. But Kellis' own obsession with the murder outlived his enemies' memories. Wherever he served, the bitter aftertaste of a job half done continued to haunt this scrupulous man.

From Naples, Italy, where he was on assignment for the Air Force, in March 1952, he wrote to Ernest Lindley, Lippmann's aide on the investigating committee.

> You undoubtedly remember that I expressed some misgivings about the whole affair and as a result of it I was pulled out of the investigation. To be perfectly frank, I tried to be

as honest as I could with the Correspondents Association, but the odds were against me.

I recently met the director of the newspaper *Akropolis*, Mr. Botsis (his paper is a right-wing paper). He has been conducting an investigation of the Polk case and he appears to have considerable doubt as to whether the truth ever came out of that investigation, and later the trial.

In case you or Mr. Lippmann are interested in getting Mr. Botsis' views, you can contact him at the *Akropolis*, Athens, Greece.

There is no record of either journalist pursuing this lead.

"Let's hope that the whole truth may come to light this time," Kellis wrote Lippmann and Lindley in 1956 from Astoria, Long Island, enclosing a clipping from an Athens paper which had begun its own investigation, "which I know you and the committee have been striving for.

"Unfortunately, in 1948 there were too many obstructing hands who made our job very difficult, if not impossible.

"I can tell you now," Kellis wrote, as if Lippmann and Lindley had been oblivious to this fact, "that I was under considerable pressure to get out of the investigation and shut up."

He went on:

When it was realized that I expressed some doubts to you, General Donovan, and the committee, certain individuals attempted to label me "leftist" and I was investigated. My phone was tapped and I and my family were placed under surveillance. Needless to say, the charge did not stick because my political beliefs are moderate. Finally, I asked to be given a lie detector test which removed any doubts.

Looking back at this whole bad dream I am proud of the stand I took and hope that in my small way I have shown integrity and courage in the job assigned me. More important yet, I did not betray the committee and the principles you stand for.

Although I am only a small fry, I have enough sense to

realize that without freedom of the press, our country and the Western World may not survive.

As time went by, Kellis' anger became more and not less sharply focused. In May 1975, retired from the CIA and working as vice president of United Technologies Corporation in Connecticut, Kellis wrote to Professor John O. Iatrides, the eminent historian of contemporary Greece:

> Needless to say, my experience in dealing with Greece through the OSS, the CIA, and NATO pointed to heavy American official influence. We were so obsessed with the Communists that we were willing to get in bed with anyone who claimed to be anti-Communist, and this included Nazi collaborators, extreme right-wingers, crooks, inept people, etc. We should thank God Greece did not turn out to be like Vietnam, because things at times were very bleak. Some of our people at the U.S. Embassy and other American Missions resembled the British Colonial Service in India!

In another letter that same spring, this time to Costas Hadjiargyris in Athens, Kellis wrote:

> The reasons for my sudden return [in the middle of the Polk investigation] are that my investigation was leading to embarrassing consequences to the Greek Government and the British and American Missions in Greece.
> I was not able to conclude my investigation but at the time of my departure it appeared to me that George Polk was trapped. The participants to this feat were some right-wing officials in the Greek Government and two British officials in Salonika. It is my opinion that the execution of Polk and the condition his body was left in intended to attribute his death to the Communists to gain some political/psychological advantage.
> You may or may not know, I am active in politics in America and I consider myself a liberal Democrat. I have no sympathy

for the Communists or their tenets. Nevertheless, it is hard for me to accept the methods of operations of some American officials at that time. Karl Rankin of the U.S. Embassy, Frederick Ayer of AMAG, and Christian Freer of the CIA in Athens are examples of the worst America can offer to our friends and allies abroad. These people were obsessed by the Cold War and disregarded morality and ethics to attain their ends. Unfortunately, they and their successors caused many problems for Greece and America.

Let me say categorically that all Greek, British, and American government investigators aimed at one objective: to cover up the facts. The trial that followed was aimed at the same direction. It was a shambles.

In 1977, Jim Kellis, in a final attempt to right the wrong of the Polk case, and spurred by renewed interest in the case, including a May 1977 cover story in *More* magazine, marched into the Greek Consulate in New York and presented the surprised consul general with a sworn affidavit. In this document, the former investigator outlined his conclusion that the murder of George Polk was the work of a handful of right-wing fanatics and their British allies. He further stated that American officials tried to pin the murder on Communists for the sake of "national security." Kellis called for a retrial of Staktopoulos, whom he deemed to be an innocent scapegoat.

On September 17, 1977, he restated the findings of his investigation in a New York *Times* Op-Ed piece, in which he concluded:

> While I was in Greece in 1948, I often heard the statement that national interests had to be given a higher priority than discovering the real murderers of George Polk. I could not accept then, and I do not accept today, that we could support national interests by disregarding moral principles.

Colonel Kellis was spared perhaps the most painful aspect of his own character assassination. None other than General Donovan implied to some that the man's honesty was open to question.

Colonel "Ace" Miller, assistant Air Force attaché in 1948 and George Polk's friend, recalled Donovan telling him in the early 1950s that Kellis was not a man to be trusted.

Kellis died of a heart ailment in 1986 at the age of sixty-eight, still proud of his association with Donovan and the CIA he served for so many years.

By 1956, Gregory Staktopoulos, in police custody for eight years, was ready to reveal his own version of the sham trial. Encouraged by Athens police chief John Panopoulos' startling revelation (during an unrelated trial) that Staktopoulos' conviction had been rigged, the prisoner wrote an Athens newspaper retracting his confession. He claimed that his confession, extracted under torture, was worthless.

In 1961, after several suicide attempts, Staktopoulos' plea was finally heard. Under a more favorable domestic political climate, he was pardoned. He walked out of prison an old man of fifty, his hearing half gone, a man made wary of his fellow man. His beloved mother was dead. Anna Staktopoulos, though acquitted by the Salonika court, never recovered from her harsh treatment at the hands of the authorities in the weeks when they applied themselves to breaking her son. Both she and Staktopoulos' sister died while he was incarcerated.

By 1977, thanks to the dogged Stylianos Papathemiles, a young and influential Salonika politician who made the case his own, the entire malodorous case had begun to unravel. Now the Minister for Northern Greece, Papathemiles found the man who had actually addressed the envelope mailed to the police station. This time the Greeks called in a graphologist, who confirmed that a Salonika grocer, Savas Karamichalis, was the man. Though the grocer himself was by now dead, his wife and son were ready to swear he had addressed the envelope with George Polk's identification card, which his friend Efthemios Bamias stumbled upon on the quay.

At the same time, Anna Staktopoulos, many years dead, was posthumously absolved of any wrongdoing. Only Staktopoulos' own confession was then left as evidence against him.

In April 1977, almost twenty-nine years after the murder of George Polk, Gregory Staktopoulos faced the bright light of the world's media and declared himself innocent of any wrongdoing. He revealed the whole nightmarish story of how he was beaten and brutalized by Salonika police until they extracted the confession they wanted from him.

Gradually, Staktopoulos picked up the pieces of his former life. He was hired back by his old newspaper, *Makedonia*, and eventually he married. Encouraged by the Liberal Prime Minister Panayotis Kanellopoulos, he began the agonizing reconstruction of his arrest and torture at Mouscoundis' hands. The result was a book, steeped in anger and grief, the cry of a man still bewildered by his own unjust fate. Published in 1984, it was entitled *The Polk Affair: My Personal Testimony*.

Simultaneously, from outside Bucharest, Rumania, Vasvanas joined Staktopoulos in calling for a retrial, in which both men pronounced themselves ready to participate.

Greece, it seemed, however, was not yet ready for such a painful look backward. By a vote of 7–2, the country's highest court rejected the bid for a retrial. Forty years have passed since those days of Greek betraying Greek. Moreover, since 1981, Greece's Socialist PASOK government has shown great sympathy for veterans of the civil war. General Markos himself returned to Athens from exile in the Soviet Union. The Polk case, with its reminders of British and American manipulation of Athens, would roil today's still fragile political equilibrium.

Chargé Karl Rankin emerged as one of the few high-ranking foreign service officers unscathed by either the Cold War or the ensuing witch-hunt that swept the State Department clean of its best and brightest. He was regularly promoted, winning ambassadorial posts in such East-West trouble spots as Taiwan and Yugoslavia.

Walter Lippmann severed his connection to the case long before it all began to unravel. On the evening of September 15, 1949, Lippmann and the other distinguished members of the Overseas Writers Special Committee to Inquire into the Murder of George Polk met in the elegant private dining room of one of the capital's great hotels. Lippmann, sleek in black tie, proclaimed that evening that, although the case left many questions unanswered, "we can at least say that one of the guilty men has been caught and that no innocent man has been made the scapegoat for a crime of which he is innocent."

Oblivious to the irony of his proud pronouncement, he turned to the man who sat at his right on the dais and said, "General Donovan, I present you with this bowl on which are inscribed the signatures of the men who had the pleasure of working with you and an inscription which records our recognition of your work in defense of freedom of the press.

"If we cannot add to your long list of honors," Lippmann went on, "we can at least say on behalf of the men whose profession it is to have few illusions that in this undertaking we have learned that your sense of justice is the equal of your courage."

One last unfinished piece of business remained for the eminent Washington elder: the long-promised publication of a final report of the Lippmann committee's efforts and, particularly, General Donovan's role in the case. The many people who contributed time and money ($43,000, a substantial sum forty years ago) eagerly anticipated such a document.

Nearly two years after the murder, however, General Donovan had still not produced the desired White Paper. Pressure from Eugene Meyer, chairman of the Washington *Post*, finally prompted Donovan to act. On March 14, 1950, Meyer wrote to Donovan:

> My dear Bill, I ran into Walter Lippmann at the Metropolitan Club today. He feels rather strongly that the Overseas Writers Committee . . . should make a report to its subscribers. He said you have the matter in mind, but haven't found time to do anything about it.
>
> While I am not chairman of the Committee, I did have to do with raising the money to finance the operation to which you contributed so liberally by your invaluable service. Don't you think people who came forward so generously with the underwriting, and some of whom extended it in part until July, ought to hear from the Committee?
>
> With your high IQ and fame for facile power of expression, this should not be too troublesome.

Despite such well-advertised qualities, the general did in fact find this task "troublesome." In the end he entrusted the task to one of the bright young lawyers on his staff, Mary G. Jones. "Take it and make something out of it," Donovan instructed her, thrusting his files at her. She was empowered neither to conduct any interviews of her own nor to see his private correspondence. Her report was based entirely on diplomatic cables, unclassified correspondence and documents, the indictment of Staktopoulos, and the trial transcript. She worked for three months on a paper that in the end neither Lippmann nor Donovan chose to circulate. Without ever saying so, neither man could have taken much pride in the effort's skimpy result.

"I never knew what the general thought of the case," Mary Jones recalled, "but you never did know with him. There were so many wheels within wheels working in that brain."

Jones had an uneasy feeling about the report, which failed to pronounce the trial either fair or unfair. "I had strong misgivings about it, even with the minimal information I had at hand. I just wasn't sure what to think."

But once again, with the report filed, though undistributed, both Lippmann and Donovan were seen to have done the right thing. In August 1952, Lippmann wrote "finis" to the case. With Donovan's final report in hand, the eminent columnist announced to the press: "My personal opinion is that Polk's murder was planned by the Cominform and was carried out by the Communist Party of Greece in order to throw the blame of the murder to the Right, thus to defame Greece abroad and to stop the application of the Marshall Plan to Greece by protest in the United States against Greece, and also to frustrate military aid to Greece."

Lippmann's "personal opinion" is an almost verbatim translation of Staktopoulos' mea culpa dictated by Major Mouscoundis and Colonel Martin.

Walter Lippmann, who died in 1974, did not live long enough to learn just how many illusions obscured his vision during those ill-tempered days.

Lippmann's was not the only tribute Donovan was to receive for his part in the case. The Greek government, with the king's full accordance, awarded him the highest medal Greece can bestow on an individual.

From Major Mouscoundis, Donovan received yet another token of gratitude. On April 21, 1949, the police major inscribed an album of mug shots of Greek Communists still at large: "To General Donovan, representative of writers from across the seas, a great friend of democracy, supporter and advisor in solving the heinous murder of George Polk, I offer this as a symbol of my boundless respect."

General Donovan died following an incapacitating heart attack in 1959. His final moments were clouded by a terrible hallucination. The old spymaster imagined the Red Army marching across Washington's Connecticut Avenue Bridge.

Major Mouscoundis, promoted to colonel, lived just long enough to benefit from the pension that he feared he might lose because of the Polk case.

The official harassment of Costas Hadjiargyris did not end with the conclusion of the trial. Long before the murder of George Polk, the Greek newsman had been an irritant to the Greek right. With the Polk case, however, the Royalists felt confident they could finally incriminate Hadjiargyris. Newspaper articles alleging his connection to the murder continued, as did relentless hounding by the police.

By May 3, 1949, Hadjiargyris had had enough. In a four-and-a-half-page typed letter, he laid out his case to the highest judicial officer in Salonika, Attorney General Panayotis Constantinides, the chief public prosecutor.

"My silence in Salonika," he wrote, referring to his "discretion" during the Staktopoulos trial, "has been more than enough so far as my duty to my country is concerned. I therefore consider it necessary to transmit to you in writing all those facts which I did not mention in court, or only fleetingly, in accordance with your advice."

Hadjiargyris then proceeded to outline the absurdity of the government's case in light of his familiarity with Polk's movements. He also described the behavior of several people he deemed "suspicious." The Greek journalist strongly suspected British involvement, though he could not fathom at which level.

It is a measure of the continued influence of Britain in Greek affairs at that late date that, following Hadjiargyris' letter, his harassment ceased almost overnight. For in the case of the maverick Greek newsman, British and Greek interests diverged. While the Greeks were anxious to pursue the troublesome Hadjiargyris, the British wanted the Polk case closed.

Raleigh Gibson informed Secretary of State Marshall in a secret memorandum dated June 1, 1949:

> Sir Charles Wickham, chief of the British Police and Prisons Mission, called on me on May 21 and informed me that he had a translation of Hadjiargyris' letter, and stated that he considered it nothing but blackmail. He did not feel that the letter brought out anything especially detrimental to the findings of the court.
>
> He further states, however, that the action of the Salonika officials in continuing the inquiries [into Hadjiargyris' role in the murder] was not wise.

The official Greek investigation was thus pronounced closed.

In 1952, Sir Charles Wickham returned to Britain after seven years as head of the British Police and Prisons Mission in Greece. In his eighties, the much decorated Sir Charles became High Sheriff of County Down, his final position as guardian of Imperial values and standards. He died at the age of ninety-two at his estate in County Down.

Sir Charles's friend Mary Barber, now Lady Nicholas Henderson, lives with her British diplomat husband in London. Through the intervention of mutual friends, she granted this author an interview. However, the former *Time* correspondent subsequently dispatched a registered, special delivery letter requesting that her name not be used anywhere in this book.

The MI6 Athens station chief at the time, Nigel Clive, sent the author a letter similar in language and tone.

J. Edgar Hoover's FBI and the State Department persisted in their effort to tar not only the murdered man but his whole family with the brush of Communism. A confidential cable from the U.S.

Embassy in Ankara, Turkey, dated July 24, 1950, informs the Secretary of State that "William Polk, brother of the late journalist George Polk, now in Turkey as representative of the National Students' Association of the U.S., states he is touring the Middle East to make contacts with other student organizations . . . Embassy would appreciate any information in Department's files concerning Polk, whether or not he is a *fellow traveler*."

Despite General Donovan's warning that he would spoil his chances for professional success if he pursued his brother's case, William Polk went on to a distinguished academic career at Harvard and the University of Chicago. He has written several books about the Middle East, the region first revealed to him by his brother when the two shared an apartment in Cairo in 1946.

As late as 1955, the FBI continued its surveillance of the Polk family. A classified memorandum, still highly sanitized in 1989, says:

> The following items regarding the Polk case may be of interest as indication of possible Communist involvement on the part of the Polks, though they do not provide substantial evidence.
>
> George Polk was considered by some in Greece to be Communist leaning because of his critical attitude toward the Greek government, which was at the time engaged in civil war with Communist guerrillas in the north.
>
> The opinion has been voiced repeatedly since the trial that much of the truth was hidden. In a reexamination of the case, a Greek journalist named Tsimbidaros pointed out what he considered the strange behavior of Rea Polk and suggested she knew more than she told.
>
> The Attorney General of Greece was of the belief that Rea Polk was responsible for the removal of certain missing files from George Polk's office in Athens.
>
> A confidential informant of unknown reliability stated that Rea Polk had stated at Columbia University in the summer of 1948 that the Royalists killed her husband and she wanted to avenge his death.

Rea Polk tried to leave Greece in June 1948 and AMAG [American Mission for Aid to Greece] tried to prevent her departure.

There is no information available here on the recent activities of the subject. Nor is there any information which would shed light on the purpose of her present visit to Egypt.

We would be interested in any suspicious activity on the part of the subject that might come to your attention.

If Hoover had been as richly endowed with "confidential informants of unknown reliability" in Cairo as he was in his own country, he would have known that Rea Polk's mother lived in Egypt. The former Mrs. Polk, a widow for the second time, suffering from multiple sclerosis, has recently returned to live in Athens. Her apartment is a few blocks from Skoufa Street, where she lived with George Polk.

Athanasios Tsaldaris, the son of the head of the Royalist Party, who himself had threatened Rea Polk, is today a prominent member of the Greek Parliament and a leading elder of the conservative New Democracy Party.

Such was the human cost of shielding an inconsequential politician named Constantine Tsaldaris. He survived this brush with personal and political ruin; he would not survive others. In 1950, a scandal involving massive corruption in the port of Piraeus, Tsaldaris' political power base, run by his son, exploded in Parliament. The civil war was over, British influence was distinctly on the wane, and Washington no longer felt obliged to back any second-rate politician with solid anti-Communist credentials. Tsaldaris had also outlasted his usefulness to his powerful military allies. This time, there were no accommodating zealots available to rescue him. Few in Athens were surprised at the precipitous political decline in the early 1950s of this mediocre man.

The secret network of military, police, and intelligence operatives responsible for George Polk's murder and Staktopoulos' death-in-life continued, however, to dominate Greek life. American support remained foursquare behind the politics of "internal security" at the expense of most other aspects of Greek reconstruction. Sir

Charles Wickham, Colonel Thomas Martin, General "Wild Bill" Donovan, Karl Rankin, Christian Freer, Raleigh Gibson, and their harsh Cold War mentality made a deep imprint on the evolution of this fragile state. KYP, the child of the CIA, continued to work hand in glove with its parent organization. By the 1960s, all key political decisions passed through American hands in Athens.

On a bright spring morning in 1967, Athens awoke to the menacing rumble of tanks. Telephone lines had been cut and hard voices announced through loudspeakers that movement on the streets was forbidden. Combat-equipped troops controlled every radio transmitter, airport, rail terminal, power plant, and police station in the land. The nightmare that George Polk had warned against two decades earlier had been realized.

A group of fanatic right-wing colonels had seized power. Their goal: to achieve the highest form of "internal security." One of the colonels, a middle-level officer in KYP, told the CIA's John M. Maury, "Look, we have done you and the king a great service. We have done what you know was necessary. But you didn't want to get your hands dirty." The colonels' justification for terror echoed the thinking of Polk's murderers. They, too, assumed ultimate American support for and collusion in their crime.

But the newly installed junta repelled even the CIA, which found itself in the odd position of reporting on the new regime's most repugnant aspects. The CIA provided well-documented evidence of torture, arbitrary police action, purges of respected military men and civil servants, and the almost complete suppression of academic and press freedom.

The American Factor, as Greeks continue to refer to Washington's influence on Greek affairs, continues to haunt a scarred national psyche and poisons chances for normal relations between the two countries. The origins of the American Factor can be traced directly to the arrogant men who thought that one honest reporter's life was a small price to pay for their vision of security, national and international. It proved a Faustian bargain. They and their successors are still paying the cost.

Acknowledgments

———◆———

The process of piecing together and attempting to solve a forty-year-old murder requires both the help of many people and a great deal of luck. I had both in extraordinary measure. First and foremost, I am indebted to William R. Polk, George Polk's younger brother. Mr. Polk gave generously of his time and allowed the author free access to his family's voluminous collection of letters and journals.

Mr. Polk's memories of his brother and his insights into the painful period following his murder enabled me to penetrate to an unusual degree the psyche of the murdered man as well as that of his murderers.

I am also deeply grateful to the Gannett Foundation for providing me with a fellowship to research this book in the congenial atmosphere of Gannett's Columbia University Center. Thanks to the unstinting support of Everett Dennis, director of the Gannett Center for Media Studies, I had unlimited access to Columbia's libraries. Of particular value was the School of Journalism collection of forty years of back issues of the New York *Times*, the New York *Herald Tribune*, the Washington *Post*, and *Time* and *Newsweek* magazines. Through the Gannett Center, I was also fortunate to be aided by a Greek researcher, Eleni Coundouriotis, who translated for me all Greek books and periodicals on the George Polk case.

Laura Kapnick at the CBS Archives and Sally Marks at the National Archives in Washington were both exceedingly helpful in locating material for this book. Quinlan J. Shea at the National Security Archives in Washington counseled the author on the sometimes frustrating limitations of operating under the restrictions of the Freedom of Information Act.

British researcher and historian Michael Kettle provided invaluable assistance in the byzantine byways of London's Public Record Office, where British diplomatic files are stored.

Nicholas Gage offered his support and enthusiasm, as well as some valuable research material he had collected. I thank him for all three.

Professor John O. Iatrides, the eminent historian of contemporary Greece, was the author's patient tutor and guide through a period which to a great many Greeks is still a field mined with unspent passions. I thank him for his tireless effort, though any glaring historical mistakes in this work are mine alone.

I am also indebted to Lawrence S. Wittner, history professor at the State University of New York in Albany, whose seminal work on the subject of Greek-American relations, *American Intervention in Greece, 1943–1949,* provided me a good background to the drama of the Polk case. Professor Wittner was also kind enough to check my manuscript for historical inaccuracies.

A great many friends and colleagues provided me with advice and counsel as I proceeded with this investigation. In particular I wish to express my appreciation to William vanden Heuvel, who shared with me his memories, documents, and his own diary, which detailed his time with General William Donovan. I am grateful to many others who were extraordinarily helpful: Edward Bliss, Howard K. Smith, Don Hewitt, Eric Sevareid, Douglas Edwards, David Schoenbrun, Helene-Maria Lekas, William L. Shirer, George Seldes, I. F. Stone, Bob Woodward, Barbara Feinman, Theodore White, Joseph Wershba, Ted Berkman, Homer Bigart, Elias Demetrokopoulos, Gerold Frank, Ruth Gruber, Christopher Hitchens, Charles Glass, Seymour Freidin, Norman Corwin, Alexander Kendrick, A. M. Sperber, Ellen James, Ronald Steel, Peter Tomkins, Cali Doxiades, Simoni Zafiropoulos, William Price, George Price, Jefferson Price, Milbry Polk, Jeanne Marie Polk Roberts, Senator William Cohen of Maine, Nigel West, Natalie Bocock (of the Senate Intelligence Subcommittee), Alexandros Lykourezos, Anna Lee, Ambassador George Vest, Colonel Allen Miller, Donald Matchan, Ed Clark, Clark Clifford, Daniel Thrapp, Lawrence R. Houston, Nicholas Elliott (retired MI6 officer), George Vournas,

Richard Holbrooke, Simon Jenkins, Phillip Knightley, Harold Evans, and Harrison Salisbury.

A special note of thanks goes to Stephen Smith for his many editorial suggestions and his patient grooming of my manuscript.

This is the second book that I have had the good fortune to write under the guidance of my editor, Linda Healey. It was once again both a stimulating and an enjoyable experience, which I hope shall be repeated. No writer could ask for a more courageous or compassionate editor, able to nurse a germ of an idea into a book.

My agent and friend, Amanda Urban, played an unusually active part in cheering on this project from the very beginning. I thank her for unlimited personal and professional support.

My husband, Peter Jennings, has allowed this book to occupy center stage of our family life. He has played his usual critical part as first reader, resident editor, and provider of emotional sustenance.

Primary Sources

—————

Much of the material relating to George Polk's personal and professional life has been drawn from Polk's diary of his early years and from his extensive collection of letters to his mother, Adelaide Polk, and his brother, William Roe Polk. I also made use of the private journal of George Polk's mother, entitled "Some Remembrances of George as a Child and Young Man by Relatives and Friends," dated Spring 1963. Made available to me by William Polk, this material provided invaluable glimpses into Polk's personal life.

Documentation regarding Polk's CBS years I obtained from the CBS Archives and the Stanton files on the murder of George Polk, in the possession of former CBS president Frank Stanton. The Edward R. Murrow papers, housed at the Fletcher School of Law and Diplomacy, Tufts University, rounded out the CBS material.

In order to trace America's deepening involvement in the Greek Civil War and in Greece's political future, as well as the role played by American officials in the Polk murder investigation, I made extensive use of the Freedom of Information Act. I thus obtained hundreds of documents (a frustrating number of them still heavily sanitized) from the Central Intelligence Agency, the Federal Bureau of Investigation, and the Department of State. In addition, I have throughout the book made use of recently declassified and non-classified diplomatic cables relating to the Polk case on file at the National Archives (under 368.113, Polk, George, or under 811.91268) in Washington.

The official but secret correspondence of Colonel James Kellis, furnished to me by the colonel's former associates, was critical in documenting the conspiracy behind George Polk's murder. I cannot publicly thank those who made these documents available to me, for I have assured them anonymity.

For an analysis of General "Wild Bill" Donovan's part in the Greek and American investigation and the murder trial I drew on Donovan's files, which I obtained from Anthony Cave Brown, his biographer.*

James Withrow, one of General Donovan's former law partners at Donovan and Leisure, provided me with other pieces of the general's correspondence and memoranda regarding the Polk case.

For a record of Walter Lippmann's relationship with George Polk, as well as the columnist's role in the investigation of the murder, I drew on the Lippmann papers, on file at the Sterling Memorial Library of Yale University.

The diary of Mrs. Waide (Geneal) Condon, wife of the USIS Athens officer at the time of the case, and friend of George Polk, provides a detailed record of the events preceding and immediately following Polk's murder, from the perspective of two Americans involved in the crime's aftermath. My thanks to Celia Straus, the Condons' granddaughter, for making this material available to me.

British involvement and interest in the case I researched at the London Public Record Office, Kew Gardens, where recently de-classified British diplomatic papers are on file. For an analysis of the role of the British Police Mission in Greece and the Greek right wing I relied in part on the study of Dr. David Close, senior lecturer in history, University of Flinders, South Australia.

I conducted over one hundred interviews with participants, eyewitnesses, and others with firsthand information regarding the Polk case. All dialogue in the book is drawn from those accounts, correspondence, or the transcripts of testimony taken by Greek investigators prior to the trial of Gregory Staktopoulos.

---

* When I queried Mr. Cave Brown why, despite the possession of so much valuable doc-umentation on the Polk case, he did not even mention George Polk in his own work, *The Last Hero*, Mr. Cave Brown answered, "There were third party obligations involved." The "third party" turned out to have been the CIA in the person of William J. Casey, former director of Central Intelligence. It was Casey, as Cave Brown himself points out in the foreword to *The Last Hero*, who approached him to write the biography of Donovan and subsequently provided him access to the general's files.

While these interviews were critical in capturing the atmosphere of those times, memory fades and can play tricks after so many years. Thus I have relied primarily on documents, letters, and sworn statements written at the time of the crime or shortly following it for the factual basis of the book.

I have taken the liberty of eliminating garbled punctuation and the use of technical formulations in the many telexes and cables I quote throughout the book. I did this purely for the sake of a smoother narrative flow without in any way altering the body of these cables.

Introduction

The description of the funeral is based on the author's interview with Rea Polk Venn and the letters of Adelaide Polk from Athens to her family, particularly the letter of May 23, 1948. These accounts were supplemented by wire service articles and photos of the rites (files of William R. Polk and Jefferson Price, nephew of George Polk).

Chapter 1

For an account of Polk's final days in Athens and Salonika, the author relied on interviews with Robert Skedgell, Rea Polk Venn, Ambassador Oliver Crosby, Col. Allen "Ace" Miller, Christopher Nicholas Halkias of the British Consulate, Salonika, Gregory Staktopoulos, and Donald Matchan. Randoll Coate, living in retirement in London, gave the author several interviews on the subject of Polk and his own alleged involvement in the murder. It was the first time Mr. Coate has given his version of events to any author or reporter since 1948.

A careful breakdown of George Polk's last days in Greece is contained in the eleven-page letter of Col. James Kellis to Gen. "Wild Bill" Donovan, dated July 22, 1948, which was among the Kellis papers (confidential source).

In addition, the author drew on the CBS Archives for Polk's final broadcast. Also "Report to Mr. Wells Church and Mr. Davidson Taylor," marked "Confidential," by Winston Burdett and John Secondari in the Stanton files, has more material on how Polk spent his time in Salonika.

Diplomatic cables from Athens and Salonika to Washington were drawn from the Diplomatic Files, National Archives, Athens Post Files, 1948 (368.113, Polk, George).

The letters of George Polk to Edward R. Murrow and to his family were in the files of William R. Polk.

Chapter 2

For a record of the Polk family's early history, the author has used the journal of George Polk's grandmother, Mary Harding Polk (files of George Polk's niece, Milbry Polk). For a description of Fort Worth in the 1920s and 1930s, the author relied on interviews with William R. Polk and the personal journal of George Polk, which he began as an eleven-year-old and continued well into his twenties (files of William R. Polk). An interview with Texas-born author Dan Jenkins provided more information about Fort Worth in the 1920s and 1930s.

Chapter 3

For material on China in the 1930s, the author interviewed Theodore White and Mary Catherine Polk Hill. Adelaide Polk's unpublished journal, "Remembrances of George Polk as a Child and Young Man by Relatives and Friends," dated Spring 1963, provided further material for this chapter.

For more background for this chapter the author relied on William Manchester's *The Glory and the Dream: A Narrative History of America, 1932–1972.*

The author interviewed Warren Hafer, George Polk's former student, for background on Polk the teacher.

Chapter 4

The author's interviews with George Polk's cousins, George and William Price, and Mary Catherine Polk Hill and Manchester's *The Glory and the Dream* provided material on George Polk's decision to enlist, as well as the general climate of the times.

William R. Polk described his brother's visit with his father in an interview with the author.

The author drew upon George Polk's detailed correspondence from Guadalcanal to his family (especially his letter to his wife dated December 21, 1942, and his letters to Mrs. Adelaide Polk dated September 30 and August 1, 1942) for the description of his war experience.

Chapter 5

George Polk's letters of 1944 to his cousin William Price (files of Jefferson Price) and interviews with the former Mrs. Polk and with author Ruth Gruber, Polk's friend and Washington neighbor, provided material regarding Polk's postwar readjustment problems.

The quotes from *Good Housekeeping* and *House Beautiful* are excerpted from p. 426 of Manchester's *The Glory and the Dream.*

The incident describing General Patton's slapping of a soldier is from p. 320 of *The First Casualty*, by Phillip Knightley.

Material on Polk's married life came from Mary Catherine Polk Hill and his cousins William and George Price.

The author relied on the Lippmann papers (Sterling Memorial Library, Yale

University) as well as an interview with Ronald Steel, Lippmann's biographer, for the section on the distinguished columnist.

For more on Lippmann's view of the immediate postwar political landscape, including the passage regarding "the British-Russian" conflict, see p. 422 of Steel's *Walter Lippmann and the American Century*.

For a description of life at the New York *Herald Tribune*, the author drew on the memories of Ruth Gruber, former *Tribune* correspondent. Ms. Gruber also provided background material regarding George Polk's Washington social and professional life. The author also relied on Richard Kluger's *The Paper* for an excellent description of the *Tribune* in the late 1940s, and David Brinkley's *Washington Goes to War* for a flavor of the capital in transition.

Chapter 6

For a description of Polk's London visit and the impression George made on his CBS colleagues, the author interviewed Howard K. Smith, Eric Sevareid, Douglas Edwards, Winston Burdett, David Schoenbrun, and William Shirer.

A. M. Sperber, Murrow's biographer, provided the author with some of her own exhaustive research in the field. Her book, *Murrow: His Life and Times*, is replete with original material. Joseph E. Persico's account, *Edward R. Murrow: An American Original*, provided the author a study of Murrow's complex character. The author again used the Murrow scripts (on file at the Fletcher School, Tufts University).

Interviews with Mary Catherine Polk Hill and Polk's correspondence, as well as Robert G. Kaiser's account of war-ravaged London, *Cold Winter, Cold War*, and Alan Bullock's *Ernest Bevin, Foreign Secretary, 1945–1951*, were sources on postwar Britain.

On the subject of Greece's primacy for British foreign policy, see also Eugene J. Meehan, *The British Left Wing and Foreign Policy* (New Brunswick, N.J.: Rutgers University Press, 1960), pp. 66–69.

In addition to drawing on Polk's CBS colleagues Shirer, Smith, and Sevareid for their memories of Polk in London, the author also relied on A. M. Sperber's interviews with John Donovan for a description of Polk's character and temperament.

Chapter 7

The letters of George Polk and his wife to their families (especially the letter of December 8, 1945, from both George and Kay to their parents, and Polk's letters of January 5, 1946, from Cairo, January 23, 1946, from Turkey, and June 30, 1946, from Jerusalem, all addressed "Dear Family") were the best sources for rendering Polk's European journey as well as his early days in the Middle East (collection of William R. Polk).

The author interviewed I. F. Stone for a description of George Polk in Cairo and the impression he made on the iconoclastic publisher.

Polk's letters and the radio scripts for CBS from this period are in the files of William R. Polk.

For more on Polk in the Middle East, the author interviewed and exchanged correspondence with Ted Berkman, Gerold Frank, Norman Corwin, and Ruth Gruber. The incident at Allenby Bridge was described to the author by Gerold Frank.

The author also wishes to thank A. M. Sperber for making available her extensive interviews with NBC's John Donovan (conducted in September and October 1982) on the subject of George Polk. Sadly, Mr. Donovan, suffering from a number of disabling diseases, was no longer physically able to participate in an interview by the time this author began her research.

For more on Turkey and America's sudden preoccupation with the Dardanelles, the author relied on Harry Truman's *Memoirs*. For a description of the circumstances of Churchill's Fulton speech, see Martin Gilbert's biography, *Winston S. Churchill: Never Despair*.

The former Mrs. Polk provided the description of the end of her marriage.

Chapter 8

Greek newspaper accounts of the return of King George II found in the files of both Gen. Donovan and William R. Polk were translated for the author by Eleni Coundouriotis.

Polk's radio scripts (CBS Archives) and the author's interviews with John O. Iatrides (professor of contemporary Greek studies, Southern Connecticut State University), Prof. George Mavrogordatos (University of Athens), and Elias Demetrokopoulos, former Salonika newspaper editor, form the background for the remainder of the chapter regarding the volatile Greek political landscape in the late 1940s.

Kevin Andrews, *The Flight of Ikaros: Travels in Greece During a Civil War*, and Kenneth Matthews, *Memories of a Mountain War*, as well as Nigel Clive, *A Greek Experience, 1943–1948*, were also vital secondary sources for this chapter.

William R. Polk provided the author with vivid descriptions of his brother's life in Cairo, as well as a collection of George's letters home and to CBS from this period.

Chapter 9

For a description of the origins of the Truman Doctrine the author interviewed Clark Clifford.

The Forrestal Diaries, ed. by Walter Millis, describes the role played by this first among Cold Warriors in shaping public opinion of the day.

For a more scholarly look at America's deepening involvement in Greece, the author interviewed L. S. Stavrianos and relied on his account, *Greece: American Dilemma and Opportunity* (Chicago: Henry Regnery, 1952).

More background for this chapter came from *Foreign Relations of the United States: Diplomatic Papers* (Washington, D.C.: U.S. Government Printing Office), 1945, 1946, 1947, as well as from George Kennan's *Memoirs, 1925–1950*.

The author also used Walter Isaacson and Evan Thomas, *The Wise Men: Six Friends and the World They Made*, an excellent study of the key Washington players and their motives in the Greek-American drama, including Marshall, Kennan, Acheson, and Bohlen.

Robert Donovan's *Conflict and Crisis: The Presidency of Harry S. Truman, 1945–1948* was drawn on for more on Truman's role in shaping America's Greek policy and also for a description of Truman's treatment of Soviet Foreign Minister Molotov.

For the perspective of the Greek right wing, the author used Greek newspaper accounts of the period found among the Donovan papers.

For background on Stalin's singular lack of enthusiasm for deeper involvement in the Greek Civil War, the author drew on *Conversations with Stalin*, by Milovan Djilas.

Throughout this chapter the author relied on the diplomatic cables on file at the National Archives, Athens Post Files, for rendering the mood of both the State Department and Washington's diplomats in Athens.

For more background on one American observer's reactions to the mire of Greek politics and its impact on Washington, see the Paul A. Porter papers, at the Truman Library, Independence, Mo.

Dean Acheson's memoirs, *Present at the Creation*, provide a good description of right-wing politician Constantine Tsaldaris and how and why the State Department shaped American thinking on the subject of American intervention in Greece. The former Secretary of State provides an equally memorable description of Lord Inverchapel and his sad mission. Acheson also captures the high drama of the White House's presentation of its radical new policy toward Greece and Turkey to an initially reluctant Congress.

President Truman describes the evolution of his own thinking on the subject of Greece and Washington's need to bolster the Athens regime in his *Memoirs*.

The author interviewed Richard C. A. Holbrooke, biographer of Clark Clifford, on the Truman Doctrine and Clifford's role and motives in its shaping.

Chapter 10

To document Polk's professional rise during 1947, the author relied on William R. Polk's memories and his files of letters from his brother. Here, as elsewhere in the book, Polk's CBS colleagues Eric Sevareid, Howard K. Smith, David Schoenbrun, and Winston Burdett supplied additional background regarding the news business and Ed Murrow's critical role as mentor.

For background on the Loyalty Oath, Truman's *Memoirs*, Robert J. Donovan's *Conflict and Crisis*, and Carl Bernstein's *Loyalties*, as well as William Manchester's *The Glory and the Dream*, provided a wealth of documentation.

The author interviewed I. F. Stone, William Shirer, William Price (New York *Daily News* correspondent and cousin of George Polk), and A. M. Sperber on the effect of the Truman Doctrine and the Loyalty Oath on journalists and journalism.

Murrow's letter of April 1948 to Lady Milner bemoaning the rising temperature of the anti-Red hysteria is among the Murrow papers, Fletcher School, Tufts University.

The description of Dr. Edward U. Condon's harassment is from Manchester's *The Glory and the Dream*, p. 490.

Chapter 11

George Polk's letters of 1947 to his family (files of William R. Polk) form the bulk of the background for the material on Palestine and for Polk's views on the British (especially his letter of October 2, 1947, which provides a detailed picture of his confrontation with Sir Henry Gurney) and the description of his crash landing in Lebanon, as well as his treatment by Dr. Wodak (letter of April 28, 1947).

James Morris's study, *Farewell the Trumpets: An Imperial Retreat*, provided the author with further background on the British presence in the Middle East.

The author relied in part on Lawrence Wittner's *American Intervention in Greece* for a solid chronicle of the Greek Civil War and the rise of General Markos.

The material on Lt. Col. Floyd A. Spencer is from the Donovan files. In a nine-page confidential memorandum (found among Donovan's papers) which Spencer addressed to Lippmann, dated April 15, 1948, the colonel outlined his relationship to Polk and the precise advice and counsel he provided the CBS reporter regarding the Communist guerrillas.

The documentation on Theodoros Ksingakos, secret agent, is from the private papers of Col. Kellis (Kellis' memo to Gen. Donovan dated July 22, 1948).

Chapter 12

The description of George Polk's meeting and romancing of Rea Cocconis is from the author's interview with the former Mrs. Polk.

For a reference to George Drossos working for the Greek right, the author relied on embassy secretary Oliver Marcy's confidential memo to Rankin (dated August 4, 1948), with a copy to CIA agent Driscoll (National Archives).

Further material depicting Greece in the fall of 1947 came from Kenneth Matthews, *Memories of a Mountain War*.

George's troubles with Egyptian officialdom are described in Polk's letter to his brother William.

The background on Polk's plans to do a book on the Middle East is from the October 25, 1947, letter to CBS's George Herman (files of William R. Polk).

The Lippmann-Polk exchange of correspondence is from the Lippmann papers (Sterling Memorial Library, Yale University).

For documentation of Churchill's shifting views on Greece, the author used the Prime Minister's letter to Sir Orme Sargent, Permanent Under Secretary of State, Foreign Office, dated October 31, 1947 (in *Winston S. Churchill*, by Martin Gilbert).

Churchill's relationship with Queen Frederika is described by C. L. Sulzberger in his *A Long Row of Candles* (New York: Macmillan, 1969), pp. 392–93.

The diplomatic cables from Dean Acheson and Karl Rankin are from the National Archives, Athens Post Files, 1947.

Polk's letter to *Newsweek* dated December 6, 1947, is in William R. Polk's files.

Chapter 13

Ambassador Dendramis' letter of December 31, 1947, to CBS president Frank Stanton is from the Stanton files.

Polk's letter answering Dendramis' charges (addressed to Stanton), February 7, 1948, is also found in the Stanton files.

On the subject of CBS's attitude toward Polk, the author interviewed Howard K. Smith and Winston Burdett.

Transcripts of Nicholas Lelis' attack on Polk aired by CBS News are from the Stanton files.

For material regarding some correspondents questioning why CBS was giving airtime to official Greek spokesmen, the author relied on the (undated) 1948 letter of CBS's George Herman addressed to George Polk (from William R. Polk's files).

For more on the tension between U.S. diplomats and the press, the author quotes from the 1946 memo from the U.S. military attaché to the Secretary of State, from the National Archives, Athens Post Files, 1946.

The author interviewed Homer Bigart for material regarding his own troubles with Chargé Rankin and others at the Athens embassy. For more on the tension between the American press corps and the embassy, the author interviewed the then Athens UP correspondent, Edward Clark.

The transcript of the conversation of Chargé Rankin, Bigart, and Costas Hadjiargyris is found in Rankin's secret memorandum of January 22, 1948, to the Secretary of State. This memo and other diplomatic cables cited in this chapter are located in the National Archives, Athens Post Files.

Lippmann's comments touching on the anxiety of the early months of 1948 are quoted from his column, "Today and Tomorrow," of March 15, 1948, and from a letter to the commander of the Sixth Fleet (also dated March 1948), which is in the Lippmann papers (Sterling Memorial Library, Yale University).

For additional material on the Berlin and Czech crisis, the author drew on Charles Bohlen's *Witness to History*, Dean Acheson's *Present at the Creation*, Allan Bullock's biography, *Ernest Bevin*, and Truman's *Memoirs*.

Chapter 14

A transcript of "CBS Views the Press," January 17, 1948, on the subject of the confrontation between George Polk and Maxwell Anderson is in the Stanton files.

George Polk's letter of February 5, 1948, to Don Hollenbeck describes his reaction to his colleagues' supportive message. The author also relied on A. M. Sperber's account of Hollenbeck's suicide (pp. 469–70 in *Murrow: His Life and Times*).

For a description of Michael Kourtessis, the author used the official deposition of Despina Vroutsis, the Polks' maid, taken by Greek authorities on June 5, 1948, contained in the Donovan files.

For additional material on Kourtessis, the author drew on a memorandum (also found among Donovan's files) entitled "Items Discussed with [Minister of Public Order] Rendis," dated August 10, 1948, a two-page summary of a conversation with the Greek minister in which Michael Kourtessis is alleged to "fit the description of the man who according to Polk's maid came to Polk's house with a letter for Polk and refused to leave the letter and waited and gave it to Polk in person. This took place just a few days before Polk's assassination."

The author relied on this same memorandum for a description of the Organization of the Port of Piraeus, which it compares to the better-known terror group X.

For a description of the Royalist security forces and their many official and semi-official tentacles, the author relied in part on a four-page "Strictly Confidential" unsigned memorandum, presumably of CIA origin, dated July 26, 1948, Athens, on the subject of the Greek "military league" (among Gen. Donovan's papers).

For additional material on the subject of the Greek right wing and its various paramilitary offshoots, the author interviewed Dr. David Close, Australian scholar of the Greek secret right-wing organizations (University of Flinders) and Prof. George Mavrogordatos (University of Athens) on the subject of the rise of the Greek extreme right.

The scene describing Tsaldaris and Zervas dancing in Piraeus is from Willie Etheridge's account of life in Athens in the mid-1940s, *It's Greek to Me*, pp. 99–100.

On the subject of Kourtessis and his front organization, the author also drew information from the August 20, 1948, letter of former OSS agent Lambros Antoniou to Col. Kellis, as well as Kellis' letter of September 3, 1948, to Gen. Donovan.

Also, notes found in Gen. Donovan's files dated August 10, 1948, entitled "Items Discussed with Mr. Rendis," regarding Kourtessis, X, and the Organization of the Port of Piraeus, provided crucial information.

John Colville's *The Fringes of Power: 10 Downing Street Diaries, 1939–1955*, especially pp. 532–33, provides a first-person account of Churchill's uncompromising attitude toward the Greek Communists.

The author also relied on interviews with Prof. John O. Iatrides for a historical assessment of the 1944 massacre of Greek leftists called *Dekemvriana*.

For additional material on the confrontation between the British and the Greek left, the author used Winston Churchill's own account, *Triumph and Tragedy* (Vol. VI of *The Second World War*, especially the chapter entitled "Christmas at Athens").

Chapter 15

On the relationship between the intelligence world and journalists, the author relied on interviews with a number of intelligence agents, British and American, most of whom asked for and were assured confidentiality. James McCargar, retired diplomat and CIA agent, and currently author of books on intelligence-related subjects, was particularly informative in this regard.

The author interviewed former Athens correspondents Daniel Thrapp, Ed Clark, and Seymour Freidin, who provided insights into the mood of the American and British press corps in Greece during the civil war.

The author also interviewed Lord Nicholas Bethel for material regarding Robert

Low of *Time* magazine. (See Bethel's *The Great Betrayal*, London: Hodder and Stoughton, 1984.)

Also, C. L. Sulzberger's *A Long Row of Candles* was a good source on the British preference for recruiting reporters as agents in the field, especially his revelation (p. 472) regarding Mary Barber's close friend, and George Polk's alleged (by his wife, Rea) "enemy," Frank Macaskie, "on special assignment for British intelligence."

The author interviewed New York *Times* correspondent Harrison Salisbury for additional material on Sedgwick's pro-British and pro-Greek Royalist bent, and former *Time* reporter Mary Barber and retired British intelligence agent Nigel Clive on their views of the Polk case. Both Barber and Clive denied any personal involvement in the cover-up or any knowledge of a British role in the Polk affair.

The author interviewed Rea Cocconis Polk for material regarding her marriage and her husband's continued nightmares.

For material relating to Polk's early 1948 trip to northern Greece, the author used transcripts of Polk's CBS broadcasts of January and February 1948 (CBS Archives).

In tracing Polk's telephone threats the author interviewed Rea Polk and William Polk and studied Costas Hadjiargyris' trial testimony (Donovan files and National Archives Diplomatic Files, 1948). Hadjiargyris' letter to the *Christian Science Monitor*, London bureau, dated May 24, 1948, addressed to William Stringer, also confirms Polk's telephone threats (files of William R. Polk).

The personal journal of Adelaide Polk describes her trip to Turkey and then Greece with her son and daughter-in-law (William R. Polk's files).

For additional background on the Polks in Turkey, the author interviewed Talia Donas (former CBS News Istanbul office manager) and Genevieve Hochstetter (widow of the CBS News Istanbul correspondent).

For more on George Polk's final months in Athens, the author drew on the letters of Adelaide Polk dated March 6, March 8, March 10, and March 11, 1948, from Athens to her family in America.

Polk's broadcast on Yanni, dated February 19, 1948, is in the CBS Archives.

Polk's broadcast on the Truman Doctrine's first anniversary, March , 1948.

Regarding Polk's late April death threats, the author drew on Hadjiargyris' trial testimony (National Archives).

Chapter 16

For material regarding the letter informing Polk of Tsaldaris' New York bank account, the author interviewed Rea Polk and William Polk. The information is also confirmed in the interviews A. M. Sperber conducted with John Donovan in 1982. For additional information on this crucial episode, the author consulted the eleven-page letter (marked "Secret: For General Donovan's Eyes Alone") written by Col. Kellis to Gen. Donovan and dated July 22, 1948.

The author interviewed Clark Clifford for his reaction to the illegal Tsaldaris bank account.

Rea Polk reconstructed the interview between the Foreign Minister and her husband for the author. William Polk and John Donovan's version (interviews of fall 1982) confirmed Mrs. Polk's.

Chapter 17

Kourtessis' movements are described in a letter from OSS veteran Lambros Antoniou to Col. Kellis dated August 20, 1948 (Kellis papers).

Kourtessis' travel to Salonika just before and right after Polk's murder is confirmed in Gen. Donovan's memorandum in his files entitled "Items Discussed with Mr. Rendis," dated August 10, 1948, which refers to Kourtessis as one of the OLP's "leading members . . . supposedly taken to Salonika by Mouscoundis five days after the crime and possibly before. . . . OLP is government controlled and operated port authority headed by Yenimatas, a Populist (Royalist Party) deputy. Yenimatas right-hand man in this undercover rightist organization is a top employee of OLP named Triandaphion. A man named Georgopoulos of the Organization of the Port of Piraeus says that Polk's murderer walks between the Wasiliades well and Glyfada . . . and another man two days later told our [Donovan's] informer that he knows the murderer and he is an OLP member." The Wasiliades well is not a landmark of any sort and must have been the private well of a man of that name. Wasiliades is not an uncommon Greek name. Glyfada is a well-known area just outside Athens.

The relationship between X, Sir Charles Wickham, and the British Police Mission is detailed in *The New Statesman and Nation*, February 1, 1947, pp. 88–89.

For additional material relating to the extreme right wing and the British, the author interviewed Prof. George Mavrogordatos (University of Athens) and used the unpublished articles of Prof. David Close (University of Flinders).

For still more on this subject, the author also drew on a memo of a conversation between Sir Charles Wickham and A. L. Moffat, January 1948, National Archives Athens Post Files.

Pretrial testimony of Polk's maid, Despina Vroutsis, June 5, 1948, contains material regarding the letter personally delivered to Polk (Donovan files on the Greek investigation).

The Kourtessis and Mouscoundis relationship is described in Lambros Antoniou's letter to Col. Kellis, dated August 29, 1948 (Kellis papers). This incident is also referred to in Donovan's notes of the meeting with Minister Rendis on August 10, 1948 (Donovan files).

The activities of the British Police Mission before and after Polk's murder are described in a memorandum, marked "Secret," from Oliver Marcy, embassy secretary in Athens, to the Secretary of State, dated August 25, 1948.

The description of Sir Charles Wickham is from Nicholas Halkias, retired consular officer, British Consulate, Salonika, during an interview with the author in Salonika. The memoirs of Mary Barber Henderson, *Xenia*, also contain relevant material on Wickham.

Cables from Ambassador Clifford Norton and Sir Reginald Leeper to the Foreign Office are from the Public Record Office, Kew Gardens, London.

Chapter 18

For a breakdown of Polk's last days and hours in Salonika the author relied on Col. Kellis' reconstruction of events in a letter to Gen. Donovan dated July 22, 1948.

For Kourtessis' role and sudden disappearance, the author used Lambros Antoniou's letter to Kellis of August 20, 1948, and Donovan's memorandum of August 10, 1948, "Items Discussed with Mr. Rendis."

The author also made use of the diary of Mrs. Waide Condon for the private thoughts of one American official deeply involved in the murder's aftermath, whose husband (the Athens USIS officer) speculates on how the murder was likely to have been executed.

Polk's unmailed letter to Murrow is in the files of William R. Polk.

The story of the missing pajamas is from the trial testimony of Gregory Staktopoulos.

Chapter 19

The story of Polk's ID card being mailed to the Salonika police is from the indictment of Gregory Staktopoulos, Donovan files, and National Archives, Diplomatic Papers.

The author relied on CBS's Stanton files for Davidson Taylor's cable to the Greek Foreign Ministry asking for information about Mrs. Polk.

The author interviewed Rea Polk for a description of her early days in Salonika following her husband's murder.

Mrs. Waide Condon's diary contains detailed material (with nearly verbatim reconstructions of conversations between the Condons and the widow) regarding Mrs. Polk's travails in Salonika.

The author interviewed Gregory Staktopoulos for material regarding the Greek newsman's brief meeting with Polk.

The story of Rea Polk's episode of terror at the hands of security men was related by the widow to William E. Colby on September 30, 1948 (transcript in Donovan files).

The author interviewed Don Matchan for his memories of George Polk and the days immediately following the murder when Matchan was in Salonika.

The official report of the autopsy of George Polk, dated May 16, 1948, was cabled by Raleigh Gibson to Secretary Marshall on May 26, 1948 (National Archives).

Waide Condon's reaction to the autopsy is described in his wife's diary.

George Herman's telephone call to Mrs. Polk breaking the news of her son's murder is drawn from Adelaide Polk's private journal (William R. Polk files).

Chapter 20

Maj. Mouscoundis' confidential report on the Polk investigation is located among the Donovan files.

A. C. Sedgwick's report is in the New York *Times*, May 16, 1948, and *Newsweek* and *Time* reports on Polk's death are from the week of May 17, 1948.

Ed Murrow's May 17, 1948, broadcast on the death of George Polk is found in the CBS Archives as well as among William Polk's private papers. It has also been excerpted by A. M. Sperber in her account, *Murrow: His Life and Times*, p. 311.

Chapter 21

Material regarding the Condons in Salonika is largely drawn from the diary of Mrs. Waide Condon.

The author's interview with Rea Polk (as well as the diary of Mrs. Condon) provided information regarding the widow's own traumatic experiences during the week following her husband's murder.

The transcript of Don Hollenbeck on "CBS Views the Press" is from the CBS Archives.

The letter of Ray Daniell to Ed Murrow is dated May 18, 1948, and gives voice to Daniell's own views on who might have murdered their colleague (Donovan files).

The author's interviews with Eric Sevareid, Winston Burdett, and Howard K. Smith provided information regarding their own as well as Ed Murrow's reaction to their colleague's slaying.

The author interviewed Winston Burdett and Alexander Kendrick and drew on A. M. Sperber's *Murrow: His Life and Times* for the material on Burdett's complicated history.

The author's interview with Peter Tomkins was the source for the former OSS agent's role in the Polk investigation.

The author's interviews and correspondence with Alexander Kendrick illuminated the CBS veteran's own views on Burdett and the Polk case.

The author interviewed Homer Bigart to learn of his experience with Gen. Markos in the mountains and his subsequent treatment at the hands of Greek and American authorities, including his own newspaper, the *Herald Tribune*.

Bigart's letter of June 1948 to Bill Polk, undated, is found in William R. Polk's files.

The cable regarding Bigart from Secretary Marshall to U.S. Embassy in Athens, marked "Secret," July 1, 1948, is in the National Archives.

The material regarding Lippmann's role as head of the investigative team of eminent journalists, including their meeting of May 24, 1948, with Secretary Marshall, is from the Lippmann papers (Sterling Memorial Library, Yale University).

The CIA's role (in the persons of agents Christian Freer and Robert Driscoll) in the Polk case is from Karl Rankin's secret cable to Secretary Marshall dated June 2, 1948 (National Archives).

Sir Charles Wickham's "extraordinary" interest in the Polk case is described by Karl Rankin's secret cable to Secretary of State Marshall dated May 21, 1948, as well as Consul Raleigh Gibson's cable (marked "Restricted"), also dated May 21, 1948, to Marshall.

For a good summary of British involvement in the investigation the author also studied embassy secretary Oliver Marcy's secret cable to Secretary Marshall dated August 25, 1948 (National Archives).

For information regarding the background to the selection of Gen. Donovan as head of the Overseas Writers Committee, the author relied on interviews with Joseph Harsch, a member of that committee, William vanden Heuvel, Donovan's former aide, James Withrow, his law partner, and Mary G. Jones, his legal assistant at the time of the Polk case.

For material on Donovan's continued loyalty to the CIA, the author drew on interviews with James Withrow, William vanden Heuvel, Lawrence R. Houston, and William Colby.

For the material regarding Donovan's 1948 service on Forrestal's secret committee, the author drew on Anthony Cave Brown's account of the same in his biography of Donovan, *The Last Hero*, p. 802.

Chapter 22

The author is indebted to Forrest C. Pogue's portrait, *George C. Marshall: Statesman, 1945–1959.*

The author based her account of President Truman's personal attitude toward Greece on an interview with Clark Clifford.

Interviews with Shana Alexander, William Price, Jefferson Price, and William Polk provided the author with the material on the Newsmen's Commission to Investigate the Murder of George Polk, as well as the information regarding Ernest Hemingway, Claude Pepper, Henry Cabot Lodge, and Wayne Morse.

For additional material on the same ill-fated effort, the author relied on the 1982 John Donovan interviews.

Secretary of State Marshall's cable to the Athens embassy explaining the strong American public reaction to the Polk murder, dated May 28, 1948, is from the National Archives.

Material on Ayer is drawn from his autobiography, *Yankee G-Man* (Chicago: Henry Regnery, 1957), pp. 289–290, and from William Polk, based on his several personal meetings with the FBI agent.

Also "Memorandum on Ayer" for Gen. Donovan dated May 30, 1948, from Governor Griswold to FBI agent Brick at Lexington Hotel, is found among the Donovan papers.

The information regarding Ayer's aide Papadopoulos is drawn from Gen. Donovan's papers (handwritten note by Donovan, apparently meant for his own eyes only).

For more background and descriptions of Col. James Kellis, the author relied on interviews with Winston Burdett, Peter Tomkins, Prof. John O. Iatrides, Congressman John Blatnik, and Mrs. James Kellis.

A transcript of the May 31, 1948, interview between Kellis and Jack Anderson is among the Kellis papers.

The Donovan papers contained a copy of the cable of Ambassador Dendramis of early June 1948 attempting to prevent Kellis from going to Greece.

Chapter 23

The author's interview with Rea Polk and the diary of Mrs. Waide Condon, as well as Costas Hadjiargyris' lengthy testimony before and during the trial of Gregory Staktopoulos (April 1949), were used for the description of Rea Polk's trip from Salonika and arrival in Athens.

Costas Hadjiargyris described the activities of the Barbers to William Polk (letter of July 17, 1950, papers of William R. Polk). In an interview with the author, Rea Polk confirmed the Barbers' preoccupation with Sir Charles Wickham. Mrs. Barber (Lady Nicholas Henderson) declined to comment on any aspect of this book (letter of Lady Henderson to author dated March 20, 1987). Adelaide Polk's letter of May 23, 1948, from Athens to her family describes the police activities surrounding George's death. Mrs. Polk also mentions Mary Barber's constant presence at Rea's side.

The story of Mary Barber retrieving the Polk files is from the author's interviews with Rea Polk, Winston Burdett, and Edward Clark, UP correspondent in Athens during this period. Also Hadjiargyris' sworn testimony of June 8, 1948 (Donovan papers), and Attorney General Constantinides' report to Raleigh Gibson (National Archives).

Following publication of the hardcover edition of this book, Mary Barber offered several possible explanations for the missing files, including the possibility that Rea Polk had asked her to collect George's book research notes. She said that she had sent the following cable to *Time* after Polk's death:

"Touchingly, Rea Polk's ambition now is to collect up George's notes and papers for the book he was working on entitled, *Middle East Mosaic*. She wants to go to some journalism school in the United States, 'so that I can finish George's work.' "

The author relied on Adelaide Polk's letter to her family dated May 25, 1948, for more material regarding the missing files, and Hadjiargyris' letter of July 17, 1950 (files of William R. Polk), regarding his unwillingness to be alone in Polk's office or to search through the papers himself.

The author's interview with Rea Polk gained information regarding her treatment at the hands of the Greek police.

Ayer's memoirs, *Yankee G-Man*, provided information on the subject of Major Mouscoundis' zeal as investigator.

Mouscoundis' report on the official investigation, dated June 2, 1948, marked "Confidential," is part of a cable from Consul Gibson to Secretary Marshall (National Archives).

The June 10, 1948, secret cable from Rankin to Marshall outlines Mouscoundis' frenetic activity and the British role in the murder investigation (National Archives).

Sir Charles Wickham's monthly report to the British Foreign Office (Public Record Office, Kew Gardens, London) documents how little information Wickham was passing on to his superiors in the Foreign Office and Scotland Yard regarding his deep involvement in the management of the murder investigation.

For an analysis of the State Department's anxiety regarding American public opinion on the Polk case, the author drew on Robert Lovett's confidential cable to the Athens embassy dated May 28, 1948 (FOIA).

The relationship of Col. Martin and Maj. Mouscoundis is described in (among other places) a secret cable from Frederick Ayer to Secretary Marshall dated June 26, 1948 (FOIA).

Also, in a Memorandum of Conversation between Salonika police chief Xanthopoulos and Consul Gibson (dated June 7, 1948), Col. Martin's early (May 8, 1948) spreading of disinformation regarding the Polk murder is described (National Archives).

Wickham's comment to Hadjiargyris that "the Americans wanted blood" is in the latter's account of the Polk case, published in Greece, entitled *The Polk Affair: The Role of the Foreign Agencies in Greece.*

All State Department cables used in this chapter are located in the National Archives or were obtained by the author under the Freedom of Information Act, with dates as provided in the text. All CIA cables were obtained under the Freedom of Information Act, CIA Polk file.

For diplomatic cables on the subject of Rea Polk and Costas Hadjiargyris as potential suspects, the author drew on Rankin's cables to Secretary Marshall dated May 19, June 2, and June 17, 1948, as well as Consul Gibson's cables to Marshall dated June 8 and June 9, 1948, and Ayer's messages to Secretary Marshall dated June 24, June 26, and July 4, 1948.

Chapter 24

The author interviewed Winston Burdett and Peter Tomkins, and drew on Kellis' five-page report dated September 22, 1948, entitled "A Report of Maj. Gen. Donovan's Activities in Connection with the Investigation of the Polk Case" (Kellis papers), for material describing Donovan's Salonika trip.

The author interviewed William vanden Heuvel and James Withrow regarding Gen. Donovan's motives and philosophy.

Memorandum from A outlining possible suspects in the case is among the Donovan papers.

Kellis' letter of June 19, 1948, to Gen. Donovan, pertaining in part to Col. Martin of the British Police Mission, is among the Donovan papers.

Two letters (one undated) of Lambros Antoniou to James Kellis of August 1948 are among the Kellis papers.

Gen. Donovan's meeting with Sir Charles Wickham is described in a letter dated September 22, 1948, from Kellis to Donovan and is among the Kellis papers.

The author learned of the story of Tsaldaris' interview with Donovan from her interview with embassy secretary Robert Miner.

Ayer's report on the investigation, addressed to Secretary Marshall, dated August 13, 1948, was obtained by the author through the FOIA.

The author's interviews with Rea Polk and William Colby provided the background for the material regarding the young widow's early days in New York.

Mrs. Barber's message of September 17, 1948, to Rea Polk was among Gen. Donovan's papers.

The story of how Rea Polk finally broke down and agreed to point an accusing finger at the Communists is in the June 26, 1948, cable from Ayer to Secretary Marshall (obtained by the author under the FOIA).

Material on John Panopoulos is from the author's interviews with Cali Doxiades and Vaios Papastathopoulos (Greek security agent and aide to Panopoulos) and is also taken from the letter of August 23, 1948, from Theodore Lambron to Gen. Donovan (Donovan papers).

Additional material on Panopoulos is drawn from the secret memorandum of August 25, 1948, of embassy secretary Oliver Marcy to the State Department.

The author's interview with former UP correspondent Daniel Thrapp was the source for the description of the journalist's own difficulties at the hands of Greek and American investigators. Mr. Thrapp's letter to his boss, Clifford Day, was among the Donovan papers.

Chapter 25

Much of the material for Kellis' shifting views on Maj. Mouscoundis is drawn from Kellis' own detailed accounts of June 28, July 22, and August 10, 1948, to Gen. Donovan (Kellis papers).

For further material regarding Col. Kellis' thinking, the author also made use of a lengthy interview given by Col. Kellis in April 1985, not long before his death, to Bob Woodward's researcher, Barbara Feinman, which Mr. Woodward kindly made available to the author.

For a description of Consul Gibson and his socializing, the author drew on material from an interview with Col. "Ace" Miller, former assistant Air Force Attaché, Athens.

The author's interviews with British intelligence expert and author Nigel West and Lord Nicholas Bethel were useful in backgrounding the mentality of the British intelligence service.

The CIA memorandum of December 3, 1953, regarding Gen. Donovan's selection of Staktopoulos as a suspect was obtained by the author under the FOIA.

The author interviewed Peter Tomkins for information about Col. Kellis' suspicions about the Greek right.

Rankin's telex urging Kellis' removal is quoted by *More* magazine, May 1977, and has since disappeared from the National Archives.

Chapter 26

The full transcript of the conversation of July 24, 1948, of Maj. Mouscoundis, Col. Kellis, Gen. Donovan, and Winston Burdett is in the National Archives.

The author conducted several interviews with Randoll Coate in 1987 and 1988 in order to understand the retired British diplomat's heretofore mysterious role in the Polk case.

The telegram of Stuart Symington telling Kellis to return to Washington is dated July 22, 1948 (National Archives).

Col. Kellis' letter to Gen. Donovan, dated August 5, 1948, is among the Kellis papers.

Ernest Lindley's memorandum to Walter Lippmann, dated July 29, 1948, explains Kellis' position regarding the derailed investigation and is among the Lippmann papers (Sterling Memorial Library, Yale University).

The fact that Rendis told Donovan that Fred Ayer asked for Mouscoundis to be in charge of the investigation is contained in the memo of Wednesday, July 28, 1948, written by Theodore Lambron to Gen. Donovan (Donovan papers).

Lambros Antoniou's letter of August 20, 1948, describing Kourtessis' role in the Polk murder is among the Kellis papers.

Kellis' letter of August 10, 1948, outlining his suggestions to Gen. Donovan for getting a real investigation going is also among the Kellis papers.

Gen. Donovan's memo of July 31, 1948, to the U.S. Embassy regarding Donovan's idea for a Royal Commission to investigate the murder of George Polk is found among the Donovan papers.

Marcy's memorandum to Rankin on the subject of Lambron, dated August 4, 1948, is marked "Confidential" and is found in the National Archives.

Chapter 27

Gen. Donovan's views on the Polk murder were related to the author by William Polk on the basis of his many conversations with the general at the time of the trial.

CBS broadcasts regarding the Polk case are from the CBS Archives.

The author interviewed Gregory Staktopoulos regarding his arrest, torture, and incarceration.

For more on Burdett and Secondari's approach to the investigation, the author relied on the June 8, 1948, Memorandum for the Director of Central Intelligence, Subject: George Polk Murder, which praises the two CBS men for their "excellent" work. This document was obtained by the author under the FOIA.

The letter of September 7, 1948, from Klara Goldzieher-Roman to Gen. Donovan regarding the handwriting on the envelope containing Polk's ID card is among the Donovan papers.

The author interviewed Minister for Northern Greece Stylianos Papathemiles for material regarding his search for the real owner of the writing on the envelope.

Chapter 28

The transcript of the conversation of Gen. Donovan, Maj. Mouscoundis, et al., of October 12, 1948, is on file at the National Archives.

The interview with Evangelos Vasvanas was conducted by the Greek journalist Dimitoris Gousidis and carried by UPI wires (files of Nicholas Gage).

The Greek communiqué on Staktopoulos' indictment is in the National Archives.

Floyd A. Spencer's letter to Walter Lippmann explaining in great detail that Staktopoulos' "confession" is implausible is in the Donovan files.

The description of Secretary Marshall's trip to Greece is from Forrest Pogue's biography of Marshall, pp. 394–403, and from issues of *Time* magazine from October 1948.

The author's interview with Prof. John O. Iatrides was one source for the impact on the Greek Civil War of the Tito-Stalin split. (See Bibliography for other historical material on this subject.)

The letter of October 27, 1948, from William Baxter to Gen. Donovan regarding his *Herald Tribune* interview is located in the Donovan papers.

Lippmann's letter to Donovan stating that "we have ugly documentary evidence" on the official treatment of Col. Kellis is dated November 1, 1948, and is among the Lippmann papers (Sterling Memorial Library, Yale University).

Lippmann's letter of October 21 to Gen. Donovan is also among Lippmann's papers.

Rea Polk gave William Colby a sworn statement regarding young Tsaldaris' threats to her on October 20, 1948. These affidavits are among the Donovan papers.

William Baxter's secret cable of December 9, 1948, to Oliver Marcy is on file at the National Archives.

Lippmann's letter of October 4, 1948, to Irving Gilman regarding his unwillingness to join forces with the Newsmen's Commission is among Lippmann's papers.

Chapter 29

The author's interview with Ronald Steel, as well as Mr. Steel's excellent biography of Lippmann, provided some of the background for the author's analysis of the distinguished pundit.

E. M. Morgan's letter of May 17, 1949, regarding Staktopoulos' "confession" is among the Lippmann papers (Sterling Memorial Library, Yale University).

The author interviewed Alexander Kendrick, Winston Burdett, and William Polk, all of whom attended the Salonika murder trial, for background and descriptions of this event.

"Who Killed George Polk?" by Constantine Poulos (who also attended the trial) is from *The Nation*, May 28, 1949, and contains a rich store of material on the trial.

The private trial notes of William Polk (from the files of William R. Polk and Jefferson Price) provided material on the atmosphere inside the courtroom, including the daily barrage of press coverage of Greek denouncing Greek.

For additional remembrances of the trial and of Salonika during that period, the author interviewed Edward Clark, who covered the trial for UP.

Raleigh Gibson's cable to the State Department describing the trial, dated April 20, 1949, is in the National Archives.

The bulk of this chapter is drawn from the actual trial transcripts, which are on file in the National Archives.

Subsequent to the hardcover publication of this book, Mary Barber stated that she does "not recall making the statement to which the judge refers." She said "it is possible" that her purported statement refers to book research notes which Rea requested. She said she is "prepared to swear under oath that if [she] took any papers it would only have been those requested."

For material on Rea Polk's mental condition during this period, the author relied on the correspondence of Dr. Louise Brush and Gen. Donovan (Donovan files), especially the letters dated April 6 and April 11, 1948.

Also, Gen. Donovan's letter of April 10, 1949, addressed to William Baxter, Division of Greek, Turkish, and Iranian Affairs, State Department (Donovan files), expresses his views on the proceedings.

Gibson and Donovan's satisfaction with the trial verdict is outlined in their

April 21, 1948, cable addressed: Salonika to State Department (National Archives).

Burdett's report on the trial was broadcast on CBS's "World News Roundup," April 11, 1948, and is located in the CBS Archives.

William Polk's despair following the trial is expressed in a letter (dated April 23, 1949) addressed to his cousin William Price (William R. Polk papers).

The author's interviews with William Polk was the source for the story of Polk's confrontation with Gen. Donovan in Athens. Memorandum of Conversation between William Baxter and Gen. Donovan (Department of State, "Restricted") dated October 26, 1948, quotes Gen. Donovan as saying, "Bill Polk seems to have sold out completely to the Commies."

Aftermath

CBS News ("World News Roundup") transcripts of April 12 through April 21, 1949, as well as "Edward R. Murrow and the News," April 18, 19, and 20, 1948, are located in the CBS Archives.

The author's interview with Alexander Kendrick provided more on Murrow and Kendrick's reaction to the trial's aftermath.

The CBS reports on the murder of George Polk of June, July, and September 1948 and April 1949 were the source for certain CBS correspondents' preoccupation with the Polk case.

Kellis' letter of June 21, 1949, to Gen. Donovan (Kellis papers) is the source for the colonel's attitude of resignation following the trial.

The source for Kellis' life following his involvement with the Polk investigation is from his unedited article (seven pages) of 1977, written for the New York *Times* Op-Ed page, which appeared in much abbreviated form on September 17, 1977, entitled "Murder in Salonika Bay" (Kellis papers).

The letters of Col. Kellis to Prof. Iatrides and to Costas Hadjiargyris are in the files of John O. Iatrides.

The author's interviews with Col. "Ace" Miller revealed Donovan's distrust of Kellis.

The author's interview with Gregory Staktopoulos was the source for the Greek journalist's life subsequent to his murder conviction.

The author interviewed Stylianos Papathemiles for information regarding Staktopoulos' pardon by the Greek government and subsequent efforts to bring his case to a retrial.

The Vasvanas interview is from the files of Nicholas Gage.

Lippmann's role in the Polk investigation is documented in the (undistributed) report of the Overseas Writers Special Committee to Inquire into the Murder at Salonika, Greece, May 16, 1948, of CBS Correspondent George Polk and is among the Lippmann papers (Sterling Memorial Library, Yale University).

Eugene Meyer's letter urging Donovan to publish a final report on the Polk case is among the Donovan papers.

The author interviewed Mary G. Jones for information regarding Gen. Donovan's final years.

The author relied on the August 1952 account of Lippmann's view of the trial, which was published in the New York *Herald Tribune*.

The May 3, 1949, letter of Hadjiargyris to the Salonika public prosecutor is in the National Archives.

The FBI letters regarding continued surveillance of William Polk and Rea Polk was obtained by the author under the FOIA.

For background on the CIA's role in Greek life, the author drew on Trevor Barnes' account, "The Secret Cold War: The CIA and American Foreign Policy in Europe" (Parts I and II: 1946–1956), *The Historical Journal*, 1981, pp. 649–70, and 1982, pp. 399–415.

For additional material on this subject, the author drew on "The Greek Coup: A Case of CIA Intervention? No, Says Our Man in Athens," by John M. Maury (former CIA agent), in the Washington *Post*, May 1, 1977.

Bibliography

Acheson, Dean. *Present at the Creation: My Years in the State Department*. New York: Norton, 1969.

Agee, Philip. *On the Run*. Secaucus, N.J.: Lyle Stuart, 1987.

———. *Inside the Company: CIA Diary*. New York: Stonehill Publishing, 1975.

Alexander, G. M. *The Prelude to the Truman Doctrine: British Policy in Greece, 1944–1947*.

Anderson, Terry H. *The U.S., Great Britain, and the Cold War, 1944–1947*. Columbia: University of Missouri Press, 1981.

Andrew, Christopher. *Secret Service: The Making of the British Intelligence Community*. London: Heinemann, 1985.

Andrews, Kevin. *The Flight of Ikaros: Travels in Greece During a Civil War*. London: Penguin, 1984.

Bernstein, Carl. *Loyalties*. New York: Simon & Schuster, 1988.

Bohlen, Charles E. *Witness to History, 1929–1969*. New York: Norton, 1973.

———. *The Transformation of American Foreign Policy*. New York: Norton, 1969.

Brinkley, David. *Washington Goes to War*. New York: Knopf, 1988.

Bullock, Alan. *Ernest Bevin: Foreign Secretary, 1945–1951*. New York: Norton, 1983.

Cave Brown, Anthony. *The Last Hero: "Wild Bill" Donovan*. New York, Vintage, 1984.

Churchill, Winston. *Triumph and Tragedy*, Vol. VI of *The Second World War*. Boston: Houghton Mifflin, 1953.

Clive, Nigel. *A Greek Experience, 1943–1948*. London: Michael Russell, 1985.

Clogg, Richard. *A Short History of Modern Greece*. Cambridge, Eng.: Cambridge University Press, 1979.

Colby, William. *Honorable Men*. New York: Simon & Schuster, 1978.

Colville, John. *The Fringes of Power: 10 Downing Street Diaries, 1939–1955*. New York: Norton, 1985.

Dimbleby, David, and David Reynolds. *An Ocean Apart: The Relationship Between Britain and America in the Twentieth Century*. New York: Random House, 1988.

Djilas, Milovan. *Conversations with Stalin*. New York, Harcourt, Brace & World, 1962.

Donovan, Robert J. *Conflict and Crisis* and *The Tumultuous Years: The Presidency of Harry S. Truman (1945–1948 and 1949–1953)*. New York: Norton, 1982.

Etheridge, Willie. *It's Greek to Me*. New York: Vanguard, 1948.

Eudes, Dominique. *The Kapetanios*. New York: Monthly Review Press, 1972.

Forrestal, James. *The Forrestal Diaries*, ed. Walter Millis. New York: Viking, 1951.

Fourtouni, Eleni. *Greek Women in Resistance: Journals, Oral Histories*. Athens: Thelphini Press, 1986.

Gaddis, John L. *The United States and the Origins of the Cold War, 1941–1947*. New York: Columbia University Press, 1972.

Gage, Nicholas. *Eleni*. New York: Ballantine, 1983.

———. *Hellas: A Portrait of Greece*. Athens: Efstathiadis Group, 1987.

Gilbert, Martin. *Winston S. Churchill: Never Despair, 1945–1965*. Boston: Houghton Mifflin, 1988.

Hadjiargyris, Costas. *The Polk Affair: The Role of the Foreign Agencies in Greece*. Athens: Gnosi, 1984.

Halle, Louis J. *The Cold War as History*. New York: Harper & Row, 1967.

Harriman, W. Averell, and Elie Abel. *Special Envoy to Churchill and Stalin, 1941–1946*. New York: Random House, 1975.

Henderson, Mary. *Xenia: A Memoir*. London: Weidenfeld and Nicolson, 1988.

Iatrides, John O., ed. *Ambassador MacVeagh Reports: Greece, 1933–1947*. Princeton, N.J.: Princeton University Press, 1980.

———. *Greek-American Relations: A Critical Review*. New York: Pella, 1980.

———. "Greece and the Origins of the Cold War," in Robert G. Kaiser, *Cold Winter, Cold War*. New York: Stein & Day, 1974.

Isaacson, Walter, and Evan Thomas. *The Wise Men: Six Friends and the World They Made*. New York: Simon & Schuster, 1987.

Kendrick, Alexander. *Prime Time: The Life of Edward R. Murrow*. Boston: Little, Brown, 1969.

Kennan, George. *American Diplomacy, 1900–1950*. New York: Mentor, 1950.

———. *Memoirs, 1925–1950*. Boston: Little, Brown, 1967.

Kluger, Richard. *The Paper: The Life and Death of the New York Herald Tribune*. New York: Knopf, 1986.

Knightley, Phillip. *The First Casualty*. New York: Harcourt Brace Jovanovich, 1975.

———. *The Second Oldest Profession: Spies and Spying in the Twentieth Century*. New York: Norton, 1986.

Koumoulides, ed. *Greece in Transition*. London: Zeno, 1977.

———. *Revolt in Athens: The Greek Communist Second Round, 1944–45*. Princeton, N.J.: Princeton University Press, 1972.

Kousoulas, D. George. *Revolution and Defeat: The Story of the Greek Communist Party*. London: Oxford University Press, 1965.

Marchetti, Victor, and John D. Marks. *The CIA and the Cult of Intelligence*. New York: Dell, 1974.

Matthews, Kenneth. *Greece, 1944–1949: Memories of a Mountain War*. London: Longman Group, 1972.

Mead, Walter Russell. *Mortal Splendor: The American Empire in Transition*. Boston: Houghton Mifflin, 1987.

Morris, James. *Farewell the Trumpets: An Imperial Retreat*. New York: Harcourt Brace Jovanovich, 1978.

O'Ballance, Edgar. *The Greek Civil War, 1944–1949*. New York: Praeger, 1966.

Persico, Joseph E. *Edward R. Murrow: An American Original*. New York: McGraw-Hill, 1988.

Pogue, Forrest C. *George C. Marshall: Statesman, 1945–1959*. New York: Viking, 1988.

Ranelagh, John. *The Agency: The Rise and Decline of the CIA*. New York: Simon & Schuster, 1986.

Reeves, Thomas C. *The Life and Times of Joe McCarthy*. Briarcliff Manor, N.Y.: Stein & Day, 1982.

Richter, Heinz. *British Intervention in Greece: From Varkiza to Civil War*. London: Merlin Press, 1985.

Roubatis, Yiannis, P. *Tangled Webs: The U.S. in Greece, 1947–1967*. New York: Pella, 1987.

Spanier, John. *American Foreign Policy Since World War II*. New York: Praeger, 1960.

Sperber, A. M. *Murrow: His Life and Times*. New York: Freundlich Books, 1986.

Staktopoulos, Gregory. *The Polk Affair: My Personal Testimony*. Athens: Gutenberg, 1984.

Steel, Ronald. *Walter Lippmann and the American Century*. New York: Vintage, 1981.

Stern, Laurence. *The Wrong Horse: The Politics of Intervention and the Failure of American Diplomacy*. New York: Times Books, 1977.

Thomas, Hugh. *Armed Truce: The Beginnings of the Cold War, 1945–46*. London: Spectre Books, 1986.

Troy, Thomas F. *Donovan and the CIA*. Frederick, Md.: University Publications of America, 1984.

Truman, Harry S. *Memoirs*, Vols. I and II. Garden City, N.Y.: Doubleday, 1956.

Wise, David, and Thomas B. Ross. *The Espionage Establishment*. New York: Random House, 1967.

Wittner, Lawrence S. *American Intervention in Greece*. New York: Columbia University Press, 1982.

Index

Photograph Credits